International Compendium of Numerical Data Projects

A Survey and Analysis

Produced by CODATA

The Committee on Data for Science and Technology
of the

International Council of Scientific Unions. *Committee on Data for Science and Technology,*

Q223
I. 6l2i
1969

Springer-Verlag
New York · Heidelberg · Berlin 1969

Title No. 1611

Foreword

At the time of its establishment in 1966, by the International Council of Scientific Unions (ICSU), the Committee on Data for Science and Technology (CODATA) was given the basic mission of promoting and encouraging, on a worldwide basis, the production and distribution of compendia and other forms of collections of critically selected numerical data on substances of interest and importance to science and technology. To accomplish this aim, the following tasks were assigned to CODATA:

(1) To ascertain, on a worldwide basis, what work on compilation of numerical data is being carried on in each country and under each union, and from this information, to prepare and distribute a Directory or Compendium of the Data-Compiling Projects and Related Publications of the World;

(2) To achieve coordination of existing programs and to recommend new programs;

(3) To encourage, from all appropriate sources, financial support for work on compilation;

(4) To encourage the use of internationally approved symbols, units, constants, terminology, and nomenclature;

(5) To encourage and coordinate research on new methods for preparing and disseminating data for science and technology.

In its first two years of operation, 1966 to 1968, in Washington, D. C., U.S.A., CODATA fortunately had as its Director Dr. GUY WADDINGTON, who was also Director of the Office of Critical Tables of the National Research Council (NRC), U.S.A. Dr. WADDINGTON brought to CODATA the knowledge and experience gained in the supervision of the preparation and publication of two similar compendia covering the status of compilation work in the U.S.A., which had been prepared by the NRC Office of Critical Tables and published in the years 1961 and 1966. As of July 1, 1968, according to plans previously made by the Bureau of CODATA, the Central Office of CODATA was moved to Frankfurt, Germany, with Dr. CHRISTOPH SCHÄFER advancing to Director. Meanwhile, Dr. WADDINGTON, with the continuous able work of Mrs. BARBARA JAMES, in Washington, D.C., completed preparation of this first CODATA Compendium. During the last two months of the work, Mr. MARTIN LEWIS, of the Central Office of CODATA, went to Washington, D.C., to prepare the index cards later assembled in Frankfurt. Credit for the typing and related work goes to Mrs. ELOISE BATCHELOR, Mrs. ALICE MACINTYRE, and Mrs. FLORENCE SCHIFTER.

With this first CODATA Compendium now available to the scientific and technical community of the world, CODATA can proceed more expeditiously on the other tasks that have been assigned to it. It is hoped to have a revision of the CODATA Compendium published every two years.

FREDERICK D. ROSSINI
President
Committee on Data for Science and Technology (CODATA)
International Council of Scientific Unions

The Committee on Data for Science and Technology
of the
International Council of Scientific Unions

Organization and Membership

The Committee on Data for Science and Technology (CODATA) of the International Council of Scientific Unions (ICSU) was formally established by the Eleventh General Assembly of ICSU held in Bombay, India, in January 1966. It consists of Union Members designated by member unions of ICSU; National Members, designated by the national organizations adhering to ICSU; co-opted Members; and Liaison Representatives from other organized international groups. The officers of CODATA are: President, two Vice Presidents, and a Secretary-Treasurer. The Bureau of CODATA, which functions as an executive committee, consists of the elected officers plus two others elected from and by members of the Committee. A Central Office with a professional staff carries out the program decided on by the Committee. The 1969 membership is as follows:

Union Members

Dr. R. I. CURRIE: International Union of Biological Sciences (IUBS);

Prof. J. T. EDSALL: International Union of Pure and Applied Biophysics (IUPAB);

Prof. G. GARLAND: International Union of Geodesy and Geophysics (IUGG);

Prof. W. GARRISON: International Geographical Union (IGU);

Dr. OLGA KENNARD: International Union of Crystallography (IUCr);

Prof. W. KLEMM: International Union of Pure and Applied Chemistry (IUPAC);

Prof. F. ODQVIST: International Union of Theoretical and Applied Mechanics (IUTAM);

Prof. M. ROUBAULT: International Union of Geological Sciences (IUGS);

Dr. CHARLOTTE SITTERLY: International Astronomical Union (IAU);

Prof. B. VODAR: International Union of Pure and Applied Physics (IUPAP).

Organization and Membership

National Members

Dr. R. N. JONES, Canada;

Prof. Dr. W. KLEMM*, Secretary-Treasurer, Germany (B.R.D.);

Prof. M. KOTANI*, Japan;

Prof. F. D. ROSSINI*, President, U.S.A.;

Academician M. A. STYRIKOVICH*, U.S.S.R.;

Sir GORDON SUTHERLAND*, Vice President, U.K.;

Prof. B. VODAR*, Vice President, France.

* Member of Bureau of CODATA.

Co-opted Member

Dr. GUY WADDINGTON (U.S.A.).

Liaison Organizations

ICSU Abstracting Board (IAB);

Federation of Astronomical and Geophysical Services (FAGS);

International Federation for Documentation (FID);

International Atomic Energy Agency (IAEA);

World Meteorological Organization (WMO);

Organization for Economic Cooperation and Development (OECD).

Central Office

Dr. CHRISTOPH D. E. SCHÄFER, Executive Director
ICSU-CODATA
Westendstrasse 19
6 Frankfurt/Main, Germany (B.R.D.)

Contents

Introduction XVII

List of Abbreviations XXI

Chapter 1. *National Data Programs and National Committees for CODATA*

1.1. **National Data Programs** 1

1.1.1. National Standard Reference Data System (NSRDS): U.S. . 1

1.1.2. Office for Scientific and Technical Information (OSTI): U.K. 3

1.1.3. The State Service for Standard and Reference Data (GSSSD): U.S.S.R. 3

1.2. **National Committees for CODATA** 4

1.2.1. The Canadian National Committee for CODATA 4

1.2.2. The German National Committee for CODATA 4

1.2.3. The Japanese National Committee for CODATA 4

1.2.4. The U.K. National Committee for CODATA 5

1.2.5. The U.S. National Committee for CODATA 5

1.2.6. The U.S.S.R. National Committee for CODATA 5

Chapter 2. *Centers Covering a Number of Areas of Science*

2.1. **Landolt-Börnstein** 6

2.2. **Tables de Constantes Sélectionnées** 10

2.3. **Thermodynamics Research Center** 13

2.3.1. The American Petroleum Institute Research Project 44 (API RP 44) 14

2.3.2. The Thermodynamics Research Center (TRC) Data Project . . 14

Contents

Chapter 3. *Continuing Numerical Data Projects and Their Publications*

3.1.	**Nuclear Properties**	16
	General Nuclear Properties	16
3.1.1.	Nuclear Data Project	16
3.1.2.	Nuclear Tables (Tabellen der Atomkerne)	20
3.1.3.	Nuclear Constants Group	21
3.1.4.	Table of Isotopes	23
3.1.5.	Nuclear Radii.	24
3.1.6.	Reactor Physics Constants Center	26
	Properties of Neutrons	27
3.1.7.	National Neutron Cross Section Center	27
3.1.8.	IAEA Nuclear Data Unit	29
3.1.9.	Neutron Cross Sections for Fast Reactor Materials	31
3.1.10.	UKAEA Nuclear Data Library	32
3.1.11.	ENEA Neutron Data Compilation Centre	33
3.1.12.	U.S.S.R. Nuclear Data Information Centre.	34
	Properties of Nuclides	34
3.1.13.	Charged-Particle Cross Sections	34
3.1.14.	Decay Schemes of Radioactive Nuclei	36
3.1.15.	Energy Levels of Light Nuclei	38
3.1.16.	Energy Levels of $Z = 11-21$ Nuclei	39
3.1.17.	Energy Levels of Nuclei: $A = 5$ to $A = 257$	40
3.1.18.	Photonuclear Data Center	43
	Indexes	44
3.1.19.	CINDA (Computer Index of Neutron Data): An Index to the Literature on Microscopic Neutron Data	44
3.2.	**Atomic and Molecular Properties**	46
	Atomic Properties Including Spectra	46
3.2.1.	Atomic Energy Levels Data and Information Center	46
3.2.2.	Atomic Transition Probabilities Data Center	49
3.2.3.	X-Ray Wavelengths and X-Ray Atomic Energy Levels	51
3.2.4.	M.I.T. Wavelength Tables	52
3.2.5.	Atomic Collision Information Center	53

Molecular Properties Including Spectra 55

3.2.6. Diatomic Molecule Spectra and Energy Levels Data Center . 55

3.2.7. Données Spectroscopiques concernant les Molécules Diatomiques 56

3.2.8. Atlas des Longueurs d'Onde Caractéristiques des Bandes d'Emission et d'Absorption des Molécules Diatomiques . . 57

3.2.9. Molecular Spectra and Molecular Structure 58

3.2.10. Tables of Molecular Vibrational Frequencies 59

3.2.11. Atomic and Molecular Processes Information Center 61

3.2.12. Data Center for Atomic and Molecular Ionization Processes 62

3.2.13. Compendium of *ab initio* Calculations of Molecular Energies and Properties 63

3.2.14. Digest of Literature on Dielectrics 64

3.2.15. Selected Values of Electric Dipole Moments for Molecules in the Gas Phase 66

Infrared and Microwave Spectra 67

3.2.16. Selected Infrared Spectral Data: American Petroleum Institute Research Project 44 67

3.2.17. Selected Infrared Spectral Data: Thermodynamics Research Center Data Project 69

3.2.18. Coblentz Society Infrared Absorption Spectra 70

3.2.19. Documentation of Molecular Spectroscopy 71

3.2.20. The Infrared Data Committee of Japan 74

3.2.21. Infrared Spectra, Sadtler Research Laboratories, Inc. . . . 75

3.2.22. Berkeley Analyses of Molecular Spectra 78

3.2.23. Spectral Data and Physical Constants of Alkaloids 79

3.2.24. Tables of Wavenumbers for the Calibration of Infra-red Spectrometers 81

3.2.25. Microwave Spectral Tables 82

3.2.26. Molecular Constants from Microwave Spectroscopy 85

Raman Spectra 86

3.2.27. Selected Raman Spectral Data: American Petroleum Institute Research Project 44 86

3.2.28. Selected Raman Spectral Data: Thermodynamics Research Center Data Project 87

Contents

Electronic Spectra — Ultraviolet (UV) and Visible . . 88

3.2.29. Selected Ultraviolet Spectral Data: American Petroleum Institute Research Project 44 88

3.2.30. Selected Ultraviolet Spectral Data: Thermodynamics Research Center Data Project 90

3.2.31. Organic Electronic Spectral Data 91

3.2.32. Ultraviolet Spectra, Sadtler Research Laboratories, Inc. . . . 92

3.2.33. Absorption Spectra in the Ultraviolet and Visible Region . . 94

3.2.34. The UV Atlas of Organic Compounds/UV-Atlas organischer Verbindungen 96

Mass Spectra 97

3.2.35. Selected Mass Spectral Data: American Petroleum Institute Research Project 44 97

3.2.36. Selected Mass Spectral Data: Thermodynamics Research Center Data Project 99

3.2.37. Compilation of Mass Spectral Data (Index de Spectres de Masse) 101

3.2.38. Mass Spectrometry Data Centre 102

Nuclear Magnetic Resonance (NMR) Spectra 103

3.2.39. Selected Nuclear Magnetic Resonance Spectral Data: American Petroleum Institute Research Project 44 103

3.2.40. Selected Nuclear Magnetic Resonance Spectral Data: Thermodynamics Research Center Data Project 104

3.2.41. Nuclear Magnetic Resonance Spectra, Sadtler Research Laboratories, Inc. 106

3.2.42. High Resolution NMR Spectra Catalog 107

3.2.43. JEOL High Resolution NMR Spectra 108

Other Atomic and Molecular Projects 110

3.2.44. Interatomic Distances and Configurations in Molecules and Ions 110

3.2.45. Bond Energies, Ionization Potentials, and Electron Affinities 111

3.2.46. Bond Dissociation Energies in Simple Molecules 112

3.2.47. X-Ray Attenuation Coefficient Information Center 113

3.2.48. Data relative to Sesquiterpenoids 114

3.2.49. Luminescence of Organic Substances 115

3.2.50. Magnetic Properties of Free Radicals 117

Indexes to Compilations 118

3.2.51. Indexes to Infrared Spectral Data Compilations 118

3.2.52. Indexes to Ultraviolet-Visible Spectral Data Compilations . . 118

3.2.53. Indexes to Mass Spectral Data Compilations 119

3.3. Solid State, Including Crystallographic, Mineralogical, Electrical and Magnetic, and Related Properties . . . 119

Crystallographic Properties 119

3.3.1. Crystal Data 119

3.3.2. Crystal Structures 122

3.3.3. Powder Diffraction File: Joint Committee on Powder Diffraction Standards 124

3.3.4. Structure Reports 128

3.3.5. A Handbook of Lattice Spacings and Structures of Metals and Alloys 130

3.3.6. International Tables for X-Ray Crystallography 132

3.3.7. International Data Centre for Work on Crystallography . . . 134

3.3.8. The Barker Index of Crystals 135

3.3.9. Elastic, Piezoelectric, Piezooptic and Electrooptic Constants of Crystals 137

Mineralogical Properties 138

3.3.10. Dana's System of Mineralogy 138

3.3.11. Rock-Forming Minerals 140

Electrical and Magnetic Properties 141

3.3.12. Electrical Resistivity of Metals at Low Temperatures 141

3.3.13. Selected Constants relative to Semi-Conductors 142

3.3.14. Magnetic Properties of Coordination and Organo-Metallic Transition Metal Compounds 143

3.3.15. Diamagnétisme et Paramagnétisme, and Relaxation Para-magnétique 145

3.3.16. Pouvoir Rotatoire Magnétique, and Effet Magnéto-Optique de Kerr 146

Other Solid State 146

3.3.17. Superconductive Materials Data Center 146

3.4. Thermodynamic and Transport Properties, Including Solution Properties 147

Thermodynamic Properties 147

Contents

3.4.1. Selected Values of Chemical Thermodynamic Properties . . 147

3.4.2. Selected Values of Properties of Hydrocarbons and Related Compounds 150

3.4.3. Selected Values of Properties of Chemical Compounds . . . 152

3.4.4. JANAF Thermochemical Tables 154

3.4.5. Contributions to the Data on Theoretical Metallurgy 156

3.4.6. Thermodynamic Properties of Chemical Substances 158

3.4.7. Thermodynamic Constants of Substances 160

3.4.8. Chemical Thermodynamics in Nonferrous Metallurgy . . . 161

3.4.9. Selected Values for the Thermodynamic Properties of Metals and Alloys 163

3.4.10. Thermochemistry for Steelmaking 165

3.4.11. Binary Metal and Metalloid Constitution Data Center 167

3.4.12. Phase Diagrams for Ceramists 168

3.4.13. High Temperature Behavior of Inorganic Salts 170

3.4.14. Low Temperature Specific Heats Data Center 172

3.4.15. The Thermodynamic Tables Project of the International Union of Pure and Applied Chemistry 173

3.4.16. International Conference on the Properties of Steam 174

3.4.17. Thermodynamic Functions of Gases 178

3.4.18. Thermodynamic Properties of Ammonia 180

3.4.19. Thermodynamic Functions of Air 180

Transport (including Thermophysical) Properties . . . 182

3.4.20. Thermophysical Properties Research Center 182

3.4.21. Cryogenic Data Center 187

3.4.22. Molten Salts Data Center 189

Solution Properties 191

3.4.23. Seidell's Solubilities of Inorganic, Metal-Organic, and Organic Compounds 191

3.4.24. Stability Constants of Metal-Ion Complexes 193

3.4.25. Dissociation Constants of Acids and Bases 194

3.4.26. Potentiels d'Oxydo-Réduction 196

Indexes to Compilations 197

3.4.27. Consolidated Index of Selected Property Values: Physical Chemistry and Thermodynamics 197

3.5. **Properties Relating to Chemical Reaction Rates** 197

Chemical Kinetics 197
3.5.1. Chemical Kinetics Information Center 197
3.5.2. Tables of Bimolecular Gas Reactions 198
3.5.3. Hydrogenation of Ethylene on Metallic Catalysts 199
3.5.4. Radiolytic Yields 200
3.5.5. Gas Phase Reaction Kinetics of Neutral Oxygen Species . . 201

3.6. **Miscellaneous Projects and Their Publications** 202

Gas Chromatographic Data 202
3.6.1. Gas Chromatographic Data Committee of Japan 202
3.6.2. Gas Chromatographic Data Compilation 203

Optical Properties 204
3.6.3. Optical Rotatory Power, I. a — Steroids 204
3.6.4. Optical Rotatory Power, II. — Triterpenes 205
3.6.5. Optical Rotatory Power, III. — Amino-acids 206
3.6.6. Optical Rotatory Power, IV. — Alkaloids 207

Other Properties 208
3.6.7. Handbook of the Physicochemical Properties of the Elements 208

Chapter 4. *New and Secondary Centers*

4.1. **Secondary Nuclear Data Centers** 210
4.1.1. The Nuclear Codes Center 210
4.1.2. The Central Bureau of Nuclear Measurements 210
4.1.3. The Swedish A. B. Atomenergi and the Research Institute of National Defense 211
4.1.4. Mainz — Amsterdam 211
4.1.5. Japan Nuclear Data Committee (JNDC) 211

4.2. **Colloid and Surface Properties** 211
4.2.1. Electrical Properties of Interfaces 211
4.2.2. Surface Tension Data of Pure Liquids 212
4.2.3. Data for the Field of Critical Micelle Concentrations 212
4.2.4. Light Scattering Critical Data Center 213

Contents

4.3.   **Other Specialized Centers** 213

4.3.1. High Pressure Data Center (U.S.) 213

4.3.2. High Pressure Data Center of Japan 214

4.3.3. Radiation Chemistry Data Center 214

4.3.4. The Groth Institute 215

4.3.5. Diffusion in Metals and Alloys Data Center 215

4.3.6. Alloy Data Center 215

4.3.7. Equilibrium Constants of Molten Steel (JAPAN) 217

4.3.8. Molecular Weights of Polymers (JAPAN) 217

4.3.9. Properties of Electrolyte Solutions 217

Chapter 5. *Handbooks and Other Sources of Useful Tabular Data*

5.1.   **Comprehensive Multi-volume Handbooks** 218

5.2.   **Desk Handbooks for Broad Fields of Science** 219

Chemistry and Physics 219

Biology 220

Earth Sciences 220

5.3.   **Handbooks for Special Areas of Science** 221

Nuclear Properties 221

Spectroscopic Properties 222

Solid State Properties; Including Crystallographic, Mineralogical, and Electrical and Magnetic 223

Thermodynamic and Transport Properties; Including Solution
Properties 224

5.4.   **Handbooks for Special Substance Categories** 227

5.5.   **Handbooks for Analytical Chemistry** 228

Chapter 6. *Physical Quantities, Units and Symbols;*
Basic Physical Constants; Nomenclature; and Related Matters

6.1.   Organizations (CIPM, ISO, ICSU Unions) 230

6.2.   Physical Quantities, Units, and Symbols; and Basic Physical
Constants 232

6.3. Nomenclature 236

6.4. Recommendations on the Publication of Numerical Property
      Values 240

Author Index 241

Subject Index 249

Country Index 293

International Projects — International Unions Index . . . 295

Introduction

This International Compendium of Numerical Data Projects is a key part of the program of the Committee on Data for Science and Technology (CODATA) of the International Council of Scientific Unions. The general purpose of CODATA is to promote and encourage on a world-wide basis, the production and distribution of collections of critically selected numerical and other quantitatively expressed values of properties of substances, and systems of substances, of importance to science and technology. As a start toward the attainment of this goal the present Compendium has been assembled from the results of questionnaires submitted to National and Union Members of CODATA and other key people throughout the world. Of particular value has been "Continuing Numerical Data Projects, A Survey and Analysis" prepared in the Office of Critical Tables of the U. S. A. National Academy of Sciences.

The term "numerical data of science and technology" if taken in its broadest sense would include an enormous amount and variety of quantitative information. CODATA recognizes this fact, and believes that the initial step in its task must be restricted in the main to consideration of critically evaluated quantitative data for pure substances and simple, characterized systems of pure substances. Such data constitute the building blocks on which depend properties of more complex systems.

The material in the Compendium attempts to answer the following general questions: what compilations containing critically evaluated data are now available; what centers or organizations produce or aid production of such data for publication on a continuing basis; what national programs exist for financial support and encouragement of data compilation work; and what guidelines are available to compilers of all countries so that their products may be compatible. Information about centers will be restricted to those centers that regularly publish data compilations, or have well advanced programs for publishing such compilations, or have a supporting role for compilers such as the preparation of bibliographies of papers that contain numerical data. Centers that may have files of data, but only answer questions on request are not included. Publications otherwise suitable but not generally available are also excluded.

The primary emphasis is on projects that systematically extract, evaluate, and publish data for selected fields on a continuing basis.

Except for a few special categories of publications the entries in the Compendium are grouped by fields of science as may be seen in the Table of Contents. The classification employed is arbitrary to some extent but in most cases will guide the user to the categories of properties in which he is interested. For information on specific properties or classes of substances an index is provided which can do no more than point to categories of substances and properties referred to in Compendium entries.

Unfortunately, it is beyond the scope of this volume to index every substance and every property value given in the many publications covered no matter how useful and desirable such a generalized index would be.

The entries in Chapter 3 of the Compendium, which is the most important part, are organized under the following headings: 1) Organization; 2) Coverage; 3) Analysis; and 4) Publications.

The first heading presents briefly information about the organization under which the work is done, i.e., the name of the director and number of his staff, sources of support and guidance, and history. The second gives factual information as to the substances covered and their states, the properties covered and the range of variables if appropriate, and the period of time covered. Under the term "Analysis" an effort is made to present facts and observations that reflect the aims of the compiler in evaluating and distributing the results of his work. Finally under "Publications" information is given leading the user to the source of the publication and its cost.

Under the term Analysis the concept of "critical evaluation of data" is included. Since CODATA has a primary interest in evaluated data a few words on evaluation are in order. The earliest compilations of numerical data did no more than extract reported property values from the literature and present these in tabular form to the user. Not infrequently several values for the same property determined under similar conditions by different investigators were presented without comment. Thus the user had no basis for differentiation without intensive effort on his part. With the publication of the International Critical Tables the concept of critical evaluation of data and critical tables emerged. In the preparation of such tables each datum is the result of appraisal by experts of all available pertinent information. The value presented is that which in the opinion of the evaluating person or group best represents the numerical value of the property in question. Today, more and more compilers of numerical data are striving to achieve high standards in the evaluation of data. However, among the many compilations available there exists a spectrum of quality ranging from excellent to mediocre. In some cases the cause of less than optimum quality is simply that the state of development of measurement in a given field does not permit meaningful evaluation. But in other situations economic factors or urgent need may prevent expenditure of the time needed for careful evaluation; or the experience and competence of the compiling group may be at fault.

CODATA makes no claim of omniscience in judging the quality of data compilations. The criteria used in selecting entries for the Compendium have had to be flexible. Ideally every entry should meet the highest standards of quality. Actually most entries describe products of high reliability. However, some publications are included that could be improved. Justifications for including publications of less than top quality are based on criteria such as the following: (a) the data are adequate for their main use and are acceptable to a large body of users; (b) the output of new projects initially may lack the highest quality but the anticipation is that experience will bring improvement; and (c) a continuing series of publications, with volumes written on different topics by different authors, may not be uniform in quality but the policy is to include all volumes of a given series.

This Compendium is addressed to two principal audiences. First, it aims to help the compiler, would-be-compiler, or planner who must know what activities and compilations exist so that new work can be planned effectively. This audience will probably be reasonably well satisfied by the present Compendium. The other audience comprises all scientists and engineers who must find reliable data for their calculations and research. The needs of this audience are usually highly specific. It will seek numerical property values of specific substances under particular conditions. The Compendium narrows the search for such users but can give only a source — not the actual data required.

CODATA plans revisions of this volume from time to time. Readers are requested to submit information about errors and omissions, and other suggestions for improvement to the Central Office of CODATA in Frankfurt, Germany.

List of Abbreviations

ACA	American Crystallographic Association
API RP 44	American Petroleum Institute Research Project 44
ARPA	Advanced Research Projects Agency, Department of Defense, U.S.A.
ASME	American Society of Mechanical Engineers
ASTM	American Society for Testing and Materials
AWRE	Atomic Weapons Research Establishment, U.K.
BNL	Brookhaven National Laboratory, U.S.A.
CCITT	Comité Consultatif International Télégraphique et Téléphonique (International Consultative Committee on Telegraphy and Telephony)
CINDA	Computer Index of Neutron Data
CINDU	Catalog of IAEA Nuclear Data Unit
CIPM	Comité International des Poids et Mesures (International Committee on Weights and Measures)
CODATA	Committee on Data for Science and Technology, ICSU
CPX	Charged-Particle Cross Sections, Oak Ridge National Laboratory, U.S.A.
CSISRS	Cross Section Information Storage and Retrieval System, National Neutron Cross Section Center, U.S.A.
DASTAR	Data Storage and Retrieval System, International Atomic Energy Agency
DMS	Documentation of Molecular Spectroscopy
ECSIL	Experimental Cross Section Information Library, Nuclear Constants Group, Livermore, U.S.A.
ENDF	Evaluated Nuclear Data File, National Neutron Cross Section Center, U.S.A.
ENEA	European Nuclear Energy Agency
GCDC	Gas Chromatographic Data Committee of Japan

GSSSD	Gosudarstevennaya Sluzhba Standartnykh i Spravochnykh Dannykh (State Service for Standard and Reference Data, U.S.S.R.)
IAEA	International Atomic Energy Agency
IAU	International Astronomical Union
ICI	International Commission on Illumination
ICPS	International Conference on the Properties of Steam
ICRU	International Commission on Radiological Units
ICSU	International Council of Scientific Unions
IEC	International Electrotechnical Commission
IFC	International Formulation Committee, International Conference on the Properties of Steam
IRDC	Infrared Data Committee of Japan
ISO (TC 12)	International Organization for Standardization (Technical Committee 12)
IUB	International Union of Biochemistry
IUCr	International Union of Crystallography
IUPAC	International Union of Pure and Applied Chemistry
IUPAP	International Union of Pure and Applied Physics
JANAF	Joint Army-Navy-Air Force, U.S.A.
JEOL	Japan Electron Optics Laboratory
JILA	Joint Institute for Laboratory Astrophysics, U.S.A.
JNDC	Japan Nuclear Data Committee
KEDAK	Kerndaten Karlsruhe (Karlsruhe Nuclear Data File, Germany-B.R.D.)
LRL	Lawrence Radiation Laboratory, U.S.A.
MCA	Manufacturing Chemists Association, U.S.A.
MIT	Massachusetts Institute of Technology, U.S.A.
NASA	National Aeronautics and Space Administration, U.S.A.
NAS-NAE-NRC	National Academy of Sciences, National Academy of Engineering, National Research Council, U.S.A.
NBS	National Bureau of Standards, U.S.A.
NNCSC	National Neutron Cross Section Center, U.S.A.
NSF	National Science Foundation, U.S.A.
NSRDS	National Standard Reference Data System, U.S.A.
NSRDS-NBS	National Standard Reference Data Series, National Bureau of Standards, U.S.A.
OECD	Organization for Economic Cooperation and Development
OIML	Organization Internationale de Métrologie Légale (International Organization for Legal Metrology)

ORNL	Oak Ridge National Laboratory, U.S.A.
OSRD	Office of Standard Reference Data, National Bureau of Standards, U.S.A.
OSTI	Office for Scientific and Technical Information, U.K.
RPCC	Reactor Physics Constants Center, U.S.A.
SIRCH	Infrared File Searching System, American Society for Testing and Materials
SUN Commission	Commission for Symbols, Units and Nomenclature, International Union of Pure and Applied Physics
TPRC	Thermophysical Properties Research Center, U.S.A.
TRC	Thermodynamics Research Center, U.S.A.
UKAEA	United Kingdom Atomic Energy Authority
UNESCO	United Nations Educational, Scientific and Cultural Organization
USAEC	United States Atomic Energy Commission
WMO	World Meteorological Organization
ZWA	Nederlandse Organisatie voor Zuiver Wetenschappelijk Anderzoek (Netherlands Organization for Pure Scientific Research)

CHAPTER 1

National Data Programs and National Committees for CODATA

1.1. National Data Programs

With the growth of science as a major factor in the life of nations, governments are participating in efforts to assure the flow of reliable scientific data to scientists and engineers. Three major countries have established offices having the function of funding and monitoring projects for the production of tables of reliable numerical data in the physical sciences. The countries are the U.K., the U.S.A., and the U.S.S.R. Brief descriptions of the three national programs follow. Descriptions of specific projects sponsored within the national programs are given at appropriate places in this volume. Each of these countries also has a national committee for CODATA which may provide advice to the national program and also avenues of communication with activities in other countries and with international organizations.

1.1.1. National Standard Reference Data System (NSRDS): United States

The National Standard Reference Data System (NSRDS) was established in 1963 at the U.S. National Bureau of Standards (Washington, D.C. 20234) by action of the President's Office of Science and Technology and the Federal Council for Science and Technology to make critically evaluated numerical data in the physical sciences available to science and technology on a national basis. In 1968, this national policy was affirmed by the Congress of the United States in the "Standard Reference Data Act" which provides formal authority for funding and implementing the program. The National Bureau of Standards administers NSRDS through the Office of Standard Reference Data, which, since January 1969, has been directed by DAVID R. LIDE, JR. It is part of the responsibility of the Associate Director for Information Programs; EDWARD L. BRADY, formerly Director of OSRD, is the Associate Director.

Under its directive, the Office of Standard Reference Data serves to coordinate data evaluation and compilation activities in the U.S.A., particularly those sponsored by Federal Government agencies. The Office has also undertaken to provide information on existing activities in this area, to identify technical areas where work is needed, to help develop standards, and to set up an effective system for disseminating results of these data activities to the technical and scientific community. The Office also provides partial or complete support for a significant number of compilation programs in both governmental and non-governmental organizations.

The NSRDS is conducted as a decentralized operation of nationwide scope. It comprises a complex of data centers and other activities, carried on in government agencies, academic institutions, and non-governmental laboratories. The independent operational status of existing critical data projects is maintained and encouraged. Data centers that are components of the NSRDS produce compilations of critically evaluated data, critical reviews of the state of quantitative knowledge in specialized areas, computations of useful functions derived from standard reference data, and useful bibliographies.

An important aspect of the NSRDS is the advice and planning assistance which the National Research Council of the National Academy of Sciences - National Academy of Engineering provides. These services are organized under an overall Advisory Committee which considers the program as a whole and makes recommendations on policy, long-term planning, and international collaboration. Advisory panels, each concerned with a single technical area, meet regularly to examine major portions of the program, recommend relative priorities, and identify specific key problems in need of further attention. Subpanels make detailed studies of specific topics.

The technical scope of NSRDS is delineated by seven property categories: nuclear, atomic and molecular, solid state, thermodynamic and transport, chemical kinetics, colloid and surface, and mechanical. The data publications of NSRDS, which may be monographs, loose-leaf sheets, computer tapes, journal articles, and some special forms, will be classified in these categories. Most compilations of critically evaluated data, and critical reviews are published in the National Standard Reference Data Series which has been initiated within the NBS publication series (NSRDS—NBS). Currently available publications, and the centers that produce them, are described in this compendium under the appropriate subject category. Additional details and information on specific accomplishments of the program may be found in *Status Report: National Standard Reference Data System, April 1968* (NBS Technical Note 448, E. L. BRADY, Ed., U. S. Government Printing Office, Washington, D. C. 20204, June 1968, 129 pp, US $ 0.70).

1.1.2. Office for Scientific and Technical Information (OSTI): United Kingdom

The Office for Scientific and Technical Information (OSTI) forms part of the Department of Education and Science and was established in 1965. OSTI supports U. K. activities in scientific and technical information over the whole field of the natural and social sciences and their related technologies and within this has a responsibility for work on numerical data compilation. Funds are provided for approved projects in universities, learned societies, research associations and Government agencies.

OSTI coordinates and stimulates data compilation activities by publishing periodically a list of ongoing numerical data projects in the U. K. The latest edition of this list entitled "Critical Data in Britain 1966 to 1967" was issued in May 1967 and was available free of charge from OSTI. A new edition will be prepared in 1969. It is a function of OSTI policy to coordinate the U. K. effort with international data activities. Several of the data compilation projects in the U. K. are international in scope though funded by OSTI. Advice on national and international policy on data is also given by the U. K. National Committee for CODATA (see 1.2.4.) sponsored by the Royal Society. Major OSTI policies, including those concerned with data, are reviewed from time to time by the Advisory Committee for Scientific and Technical Information comprised of members from academic, industrial, and other interested institutions. A number of publications and centers sponsored by OSTI are described elsewhere in this volume.

1.1.3. The State Service for Standard and Reference Data (GSSSD): U.S.S.R.

This program is one of the responsibilities of the State Committee on Standards which also has cognizance over a corresponding program on Standard Reference Materials. The purpose of the GSSSD is to provide science and technology in the U. S. S. R. with standard and reference data of materials on a broad scale. In the context of this program *reference data* are conceived of as being somewhat equivalent to critically evaluated property values whereas *standard data* have the connotation of prescribed specifications for materials used in manufacturing. The GSSSD will also cover properties of complex industrial materials, customarily designated engineering properties.

The headquarters of the GSSSD will serve as a focal point to coordinate activities, to determine data requirements of science and industry, and to establish priorities. It will not only develop standards of testing and evaluation of data, but also identify centers to compile and evaluate standard data. To support its function as an information center, it is developing methods of storing and retrieving data.

The program of the GSSSD is still in the formative stage. However, about a hundred titles of compilations to be assembled under its aegis have been projected with the first publications scheduled for 1968. A number of these titles which seem to fall within the scope of CODATA are listed in Chapter 5.

Primary guidance and coordination in the U.S.S.R. for compilations covering well defined properties of simple substances are vested in the National Committee for CODATA (see 1.2.6.) which functions within the Academy of Sciences of the U. S. S. R.

1.2. National Committees for CODATA

One of the conditions for national membership on CODATA is that the country shall have a national committee for CODATA attached to the organization which adheres to ICSU. Usually such organizations are non-governmental. These national committees provide support on an inter-disciplinary basis to the CODATA National Member and also are available to provide advice and guidance to data compilation activities within their countries. Eventually all member countries of CODATA will have such committees. To date six countries have formally established committees. For several of these committees, but not all, the Chairman is also the National Representative for his country on CODATA. In 1969 the individuals named below were chairmen of their respective national committees:

1.2.1. The Canadian National Committee for CODATA

Chairman: Dr. R. N. JONES. Sponsoring organization: National Research Council of Canada, Sussex Drive, Ottawa, Ontario.

1.2.2. The German National Committee for CODATA

Chairman: Professor Dr. W. KLEMM. Sponsoring organization: Deutsche Forschungsgemeinschaft, Kennedyallee 40, 5320 Bad Godesberg, Germany, B. R. D.

1.2.3. The Japanese National Committee for CODATA

Chairman: Professor MASAO KOTANI. Sponsoring organization: The Science Council of Japan, Ueno Park, Tokyo.

1.2.4. The U. K. National Committee for CODATA

Chairman: Dame KATHLEEN LONSDALE. Sponsoring organization: The Royal Society, 6 Carlton House Terrace, London, S. W. 1.

1.2.5. The U.S. National Committee for CODATA

Chairman: Professor FREDERICK D. ROSSINI. Sponsoring organization: National Research Council of the National Academy of Sciences - National Academy of Engineering, 2101 Constitution Avenue, Washington, D. C., 20418.

1.2.6. The U. S. S. R. National Committee for CODATA

Chairman: Academician M. A. STYRIKOVICH. Sponsoring organization: The Academy of Sciences of the U. S. S. R., Leninsky Prospekt 14, Moscow B—17.

CHAPTER 2

Centers Covering a Number of Areas of Science

At one time, years ago, it was possible for a single organization to undertake the compilation of all existing numerical data for the physical sciences. The International Critical Tables completed such an endeavor. The LANDOLT-BÖRNSTEIN Tabellen (2.1) through the sixth edition aimed at covering all of the physical sciences. The Tables Annuelles des Constantes Sélectionées (2.2) also originally had wide coverage. But today no single organization can dream of tackling the evaluation and publication of data for all major areas of science. However, some current publication efforts do cover numerical property values in several, or many, areas of science. The organizations with such programs are described in this section. Their individual publications are discussed in detail under the pertinent sections of this volume.

2.1. Landolt-Börnstein

Zahlenwerte und Funktionen aus Physik, Chemie, Astronomie, Geophysik und Technik; and Zahlenwerte und Funktionen aus Naturwissenschaften und Technik — Neue Serie (Numerical Data and Functional Relationships in Science and Technology — New Series).

Organization

In 1883, HANS LANDOLT, with the collaboration of RICHARD BÖRNSTEIN, issued the first (one volume) edition of "Physikalisch-Chemische Tabellen". Work on the sixth edition of LANDOLT-BÖRNSTEIN, "Zahlenwerte und Funktionen aus Physik, Chemie, Astronomie, Geophysik und Technik", started soon after the last volume of the fifth edition was published in 1936. Publication began in 1950 under the editorship of the late ARNOLD EUCKEN. Editorial responsibility for recent volumes has been shared by H. BORCHERS, H. HAUSEN, K.-H. HELLWEGE, KL. SCHÄFER, E. SCHMIDT, and the late J. BARTELS. The rapid advance in existing fields of physical science and the growth of important new fields made it evident that after publication of the sixth edition it would be practically impossible to resume publishing with such a comprehensive coverage of all fields of science. Beginning in 1961, publication of a new series of volumes was started. These volumes will appear under the general title "Numerical Data and Functional Relationships in Science and Technology" and are, at present, under the general editorship of K.-H. HELLWEGE. The editorial office is in the Technische Hochschule, Institut für Technische Physik, 61 Darmstadt, Germany. The selection of topics for this series is determined by the current trends and needs of science. Thus active fields will be the subject of frequently published volumes, and inactive fields may receive no attention for many years.

Coverage

Very wide coverage is attained including the elements (all nuclides), organic and inorganic compounds, and characterized systems of compounds as necessitated by the subject matter of the individual volumes.

The goal of the editors of the sixth edition has been to present comprehensively all the important fundamental properties of physics, chemistry, astronomy, geophysics, and technology. In the new series an entire volume may be devoted to a limited area of research.

Sources of data are from the literature. The lists of references are very complete and provide a useful guide to the literature in specific fields.

Analysis

Data for the sixth edition have been more critically examined than those in previous editions. There is no overall standard by which data are evaluated, the standard for each volume depending upon the individual compilers and editors.

All the volumes of a compilation with publication extending over more than 15 years cannot possibly be current. The establishment of the new series is an attempt to bring the earlier volumes of the sixth edition up to date in the most important areas and to present data in new fields of interest.

The volumes of the sixth edition are published as cloth-bound books, divided into sections. The individual volumes have no indexes (except Vol. II/9), but an index for the entire sixth edition is in preparation. A table of contents is given in each book, with the applicable part repeated at the beginning of each section in some of the volumes. Data are presented in tables and graphs. References either accompany the individual tables or graphs, or are placed at the end of the section. Earlier editions and most volumes of the sixth edition are in German. A welcome trend evident in some recent volumes, and planned for all volumes of the new series, is to have the introductory material and a large part of the data and explanatory paragraphs in both German and English.

2.1.

Description of the volumes listed under "New Series" are to be found under the appropriate classification elsewhere in this compendium.

Publications

LANDOLT-BÖRNSTEIN: *Zahlenwerte und Funktionen aus Physik, Chemie, Astronomie, und Technik,* sixth edition, published by Springer-Verlag, Berlin and Heidelberg. Also available from Springer-Verlag New York Inc., 175 Fifth Avenue, New York, N. Y. 10010.

Vol. I: Atom- und Molekularphysik.

Part 1, Atome und Ionen, 1950, XII, 441 pp, DM 126 (US $ 31.50).
Part 2, Molekeln I: Kerngerüst, 1951, VIII, 571 pp, DM 168 (US $ 42.00).
Part 3, Molekeln II: Elektronenhülle, 1951, XI, 724 pp, DM 218 (US $ 54.50).
Part 4, Kristalle, 1955, XI, 1.007 pp, DM 318 (US $ 79.50).
Part 5, Atomkerne und Elementarteilchen, 1952, VIII, 470 pp, DM 148 (US $ 37.00).

Vol. II: Eigenschaften der Materie in ihren Aggregatzuständen.

Part 1, Mechanisch-thermische Zustandgrößen (in preparation).
Part 2, Gleichgewichte außer Schmelzgleichgewichten.
Part 2a, Gleichgewichte Dampf-Kondensat und osmotische Phänomene, 1960, XII, 974 pp, DM 448 (US $ 112.00).
Part 2b, Lösungsgleichgewichte I., 1962, XII, 984 pp, DM 510 (US $ 127.50).
Part 2c, Lösungsgleichgewichte II., 1964, VIII, 731 pp, DM 388 (US $ 97.00).
Part 3, Schmelzgleichgewichte und Grenzflächenerscheinungen, 1956, XII, 535 pp, DM 198 (US $ 49.50).
Part 4, Kalorische Zustandgrößen, 1961, XII, 863 pp, DM 438 (US $ 109.50).
Part 5, Transportphänomene. Kinetik. Homogene Gasgleichgewichte.
Part 5a, Transportphänomene I (in preparation).
Part 5b, Transportphänomene II. Kinetik. Homogene Gasgleichgewichte, 1968, ca. 410 pp, ca. DM 228 (US $ 57.00).
Part 6, Elektrische Eigenschaften I., 1959, XVI, 1018 pp, DM 448 (US$ 112.00).
Part 7, Elektrische Eigenschaften II., 1960, XII, 959 pp, DM 478 (US $ 119.50).
Part 8, Optische Konstanten, 1962, XVI, 901 pp, DM 476 (US $ 119.00).
Part 9, Magnetische Eigenschaften I — Magnetic Properties I, 1962, XXVI, 935 pp, DM 496 (US $ 124.00).
Part 10, Magnetische Eigenschaften II — Magnetic Properties II — Propriétés magnétiques II, 1967, VIII, 173 pp, DM 106 (US $ 26.50).

Vol. III: Astronomie und Geophysik, 1952, XVIII, 795 pp, DM 248 (US $ 62.00).

Vol. IV: Technik.

Part 1, Stoffwerte und mechanisches Verhalten von Nichtmetallen, 1955, XVI, 881 pp, DM 288 (US $ 72.00).
Part 2, Stoffwerte und Verhalten von metallischen Werkstoffen.
Part 2a, Grundlagen, Prüfverfahren, Eisenwerkstoffe, 1963, XII, 888 pp, DM 468 (US $ 117.00).
Part 2b, Sinterwerkstoffe, Schwermetalle (ohne Sonderwerkstoffe), 1964, XX, 1000 pp, DM 530 (US $ 132.50).
Part 2c, Leichtmetalle, Sonderwerkstoffe, Halbleiter, Korrosion, 1965, XX, 976 pp, DM 518 (US $ 129.50).

Part 3, Elektrotechnik, Lichttechnik, Röntgentechnik, 1957, XVI, 1076 pp, DM 396 (US $ 99.00).

Part 4, Wärmetechnik

Part 4a, Wärmetechnische Meßverfahren. Thermodynamische Eigenschaften homogener Stoffe, 1967, XII, 944 pp, DM 510 (US $ 127.50).

Part 4b, Thermodynamische Eigenschaften von Gemischen; Verbrennung; Wärmeübertragung (in preparation).

LANDOLT-BÖRNSTEIN: *Zahlenwerte und Funktionen aus Naturwissenschaften und Technik* — *Numerical Data and Functional Relationships in Science and Technology*, Neue Serie — New Series, Editor-in-Chief: K.-H. HELLWEGE.

Group I: Kernphysik und Kerntechnik — Nuclear Physics and Technology.

Vol. 1, Energie-Niveaus der Kerne: $A = 5$ bis $A = 257$ — Energy Levels of Nuclei: $A = 5$ to $A = 257$, 1961, XII, 814 pp, DM 212 (US $ 53.00), see 3.1.17.

Vol. 2, Kernradien — Nuclear Radii, 1967, VIII, 54 pp, DM 38 (US $ 9.50), see 3.1.5.

Vol. 3, Numerische Tabellen für die Berechnung von Winkelkorrelationen in der α-, β- und γ-Spektroskopie — Numerical Tables for Angular Correlation Computations in α-, β- and γ-Spectroscopy, 1968, VI, 1202 pp, DM 328 (US $ 82.00).

Vol. 4, Numerische Tabellen für Beta-Zerfall und Elektronen-Einfang — Numerical Tables for Beta-Decay and Electron Capture, 1969, VII, 316 pp, DM 118 (US $ 29.50).

Group II: Atom- und Molekularphysik — Atomic and Molecular Physics.

Vol. 1, Magnetische Eigenschaften freier Radikale — Magnetic Properties of Free Radicals, 1965, X, 154 pp, DM 68 (US $ 17.00), see 3.2.50.

Vol. 2, Magnetische Eigenschaften der Koordinations- und metallorganischen Verbindungen der Übergangselemente — Magnetic Properties of Coordination and Organo-Metallic Transition Metal Compounds, 1966, XII, 578 pp, DM 232 (US $ 58.00), see 3.3.14.

Vol. 3, Lumineszenz organischer Substanzen — Luminescence of Organic Substances, 1967, VIII, 416 pp, DM 196 (US $ 49.00), see 3.2.49.

Vol. 4, Molekelkonstanten aus mikrowellenspektroskopischen Messungen — Molecular Constants from Microwave Spectroscopy, 1967, X, 225 pp, DM 110 (US $ 27.50), see 3.2.26.

Vol. 5, Molekularakustik — Molecular Acoustics, 1967, XII, 286 pp, DM 156 (US $ 39.00).

Group III: Kristall- und Festkörperphysik — Crystal and Solid State Physics.

Vol. 1, Elastische, piezoelektrische, piezooptische und elektrooptische Konstanten von Kristallen — Elastic, Piezoelectric, Piezooptic and Electrooptic Constants of Crystals, 1966, X, 160 pp, DM 68 (US $ 17.00), see 3.3.9.

Vol. 2 (Supplement and extension to Vol. III/1), Elastische, piezoelektrische, piezooptische, elektrooptische Konstanten und nichtlineare dielektrische Suszeptibilitäten von Kristallen — Elastic, Piezoelectric, Piezooptic, Electrooptic Constants, and Nonlinear Dielectric Susceptibility of Crystals (in preparation).

Vol. 3, Ferro- und antiferroelektrische Substanzen — Ferro- and Antiferroelectric Substances (in preparation).

Vol. 4, Magnetische und andere Eigenschaften von Oxidsystemen — Magnetic and other Properties of Oxide Systems (in preparation).

Vol. 5, Strukturdaten organischer Kristalle — Structural Data of Organic Crystals (in preparation).

Group IV: Makroskopische und technische Eigenschaften der Materie — Macroscopic and Technical Properties of Matter.

Vol. 1, Phosphoreszenz anorganischer Substanzen — Phosphorescence of Inorganic Substances (in preparation).

Group V: Geophysik und Weltraumforschung — Geophysics and Space Research (in preparation).

Group VI: Astronomie, Astrophysik und Weltraumforschung — Astronomy, Astrophysics and Space Research.

Vol. 1, Astronomie und Astrophysik — Astronomy and Astrophysics, 1965, XL, 711 pp, DM 314 (US $ 78.50).

2.2. Tables de Constantes Sélectionnées

Organization

Publication of "Tables Annuelles de Constantes et Données Numériques" began in 1909 under the aegis of the International Union of Pure and Applied Chemistry (IUPAC) and the editorship of CH. MARIE. The tables were to bring together all the numerical data published in chemistry, physics, biology, and technology. Ten volumes appeared between 1910 and 1930, and these were indexed in two separate volumes. Between 1936 and 1945, 40 installments of the Tables Annuelles appeared. Each contained one or more chapters on special topics, some covering data of the periods 1931 to 1934 or 1935 to 1936, some the whole period 1931 to 1936, and No. 40 only, 1931 to 1939. Later, 8 of these were issued as Volume XI and 12, as Volume XII. In 1947 publication was resumed under the title "Tables de Constantes Sélectionnées". To date, expert collaborators have compiled 15 numbered monographs in this new series. The present director is Dr. P. KHODADAD, 250 rue Saint Jacques, Paris Ve, France. Guidance is provided by an advisory committee composed of eminent scientists. Publication of the new series has been supported by governmental grants, by contributions from industrial concerns, and by profits from sales.

Coverage

The subject matter of a given monograph, both as to substance and properties, is designed to meet a current demand of science or industry for specialized tables. Both organic and inorganic substances have been covered (see list of publications at end of this section).

The list of publications below shows the variety of properties covered since 1947. In recent years efforts have been directed toward rapidly moving fields of science, the properties reported being those of greatest significance in the selected fields.

Sources of data are from the literature.

Analysis

There is some selection of values, but the criticality varies from one monograph to another being largely a function of the type of data. The goal is to produce "useful" as well as critical values. Where doubt exists, attention is called to the uncertainty. The editorial staff avails itself of guidance from collaborating scientists.

As far as possible, IUPAC usage is adhered to for nomenclature, symbols, units, and physical constants. If no rules exist, well-known and able authorities are followed.

There has been no definite plan to bring the earlier tables of the current series up to date. However, some subjects, particularly those for which few if any other compilations exist, are treated somewhat as a series, for example, Optical Rotatory Power, for which five volumes have been issued.

Volumes 1 to 5 of the recent series of publications were papercovered, Volumes 6 and 7 were issued with both paper and hard covers, and those since Volume 8 have hard covers, 21.1×27.9 cm. The data are presented in tables. Arrangement of material varies because different substances and properties are treated in each monograph. A bibliographic column in the tables guides the user to the pertinent literature reference in the general bibliography at the end of the monograph. General indexes vary in type, some being indexed by name, others by formula, and some by author with references to the general bibliography. Although the tables are in French, the title page and, beginning with Volume 6, the preface, introduction, and other explanatory sections such as those for symbols and abbreviations are given in both French and English. Descriptions of the volumes listed below are given elsewhere in this compendium under the appropriate subject classification except for out-of-print or superseded volumes.

2.2.

Publications

Tables de Constantes Sélectionnées — Tables of Selected Constants

Vol. 1. Longueurs d'Onde d'Emissions X et des Discontinuités d'Absorption X — Wavelengths of Emission and Discontinuities in Absorption of X-Rays, Y. Cauchois and H. Hulubei, 1947, 199 pp (out of print).

Vol. 2. Physique Nucléaire — Nuclear Physics, R. Grégoire, F. Joliot-Curie, and I. Joliot-Curie, 1948, 131 pp (out of print).

Vol. 3. Pouvoir Rotatoire Magnétique (Effet Faraday) — Magnetic Rotatory Power (Faraday Effect), R. de Mallemann; Effet Magnéto-Optique de Kerr — Magneto-Optic Effect (Kerr), F. Suhner, 1951, 137 pp, 15 F, £ 1.10.0. (US $ 4.50), see 3.3.16.

Vol. 4. Données Spectroscopiques concernant les Molécules Diatomiques — Spectroscopic Data for Diatomic Molecules, B. Rosen, R. F. Barrow, A. D. Caunt, A. R. Downie, R. Herman, E. Huldt, A. McKellar, E. Miescher, and K. Wieland, 1951, 361 pp, 48 F, £ 5.0.0. (US $ 15.00), see 3.2.7.

Vol. 5. Atlas des Longueurs d'Onde Caractéristiques de Bandes d'Emission et d'Absorption des Molécules Diatomiques — Atlas of Characteristic Wavelengths for Emission and Absorption Bands of Diatomic Molecules (a continuation of Vol. 4 by the same authors), 1952, 389 pp, 56 F, £ 5.15.0. (US $ 17.50), see 3.2.8.

Vol. 6. Pouvoir Rotatoire Naturel I. — Steroïdes — Optical Rotatory Power I. — Steroids, J.-P. Mathieu and A. Petit, 1956, 507 pp (out of print, superseded by Vol. 14).

Vol. 7. Diamagnétisme et Paramagnétisme — Diamagnetism and Paramagnetism, G. Foëx; Relaxation Paramagnétique — Paramagnetic Relaxation, C. J. Gorter and L. J. Smits, 1957, 317 pp, 97 F, £ 9.15.9. (US $ 29.00), see 3.3.15.

Vol. 8. Potentiels d'Oxydo-Réduction — Oxidation-Reduction Potentials, G. Charlot, D. Bézier, and J. Courtot, 1958, 41 pp, 21.60 F, £ 1.10.0. (US $ 5.00), see 3.4.26.

Vol. 9. Pouvoir Rotatoire Naturel II. — Triterpénoïdes — Optical Rotatory Power II. — Triterpenoids, J.-P. Mathieu and G. Ourisson, 1958, 302 pp, 93.60 F, £ 7.0.0. (US $ 21.00), see 3.6.4.

Vol. 10. Pouvoir Rotatoire Naturel III. — Amino-acides — Optical Rotatory Power III. — Amino Acids, J.-P. Mathieu, J. Roche, and P. Desnuelle, 1959, 61 pp, 28 F, £ 2.0.0. (US $ 6.50), see 3.6.5.

Vol. 11. Pouvoir Rotatoire Naturel IV. — Alcaloïdes — Optical Rotatory Power IV. — Alkaloids, J.-P. Mathieu and M. M. Janot, 1959, 211 pp, 110.40 F, £ 8.0.0. (US $ 24.00), see 3.6.6.

Vol. 12. Semi-Conducteurs — Semi-Conductors, P. Aigrain and M. Balkanski, 1961, 78 pp, 27 F, £ 2.0.0. (US $ 6.50), see 3.3.13.

Vol. 13. Rendements Radiolytiques — Radiolytic Yields, M. Haissinsky and M. Magat, 1963, 230 pp, 114 F, £ 8.10.0. (US $ 25.50), see 3.5.4.

Vol. 14. Pouvoir Rotatoire Naturel I. a — Stéroïdes — Optical Rotatory Power I. a — Steroids, J. Jacques, H. Kagan, G. Ourisson, and S. Allard, 1965, 1,046 pp, 258 F (Supersedes Vol. 6), see 3.6.3.

Vol. 15. Données relatives aux Sesquiterpenoïdes — Data relative to Sesquiterpenoids, G. OURISSON, S. MUNAVALLI, and C. EHRET, 1966, 70 pp + 28 pp
structural formulas, 63 F, see 3.2.48.

In Press

Metals.
  Part I: Thermal and Mechanical Data.

In Preparation

Metals.
  Part II: Crystal Data.
  Part III: Electric and Magnetic Data.

Data on Molecular Spectroscopy (Supersedes Vol. 4).
  Part I: Diatomic Molecules.
  Part II: Polyatomic Molecules.

Refractory Compounds.

Optical Rotatory Power and Structures of Compounds with one asymmetric
carbon atom.

Wavelengths of Emission and Discontinuities in Absorption of X-Rays (Supersedes Vol. 1).

There have been several publishers for the present series. Volume 8 and
later volumes have been published by Pergamon Press from whom the
earlier volumes as well as the titles, availability, and prices of the 40 installments of Tables Annuelles, covering the period 1931 to 1936, may be
obtained.

Published by Pergamon Press, London, (4 & 5 Fitzroy Square), Paris
(24 rue des Ecoles), New York (Maxwell House, Fairview Park, Elmsford,
N. Y. 10523).

2.3. Thermodynamics Research Center

Organization

The Thermodynamics Research Center (TRC) is located in the Research
Center of Texas A & M University, College Station, Texas 77843, and is
directed by BRUNO J. ZWOLINSKI. The activities of TRC encompass data
evaluation and compilation, and theoretical and experimental research. The
data compilation projects include not only thermodynamic and other
physico-chemical properties, but also several types of spectral data which
are becoming increasingly important: infrared, ultraviolet, Raman, mass,
and nuclear magnetic resonance spectral data. These activities are supported
by a staff of some 14 professional workers plus editorial and office personnel.
Research carried out by staff members and graduate students produce, in

part, new or more reliable data for the compilations. In addition, literature searches are routinely carried out. Three distinct projects operate within TRC: the American Petroleum Institute Research Project 44, the Thermodynamics Research Center Data Project, and a project supported by the Office of Standard Reference Data of the National Bureau of Standards (NBS). These projects are described below; the various subject areas and their products are described in detail in the appropriate sections of the compendium.

2.3.1. The American Petroleum Institute Research Project 44 (API RP 44)

Was established in 1942 at NBS with the sponsorship and financial support of the API (an industrial association); and was directed by FREDERICK D. ROSSINI from its inception until 1960. In 1950, the project was moved to Carnegie Institute of Technology (now Carnegie-Mellon University); and in 1960, to its present TRC location. The project was put on a self-supporting basis in 1966, with API guaranteeing a definite support level. An API appointed Advisory Committee provides scientific guidance, and liaison with data users and sponsors. This project is closely allied, and in some respects complementary, to the other two projects, and differs mainly in the classes of compounds studied. API RP 44 covers all classes of hydrocarbons and certain classes of organic sulfur and nitrogen compounds.

Publications

Selected Values of Properties of Hydrocarbons and Related Compounds (see 3.4.2).
Catalog of Selected Infrared Spectral Data (see 3.2.16).
Catalog of Selected Raman Spectral Data (see 3.2.27).
Catalog of Selected Ultraviolet Spectral Data (see 3.2.29).
Catalog of Selected Mass Spectral Data (see 3.2.35).
Catalog of Selected Nuclear Magnetic Resonance Spectral Data (see 3.2.39).

2.3.2. The Thermodynamics Research Center (TRC) Data Project

Was known until 1963 as the Manufacturing Chemists Association (MCA) Research Project. The project was established in 1955 at the Carnegie Institute of Technology (now Carnegie-Mellon University), and moved in 1961 to its present TRC location. FREDERICK D. ROSSINI directed the project until 1960 when he was succeeded by BRUNO J. ZWOLINSKI. The project was supported by MCA (an industrial association) until 1963 at which time it assumed a self-supporting basis from the sale of data sheets. The TRC

14

Data Project covers many of the same properties as API RP 44, but for inorganic and certain classes of organic compounds, not duplicated by API RP 44.

Publications

Selected Values of Properties of Chemical Compounds (see 3.4.3).
Catalog of Selected Infrared Spectral Data (see 3.2.17).
Catalog of Selected Raman Spectral Data (see 3.2.28).
Catalog of Selected Ultraviolet Spectral Data (see 3.2.30).
Catalog of Selected Mass Spectral Data (see 3.2.36).
Catalog of Selected Nuclear Magnetic Resonance Spectral Data (see 3.2.40).

A research project supported by the Office of Standard Reference Data of NBS was initiated in 1963, and is thus linked to the National Standard Reference Data System (NSRDS, see 1.1.1.). Thermodynamic data for selected families of oxygen compounds are critically evaluated in depth. A detailed report on aliphatic alcohols is now under review.

In addition to these three projects, TRC contributes substantially to the "Annual Substance-Property Index and Bibliography" in *IUPAC Bulletin of Thermodynamics and Thermochemistry* (University of Michigan, Publications Distribution Service, 615 East University Avenue, Ann Arbor, Michigan 48106).

Other Publications

The Thermodynamics Research Center has issued *Comprehensive Index of API 44 — TRC Selected Data on Thermodynamics and Spectroscopy* which is a key to the contents of publications presenting critically evaluated numerical property values and selected spectral data that are prepared, compiled, published, and distributed by TRC. The first edition covers the 12 publications listed under API RP 44 and TRC Data Project.

Comprehensive Index of API 44 — TRC Selected Data on Thermodynamics and Spectroscopy.

Publication 100, B. J. ZWOLINSKI, Director, Thermodynamics Research Center, Texas A & M University, 1968, XVII, 507 pp, US $ 14.00. Order from the TRC Data Distribution Office, Texas A & M Research Foundation, F. E. Box 130, College Station, Texas 77843.

CHAPTER 3

Continuing Numerical Data Projects and Their Publications

The entries in this chapter comprise the bulk of the data compiling activity going on in the world today. Ideally each entry should describe a continuing data compiling activity carried out by experts in a center of excellence. However, some of the publications are not continuing in a strict sense of the word and others are included because of their usefulness even though they fall short of the highest attainable standards. The important thing is that this substantial group of activities represents what is available now on which to develop a better, more complete and hopefully coordinated system of evaluated tables of data for scientists and engineers of the world.

3.1. Nuclear Properties

General Nuclear Properties

3.1.1. Nuclear Data Project

Organization

This project is located in the Oak Ridge National Laboratory, Oak Ridge, Tennessee 37831. From 1953 to 1964, it was housed in the National Academy of Sciences - National Research Council, where it had been moved from the National Bureau of Standards. KATHARINE WAY directed the project from its inception in 1948 to July 1968; the acting director is ARTHUR SNELL. Dr. WAY is also an editor of the journal *Nuclear Data*. Financial support is supplied by the Atomic Energy Commission. The staff of the project includes eight professional members plus supporting personnel.

Coverage

Substances covered include all nuclides, but especially those with $A \geq 40$. The lower ranges are covered in particular by "Energy Levels of Light Nuclei", T. LAURITSEN and F. AJZENBERG-SELOVE (see 3.1.15.) and "Energy Levels of $Z = 11 - 21$ Nuclei", P. M. ENDT (see 3.1.16.).

The principal publication, "Nuclear Data Sheets", presents experimental results on radioactivity, nuclear moments, and nuclear reactions which give information about nuclear energy levels. The results for all nuclei of one mass number (or A-number) are grouped together into an "A-chain". The material for each A-chain includes (in order): Title Page giving the name of the compiler, nuclei discussed, and literature cut-off date; Drawings of Level Schemes; Summary Sheets; and Data Sheets.

The types of data currently presented are ground state, ground state decay, metastable state, metastable-state decay, reaction data.

Supplementary data and information provided before 1966 included nuclear moments, relative isotope abundances, adjusted mass differences, beta disintegration energy charts, energies of first 2^+-states in even-even nuclei, E2 mean-lines in even-even nuclei, a nomograph for estimating half-lives in alpha decay, beta-decay transition probabilities, and ground-state Q-values.

Sources of data include pertinent journals, abstracts, conference proceedings, and reports in the primary literature.

Analysis

All known experimental results are reported. The compilers construct level schemes to give, in their views, the most consistent and plausible interpretations of the experimental determinations. Where choices are possible, comments on the Summary Sheets indicate which data were selected in preparing the level schemes. Summary Sheets also include reasons for all spin-parity assignments. The numerical data are presented in tabular form on the Data Sheets with a literature reference for each entry. Level schemes diagrammed for an entire A-chain precede the tables. In general the group follows the recommendations of the Commission for Symbols, Units and Nomenclature of the International Union of Pure and Applied Physics in its usages.

Initially, data were published in the form of "Nuclear Data Sheets". The Data Sheets are now being issued as Section B of the new journal *Nuclear Data*, begun in late 1965, devoted to compilations and evaluations of experimental and theoretical results. Policies, conventions, bases for spin-parity assignments, and cumulative index to A-chains are given in the front of each issue. Adjusted mass differences, references, and explanations of symbols and abbreviations are given at the back of each issue. A simple method of designation on the spine of each journal indicates the A-chains covered therein. Revisions will be planned so that entire superseded issues can be discarded.

3.1.1.

One issue a year is devoted to Recent References, covering all A-chains and bringing the subscriber up-to-date with references to (and a key-word description of) articles published since the last issue of Recent References. Revisions of "Radiations of Radioactive Atoms in Frequent Use", and "Nuclear Moments" (see nos. 6 and 11 under Publications) are in preparation.

Publications

The data publications of this project have appeared in the following chronological order:

1. *Nuclear Data. A Collection of Experimental Values of Half-Lives, Radiation Energies, Relative Isotopic Abundances, Nuclear Moments, and Cross Sections*, NBS Circular 499, KATHARINE WAY, LILLA FANO, M. R. SCOTT, and KARIN THEW, U. S. Government Printing Office, Washington, D. C., 1950, XIV, 309 pp, US $ 4.25; and three supplements issued April 1951, Nov. 1951, and June 1952 (out of print). Superseded by 5.

2. *New Nuclear Data, Annual Cumulations*, issues 24 B of Vols. 6 through 10 of Nuclear Science Abstracts, published for the U. S. Atomic Energy Commission by the U. S. Government Printing Office, Washington, D. C., 1952, 1953, 1954, 1955, and 1956. The sixth annual cumulation (1957) was issued as a separate publication by the U. S. Atomic Energy Commission (published by U. S. Government Printing Office, Washington, D. C.). Superseded by 5.

3. *Nuclear Data Cards*, 1954 to 1957. National Academy of Sciences-National Research Council, 2101 Constitution Avenue, Washington, D. C. 20418, US $ 20.00/year (out of print). Superseded by 5.

4. *Nuclear Level Schemes, $A = 40 - A = 92$ (Ca—Zr)*, TID-5300, K. WAY, R. W. KING, C. L. McGINNIS, R. VAN LIESHOUT, published for the U. S. Atomic Energy Commission by the U. S. Government Printing Office, Washington, D. C., 1955, XX, 221 pp, US $ 1.75 (out of print). Superseded by 5.

5. *Nuclear Data Sheets*, January 1958 to present,

(a) 1958, 1959, 1960, 1961, Vols. 5 and 6, published by the National Academy of Sciences-National Research Council, 2101 Constitution Avenue, Washington, D. C. 20418 (out of print).

(b) Complete reprint issue (1959 to 1965) in 11 volumes, KATHARINE WAY, Ed., Academic Press, New York and London (1966), US $ 55.00.

(c) Section B of the new journal *Nuclear Data*. See 12.

6. *Radiations from Radioactive Atoms in Frequent Use*, L. SLACK and K. WAY, published for the U. S. Atomic Energy Commission by the U. S. Government Printing Office, Washington, D. C. 20402, 1959, XII, 75 pp, US $ 0.55.

7. *1959 Nuclear Data Tables*, K. WAY, Ed., pub. for the U. S. Atomic Energy Commission by the U. S. Government Printing Office, Washington, D. C. 20402, VIII, 151 pp, US $ 1.00.

8. *1960 Nuclear Data Tables*, K. WAY, Ed., published for the U. S. Atomic Energy Commission by the U. S. Government Printing Office, Washington, D. C. 20402, 1960.

Part 1: Consistent Set of Q-Values, $A \leq 66$, F. EVERLING, L. A. KOENIG, J. H. E. MATTAUCH, and A. H. WAPSTRA, 1961, XVI, 214 pp, US $ 1.50.

Part 2: Consistent Set of Q-Values, $67 \leq A \leq 199$, L. A. KOENIG, J. H. E. MATTAUCH, and A. H. WAPSTRA, 1961, XII, 456 pp, US $ 2.75.

Part 3: Nuclear Reaction Graphs, J. B. MARION, 1960, XI, 181 pp, US $ 1.25 (out of print).

Part 4: Short Tables, K. W. FORD, and A. M. KAUFMAN, L. LIDOFSKY, E. DER MATEOSIAN, and M. MCKEOWN, J. B. MARION, and S. M. SHAFROTH, G. H. FULLER, and K. WAY, 1961, V, 249 pp, US $ 1.50.

9. *Energy Levels of Nuclei, $A = 21 — A = 212$*, K. WAY, N. B. GOVE, C. L. MCGINNIS, and R. NAKASIMA, (550 pp) in Volume 1, Group 1, New Series, LANDOLT-BÖRNSTEIN, A. M. HELLWEGE, and K.-H. HELLWEGE, Eds., Springer-Verlag, Berlin-Göttingen-Heidelberg, 1961, 812 pp, US $ 53.00 (see 3.1.17.).

10. *Energy Levels of Light Nuclei*, May 1962, T. LAURITSEN, and F. AJZENBERG-SELOVE (cf 3.1.15.) issued as Sets 5 and 6 of the 1961 Nuclear Data Sheets (see no. 5), essentially an addendum to a review article in *Nucl. Phys.* **11**, 1—340 (1959). A special bound volume was issued.

11. *Nuclear Moments*, G. H. FULLER, and V. W. COHEN, National Academy of Sciences-National Research Council, 2101 Constitution Avenue, Washington, D. C. 20418, 1965, XI, 134 pp. Appendix 1 to Nuclear Data Sheets covering all references to May 1964 (out of print).

12. *Nuclear Data*, Section B, K. WAY, Ed., Academic Press, New York and London. Vol. 1, 1966, US $ 20.00; Vol. 2, 1967 to 1968 (Irregular), US $ 15.00.

Other publications of the Nuclear Data Project, which are not data compilations, are:

13. *A Directory to Nuclear Data Tabulations*, U. S. Government Printing Office, Washington, D. C. 20402, 1958, XIII, 185 pp, 70 cents. Supplements to this directory appear in 7 and in 8, Part 4, listed above, the former covering the period Dec. 1957 to Dec. 1958 and the latter the period Dec. 1959 to June 1961.

14. *Nuclear Theory Index Cards*, Jan. 1958 to 1962 (out of print).

15. *Nuclear Theory Reference Book* for the following periods: 1957 and 1958, US $ 1.00; 1959 and 1960, US $ 1.00; and 1961 and 1962, US $ 1.25. All were issued in 1963 by the U. S. Government Printing Office, Washington, D. C. 20402, and are compilations of the corresponding Nuclear Theory Index Cards made by photographic reproduction.

16. *Nuclear Theory Index Booklets*, 1963 —. These booklets were issued quarterly to replace the index cards, 14. Current bibliographic items were presented under the same headings as used on the cards. Booklet 4 for 1963 was cumulative for the entire year: Nuclear Theory Index, cumulation for 1963 (TID-21133), US $ 3.00; Nuclear Theory Index, cumulation for 1964 (TID-22771), US $ 3.00; both available from the Clearinghouse for Scientific and Technical Information, Springfield, Va. 22151.

Note: All correspondence relating to the content of the Nuclear Data Sheets or to availability not indicated for publications should be addressed to the Nuclear Data Group, Oak Ridge National Laboratory, P. O. Boxx, Oak Ridge, Tenn. 37831.

3.1.2. Nuclear Tables (Tabellen der Atomkerne)

Organization

Nuclear Tables is an extensive compilation of nuclear properties and reactions, prepared by WUNIBALD KUNZ, Vienna, Austria, and JOSEF SCHINTLMEISTER, Zentralinstitut für Kernforschung of the Deutsche Akademie der Wissenschaften, Dresden, D.D.R. The Tables were originally compiled by the authors while they were in the Soviet Union, and were later brought up to date. Part I, Nuclear Properties, and Part II, Nuclear Reactions, have been published.

Coverage

Part I, "Nuclear Properties", covers the elements neutron to tin (0 to 50) in Volume 1, and antimony to nobelium (51 to 102) in Volume 2. Part I includes data concerning stable and radioactive nuclei and decay schemes. Values are given for number of nucleons (mass number), neutrons and excess neutrons ($+$ or $-$); atomic mass; isotopic abundance; decay; half-life; energy of particles; energy of gamma-ray quanta; conversion coefficients; and decay schemes (as diagrams).

Part II, "Nuclear Reactions", covers the elements neutron to magnesium (0 to 12) in Volume 1, aluminum to sulfur (13 to 16) in Volume 2 and chlorine to calcium (17 to 20) in Volume 3. Part II includes data about nuclear reactions, and gives the energy level schemes of most of the nuclides. Volumes 1 to 3 of Part II each consist of two parts, the Text Volume and the Table Volume. The Text Volume of Volumes 1 to 3 gives nuclear reactions in tabular form. Cross-sections are presented as numerical values and in graphs. The Q-values, threshold values, kinetic energies of emitted gamma-rays, energies and quanta-characteristics of the energy levels are given in detail. The Text Volumes of Volume 2 and 3 differ from Volume 1 only in some points of presentation, which are noted and discussed. Many of these are for the benefit of the user, to clarify the level schemes and to differentiate between "decay levels" and "reaction levels". The Table Volumes give detailed energy level or decay scheme diagrams.

Data are compiled from the primary literature.

Analysis

Whenever possible, the original papers were examined. In a few cases, summary reports were used. The values given first in the tables are, in the judgment of the compilers, the most probable values; and in some cases are weighted mean values of those collected. Limits of error are generally given. Values calculated by the authors are indicated. The preface and explanation of the tables in each volume are given in German, English, and Russian. Symbols and abbreviations used are defined, and complete references provided.

Part I includes data published between 1940 and 1958. Part II, Volume 1, includes many references to articles published from 1958 to 1962. Part II, Volume 2, was published in 1967 and includes references from 1964. Part II, Volume 3 was published in 1968.

Part I, Volumes 1 and 2, and Part II, Volumes 1, 2 and 3, Text Volume, are clothbound books, 22×30 cm. Part II, Volumes 1, 2 and 3, Table Volume, consist of energy level diagrams, presented on separate sheets which come in a box the same size as the books.

Publications

Tabellen der Atomkerne (Nuclear Tables), WUNIBALD KUNZ and JOSEF SCHINTL-
MEISTER, published by Akademie-Verlag, GmbH, Berlin, D.D.R.; available from Pergamon Press, Oxford, London, and New York.

Teil (Part) I, Eigenschaften der Atomkerne (Nuclear Properties):
Band (Volume) 1, Die Elemente Neutron bis Zinn (The Elements Neutron to Tin), 1958, XLIV, 465 pp, DM 105 (US $ 26.25).
Band (Volume) 2, Die Elemente Antimon bis Nobelium (The Elements Antimony to Nobelium), 1959, XLIV, 641 pp, DM 130 (US $ 32.50).

Part II, Nuclear Reactions:
Vol. 1, The Elements from Neutron to Magnesium, 1965, Text Volume, XLVI, 699 pp, and Table Volume, 36 tables, (US $ 75.00).
Vol. 2, The Elements from Aluminum to Sulphur, 1967, Text Volume, XX, 271 pp, and Table Volume, 23 tables, DM 190 (US $ 45.00, £ 15).
Vol. 3, The Elements from Chlorine to Calcium, 1968, Text Volume, X, 210 pp, and Table Volume, 32 tables, DM 200 (US $ 50.00).

3.1.3. Nuclear Constants Group

Organization

This program is carried out at the University of California Lawrence Radiation Laboratory (LRL), Livermore, California, under the direction of

3.1.3.

ROBERT J. HOWERTON of the Theoretical Physics Division. The U.S. Atomic Energy Commission (AEC) provides financial support.

Coverage

All nuclides and naturally occurring elements are included.

Experimental neutron cross sections, angular distributions and energy spectra are accumulated over the entire energy range. Semi-empirical cross section data are compiled as follows:

$$\text{neutrons} - 10^{-10} \text{ to } 20 \text{ MeV}$$

$$\text{photons} - 10^{-3} \text{ to } 100 \text{ MeV}$$

$$\text{charged particles} - \text{as required.}$$

In addition, thresholds of nuclear reactions for the various impinging particles were issued as a compilation in 1964.

Sources of experimental data include journals, AEC report literature, private communications, and contacts with other similar data centers.

Analysis

The center is set up to answer inquiries as well as to produce state-of-the-art reviews and compilations.

A tape library of experimental neutron cross section data was originated in 1960. Modifications since that time have led to the development of the ECSIL program. This is a computer system for the storage, retrieval, and display, either tabular or graphical, of experimental neutron cross section data. Currently, approximately 600,000 data points are stored in the ECSIL library which is maintained on an updated basis. Because of the large bulk of data in the system, indexes are provided for both the data as well as the associated bibliographic information.

The semiempirical cross section tape library was also started in 1960 for neutrons only. Since that time, both photons and charged particles have been incorporated into the system. The neutron data is obtained by evaluations of the information in the ECSIL system. Photon and charged particle data are obtained in conjunction with other groups within the laboratory.

Publications

Earlier publications put out by the center are no longer available.

"A Formalism for Calculation of Neutron Induced Gamma-Ray Production Cross Sections and Spectra", R. J. HOWERTON and E. F. PLECHATY, *Nuclear Science and Engineering* **32**, 178 (1968). A library of the data is available from the authors.

An Integrated System for Production of Neutronics and Photonics Calculational Constants, UCRL-50400, Lawrence Radiation Laboratory, Livermore.

Vol. I, R. J. HOWERTON et al., "ECSIL, A System for Storage, Retrieval and Display of Experimental Neutron Data" (1968).

Vol. VI, E. F. PLECHATY and J. R. TERRALL, "Photon Cross Sections 1.0 keV to 100.0 MeV" (1968).

3.1.4. Table of Isotopes

Organization

Publication of the Table of Isotopes series was begun in 1940 by GLENN T. SEABORG and his associates. Subsequent editions have been prepared at the Lawrence Radiation Laboratory of the University of California, Berkeley, California, in 1944, 1948, 1953, 1958 and 1967. The first five compilations in this series appeared in *Reviews of Modern Physics*, and the sixth edition was published in book form. The project has been supported by the U. S. Atomic Energy Commission.

Coverage

All nuclear species, stable and unstable, are included. The sixth edition is divided into two main sections: Table I, "Radioisotope Data", a listing of stable and unstable species by element or atomic number; and Table II, "Detailed Nuclear Level Properties", decay-scheme and energy-level diagrams, arranged by mass number. Table I gives: isotope, Z and A; half-life; type of decay, % abundance, mass excess, and neutron cross section (capture and fission); certainty and means of identification, genetic relationships; major radiations; and principal means of production. Table II includes tabulations of detailed information on radiations and nuclear level properties, as well as diagrams. Among the properties listed are: spin; moments; alpha, beta, and gamma radiation data (energies, intensities, internal conversion coefficients, spectroscopic methods, angular distributions); and decay schemes.

Supplementary tables of values such as fundamental constants, energy conversion factors, nuclear spectroscopy standards, atomic levels, and theoretical nuclear decay rates are given in appendices.

The literature is the primary source of data. Especially useful for the sixth edition were existing compilations.

3.1.5.

Analysis

Table I of the sixth edition provides a ready reference to the principal decay properties. Its arrangement, conciseness, and carefully limited number of properties were selected for easy use. Table II gives detailed information on nuclear states and transitions between these states. The tabulations in Table II are measurements; the decay schemes and energy level diagrams are interpretations. In general, decay schemes are based on direct experimental information. Only those levels at energies below the decay energy of the observed neighboring isobars are included.

These two tables are selective and critical; however, a complete list of references is included so that all available data may be located. Use of the tables, the properties included, symbols and nomenclature, degree of certainty, and some experimental methods are well covered in the introduction. A seven level information-rating system is used for evaluation of how well each radioisotope has been identified.

The fundamental and derived constants listed in Appendix I are those accepted by recognized international bodies.

Six tables of the series appeared between 1940 and 1966. The April 1958 table is current approximately through February 1958; the 1967 table, through January 1966. The tables have increased in size from 17 to 594 pages.

Publications

"Table of Isotopes", J. J. Livingood and G. T. Seaborg, *Rev. Mod. Phys.* **12**, 30—47 (1940).

"Table of Isotopes", G. T. Seaborg, *Rev. Mod. Phys.* **16**, 1—32 (1944).

"Table of Isotopes", G. T. Seaborg and I. Perlman, *Rev. Mod. Phys.* **20**, 585—666 (1948).

"Table of Isotopes", J. M. Hollander, I. Perlman, and G. T. Seaborg, *Rev. Mod. Phys.* **25**, 469—650 (1953).

"Table of Isotopes", D. Strominger, J. M. Hollander, and G. T. Seaborg, *Rev. Mod. Phys.* **30**, No. 2, Part 2, 585—904 (1958). Available from the American Institute of Physics, 335 East 45th Street, New York, N. Y. 10017.

Table of Isotopes, 6th ed, C. M. Lederer, J. M. Hollander, and I. Perlman, John Wiley and Sons, Inc., New York, 1967, XIII, 594 pp, US $ 4.95 paper, US $ 7.95 cloth.

3.1.5. Landolt-Börnstein, Volume 2, Group I

Nuclear Radii, H. R. Collard, L. R. B. Elton, and R. Hofstadter; edited by H. Schopper. Vol. 2 of Group I, Nuclear Physics and Technology, of Landolt-Börnstein, Numerical Data and Functional Relationships in

24

Science and Technology, New Series, Springer-Verlag, Berlin-Heidelberg, 1967, VIII, 54 pp, DM 38 (US $ 9.50).

Organization

The book is divided into two chapters. Chapter 1 was prepared by L. R. B. ELTON, University of Surrey, London; Chapter 2 by R. HOFSTADTER and H. R. COLLARD, both of Stanford University, Stanford, California, U.S.A. The description of the LANDOLT-BÖRNSTEIN series and organization may be found in 2.1.

Coverage

The book covers radii and other parameters for the distribution of the electric charge and the magnetic moment of atomic nuclei. It is divided into two independent but complementary chapters, "Nuclear charge distribution (derived from sources other than electron scattering)", and "Nuclear radii determined by electron scattering".

Chapter 1 gives the equivalent uniform radius parameters of μ-mesic atoms for spherical nuclei, from the $2p \rightarrow 1s$ transitions, and μ-mesic X-ray transitions; changes in nuclear radii by neighboring nuclides and nuclear compressibilities; radius parameters for deformed nuclei; and radii of isomers.

Chapter 2 consists of one main, extensive table of electric charge radii, and a shorter table of magnetic radii. These tables give for the listed nuclei: the type of charge distribution, the charge radius, the radius of equivalent uniform model, skin thickness, half-density radius, equivalent uniform density, and parameters of the Fermi three parameter charge distribution. Comparable information is given for the magnetic radii.

The major source of data is the primary literature. Although the compilation work was completed well ahead of the publication date, corrections and additions were incorporated into proof only a short time before publication.

Analysis

The volume is introduced as "more than a critical compilation of published data but ... rather an original contribution to the development of this field". Considerable progress is being made in this area; and this compilation serves also as a review. In this respect, it will be most useful to persons working in this area. The data have been critically evaluated. Uncertainties and accuracies are given. Extensive discussion of the field-experimental methods and validity of the data — as checked against other information — in the introduction and discussions of many of the individual data are also included.

3.1.6. Reactor Physics Constants Center

Organization

Established in 1955, this center is located in, and supported by the Argonne National Laboratory, Argonne, Illinois. ROBERT AVERY, the director of the program, is assisted by some twenty part-time contributors. A committee of consultant editors has the responsibility for the publication "Reactor Physics Constants".

Coverage

In general, the Center compiles information necessary to calculate reactor characteristics: fission properties, cross-section data, shielding, interpretation of experimental data, digital-computer codes, and several types of reactor physics data.

These data are issued in a comprehensive publication "Reactor Physics Constants". The first edition appeared in 1958, and the second, in 1963. The two editions vary only slightly in content and cover (1) well-defined reactor physics parameters and engineering properties, and (2) instrument performance characteristics. In the first category are fission properties, cross-section data, gamma-ray activity, diffusion parameters, lattice parameters, and gamma-ray spectra and attenuation cross-sections. Engineering properties and instrument performance characteristics include shielding constants, specific operating information for various types of reactors, and descriptions of photomultiplier tubes and scintillators.

"Reactor Physics Constants" was prepared by the collaboration of several persons, many in organizations other than Argonne, some from Canada and the U.K.

Analysis

The Reactor Physics Constants Center (RPCC) also acts as a clearinghouse; and encourages standardization of parameter definitions, as well as critical evaluation of data.

"Reactor Physics Constants" implements these goals. In effect, it is a state-of-the-art review; its format is more a critical review, with many substantial tables and graphs, than a data compilation. The editors note that they have evaluated the data published, but that many other factors also determined which data were included. Most indications of reliability are found in the text.

Most references are from the primary literature. The cut-off date was March 1961; however, some later references were included. Additions and corrections to the 2nd edition will be noted in the Newsletter.

Publications

Reactor Physics Constants, Argonne National Laboratory, United States Atomic Energy Commission, 1958.

Reactor Physics Constants, ANL-5800, Argonne National Laboratory, United States Atomic Energy Commission, 1963, XVII, 850 pp. For sale by the U. S. Government Printing Office, Washington, D. C. 20402, US $ 6.00.

Other Publications

RPCC Newsletter, Reactor Physics Constants Center, Argonne National Laboratory, Argonne, Illinois 60439.

Properties of Neutrons

3.1.7. National Neutron Cross Section Center

Organization

The National Neutron Cross Section Center (NNCSC) is located at the Brookhaven National Laboratory (BNL), Upton, Long Island, New York 11973. NNCSC was formed in 1967 from the merger of what was formerly the Cross Section Evaluation Center and the Sigma Center, both of which were at BNL. The Center includes 18 professional staff members and 6 supporting personnel. The director is SOL PEARLSTEIN. An advisory committee of six scientists reviews the Center's program. On the international level, NNCSC works with the European Nuclear Energy Agency (ENEA, see 3.1.11.) and the International Atomic Energy Agency (IAEA, see 3.1.8.) for the exchange of neutron data. Support for the Center is provided by the U. S. Atomic Energy Commission.

Coverage

The NNCSC covers all available neutron cross section data for all nuclides and naturally occurring mixtures of isotopes. Separate data files are maintained for experimental, and for evaluated data. The experimental data file is used to prepare the "Barn Books" — BNL 325 covers total cross section data and BNL 400 covers angular distribution. The information storage and retrieval operations of the data file have been computerized. A new computer system being developed is known as CSISRS (Cross Section Information Storage and Retrieval System).

The evaluated data are maintained on a computerized file known as ENDF (Evaluated Nuclear Data File). Originally, the ENDF was prepared as a set of evaluated neutron cross sections for all important nuclides over the entire range of energies of importance for reactor purposes, i.e., from approximately one millivolt to 15 MeV. The range of interest has now been expanded to systems other than reactors. Although formal publication of these data will be at some future date, they are available to users in the U. S. and Canada, and by agreement to those in OECD/ENEA member countries.

The Barn Books (BNL-) prepared from the experimental data file present neutron cross section data as:

(1) thermal cross sections — reaction cross sections (absorption and activation) and scattering cross sections (coherent, incoherent, bound atom, and average) for thermal or 2200 m/s neutrons;

(2) resonance parameters — light, heavy, and fissionable nuclei;

(3) cross section curves in energy ranges from zero to 10^8 eV; and

(4) angular distribution curves mainly for elastically scattered neutrons, a large number for inelastically scattered neutrons, and some for charged particles and gamma rays associated with inelastic neutron scattering.

Sources of data are the open literature and unpublished work.

Analysis

The Barn Book publications primarily serve the needs of reactor physicists and engineers, but an attempt has been made to present the data in the form most useful to other physicists as well. In recent issues, emphasis has been on nuclear processes rather than on methods of observation. Except for the recommended values and the curves, all recorded values are experimental. The recommended values are in general weighted means of the experimental values, and are given with estimated errors. Smooth curves were drawn through the points on the graphs with no attempt to achieve a least-squares fit to any predetermined shape.

The angular distribution data are plotted on linear grids. Textual references, laboratory in which the measurements were made, type of experiment, and other pertinent information are given on the left-hand page facing the graphs.

Generally, all experimental data influencing the choice of recommended values are included and referred to, so that the user can evaluate the data presented. Reference sources are provided. Older, obviously superseded data are generally not included. Most supplements must be used with the other material published in the series to insure complete coverage.

Supplements and revisions are issued at irregular intervals. Unpublished contributions and a short publication lag result in up-to-date coverage.

Publications

BNL 325, *Neutron Cross Sections*, D. J. HUGHES and J. A. HARVEY, U.S. Government Printing Office (GPO*), Washington, D. C. 20402, July 1955, V, 328 pp, US $ 3.50.

Supplement 1, D. J. HUGHES and R. B. SCHWARTZ, GPO*, Washington, D.C. 20402, January 1957, XXVII, 129 pp, US $ 1.75.

BNL 325, *Neutron Cross Sections*, 2nd ed, D. J. HUGHES and R. B. SCHWARTZ, U.S. Government Printing Office (GPO*), Washington, D.C. 20402, July 1958, V, 373 pp, US $ 4.50. Supersedes 1st ed and its supplement.

Supplement 1, D. J. HUGHES, B. A. MAGURNO, and M. K. BRUSSEL, GPO*, Washington, D.C. 20402, January 1960, IV, 129 pp, US $ 2.00.

Supplement 2, *Vol. I*, $Z = 1$ *to 20*, J. R. STEHN, M. D. GOLDBERG, B. A. MAGURNO, and R. WIENER-CHASMAN, GPO*, Washington, D.C. 20402, May 1964, sectional pagination (sec pag), US $ 2.50.

Vol. IIA, $Z = 21$ *to 40*, M. D. GOLDBERG, S. F. MUGHABGHAB, B. A. MAGURNO, and V. M. MAY, Clearinghouse for Federal Scientific and Technical Information (CFSTI**), Springfield, Virginia 22151, February 1966, sec pag, US $ 4.00.

Vol. IIB, $Z = 41$ *to 60*, M. D. GOLDBERG, S. F. MUGHABGHAB, S. N. PUROHIT, B. A. MAGURNO, and V. M. MAY, CFSTI**, Springfield, Virginia 22151, May 1966, sec pag, US $ 4.00.

Vol. IIC, $Z = 61$ *to 87*, M. D. GOLDBERG, S. F. MUGHABGHAB, S. N. PUROHIT, B. A. MAGURNO, and V. M. MAY, CFSTI**, Springfield, Virginia 22151, August 1966, sec pag, US $ 3.00 printed, US $ 0.65 microfiche.

Vol. III, $Z = 88$ *to 98*, J. H. STEHN, M. D. GOLDBERG, R. WIENER-CHASMAN, S. F. MUGHABGHAB, B. A. MAGURNO, and V. M. MAY, CFSTI**, Springfield, Virginia 22151, February 1965, sec pag, US $ 3.00.

BNL 400, *Neutron Cross Sections: Angular Distributions*, D. J. HUGHES and R. S. CARTER, Clearinghouse for Federal Scientific and Technical Information, Springfield, Virginia 22151, June 1956, 102 pp, US $ 0.50.

BNL 400, *Neutron Cross Sections: Angular Distributions in Neutron-Induced Reactions*, 2nd ed, Vols. I, $Z = 1$ to 22, and II, $Z = 23$ to 94, M. D. GOLDBERG, V. M. MAY, and J. R. STEHN, Clearinghouse for Federal Scientific and Technical Information, Springfield, Virginia 22151, October 1962, 804 pp, sec pag, US $ 8.50.

Other Publications

BNL 50066, *ENDF/B — Specifications for an Evaluated Nuclear Data File for Reactor Applications*, HENRY C. HONECK, Clearinghouse for Federal Scientific and Technical Information, Springfield, Virginia 22151, September 1967, sec pag, US $ 3.00.

3.1.8.   IAEA Nuclear Data Unit

Organization

The International Atomic Energy Agency (IAEA) is actively promoting international collaboration in the area of basic information in nuclear

---

* U.S. Government Printing Office, Washington, D.C. 20402.
** Clearinghouse for Federal Scientific and Technical Information, Springfield, Virginia 22151.

physics. To this end it established the Nuclear Data Unit at its headquarters in Vienna in 1965. The activities of this Unit are guided by the suggestions and the advice of the IAEA's standing *International Nuclear Data Committee*. Accordingly, in 1966 the Nuclear Data Unit initiated a data center for promoting worldwide compilation and exchange of numerical neutron data. In this latter effort the Nuclear Data Unit engages cooperatively with three other recognized, principal neutron data centers located respectively at Brookhaven, Obninsk and Saclay. Each center is responsible for servicing a specific area of the world as follows: the Brookhaven National Neutron Cross Section Center, U.S.A. (see 3.1.7.), services the U.S.A. and Canada; the ENEA Neutron Data Compilation Center at Saclay, France (see 3.1.11.), services countries in Western Europe and Japan; the Informacionnyj Centr po Jadernym (Nuclear Data Information Centre), Obninsk, U.S.S.R. (see 3.1.12.), services the U.S.S.R.; and the IAEA Nuclear Data Unit, Kärntner Ring 11, A—1010 Vienna, Austria, services all other countries in Eastern Europe, Asia, Africa, South and Central America, Australia and New Zealand. The Nuclear Data Unit, directed by WILFRED M. GOOD, is a section of IAEA.

Coverage

The numerical data include: measured or deduced microscopic neutron cross sections; related fission, capture and scattering parameters; and other microscopic data for a given target nucleus. Pertinent auxiliary information is also given, such as element symbol, mass number, class of neutron data, range of incident neutron energy, complete reference information, and such additional documentary information as is deemed essential by the author for significant use of his data.

The numerical and other data are maintained in a computer file, which is compatible with other large computerized systems of neutron data. The IAEA computerized system is known as "DASTAR", the *DA*ta *ST*orage *A*nd *R*etrieval System of the IAEA Nuclear Data Unit. *Data* are retrieved by means of an index which is called CINDU (*C*atalogue of the *IA*EA *N*uclear *D*ata *U*nit). CINDU is printed and distributed regularly with the information arranged by increasing Z number, from Hydrogen $Z = 1$ to Californium $Z = 98$. Information thus given includes: element, symbol and mass number; class of neutron data; cross section quantity; range of incident neutron energy; type of reference and investigation; and references, comments, and entry date. The format of CINDU is based on CINDA (see 3.1.19.), *C*omputer *I*ndex to the literature on microscopic *N*eutron *DA*ta, which is an internationally sponsored index to *literature*.

Analysis

The compilation of experimental neutron data and the evaluation of experimental neutron data are treated as separate functions. Evaluation is performed almost exclusively away from the data centers, which rather serve as coordinators; thus the distinction between experimental data and evaluated data has become very strict. The evaluator, wherever he works, uses the experimental data from the center's compiled files to make his evaluation. His product, the evaluated data, is however entered into the evaluated data file at the data center. Even though the data center's evaluation activity is limited, it nevertheless compiles evaluated data exactly as it compiles experimental data.

Some evaluations are made under the auspices of the IAEA Nuclear Data Unit, with the help of specialists' panels regularly convened for the purpose; such evaluations are presently the following:

a) Standards for neutron cross section measurements,

b) World values for certain parameters of fissile isotopes at thermal neutron energy.

The data are on magnetic tape and are available upon request in various forms. These include magnetic tape, printed lists, punched cards, and graphical plots. All data are conformed to common practice before being added to the data file.

Publications

CINDU, *Catalogue of Numerical Neutron Data available from the IAEA Nuclear Data Unit*, No. 7 (CINDU-7), IAEA Nuclear Data Unit, Vienna, May 1968, 136 pp.

3.1.9. Neutron Cross Sections for Fast Reactor Materials

Organization

This project is located in the Kernforschungszentrum (Nuclear Research Center), Karlsruhe, Germany, in the Institut für Neutronenphysik und Reaktortechnik. The author of the volumes appearing under the title name is J. J. SCHMIDT, a member of the Institut. Neutron data evaluation was started in 1960. This project has contributed to the data files of the European Nuclear Energy Agency (ENEA) located in Saclay, France (see 3.1.11.).

Coverage

Three volumes and an introductory statement have appeared under this title. Two volumes, i.e., Part II: Tables (1962) and Part III: Graphs (1963) appeared before the third volume, Part I: Evaluation (1966). Parts II and III contain recommended values for neutron cross sections for all occurring neutron nuclear interactions in the energy range 0.01 eV to 10 MeV for C, Cr, Fe, H, He, Mo, Na, Ni, O, ^{239}P, ^{235}U, and ^{238}U.

Part I: Evaluation provides documentation for Parts II and III. In addition, it contains extensive tables of resolved and statistical resonance parameters and updated level schemes for the isotopes concerned. However, a great portion of Part I is devoted to consideration of information published between 1962 and 1966, and to updating the data in Parts II and III.

The data in Part I have been added to the computerized microscopic data library called KEDAK (the Karlsruhe nuclear data file). This file has been used to produce a fourth uptadet volume *Tables of Evaluated Neutron Cross Sections for Fast Reactor Materials* (1968) which in general covers the same elements and properties — neutron cross sections and resonance parameters — included in the earlier series.

Publications

Neutron Cross Sections for Fast Reactor Materials, J. J. SCHMIDT, Kernforschungszentrum, Karlsruhe (KFK 120; EANDC — E — 35 — U).
Introduction, Part I: Evaluation, 1967, 12 pp.
Part I: Evaluation, 1966, 1300 pp.
Part II: Tables, 1962, 440 pp.
Part III: Graphs, 1963, 320 pp.

Tables of Evaluated Neutron Cross Sections for Fast Reactor Materials, I. LANGNER, J. J. SCHMIDT, and D. WOLL, Kernforschungszentrum, Karlsruhe (KFK 750; EUR 3715; EANDC — E — 88 — U), Jan. 1968, 663 pp.

3.1.10. UKAEA Nuclear Data Library

Organization

A program, several years old, of evaluating nuclear cross sections provides the data for the UKAEA Nuclear Data Library. K. PARKER and E. PENDLEBURG at the Atomic Weapons Research Establishment, Aldermaston, J. S. STORY at the Atomic Energy Establishment, Winfrith, and W. HART at the Authority Health and Safety Branch, Risley, participate in this activity. The program cooperates in international exchange of nuclear data by making its evaluated data available through the ENEA Neutron Data Compilation Centre, Saclay, France (see 3.1.11.), and the National Neutron Cross Section Center at Brookhaven National Laboratory, New York, U. S. A. (see 3.1.7.).

Coverage

Covered are neutron cross sections in the energy range 0 to 20 MeV, and photon cross sections in the energy range 10 KeV to 20 MeV.

The data are evaluated and then stored in a form for computer use. Computer programs are used to check the data filed for internal consistency.

Publications

Details concerning the library may be found in:

UKAEA Nuclear Data Library, January 1967, D. S. NORTON, J. S. STORY, Atomic Energy Establishment, Winfrith (England), February 1968, 19 pp, UK 3s. 6d.

3.1.11. ENEA Neutron Data Compilation Centre

Organization

In 1964, the European Nuclear Energy Agency established, within its framework, the Neutron Data Compilation Centre (Centre de Compilation de Données Neutroniques — CCDN) at the Centre d'Etudes Nucléaires at Saclay, France, in order to provide a coordinating point in Europe for neutron data compilation, classification, and distribution. This center is part of the Organization for Economic Cooperation and Development (OECD) and is supported by Austria, Belgium, Denmark, France, Germany (B.R.D.), Italy, Japan, the Netherlands, Norway, Spain, Sweden, Switzerland, and the United Kingdom.

The center also participates in international neutron data exchange programs; it both contributes to and publishes issues of CINDA (see 3.1.19.), and it cooperates with three other centers — Brookhaven National Neutron Cross Section Center, New York, U.S.A. (see 3.1.7.); IAEA Nuclear Data Unit, Vienna, Austria (see 3.1.8.); and the U.S.S.R. Nuclear Data Information Centre, Obninsk, U.S.S.R. (see 3.1.12.) — in servicing world neutron data needs (see 3.1.8.). The ENEA Neutron Data Compilation Centre processes both data and data requests from Western Europe and Japan — the countries listed above.

The director of the center is V. J. BELL, ENEA Neutron Data Compilation Centre, B. P. no. 9, 91-Gif-sur-Yvette, France.

Coverage

Compilation of neutron data from the 13 OECD countries is a major activity. The data are stored in computer files. The center can also provide users with CINDA, or specific searches of CINDA.

The center has built up a library of evaluated data files, notably the UKAEA Nuclear Data Library (see 3.1.10.), the Evaluated Nuclear Data File (see 3.1.7.), and the Karlsruhe KEDAK library (see 3.1.9.), among others.

Some data evaluation work is done at the center. These compilations are published in the ENEA Neutron Data Compilation Centre Newsletter.

3.1.12.   U.S.S.R. Nuclear Data Information Centre

The U.S.S.R. Nuclear Data Information Centre (Informacionnyj Centr po Jadernym) is located in the Institute of Physics and Energetics, Obninsk (Kaluga region), U.S.S.R., and is directed by A. I. ABRAMOV. This center is one of the four contributors to CINDA (see 3.1.19.). It also participates in an international effort to exchange numerical neutron data (see 3.1.8.). The other three centers are: the Brookhaven National Neutron Cross Section Center, U.S.A. (see 3.1.7.); the ENEA Neutron Data Compilation Centre, Saclay, France (see 3.1.11.); and the IAEA Nuclear Data Unit, Vienna, Austria (see 3.1.8.). As part of the international effort, the Centre services the U.S.S.R. by compiling nuclear data submitted by workers in this area and by providing data upon request.

Properties of Nuclides

3.1.13.   Charged-Particle Cross Sections

Organization

This project, sponsored by the U.S. Atomic Energy Commission (AEC), is carried on in the Charged-Particle Cross-Section (CPX) Data Center of the Physics Division at Oak Ridge National Laboratory (ORNL), Oak Ridge, Tennessee, under the supervision of FRANCIS K. McGOWAN. The program originated at Los Alamos Scientific Laboratory, University of California, Los Alamos, New Mexico, in 1955. It was discontinued in 1960, and after a brief lapse was started again at ORNL.

Coverage

Compilations include cross-section data at all energies for nuclear reactions of the type A (x, y) B, were A is the target nucleus and B the residual nucleus, x is the bombarding charged particle, and y is the outgoing particle or particles in the reaction. The mass of x must be equal to or greater than one nucleon mass. To date, only targets from hydrogen (as proton, deutron, and triton) through copper have been covered. Bombarding particles include $p, d, t, \alpha, {}^3\text{He}, {}^6\text{Li}, {}^{12}\text{C}, {}^{14}\text{N}, {}^{16}\text{O}$ and in a few isolated reactions ${}^{15}\text{N}, {}^{19}\text{F}, {}^{20}\text{Ne}$, and ${}^{22}\text{Ne}$.

Cross-section data at all energies including angular distributions and excitation functions, and data on angular dependence of polarization produced in nuclear reactions are included.

Primary sources of data consist of the open literature, AEC reports, and preprints of papers to be published. Nuclear Science Abstracts, Physics Abstracts, and Chemical Abstracts are used as secondary sources.

Analysis

In general, only one reference is given for each set of data: this is either the only set available or the best set as judged by the compiler. Errors given for cross sections are standard deviations. When the type of error was not designated by the author, the compiler has arbitrarily assumed that the errors were standard deviations. For some of the earlier cross-section data the only source is a small figure from a journal. In general, the accuracy of the data points read from the small figures depends on the accuracy of the original drawing and on the distortions resulting from publication. Captions to the tabular data include the reaction, the energy E (in the laboratory frame of reference), and the energy of the merging particle (or particles), Q taken from the 1961 *Nuclear Data Tables*, the reference, contributing laboratory, and a few experimental details. In most cases, some indication of the errors is given.

In general, the symbols used conform to those in use by the Nuclear Data Project (see 3.1.1.) and recommended by the Commission for Symbols, Units, and Nomenclature of the International Union of Pure and Applied Physics. Lists of symbols and abbreviations are given in LA—2014 and ORNL—CPX—1 (see Publications).

The first report issued in Los Alamos appeared in February 1957 and the second, January 1961. The two reports cover targets hydrogen through fluorine, and neon through chromium, respectively. The first compilation by the ORNL group, issued in July 1964, covers manganese, iron, and cobalt. The second, issued in January 1965, covers nickel and copper. Both cover the literature up to January 1964. Future plans are to finish the first cycle of the compilation — nickel through uranium — in three or four sections and, concurrently, to bring the cross-section data up to date for the light elements. Future issues of data will appear in Section A of the journal *Nuclear Data: A Journal Devoted to Compilations and Evaluations of Experimental and Theoretical Results in Nuclear Physics* (see also 3.1.1.) (see Publications).

Publications

Charged Particle Cross Sections, LA-2014, NELSON JARMIE and JOHN D. SEAGRAVE, Eds., Los Alamos (LA) Scientific Laboratory, University of California, Los Alamos, N. M., February 1957, 234 pp, US $ 1.25. Available from the Clearinghouse for Federal Scientific and Technical Information (CFSTI*), Springfield, Virginia 22151.

Charged Particle Cross Sections, LA-2424, Neon to Chromium, DARRYL B. SMITH, Compiler and Ed., NELSON JARMIE and JOHN D. SEAGRAVE, associate Eds., Los Alamos (LA) Scientific Laboratory, University of California, Los Alamos, N. M., January 1961, III, 137 pp, US $ 2.50. Available from CFSTI*, Springfield, Virginia 22151.

Nuclear Cross Sections for Charged-Particle Induced Reactions, (Mn, Fe, Co), ORNL-CPX-1, F. K. McGOWAN, W. T. MILNER, and H. J. KIM, compilers, Oak Ridge National Laboratory, Oak Ridge, Tenn. 37831, July 1964, 443 pp.

Nuclear Cross Sections for Charged-Particle Induced Reactions, (Ni, Cu), ORNL-CPX-2, F. K. McGOWAN, W. T. MILNER, and H. J. KIM, compilers, Oak Ridge National Laboratory, Oak Ridge, Tenn. 37831, Sept. 1964, III, 511 pp.

Nuclear Cross Sections for Charged-Particle-Induced Reactions, (Li, Be, B), compiled by H. J. KIM, W. T. MILNER, and F. K. McGOWAN, *Nuclear Data A1*, 203—389 (1966), issues 3 and 4 combined US $ 6.00, Academic Press, 111 Fifth Avenue, New York, N. Y. 10003.

Nuclear Cross Sections for Charged-Particle-Induced Reactions, (C), compiled by H. J. KIM, W. T. MILNER, and F. K. McGOWAN, *Nuclear Data A2*, 1—241 (1966), issues 1 and 2 combined US $ 6.00, Academic Press, 111 Fifth Avenue, New York, N. Y. 10003.

Nuclear Cross Sections for Charged-Particle-Induced Reactions, (N and O), compiled by H. J. KIM, W. T. MILNER, and F. K. McGOWAN, *Nuclear Data A3*, 123—285 (1967), issue 2, US $ 3.00, Academic Press, 111 Fifth Avenue, New York, N. Y. 10003.

"Charged Particle Cross Sections", to be published in Section A of *Nuclear Data: A Journal Devoted to Compilations and Evaluations of Experimental and Theoretical Results in Nuclear Physics*, Academic Press, New York, London. Subscription price, US $ 15.00 per volume (per section).

3.1.14. Decay Schemes of Radioactive Nuclei

Organization

Two editions with the above title have appeared since 1958. They were published by the U. S. S. R. Academy of Sciences Press. The first was by B. S. DZHELEPOV and L. K. PEKER; the second by the same authors with V. O. SERGEJEV as a coauthor. The first edition has been translated into English and published by Pergamon Press.

Coverage

The first edition included radioactive nuclei from $A = 1$ to $A = 256$; the second edition, nuclei from $A = 100$ to $A = 257$.

Decay scheme diagrams of radioactive nuclei are presented, i.e., the ground and excited states of nuclei and the probabilities of different transitions between them. The second edition, in addition to the data on levels excited in radioactive decay, includes data on levels excited in different nuclear reactions, such as Coulomb excitation (n, r), (d, p). Numerical values referring to energy levels and transitions between them are placed directly on the diagrams. Mass, isotopic abundance, half-life, transition energies, and other information are given on the diagrams. Tables at the end of the second edition give spin values, magnetic dipole and electric quadrupole moments, conventional names of radioactive isotopes, binding energies of electrons, cross sections of nuclear activation by thermal neutrons, and nomograms for calculation of $\log ft$, for β^--, β^+-, and ε-transitions.

The primary literature was surveyed for data.

Analysis

Both editions have a title page and introduction in English and Russian and give the English meanings of abbreviations. The introduction has an excellent description of the decay scheme diagrams and supplementary data. The second edition has a two-page list defining symbols in Russian only; however, the symbols throughout the book are in roman characters. On a diagram, all the isotopes with the mass number A are given at the top of the page by chemical symbol, with mass number as a right superscript, atomic number as a left superscript, and number of neutrons in the nucleus as a right subscript, in part contrary to the International Union of Pure and Applied Physics recommendations. Supplementary information and a bibliography are given for each nuclide.

The decay scheme diagrams of the first edition, published in 1958, were constructed from experimental data published up to the end of 1957. The diagrams of the second edition (1963) were based on data published and available to the authors up to April 1962. Many of the schemes of the first edition were revised for the second edition.

The first edition of the Russian text is a well-bound 18×27 cm book printed on good-quality paper. The second edition is the same size, but has a less attractive binding and paper of much poorer quality. The printing is clear in both text and diagrams. The English translation is a well-bound book 17×26 cm. Addenda of new references are given at the end of each edition.

3.1.15.

Publications

Decay Schemes of Radioactive Nuclei, B. S. Dzhelepov and L. K. Peker, U.S.S.R. Academy of Sciences Press, Moscow and Leningrad, 1958, VIII, 787 pp, English translation, Pergamon Press, New York, Oxford, London, Paris, 1961, VI, 786 pp.

Decay Schemes of Radioactive Nuclei, $A \geq 100$, B. S. Dzhelepov, L. K. Peker, and V. O. Sergejev, U.S.S.R. Academy of Sciences Press, Moscow and Leningrad, 1963, 1060 pp.

3.1.15. Energy Levels of Light Nuclei

Organization

Seven reports have been published since 1948. These reports are reviews as well as compilations, and summarize experimental information on the energy level schemes of the nuclei from ^{5}He to ^{24}Ne; the seventh (1966) was limited to $A = 5$ to 10. Thomas Lauritsen of the California Institute of Technology, Pasadena, California, and Fay Ajzenberg-Selove of Haverford College, Haverford, Pennsylvania, have been the major authors. The work has been supported in part by the Office of Scientific Research of the U.S. Air Force, by a joint program of the U.S. Office of Naval Research and U.S. Atomic Energy Commission, and by the National Science Foundation. This project complements "Energy Levels of $Z = 11 - 21$ Nuclei" (see 3.1.16.).

Coverage

Data on the light nuclei ^{5}He to ^{24}Ne ($Z = 2$ to $Z = 10$) are presented, except for VII (1966) which is limited to $A = 5$ to 10 and VII (1968) $A = 11$ to 12.

Included are: energy level diagrams, tables of values, and the nuclear reactions in which the nuclei are involved. Numerical values are given for excitation energies, masses, Q-values, binding energies (weighted mean values), resonances, γ-transitions, cross sections, and a separate table of atomic mass excesses.

Sources of data include the open literature and some prepublished data.

Analysis

These publications constitute a series of compilations summarizing experimental information on the energy levels of nuclei. The first six covered $Z = 2$ to $Z = 10$; the seventh was limited to $A = 5$ to 10 to permit more timely publication. Each publication is independent; however, for certain reactions earlier summaries may be consulted for more detailed discussion and bibliography.

38

The data upon which the level schemes are based are tabulated, analyzed, and discussed for each nuclide covered. Uncertainties and ranges of error are given; and complete references are provided. In VI (1959) and VII (1966), "best" values are indicated in tables of data when appropriate. In addition, quantities which are calculated or converted, and numbers or parameters whose identification is uncertain are indicated.

Literature references cited are very close to the date the manuscript was reviewed.

Publications

Energy Levels of Light Nuclei

I. W. F. HORNYAK and T. LAURITSEN, *Rev. Mod. Phys.* **20**, 191—227 (1948).

II. T. LAURITSEN, *Nat. Acad. Sci.-Nat. Res. Council, Nucl. Sci. Rept.* **5**, 52 pp. (1949) — (out of print).

III. W. F. HORNYAK, T. LAURITSEN, P. MORRISON, and W. A. FOWLER, *Rev. Mod. Phys.* **22**, 291—372 (1950).

IV. F. AJZENBERG and T. LAURITSEN, *Rev. Mod. Phys.* **24**, 321—402 (1952).

V. F. AJZENBERG and T. LAURITSEN, *Rev. Mod. Phys.* **27**, 77—166 (1955).

VI. F. AJZENBERG-SELOVE and T. LAURITSEN, *Nucl. Phys.* **11**, 1—340 (1959). Available for US $ 10.00 from North-Holland Publishing Company, P. O. Box 103, Amsterdam, The Netherlands (out of print). (A supplement to this was published as "Nuclear Data Sheets, Sets 5 and 6 of 1961". See Nuclear Data Project, Publications, 3.1.1.).

VII. T. LAURITSEN and F. AJZENBERG-SELOVE, "Energy Levels of Light Nuclei, $A = 5 - 10$", *Nucl. Phys.* **78**, 1—176 (1966). Available for US $ 4.00 from the North-Holland Publishing Co., P. O. Box 103, Amsterdam, The Netherlands.

VII. F. AJZENBERG-SELOVE and T. LAURITSEN, "Energy Levels of Light Nuclei, (VII), $A = 11 - 12$", *Nucl. Phys. A* **114**, 1—142 (1968). Available for US $ 5.00 from the North-Holland Publishing Co., P. O. Box 103, Amsterdam, The Netherlands.

3.1.16. Energy Levels of $Z = 11 - 21$ Nuclei

Organization

Four compilations on the above subject have been published since 1954. Compiled by P. M. ENDT and his colleagues of the Fysisch Laboratorium, Rijksuniversiteit, Utrecht, the Netherlands, this series consists of reviews as well as compilations, and complements the project "Energy Levels of Light Nuclei" (see 3.1.15.).

3.1.17.

Coverage

Substances covered are the light nuclei, $Z = 11$ to $Z = 21$. Included are: energy levels with spins, parities and isospins (both tabular and schematic form), decay modes, weighted mean values of lifetimes, excitation and resonance energies, and tables of atomic mass excesses, natural abundance, and nuclear moments.

Sources of data include the open literature and private communications.

Analysis

The evaluation of the data for each nuclide is discussed.

The articles have appeared at three- to five-year intervals. Each one brings the data up to date. However, papers of only historical interest or those which have been superseded have been omitted from the later bibliographies. Article IV, for which the manuscript was submitted 31 July 1967, contained references up to 1 July 1967.

Publications

Energy Levels of Light Nuclei, $Z = 11$ to $Z = 20$.

I. P. M. Endt and J. C. Kluyver, *Rev. Mod. Phys.* **26**, 95—166 (1954). Back issues can be ordered from the American Institute of Physics, 335 East 45th Street, New York, N.Y. 10017, at US $ 2.25 each.

II. P. M. Endt and C. M. Braams, *Rev. Mod. Phys.* **29**, No. 4, 683—756 (1957). Back issues can be ordered from the American Institute of Physics, 335 East 45th Street, New York, N.Y. 10017, at US $ 2.25 each.

III. P. M. Endt and C. van der Leun, *Nucl. Phys.* **34**, 1—324 (1962). Reprints are available for US $ 10.00 from North-Holland Publishing Company, P. O. Box 103, Amsterdam, The Netherlands.

Energy Levels of $Z = 11 — 21$ Nuclei

IV. P. M. Endt and C. van der Leun, *Nucl. Phys.* A **105**, 1—488 (1967); errata and addenda *Nucl. Phys.* A **115**, 697 (1968). Reprints are available for US $ 12.00 from North-Holland Publishing Company, P. O. Box 103, Amsterdam, The Netherlands.

3.1.17. Landolt-Börnstein, Volume 1, Group I

Energy Levels of Nuclei: $A = 5$ *to* $A = 257$ by F. Ajzenberg-Selove, N. B. Gove, T. Lauritsen, C. L. McGinnis, R. Nakasima, J. Scheer, and K. Way, edited by A. M. Hellwege and K.-H. Hellwege. Volume 1 of Group I, Nuclear Physics and Technology, of Landolt-Börnstein, Numerical Data and Functional Relationships in Science and Technology, New Series, Springer-Verlag, Berlin-Heidelberg, 1961, XII, 813 pp, DM 212 (US $ 53.00).

Organization

This volume consists of three chapters prepared by three groups of compilers in different places. Chapter 1 was prepared by F. Ajzenberg-Selove, Haverford College, Haverford, Pennsylvania, U.S.A., and T. Lauritsen, California Institute of Technology, Pasadena, California, U.S.A. (see also 3.1.15.); Chapter 2, by K. Way, N. B. Gove, C. L. McGinnis, and R. Nakasima, Nuclear Data Project, Oak Ridge National Laboratory, Oak Ridge, Tennessee, U.S.A. (see also 3.1.1.); and Chapter 3, by J. Scheer, Universität Heidelberg, Fed. Rep. of Germany, and Lawrence Radiation Laboratory, University of California, Berkeley, California, U.S.A. The modes of presentation differ slightly from one another. Each chapter has its own introduction and list of references. Uniformity of the volume has been assured by establishing a correspondence in the material content of the three chapters. The compilation was published under the auspices of "Landolt-Börnstein", described in 2.1.

Chapter I

Coverage

The first chapter (94 pages) deals with the energy levels of light nuclei from ^{5}He to ^{20}Na. The tables list the following parameters for each level as far as known: the excitation energy above the ground state; the total angular momentum quantum number and parity, and the isobaric spin quantum number; the half-life or mean life of the state or its half-width, and the known modes of decay of the states. The diagrams include information on energy levels, nuclei-forming reactions, binding energies, Q-values, thin-target excitation functions, cross sections, center-of-mass energy, as well as excitation energies, angular momentum quantum number and parity, and the isobaric spin quantum number.

Analysis

In all but a few cases, the 1960 mass tables and Q-value tables of Everling, Koenig, Mattauch and Wapstra, *Nuclear Physics* 15, 342 (1960), were used. In some cases more precise values became available after the publication of the mass tables and were used in computing Q-values and excitation energies. Tabulated probable errors indicated are generally weighted means from several determinations and include uncertainties in mass values.

In addition to specific references to data, supplementary references are provided. The brevity of the introduction implies that the user must be knowledgeable in this area. All symbols are defined and brief comments are sometimes given on the diagrams.

3.1.17.

Chapter II

Coverage

The second chapter (565 pages) deals with energy levels of atom masses $A = 21$ to $A = 212$. It was prepared by members of the U. S. Nuclear Data Project and overlaps data published by that group (see 3.1.1.). It gives in diagrammatic form the available information on the energies, decay modes, half-lives, spins, and parities of the levels of medium-weight atomic nuclei, and presents on the pages facing the diagrams reasons for making spin-parity assignments, comments on the level schemes, information on mass differences used, and literature references to basic data.

Analysis

The introduction is very useful in its presentation of detailed descriptions of the level scheme conventions, spin and parity assignments, mass links, references, general conventions — including determination of uncertainties — and symbols and abbreviations; and in general facilitates use of the material. Uncertainties are indicated on the diagrams and in the explanatory material.

Chapter III

Coverage

The third chapter (154 pages) covers the heavy-element region with mass numbers 213 to 257. The following properties are given on the energy level diagrams: energies, spins, parities, and rotational quantum numbers for each level. Also given are the energies and multipolarities of gamma-transitions. Intensities are included.

On the pages facing the figures there are presented level tables with assignments of quantum numbers to the levels and radiation tables with data on the radiation of the listed nuclide.

Analysis

A complete tabulation of all nuclear data was not intended. When information from different sources is available only a single selected value is given. In cases of serious discrepancies, the different values are listed independently. In no cases have average values been given because of the problem of assigning relative weights to the different values. Uncertain data transitions and levels are marked.

42

Arrangement of the nuclides, use of the tables, and symbols are discussed in the introduction.

3.1.18. Photonuclear Data Center

Organization

The Photonuclear Data Center was established in 1963. It is located in the LINAC Radiation Division, Center for Radiation Research, National Bureau of Standards (NBS), Washington, D.C. 20234. The program is supported by the Office of Standard Reference Data, NBS (see 1.1.1.), and directed by EVERETT G. FULLER.

Coverage

Interactions of high energy electromagnetic radiation with nuclei are covered. These include: total photon interaction cross sections, cross sections for specific photon induced reactions, spectra and angular distribution of photo-disintegration reaction products, inverse capture reactions, inelastic electron scattering cross sections, Q-values for photonuclear reactions, and abundance of stable isotopes. The energy range of primary interest is 5 to 150 MeV.

A comprehensive Photonuclear Data File is maintained that includes abstracts of significant data from each reference. The literature has been searched back to 1955 and is essentially current. Nine journals are searched for data and *Nuclear Science Abstracts* is used to cover other journals. In general, only articles published in journals are abstracted, although a few conference reports have been included. The publications to date include "Photonuclear Data Index" published in 1966, and a supplement issued in 1967. These publications differ from bibliographies in that quantitative information (numerical data) concerning the content is included. The Indexes are arranged by element and isotope from $Z = 1$ to $Z = 95$. Each entry is a line tabulation of the reference, nucleus excited, reaction, type of information, excitation energy range, source type and energy range, detector type, energy and angular range, and remarks.

Analysis

A data file on photonuclear reactions is maintained up-to-date. With the literature search well underway, the systematic evaluation of data has been started. A critical review of all available data on the s-shell nuclei is in progress. These evaluations will be published as monographs or review articles in the National Standard Reference Data Series. At present, bibliography-indexes are published periodically.

3.1.19.

Publications

Photonuclear Data Index, NBS Misc. Pub. 277, N. V. BAGGETT, T. M. COLLINS, E. G. FULLER, J. C. HOLLAND, J. H. HUBBELL, and J. S. O'CONNELL, U.S. Government Printing Office (GPO), Washington, D.C. 20402, 1966, IV, 96 pp, US $ 0.55.

Photonuclear Data Index: January 1965 through April 1967, NBS Misc. Pub. 277-Supplement 1, T. M. COLLINS, E. G. FULLER, J. D. MURPHY and J. S. O'CONNELL, GPO, Washington, D.C. 20402, 1967, IV, 66 pp, US $ 0.45.

Indexes

3.1.19. CINDA (Computer Index of Neutron Data): An Index to the Literature on Microscopic Neutron Data

Organization

CINDA is an index to the literature on microscopic neutron cross sections and allied data. Begun as a private effort by HERBERT GOLDSTEIN in 1956, today the compilation and publication of this index are the result of international cooperation involving four information centers, each of which is responsible for servicing a specific area of the world. The person to contact at the center, the name of the center, and its area of responsibility are: LAWRENCE T. WHITEHEAD, USAEC (U.S. Atomic Energy Commission), Division of Technical Information Extension, Oak Ridge, Tennessee, U.S.A: U.S.A. and Canada; VICTOR J. BELL, ENEA Neutron Data Compilation Centre, Saclay, France (see also 3.1.11.): OECD (Organization for Economic Cooperation and Development) countries, i.e., Austria, Belgium, Denmark, France, Germany, Italy, Japan, the Netherlands, Norway, Spain, Sweden, Switzerland, and the United Kingdom; WILFRED M. GOOD, IAEA (International Atomic Energy Agency), Nuclear Data Unit, Vienna, Austria (see also 3.1.8.): Eastern Europe, Asia, Australia, Africa, Latin America, and IAEA; and A. ABRAMOV, U.S.S.R. Nuclear Data Information Centre, Obninsk, U.S S.R. (see also 3.1.12.): the U.S.S.R.

In 1963, CINDA was transferred from the Nuclear Development Associates (now a part of United Nuclear Corporation) to Columbia University where it was translated into computer format, with support from the Divisions of Research and of Technical Information at the USAEC. In 1966, this operation was moved to Oak Ridge; and the Obninsk center joined the effort to make up the present distribution. HERBERT GOLDSTEIN of Columbia University (New York City, New York) is chairman of the U.S. Advisory CINDA Steering Group.

44

Coverage

CINDA covers references providing information on specific types of neutron cross sections or other microscopic data for a given target nucleus. In general, it is limited to reactions induced by neutrons of energy < 20 MeV, for specific elements and isotopes. In addition, information on (γ, n) and (γ, f) reactions has been included recently with the restriction that the γ-ray energy must be less than approximately 15 MeV, and the (γ, n) cross section greater than 0.1 mb.

The CINDA publications represent computer edits of the entire master library. The entries are ordered first by element and mass number and then by class of data quantity. Within the data quantity classes, order is chronological, with the date included. Other information listed includes the type of investigation and reference, minimum and maximum energy, the reference, laboratory, and comments.

The primary literature, as well as other sources of neutron data is monitored by the four centers. The literature has been covered thoroughly from 1956 to the present; some pre-1956 references are included.

Analysis

CINDA is an index to all neutron data within the scope indicated under "Coverage". In those cases where the reference is to the computer libraries of the four centers, a scientist may request computer retrieval of specific data from the center servicing his area. Other references are to standard compilations, journals, and unpublished work. No numerical data are given, and the original source must be used.

In indexing the data, certain editorial standards are followed. The computer files of the information centers have largely been built on this established format. CINDA and the computer files are updated and revised as new and improved data become available. Each issue supersedes the previous one. The last CINDA publication is CINDA 68. A supplement to this volume was published in January 1969. CINDA 69 will probably be published in May 1969.

Publications

CINDA 66, An Index to the Literature on Microscopic Neutron Data, by Columbia University and ENEA Neutron Data Compilation Centre, published by the ENEA Neutron Data Compilation Centre, Saclay, and the USAEC Division of Technical Information Extension, Oak Ridge, 1966, XXVIII, 1379 pp.

CINDA 66, Supplement 1, prepared and published by the ENEA Neutron Data Compilation Centre, Saclay, and the USAEC Division of Technical Information Extension, Oak Ridge, October 1966, XXXII, 327 pp.

CINDA 66, Supplement 2, prepared and published by the ENEA Neutron Data Compilation Centre, Saclay, and the USAEC Division of Technical Information Extension, Oak Ridge, March 1967, XXXIV, 561 pp (cumulative).

CINDA 67, An Index to the Literature on Microscopic Neutron Data, Parts I and II, USAEC Division of Technical Information Extension, U.S.S.R. Nuclear Data Information Centre, ENEA Neutron Data Compilation Centre, and IAEA Nuclear Data Unit, published by ENEA Neutron Data Compilation Centre, Saclay, and the Division of Technical Information Extension, USAEC, Oak Ridge, 1967, Part I, X, 868 pp, Part II, 125 pp.

CINDA 68: *An Index to the Literature on Microscopic Neutron Data,* USAEC Division of Technical Information Extension, U.S.S.R. Nuclear Data Information Centre, ENEA Neutron Data Compilation Centre, and the IAEA Nuclear Data Unit, published by ENEA Neutron Data Compilation Centre, Saclay, 1968, X, 1019 pp.

CINDA 68, Supplement, USAEC Division of Technical Information Extension, U.S.S.R. Nuclear Data Information Centre, ENEA Neutron Data Compilation Centre, and the IAEA Nuclear Data Unit, published by USAEC Division of Technical Information Extension, Oak Ridge, 1969, VIII, 181 pp.

3.2. Atomic and Molecular Properties

Atomic Properties Including Spectra

3.2.1. Atomic Energy Levels Data and Information Center

Organization

This project was established at the U.S. National Bureau of Standards (NBS) in 1946 under the sponsorship of the National Academy of Sciences-National Research Council (NAS-NRC) Committee on Line Spectra of the Elements. It entails the international responsibility for the compilation, evaluation, publication, and general dissemination of data on the energy levels as derived from the optical spectra of atoms and ions, and on the observed transitions giving rise to these levels. This program is of interest, also, to the IAU Commission 14 on Fundamental Spectroscopic Data, and the Joint ICSU Commission on Spectroscopy of IAU-IUPAC-IUPAP (International Astronomical Union-International Union of Pure and Applied Chemistry-International Union of Pure and Applied Physics). This data center is under the supervision of CHARLOTTE E. MOORE-SITTERLY of the Atomic Physics Division, Institute for Basic Standards, NBS, Washington, D.C. 20234. Support is provided by the National Standard Reference Data System (NSRDS), NBS (see 1.1.1.).

Coverage

As far as possible, atomic energy levels and multiplet tables are to be given for all the elements. The first edition of *Atomic Energy Levels* covered the elements ¹H to ⁵⁷La and ⁷²Hf to ⁸⁹Ac. Compilation of data for the lanthanide and actinide groups is still in progress. Separate multiplet tables have been published in which the selection of lines is based primarily on their astrophysical importance. These are *A Multiplet Table of Astrophysical Interest* (λ longer than 3000 Å) and *An Ultraviolet Multiplet Table* (λ shorter than 3000 Å). Both contain finding lists. In 1965, work was begun on new editions of both the atomic energy level and the multiplet tables. These tables are being issued in a NSRDS series of publications under the heading *Selected Tables of Atomic Spectra*. For each spectrum the energy levels and multiplets are listed under one cover. Thus far, data for Si ɪ, Si ɪɪ, Si ɪɪɪ and Si ɪᴠ have appeared in this NSRDS series.

The Atomic Energy Level Tables present the following information for each spectrum: general descriptive remarks, number of electrons, the isoelectronic sequence, the ground state of the atom with its complete electron configuration, the absolute value of the ground level, the atomic number Z, the ionization potential, and a selected bibliography. The data listed include: configurations, designations, J-values, atomic energy levels, intervals, and observed g-values. Hyperfine structure ascribed to atomic nuclei is not included, except for hydrogen, deuterium, and tritium.

The multiplet tables include for a given spectrum: a general grading of the analysis and a grading of the completeness of the multiplet table. For individual multiplets, wavelengths, reference sources, low and high excitation potentials, J-values, term designations, and multiplet numbers are given.

The Solar Spectrum 2935 Å to 8770 Å, which is the second revision of ROWLAND's preliminary tables of solar spectrum wavelengths, includes some 20,000 lines observed in the solar spectrum between 2935 Å and 8770 Å. This project was promoted by the IAU and was carried out in collaboration with M. MINNAERT and J. HOUTGAST at the Utrecht Observatory in The Netherlands.

The main sources of data are the open literature and unpublished contributions. The comprehensive card catalog of references maintained at NBS since 1914, used for the "Atomic Energy Levels" project has, also, provided extensive material for the revised identifications of solar lines.

Analysis

These publications were originally prepared in response to the need for a critical compendium of data, and they still serve that purpose. The data in the *Atomic Energy Levels* and *Multiplet Tables* are derived from analyses of

47

optical spectra; these data have been examined critically before publication. An effort has been made to coordinate the programs in all active spectroscopic laboratories in order to avoid duplication of effort; it is an international enterprise. Much unpublished material has been utilized owing to the collaboration of spectroscopists in the U. S. A. and many other nations.

The introductory text in *Atomic Energy Levels* on individual spectra contains an appraisal of the analysis and points out the spectra that need further observation and study. In compiling the data, special effort has been made to introduce the uniform spectroscopic notation recommended by the Joint Commission for Spectroscopy. The terminology is generally accepted by spectroscopists and is adequately explained in the introduction.

In *Selected Tables of Atomic Spectra*, the revised (1964) conversion factor from reciprocal centimeter to electron volt (0.000123981) has been used to obtain the respective ionization and excitation potentials quoted in the tables. Complete references precede each spectrum. The arrangement of the multiplet tables parallels that of the atomic energy levels: references and descriptive remarks precede tables of data. Some references for hyperfine structure are included.

Publications

A Multiplet Table of Astrophysical Interest, Contributions from the Princeton University Observatory No. 20, C. E. MOORE, Princeton University, Princeton, N. J., 1945. Reprinted as NBS Technical Note 36, 1959, 242 pp (PB 151395), Clearinghouse for Federal Scientific and Technical Information, Springfield, Virginia 22151, US $ 4.00.

An Ultraviolet Multiplet Table, NBS Circular 488, C. E. MOORE, U. S. Government Printing Office, Washington, D. C. 20402.

Section 1 (H to V, $Z = 1 — 23$), 1950, 85 pp, US $ 0.55. Reprinted 1956.

Section 2 (Cr to Nb, $Z = 24 — 41$), 1952, 120 pp, US $ 0.70. Reprinted 1956.

Sections 1 and 2 combined, reprinted 1963, US $ 1.25.

Section 3 (Mo to La, $Z = 42 — 57$, and Hf to Ra, $Z = 72 — 88$), 1962, 98 pp, US $ 0.60.

Section 4, Finding List for Spectra of the Elements Hydrogen to Niobium ($Z = 1$ to 41), 1962, 70 pp, US $ 0.45.

Section 5, Finding List for Spectra of the Elements Molybdenum to Lanthanum ($Z = 42$ to 57); Hafnium to Radium ($Z = 72$ to 88), 1962, 34 pp, US $ 0.30.

Atomic Energy Levels, As Derived from the Analyses of Optical Spectra, NBS Circular 467, C. E. MOORE, U. S. Government Printing Office, Washington, D. C. 20402.

Vol. I: Hydrogen to Vanadium ($Z = 1 — 23$), 1949, 309 pp, US $ 5.50. Reprinted 1954, 1960, 1964.

Vol. II: Chromium to Niobium ($Z = 24 — 41$), 1952, 227 pp, US $ 4.00. Reprinted 1958, 1963, 1966.

Vol. III: Molybdenum to Lanthanum ($Z = 42 — 57$) and Hafnium to Actinium ($Z = 72 — 89$), 1958, 245 pp, US $ 3.00. Reprinted 1963, 1966.

Vol. IV: Lanthanide and Actinide groups; in preparation.

Selected Tables of Atomic Spectra, NSRDS-NBS 3, C. E. MOORE, U. S. Government Printing Office, Washington, D. C. 20402.

Section 1, Atomic Energy Levels and Multiplet Tables, Si II, Si III, Si IV, 1965, US $ 0.35.

Section 2, Atomic Energy Levels and Multiplet Tables, Si I, 1967, US $ 0.20.

The Solar Spectrum 2935Å to 8770Å, Second Revision of Rowland's Preliminary Table of Solar Spectrum Wavelengths, NBS Monograph 61, C. E. MOORE, M. J. G. MINNAERT, and J. HOUTGAST, U. S. Government Printing Office, Washington, D. C. 20402, 1966, XXX, 349 pp, US $ 4.00.

Partial Grotrian Diagrams of Astrophysical Interest, NSRDS-NBS 23, C. E. MOORE and P. W. MERRILL, U. S. Government Printing Office, Washington, D. C. 20402, 1968, V, 65 pp, US $ 0.55. A reprint of Appendix A from *Lines of Chemical Elements in Astronomical Spectra*, P. W. MERRILL, Carnegie Institution of Washington, Publication 610, Washington, D. C., 1956.

Bibliography on the Analyses of Optical Atomic Spectra, NBS Special Publication 306, Section 1, ¹H—²³V, C. E. MOORE, U. S. Government Printing Office, Washington, D. C. 20402, 1968, 80 pp, US $ 1.00.

3.2.2. Atomic Transition Probabilities Data Center

Organization

In 1960, the Atomic Transition Probabilities Data Center was established in the Atomic Physics Division of the U. S. National Bureau of Standards (NBS) to survey the literature and to produce critical compilations of data in this field. The Center is directed by W. L. WIESE, and is supported by government agencies. There are three professional staff members. The first data compilation of the Center was issued as part of the NBS National Standard Reference Data Series (NSRDS, see 1.1.1.).

Coverage

The Data Center collects, evaluates, and publishes data on atomic transition probabilities. This encompasses radiative transition probabilities of atoms and atomic ions in the gas phase (intensities of spectral lines). All the elements are to be covered. The Data Center also answers inquiries from the public.

A first critical compilation of *Atomic Transition Probabilities* covers the first 10 elements of the periodic table; the second volume (in preparation) will cover the next 10. Succeeding volumes will include elements for which extensive and adequate data are available — the heavier noble gases, some of the well-known metals, the alkalies, and the alkaline earths.

The tables are arranged according to increasing atomic number and stage of ionization. Allowed and forbidden transitions appear in separate tables. The following properties are included: ground state configuration, ionization potential, spectroscopic notation, wavelength, energy levels, statistical weights (g_i and g_k), transition probability for spontaneous emission (A_{ki}), and line strength (S); for allowed transitions, in addition, the absorption oscillator strength and log gf; and for forbidden transitions, the type of transition.

Sources of data are the open literature, private communications, theoretical and experimental work at NBS, and — for the wavelengths and energy levels — NBS compilations on atomic energy levels and multiplet tables prepared by the Atomic Energy Levels Data and Information Center (see 3.2.1.). Also, numerous calculations based on the Coulomb approximation of BATES and DAMGAARD have been made to fill gaps in the data.

Analysis

The authors have compiled the "best" available transition probabilities of allowed (i.e., electric dipole) and forbidden (i.e., electric quadrupole and magnetic dipole) lines of the first ten elements, including their ions.

The introduction to *Atomic Transition Probabilities* includes useful discussions of the major experimental and theoretical methods by which the tabulated data were obtained, the methods of evaluation, and the content and arrangement of the tables. A brief introduction for each spectrum, i.e., each stage of ionization, covers the selection of the tabulated values and gives some indication of accuracy. The stronger lines characteristic of the neutral atoms and ions and additional material with estimated uncertainties less than 50 percent are listed. Data with estimated uncertainties greater than 50 percent are included only in special cases. The estimation of uncertainties is coded to indicate five levels of uncertainty covering a range from 1 to 50%. Experimental accuracies are generally not less than 10 percent, with the exception of some data obtained from lifetime measurements. When values were obtained by several methods of comparable quality, the results were averaged to obtain the "best value". Numerous units and symbols are used in the literature for transition probabilities. From these the authors have adopted the following: A_{ki} (sec^{-1}), transition probability for spontaneous emission; f_{ik} (dimensionless), absorption oscillator strength; log gf; and S (atomic units), the line strengths.

Most of the literature through 1963 to 1964 was examined for the evaluation for the first ten elements. References for each spectrum precede the tables of data. A list of pertinent materials received after the cut-off date is included.

Publications

Atomic Transition Probabilities, A Critical Data Compilation, NSRDS-NBS 4 (Vol. I: Hydrogen Through Neon), W. L. WIESE, M. W. SMITH, and B. M. GLENNON, U.S. Government Printing Office (GPO*), Washington, D.C. 20402, May 1966, XI, 154 pp, US $ 2.50.

Atomic Transition Probabilities, A Critical Data Compilation, NSRDS-NBS 22 (Vol. II: Sodium Through Calcium), W. L. WIESE, M. W. SMITH, and B. M. MILES, GPO*, Washington, D.C. 20402, to be published, 1969.

Other Publications

Bibliography on Atomic Transition Probabilities, B. M. GLENNON and W. L. WIESE, GPO*, Washington, D.C. 20402, (1) NBS Monograph 50, 1962, 44 pp, superseded by (2) NBS Miscellaneous Publication 278, 1966, 92 pp, US $ 0.55, plus (3) Supplement to NBS Miscellaneous Publication 278, 1968, 43 pp, US $ 0.30 (for the period May 1966 to December 1967).

3.2.3. National Standard Reference Data System, NSRDS-NBS 14

X-Ray Wavelengths and X-Ray Atomic Energy Levels, NSRDS-NBS 14, J. A. BEARDEN, U.S. Government Printing Office, Washington, D.C. 20402, 1967, VI, 66 pp, US $ 0.40. Reprinted from *Reviews of Modern Physics* **31**, No. 1 (January 1967).

Organization

The work at The Johns Hopkins University (Baltimore, Maryland 21218), on which these publications are based, was supported by various government agencies including the Office of Standard Reference Data (see 1.1.1.) of the National Bureau of Standards (NBS). The publication is divided into two parts: "X-Ray Wavelengths" by J. A. BEARDEN, and "Reevaluation of X-Ray Atomic Energy Levels" by J. A. BEARDEN and A. F. BURR.

Coverage

Discrepancies in the tabulations of X-ray reference lines prompted the establishment of the standard W $K\alpha_1$ wavelength as exactly 0.2090100 Å*, where Å* is a new unit, $1Å* = 1Å \pm 5$ ppm. The wavelengths of Ag $K\alpha_1$, Mo $K\alpha_1$, Cu $K\alpha_1$, and Cr $K\alpha_2$ were established as secondary standards; and 61 additional X-ray lines, as reference values. The first section includes two major tables. The first lists all emission lines of an element including the line and level designation, wavelength in Å* with probable error, and energies in keV. Elements are arranged by atomic number. The second table lists wavelengths in numerical order of the emission lines. Included are the wavelength in Å*, probable error, element, line designation, absorption edge, and energies in keV.

The second section is based on the first. The reevaluated X-ray emission lines of section one are used with photoelectron measurements to redetermine values of atomic energy levels by means of a least squares adjustment for each element. Data tabulated include values of the adjusted atomic energy levels, and probable errors in eV, photoelectron direct measurements when available, and measured values of the X-ray absorption energies. The elements are arranged by ascending atomic number.

Data were compiled from the primary literature, some secondary sources, and work done by the authors at The Johns Hopkins University.

Analysis

This work is the result of very careful examination of the theoretical and experimental bases used in the determination of X-ray wavelength standards, and a close scrutiny of the literature. After serious discrepancies were uncovered, new standards were worked out based on the critical evaluation of available data — some of which were determined by the author(s).

The standards and reference values for X-ray emission lines and atomic energy levels are well documented with references, and discussions in the introductory texts. Descriptions of errors and scrupulous definitions of the "probable error" assigned to each value are provided.

Symbols and nomenclature are those accepted by international bodies.

3.2.4. M.I.T. Wavelength Tables

G. R. HARRISON, The Technology Press (MIT), and John Wiley & Sons, Inc., New York-London, 1939, XXVIII, 429 pp, US $ 18.50.

Organization

The spectrum lines were measured and the data compiled from the literature by the staff members of the Spectroscopy Laboratory of the Massachusetts Institute of Technology (MIT), Cambridge, Massachusetts 02139. GEORGE R. HARRISON, Professor of Physics, MIT, directed the project.

Coverage

This publication includes wavelength tables with intensities in arc, spark, or discharge tube of some 109,275 spectrum lines, most strongly emitted by the atomic elements under normal conditions of excitation, between 10000 Å and 2000 Å, arranged in order of decreasing wavelengths.

The main tables give the wavelength, the intensity in arc, spark, or discharge tube, the stage of ionization of the parent atom when the line has been classified in a term array, and the wavelength authority. Atoms in only the first two stages of ionization are knowingly included. All the elements up to and including U are covered except for Tc, Pm, At, Fr, and Pa.

Most references are to the primary literature, from 1939 and earlier.

Analysis

This publication is the most comprehensive offering of its kind. The data included were based on a literature search and on measurements made at MIT to corroborate the literature values. All values included were selected by critical evaluation and carry an indication of precision.

The introduction provides discussions of the tables, precision of wavelengths, and other factors.

3.2.5. Atomic Collision Information Center

Organization

The Information Center is located in the Joint Institute for Laboratory Astrophysics (JILA), University of Colorado, Boulder, Colorado 80302, and is jointly operated by the University and the U.S. National Bureau of Standards. It receives support from the Advanced Research Projects Agency (ARPA) of the Department of Defense, and the U.S. National Bureau of Standards (NBS), through the National Standard Reference Data Program (NSRDP, see 1.1.1.). L. J. KIEFFER (NBS) supervises the Information Center activities. The staff includes faculty members (academic staff who are members of the University), NBS staff members, Visiting Fellows, Members from other institutes, graduate students, and postdoctoral appointees. There are four full-time and six part-time professional staff members, and supporting personnel.

Coverage

The Information Center collects, critically evaluates, and compiles data on collisions of electrons, and photons, with ions, atoms, and molecules which are of interest to astrophysicists, aeronomists, and plasma physicists. The scope of the program is limited to low energy atomic collision data.

53

3.2.5.

The Center maintains as complete and up-to-date a bibliographic file as possible. The main source of data is the primary literature, but abstracting journals are also used to monitor the literature.

A critical evaluation of absolute cross sections for ionization of atoms and diatomic molecules by electron impact has been published. Data fall into two main classes: total ionization cross sections and cross sections for individual ionization processes. Groups of substances covered are: the rare gases, atomic hydrogen, atomic nitrogen, atomic oxygen, atomic mercury, the alkali metals, diatomic molecular cross sections ($H_2, D_2, N_2, O_2, CO, NO$), and ion cross sections ($He^+, Li^+, N^+, Ne^+, Na^+, K^+$).

Analysis

JILA has a number of activities; the Information Center is one. Under NSRDP, the Information Center makes available to the general scientific and technical community critically evaluated data for low energy electron, photon, and heavy particle collisions with atoms and simple molecules. All information on low energy atomic collisions is collected and published in bibliographies, each new edition superseding previous ones. These bibliographies are used to prepare critical reviews of atomic collision data. In the reviews all data are critically analyzed, and scrutinized for a number of requirements including theoretical background, experimental method, and researcher's investigation of systematic errors. Data which are only of historical interest and which have been superseded are not included in the critical review.

A bibliography and a subsequent critical review have been published. The introduction to the data compilation in the critical review includes a thorough discussion of the criteria used for data evaluation — the specifics of experimental method, and systematic errors. Older data expressed as efficiency versus electron energy were converted to cross section units. The reliability and uncertainty of data is indicated, and the validity of obtaining values from graphs is considered. Complete references are included. The data for each class of atoms, atomic ions, and diatomic molecules are discussed critically. Data are presented in graphs.

Publications

"Electron Impact Ionization Cross-Section Data for Atoms, Atomic Ions, and Diatomic Molecules: I. Experimental Data", L. J. KIEFFER and G. H. DUNN, *Rev. Mod. Phys.* **38**, No. 1, 1—35 (1966).

Electron Impact Excitation of Atoms, NSRDS-NBS 25, B. L. MOISEIWITSCH and S. J. SMITH, U.S. Government Printing Office, Washington, D.C. 20402, August 1968, IV, 116 pp, US $ 2.00. Reprinted from *Rev. Mod. Phys.* **40**, No. 2, 238 (1968).

"Ionization of Atoms by Electron Impact: II. Theory", M. R. H. RUDGE, *Rev. Mod. Phys.* **40**, 564 (1968).

Bibliographies

Bibliography of Low Energy Electron Collision Cross Section Data, National Bureau of Standards Miscellaneous Publication 289, L. J. KIEFFER, U.S. Government Printing Office, Washington, D.C. 20402, 1967, VIII, 87 pp, US $ 0.50.

A Bibliography of Electron Swarm Data, JILA Information Center Report No. 4, J. DUTTON, October 1967, 57 pp.

Bibliography of Photoabsorption Cross Section Data, JILA Information Center Report No. 5, L. J. KIEFFER, April 1968, VII, 32 pp.

Molecular Properties Including Spectra

3.2.6. Diatomic Molecule Spectra and Energy Levels Data Center

Organization

This program was established in July 1966 in the Heat Division of the Institute for Basic Standards, National Bureau of Standards (NBS) in Washington, D.C. 20234. It is directed by ARNOLD M. BASS. Support is provided by the Office of Standard Reference Data of NBS (see 1.1.1.).

Coverage

The center covers optical spectroscopic data and constants for diatomic molecules in all pertinent regions of the electromagnetic spectrum, and molecular parameters derived from spectroscopic measurements. Data included are: wavelengths of characteristic bands in the electronic spectra, energy levels associated with observed transitions, spectroscopic constants for observed states, potential energy curves, and dissociation energies. Of particular interest at this time are vacuum UV band wavelengths.

An information file is maintained as complete and up-to-date as possible. The literature has been surveyed from 1900 to 1965. This included not only primary literature but also abstracting journals and a few other references. The center plans to issue bibliographies, reviews, and compilations of critically evaluated numerical data.

The first publication and data compilation, *The Band Spectrum of Carbon Monoxide*, appeared in 1966 as NSRDS-NBS 5. Observed and predicted spectroscopic data on CO, CO$^+$, and CO^{2+} in the gas phase are presented. Properties included in the first half, a critical review of the literature, are the electronic structure and spectrum of CO and CO$^+$; perturbations; dissociation energies; other spectra of CO; RAMAN, STARK, and ZEEMAN

3.2.7.

effects for CO and CO$^+$; molecular energy levels, potential energy curves; and transition probabilities and lifetimes. Seventy-four tables constitute the second half and mainly include band heads and origins, rotational constants and FRANK-CONDON factors. A few other properties are also included.

Analysis

The center performs two complementary functions: it acts as an information center by accumulating, processing, and storing data; and it produces reviews and compilations of critically evaluated data.

The Band Spectrum of Carbon Monoxide combines a literature review and a compilation of critically evaluated data. Papers from which data were taken are discussed in the text. Early data, which are assumed to be of low precision, are included only when better data are not available. The author indicates that estimates of reliability are given where possible: in the tabulations copious footnotes perform this function.

Spectrograms and topics such as infrared intensities, which are treated fully elsewhere, are not included, but references are provided. All references used are grouped together at the end, constituting a critical bibliography of the subject. Most references are to the primary literature and include the title of the paper, which enhances the usefulness of the bibliography.

The spectroscopic notation follows recommendations by the Triple Commission on Spectroscopy (now the Joint ICSU Commission on Spectroscopy, see 3.2.1.). Symbols, nomenclature, other conventions, and physical constants and conversion factors used are also indicated.

Publications

The Band Spectrum of Carbon Monoxide, NSRDS-NBS 5, P. H. KRUPENIE, U.S. Government Printing Office, Washington, D.C. 20402, 1966, VI, 87 pp, US $ 0.70.

3.2.7. Tables de Constantes Sélectionnées, Volume 4

Données Spectroscopiques concernant les Molécules Diatomiques, B. ROSEN, Ed., Volume 4 of Tables de Constantes et Données Numériques, Constantes Sélectionnées, Hermann et Cie, Paris, 1951, 361 pp, 48 F (US $ 15.00).

Organization

This volume, and Volume 5, were produced under the aegis of the Tables de Constantes organization, but also with joint sponsorship by the International Astronomical Union and the International Union of Pure and

Applied Chemistry. The editor of both volumes was B. Rosen of Liege, Belgium, and the scientific collaborators were R. F. Barrow (U.K.), A. D. Caunt (U.K.), A. R. Downie (U.K.), R. Herman (France), E. Huldt (Sweden), A. McKellar (Canada), E. Miescher (Switzerland), and K. Wieland (Switzerland). For a description of the organization of "Tables de Constantes et Données Numeriques", see 2.2.

Coverage

This volume includes information on spectra of about 400 diatomic molecules of particular interest to astrophysicists. For each molecule the following information is given in tabular form: the method(s) of production of the spectra; the band systems or groups of bands including the pertinent transition, the favorable sources, the limits of observation, the direction of shading, wavelengths of characteristic band heads, frequency values and references; molecular constants (for the most abundant isotope); information on perturbation, predissociation or preionization; and potential energy curves (a few cases only).

Analysis

A brief, but information-packed introduction presents nomenclature, symbols, conventions, and formulas applicable to the tables. The data for each molecule were assembled by the expert collaborators; and reviewed for consistency by Prof. Rosen. The bibliography is complete to July 1951 and comprises 2,625 references. A revision of this work is in progress.

3.2.8. Tables de Constantes Sélectionnées, Volume 5

Atlas des Longueurs d'Onde Caractéristiques des Bandes d'Emission et d'Absorption des Molécules Diatomiques, B. Rosen, Ed., Volume 5 of Tables de Constantes et Données Numériques, Constantes Sélectionnées, Hermann et Cie, Paris, 1952, 389 pp, 56 F (US $ 17.50).

Organization

This volume, and Volume 4, were produced under the aegis of the Tables de Constantes organization, but also with joint sponsorship by the International Astronomical Union and the International Union of Pure and Applied Chemistry. The editor of both volumes was B. Rosen of Liege, Belgium, and the scientific collaborators were R. F. Barrow (U.K.), A. D. Caunt, (U.K.), A. R. Downie (U.K.), R. Herman (France), E. Huldt (Sweden),

3.2.9.

A. McKELLAR (Canada), E. MIESCHER (Switzerland), and K. WIELAND (Switzerland). For a description of the organization of "Tables de Constantes et Données Numériques", see 2.2.

Coverage

This volume presents spectral data for essentially the same molecules treated in Volume 4. The main part is a 320-page table giving in decreasing order of wavelength, from 15000 to 700 Å the heads or maxima of bands for 299 diatomic molecules. An indication is given for each band of the mode of observation, the direction of shading, Δv, characteristic bands of the system, and a literature reference or cross index to tables of Volume 4. A separate table of 55 pages lists 4000 individual lines for H_2. Also for a small number of molecules, a complete listing of wavelengths is given for their bands (6 pages only).

Analysis

This atlas of bands and lines for diatomic molecules is an extremely useful extension of the data of Volume 4, although now out of date.

3.2.9. Molecular Spectra and Molecular Structure

GERHARD HERZBERG, D. van Nostrand Co., Inc., Princeton-Toronto-London-New York.

Vol. I. Spectra of Diatomic Molecules, 1939; 2nd ed 1950, XV, 658 pp, US $ 15.00.

Vol. II. Infrared and Raman Spectra of Polyatomic Molecules, 1945, XIII, 632 pp, US $ 15.00.

Vol. III. Electronic Spectra and Electronic Structure of Polyatomic Molecules, 1966, XVIII, 745 pp, US $ 20.00.

Organization

These volumes were prepared by GERHARD HERZBERG, National Research Council of Canada, 100 Sussex Drive, Ottawa 7, Ontario, Canada.

Coverage

Volume I covers: resume of the Elements of Atomic Structure; Observed Molecular Spectra and Their Representation by Empirical Formulae; Rotation and Vibration of Diatomic Molecules; Interpretation of Infrared and Raman Spectra; Elementary Discussion of Electronic States and Electronic Transitions; Finer Details About Electronic States and Electronic Transitions; Building-up Principles, Electron Configurations, and Valence; Continuous and Diffuse Molecular Spectra: Dissociation and Predissociation; Examples, Results, and Applications. Bibliography.

Volume II covers: Introduction; Rotation and Rotation Spectra; Vibrations, Vibrational Energy Levels, and Vibrational Eigenfunctions; Vibrational, Infrared and Raman Spectra; Interaction of Rotation and Vibration, Rotation-Vibration Spectra; Applications; Appendix; Bibliography; Author Index; Subject Index.

Volume III covers: Electronic States; Electronic Transitions; Building-Up Principles, Electronic Configurations and Stability of Electronic States; Dissociation, Predissociation and Recombination: Continuous and Diffuse Spectra; Electronic Spectra of Individual Molecules and their Interpretation; Appendices (I—VII); Bibliography; Subject Index; and Author Index.

Extensive tables of data appear as appendices in Volumes I and III. For Volume I the main table covers vibrational and rotational constants for the electronic states of all known diatomic molecules. In Volume III, the Appendices include: point groups, and for the important point groups, species of spin functions and direct products of representations (species); also, "resolution of species of linear molecules into those of molecules of lower symmetry"; "molecular orbitals formed from atomic orbitals of equivalent atoms"; and molecular constants of the electronic states of molecules.

Analysis

Volume III concludes the series "Molecular Spectra and Molecular Structure", begun in 1939. The author's primary purpose was to present a thorough exposition of the theoretical background and the empirical results necessary to a consideration of molecular spectra and structure. Also included, as part of the presentation, are diagrams, graphical reproductions of eigenfunctions and potential curves, energy level diagrams, spectrograms, and extensive tables of carefully selected data.

3.2.10. Tables of Molecular Vibrational Frequencies

Organization

This continuing numerical data program was begun in 1964 at the University of Tokyo, Tokyo, Japan. Its director, TAKEHIKO SHIMANOUCHI, is a member of the Department of Chemistry of the University, and is also the chairman

59

3.2.10.

of the Infrared Data Committee (IRDC) of Japan (see 3.2.20.). The Office of Standard Reference Data, National Bureau of Standards (NBS), (see 1.1.1.) provides financial support.

Coverage

Complete fundamental vibrational frequency values are given for a comprehensive series of selected simple inorganic and organic molecules including XY_2, XY_3 and XY_4 type molecules (where $X = O$, N, C, S, P, Si, etc., and $Y=H$, F, Cl, Br, I), simple hydrocarbons and halogen and other basic derivatives, and deuterated varieties of many of the foregoing. A table is given for each molecule; it lists the selected value of each fundamental frequency, and its symmetry class and mode (stretching, rocking, etc.). Other information provided includes: observed infrared and Raman frequencies (cm^{-1}), the molecular formula, and estimated frequency uncertainty. Coded notations indicate the strength and type of line (strong or weak, shoulder, polarized, etc.).

To date three parts of a four-part compilation have been issued in the National Standard Reference Data System (NSRDS) publications series. The publication *Tables of Molecular Vibrational Frequencies*, Parts 1, 2, and 3, includes 167 molecules. Part 4 will cover about 50 additional molecules.

Most references are from the primary literature with a few from unpublished work and secondary sources.

Analysis

It is anticipated that fundamental vibrational frequencies for several hundred key molecules will be assigned and evaluated. A consolidated volume comprised of Parts 1, 2, and 3 plus Part 4, now in preparation, will include the first 229 molecules.

The fundamental frequencies are obtained mainly from infrared and Raman spectra supplemented by microwave spectra. The assignment of vibrational frequencies are adopted only when supported by calculation of frequencies from force constants. Such calculations are also used to predict optically inactive or otherwise missing lines. Five levels of uncertainty are assigned, ranging from an uncertainty of $0 - 1$ cm^{-1} to $15 - 30$ cm^{-1} and reflect a magnitude of uncertainty characteristic of the instrumentation used.

The brief introduction refers the reader to a number of publications for the methods used in selecting force constants and in calculating normal vibrations. The use of the tables and the abbreviations and conventions employed are also discussed.

A goal of the program is to supply complete frequency assignments for use in calculation of thermodynamic functions for the ideal gas state. Also, a continuing objective is to develop a consistent set of force constants between atoms that will be transferrable between molecules of similar type.

Publications

Tables of Molecular Vibrational Frequencies, TAKEHIKO SHIMANOUCHI, U.S. Government Printing Office, Washington, D.C. 20402.

Part 1, NSRDS-NBS 6, March 1967, IV, 56 pp, US $ 0.40.

Part 2, NSRDS-NBS 11, October 1967, IV, 38 pp, US $ 0.40.

Part 3, NSRDS-NBS 17, March 1968, IV, 39 pp, US $ 0.30.

3.2.11. Atomic and Molecular Processes Information Center

Organization

The center was established in 1964 at the Oak Ridge National Laboratory, Oak Ridge, Tennessee 37831. The Atomic Energy Commission and the Office of Standard Reference Data, National Bureau of Standards (NBS, see 1.1.1.), support the center, which is directed by C. F. BARNETT. Thus far its main product has been the "Bibliography of Atomic and Molecular Processes".

Coverage

Covered are atomic collisions: heavy particle-heavy particle atomic collision cross sections, particle interactions with quasi-static electric and magnetic fields, particle penetration into macroscopic matter, and energetic particle interactions with surfaces. Molecular interactions are considered for molecules consisting of less than 5 or 6 atoms.

A file of evaluated bibliographical references has been prepared from a literature search covering the period 1950 to 1967. The Center prepares the "Bibliography of Atomic and Molecular Processes" from a survey of 76 scientific and 5 abstract journals. This annotated bibliography has been covering 6-month intervals.

The center has several publications in various stages: A critical monograph, "Ion-Atom Rearrangement Collisions" is being published by John Wiley & Sons; a critical review, "Excitation, Ionization and Dissociation by Heavy Particles", is almost completed; and "Charge Exchange" is in progress.

3.2.12.

Analysis

The center was set up to review and critically evaluate data concerning atomic collisions. A bibliographical file, noted above, is virtually complete; work on a data file of evaluated collision data is well underway.

The three publications named are described as critical review monographs.

Publications

Bibliography of Atomic and Molecular Processes for July—December 1965, ORNL-AMPIC-6, Oak Ridge National Laboratory (ORNL), Oak Ridge, Tennessee, Sept. 1967, 257 pp. Available from Clearinghouse for Scientific and Technical Information (CFSTI), Springfield, Virginia 22151 for US $ 3.00 hardcover, US $ 0.65 microfiche.

Bibliography of Atomic and Molecular Processes for January—June 1966, ORNL-AMPIC-7, ORNL, Oak Ridge, Tennessee, Oct. 1967, 195 pp. Available from CFSTI, Springfield, Virginia 22151 for US $ 3.00 hardcover, US $ 0.65 microfiche.

Bibliography of Atomic and Molecular Processes for July—December 1966, ORNL-AMPIC-8, ORNL, Oak Ridge, Tennessee, Oct. 1967, 176 pp. Available from CFSTI, Springfield, Virginia 22151 for US $ 3.00 hardcover, US $ 0.65 microfiche.

Bibliography of Atomic and Molecular Processes for January—June 1967, ORNL-AMPIC-9, ORNL, Oak Ridge, Tennessee, June 1967, 225 pp. Available from CFSTI, Springfield, Virginia 22151 for US $ 3.00 hardcover, US $ 0.65 microfiche.

3.2.12. Data Center for Atomic and Molecular Ionization Processes

Organization

The center was set up in 1965 in the Physical Chemistry Division, Institute for Basic Standards, National Bureau of Standards (NBS), Washington, D. C. 20234. It is supported by the Office of Standard Reference Data of NBS (see 1.1.1.). HENRY M. ROSENSTOCK is the director.

Coverage

Properties covered include ionization and appearance potentials, and the properties of excited ionic states — in general, the energetics of gaseous ionization. All atomic and molecular species are included.

Many of the properties covered may be measured by mass spectrometric techniques, and are of interest to mass spectroscopists. Because of this facet, the center has sometimes been called the "Mass Spectrometry Data Center". The primary literature is searched for data which are stored on punched cards.

Analysis

As part of its responsibilities, the data center answers requests from individuals for specific information, and evaluates data for specific projects. Publication of tabular compilations of evaluated data has been planned, and one on ionization potentials, appearance potentials and ionic heats of formation — in collaboration with J. L. FRANKLIN — is in press.

The literature from 1955 to 1966 has been abstracted, and work on bringing the file up to date is in progress.

Publications

A Bibliography on Ion-Molecule Reactions, January 1900 to March 1966, NBS Technical Note 291, F. N. HARLLEE, H. M. ROSENSTOCK, and J. T. HERRON, U.S. Government Printing Office, Washington, D.C. 20402, 1966, III, 38 pp. US $ 0.30.

Ionization Potentials, Appearance Potentials, and Heats of Formation of Gaseous Positive Ions, NSRDS-NBS 26, J. L. FRANKLIN, J. G. DILLARD, H. M. ROSENSTOCK, J. T. HERRON, K. DRAXL, and F. H. FIELD — In press.

3.2.13. Compendium of *ab initio* Calculations of Molecular Energies and Properties

Technical Note 438, MORRIS KRAUSS, U.S. Government Printing Office, Washington, D.C. 20402, 1967, XII, 139 pp, US $ 0.70.

Organization

This work was prepared by MORRIS KRAUSS in the Physical Chemistry Division, Institute for Basic Standards, National Bureau of Standards, Washington, D.C. 20234.

Coverage

Observable properties for which calculated data are given include: total energy, dissociation energy, electron affinity, spectroscopic constants, electric moments, field gradients, polarizabilities, magnetic constants, and orbital energies. The calculations have been assigned to two broad groups, i.e., HARTREE-FOCK, and beyond HARTREE-FOCK.

All data are referenced. Other information provided for the annotated ab initio calculations include state, method, and basis set. Gaussian basis calculations are presented for 16 molecules in the last table to illustrate the use of ab initio calculations for polyatomic molecules which range over systems such as H_2CO, C_2H_4, $C_4H_4N_2$, and C_6H_6.

Sixty-five other molecules are covered from the homonuclear diatomics to pentatomics, e.g., H_2, LiH, KCl, N_2O, HCOF, HCCCl, and HCCCN.

The data included are from the period 1960 to 1967. Unpublished material as well as the primary literature was used for the compilation.

Analysis

By virtue of its breadth, this data compilation presents an overview of the field. The author states that the best values for the several observable properties have been compiled from the mass of data available, but that the publication is not intended to be a critical review. Data are presented in tables; a few graphs are included.

3.2.14. Digest of Literature on Dielectrics

Organization

The Digest of Literature on Dielectrics has been issued annually since 1936 by the Committee on Digest of Literature of the Conference on Electrical Insulation and Dielectric Phenomena, Division of Engineering, National Research Council as a service of the National Academy of Sciences. The publication is prepared by a number of authors who contribute sections or chapters. The authors, in turn, are aided by their companies or institutions who allow the authors working time. The chairman of the Committee on Digest of Literature on Dielectrics is FREDERICK I. MOPSIK; the NAS-NRC staff office of the Conference on Electrical Insulation is located at the NAS-NAE-NRC headquarters in Washington, D. C.

Coverage

The digest is an annual compilation of information which has been published during the year on dielectric phenomena. *Chemical Abstracts, Physics Abstracts*, other abstracting services, and other sources are used to locate papers which are then examined. Although the publication is a digest of literature on dielectrics, the emphasis is on instrumentation and measurements. The content and scope of the digest reflects the interest of the Conference on Electrical Insulation.

The format of the Digest has been changed a number of times, but the basic purpose has remained the same. Volume 30 (1966) of the Digest consists of chapters which include a review of the literature highlights and an extensive bibliography listing paper titles. Other formats have used extensively annotated bibliographies.

Always included is a chapter with tables of dielectric constants and dipole moments, and more recently, dielectric relaxation times. This data compilation frequently accounts for about ten percent of the book. The classes of compounds included in the tables are inorganic, metal- and nonmetal-organic, complexed, and organic materials. Pure materials and dilute solutions only are considered. The tables in Volume 30 (1966) cover the static dielectric constants of pure liquids and pure solids, dipole moments, and unresolved and resolved relaxation times. A brief introduction, list of abbreviations and units, and methods of calculation are given.

Analysis

It is not indicated that the tables of data have been critically evaluated. The authors note that in most cases the values listed were taken from the original literature, or in some cases from the abstracts. In the cases where an uncertainty or accuracy was given in the original literature, this is included with the value listed in the table. Also included after some tables are descriptions of measurements which were not suitable to be included in the tables.

The table of dipole moments is the most substantial of the five tables, reflecting the activity in this field.

The other chapters of the Digest are literature reviews and extensive bibliographies — very useful in providing an annual up-to-date review of the areas under consideration. Volume 30 covering 1966 was published in 1967.

Publications

Digest of Literature on Dielectrics, prepared by the Committee on Digest of Literature, Conference on Electrical Insulation and Dielectric Phenomena of the Division of Engineering, National Research Council. Published by the National Academy of Sciences, 2101 Constitution Avenue, Washington, D. C. 20418.

Vol. 11, 1947		1948, VI, 94 pp, paper, US $ 5.00.
Vol. 12, 1948		1949, V, 150 pp, paper, US $ 5.00.
Vol. 13, 1949		1950, VII, 162 pp, paper, US $ 5.00.
Vol. 18, 1954	Publication	383/1955, IX, 176 pp, paper, US $ 5.00.
Vol. 19, 1955	Publication	503/1956, X, 236 pp, paper, US $ 5.00.
Vol. 20, 1956	Publication	562/1957, XV, 239 pp, paper, US $ 5.00.

Vol. 21, 1957	Publication	599/1958, XII,	283 pp, paper, US $ 5.00.
Vol. 22, 1958	Publication	713/1959, XIII,	293 pp, paper, US $ 5.00.
Vol. 23, 1959	Publication	799/1960, XIV,	423 pp, paper, US $ 8.00.
Vol. 24, 1960	Publication	917/1961, VII,	303 pp, paper, US $ 10.00.
Vol. 25, 1961	Publication	1034/1962, VII,	419 pp, paper, US $ 15.00.
Vol. 26, 1962	Publication	1139/1963, VII,	345 pp, paper, US $ 15.00.
Vol. 27, 1963	Publication	1230/1964, VII,	255 pp, paper, US $ 15.00.
Vol. 28, 1964	Publication	1342/1965, IX,	359 pp, cloth, US $ 20.00.
Vol. 29, 1965	Publication	1461/1966, (X),	257 pp, cloth, US $ 20.00.
Vol. 30, 1966	Publication	1496/1967, X,	430 pp, cloth, US $ 20.00.
Vol. 31, 1967	Publication	1595/1969,	433 pp, cloth, US $ 27.00.

3.2.15. National Standard Reference Data System, NSRDS-NBS 10

Selected Values of Electric Dipole Moments for Molecules in the Gas Phase, NSRDS-NBS 10, R. D. NELSON, JR., D. R. LIDE, JR., and A. A. MARYOTT, U. S. Government Printing Office, Washington, D. C. 20402, 1967, V, 49 pp, US $ 0.40.

Organization

This compilation was prepared in the Infrared and Microwave Spectroscopy Section, Institute for Basic Standards, National Bureau of Standards (NBS) in Washington, D. C. 20234 as a part of the National Standard Reference Data Program described in 1.1.1.

Coverage

Selected Values of Electric Dipole Moments for Molecules in the Gas Phase revises, updates, and extends the coverage of NBS Circular 537, *Tables of Dielectric Constants and Electric Dipole Moments of Substances in the Gaseous State* by A. A. MARYOTT and F. BUCKLEY (1953).

Some 600 compounds are included. Of these, 127 are inorganic compounds; halides account for over half of this group. The remaining 470 are carbon compounds, most with less than 12 carbon atoms. Table 1, inorganic, and Table 2, organic, are arranged alphabetically in ascending order by empirical formula, except in the carbon compounds in which the C and H come first.

The tables are based on data from the open literature. Data taken from compilations on dipole moments, dielectric constants, and microwave spectroscopy were also critically evaluated. The literature was covered from 1919 to the end of 1965, with some references from 1966.

Analysis

The tables present the following: the formula, the compound name, recommended value of the dipole moment, and its accuracy. The experimental values which were weighted most strongly in the final selection are also listed for each compound, accompanied by bibliographic references and a code symbol indicating the method of measurement. IUPAC nomenclature recommendations are followed; dipole moment values are expressed in the cgs system.

Values taken from the original literature have been made to conform to the current recommended values of the fundamental constants and dipole moments of reference molecules. Incorrect or irrelevant literature values were discarded or corrected. Code letters for seven levels of accuracy are assigned. In estimating accuracy, chemical purity, scope and precision of data, experimental technique and overall reliability of the laboratory were considered. The introductory text provides useful information on use of the tables, the bibliography, the definition of dipole moment, the principal methods of measuring dipole moment and a critique of these methods. The criteria used in selecting the published values are given.

Separate tables of dipole moments measured in different vibrational states and for different isotopic species appear as appendices.

Infrared and Microwave Spectra

3.2.16. Selected Infrared Spectral Data: American Petroleum Institute Research Project 44

Organization

The American Petroleum Institute (API) Research Project 44 (see 2.3.1.) initiated a catalog of infrared spectral data in 1943, the first compilation of its kind in the field. BRUNO J. ZWOLINSKI, director of the Thermodynamics Research Center (TRC, see 2.3.) at Texas A & M University, College Station, Texas 77843, is in charge of the program which is closely associated with the TRC Data Project in IR (see 3.2.17.).

Coverage

Substances covered are principally hydrocarbons, as well as certain classes of nitrogen and sulfur compounds. Prior to 1959, the collection included oxygen compounds, organometallic compounds, and certain halogen derivatives.

3.2.16.

Both infrared prism and infrared grating spectra are published. Infrared absorption spectra are recorded mostly in the wavelength range 2 to 15 microns but some, in ranges 2.5 to 40 microns, 14 to 25 microns, 14 to 40 microns. In most cases, percent transmittance is plotted against wavelength, in microns. Numerical values of principal peaks and shoulders are tabulated for some spectra. Other information given includes: state, temperature, operating characteristics, and molecular and structural formulas. Some data in the far infrared have been published. These are collected by the supporting experimental program of the Thermodynamics Research Center.

Some 51 selected industrial, academic, and governmental laboratories in the United States, Canada, England, and Japan contribute spectra. TRC also determines some spectra, mainly for correlation or filling in gaps.

Analysis

Currently, emphasis is placed on grating spectra of high resolution. Spectra are selected on the basis of the competence of the investigator, the quality of the instrumentation employed, and the purity of the compounds. The source and purity of the compound are given in the legend when possible. To upgrade quality, the project supplies contributors criteria for the determination and presentation of spectra.

Spectra are replaced as better ones become available. Revisions and additions are issued semiannually when warranted by the accumulation of new spectra.

The spectra are published on 22×29 cm loose-leaf sheets, for which special post binders are available. The sheets are arranged by serial number. The spectrograms vary slightly with contributing laboratory due to the different instruments used. The name of the contributing laboratory is given on the spectral sheet and identified in the indexes by code letters. A compound index, based on the Standard Order System (see 3.4.1.), and in turn on compound type, and a numerical index arranged in order of serial number, are revised as new sheets are issued. Cumulative compound and numerical indexes are issued every few years.

Publications

Catalog of Selected Infrared Spectral Data, American Petroleum Institute Research Project 44, B. J. ZWOLINSKI, Director, Thermodynamics Research Center, Texas A & M University, College Station, Texas 77843; 2908 loose-leaf data sheets extant December 1967, comprising 7 volumes, sold initially in complete sets only for US $ 920.60 (with binders), approximate cost of supplements per year is US $ 48.00. Discount prices are available to some educational and non-profit research institutions. Order from the TRC Data Distribution Office, Texas A & M Research Foundation, F. E. Box 130, College Station, Texas 77843.

3.2.17. Selected Infrared Spectral Data: Thermodynamics Research Center Data Project

Organization

The Thermodynamics Research Center (TRC) Data Project, formerly the Manufacturing Chemists Association Research Project is described in 2.3.2. Infrared spectral data were first published in 1959. BRUNO J. ZWOLINSKI, director of the Thermodynamics Research Center (discussed in 2.3.), Texas A & M University, College Station, Texas 77843, is in charge of the spectral data program which is closely associated with the API RP 44 program in this area (see 3.2.16.).

Coverage

Substances covered include nonhydrocarbon compounds of defined purity of interest to the chemical industry. Spectra have been issued for organic compounds containing oxygen, nitrogen, sulfur, halogen, phosphorus, boron, arsenic, sodium, silicon, and zinc, and for boric acid. The TRC infrared catalog is complementary to that of the American Petroleum Institute, and substances covered therein are not duplicated.

Infrared absorption spectra are recorded as percent transmittance versus frequency and wavelength, in general 2 to 15 microns. In addition to the spectral curve, the name, molecular and structural formulas of the compound, and the solvent and concentration (if in solution) are given in the legend on the sheet.

Spectra measured in 16 cooperating industrial and academic laboratories provide the major source of material. Some spectra are determined by TRC. Laboratories interested in cooperating in this project may consult the director.

Analysis

Spectra are selected on the basis of the competence of the investigator, the quality of the instrumentation employed, and the purity of the compounds. Currently, emphasis is placed on grating spectra of high resolution. The source and purity of the compound, molecular and semistructural formulas, cell length, and the solvent and concentration (if in solution) are given in the legend. To upgrade quality the project supplies contributors with instructions for calibration of absolute wavelengths and intensities.

Spectra are replaced as better ones become available; revisions and additions are issued when warranted by the accumulation of new spectra.

The catalog is made up of 22×29 cm loose-leaf sheets for which special post binders are available. The sheets are arranged by serial number. Charts vary slightly with contributor and instrument used.

3.2.18.

Publications

Catalog of Selected Infrared Spectral Data, Thermodynamics Research Center Data
Project, B. J. ZWOLINSKI, Director, Thermodynamics Research Center, Texas
A & M University, College Station, Texas 77843; 409 loose-leaf data
sheets extant June 1968, sold initially in complete sets only for US $ 122.70
(with binders), approximate cost of supplements per year is US $ 45.00.
Discount prices are available to some educational and non-profit research
institutions. Order from the Data Distribution Office, Texas A & M Research
Foundation, F. E. Box 130, College Station, Texas 77843.

3.2.18. Coblentz Society Infrared Absorption Spectra

Organization

The Coblentz Society was founded in 1954 by a group of persons interested
in infrared spectroscopy and related fields. Its headquarters are at 761 Main
Avenue, Norwalk, Connecticut 06851. In 1957, the Society established a
Committee on Infrared Absorption Spectra to expedite the production and
distribution of infrared spectra. Editor of the Coblentz spectra is CLARA
D. SMITH. About 5000 spectra have been published.

At the request of the Office of Standard Reference Data (see 1.1.1.) of
the National Bureau of Standards (NBS), the Coblentz Society Board of
Managers prepared recommendations for quality standards for compilations
of infrared spectral data (see Appendix II).

Coverage

Spectra of pure compounds and commercial products are issued. Many
spectra are from private collections, including members' files.

Both infrared grating and infrared prism spectra are included. The
wavelength range is generally within 2 to 40 microns. Percent transmittance
is plotted against wavelength (microns) and frequency (cm^{-1}). The name,
the empirical or semi-structural formula, or both, and sometimes values of
other properties such as boiling point and refractive index are given with
each spectrum.

Analysis

Spectra are checked for completeness, consistency of compound or material
name and structure, accuracy, and quality. More than one spectrum for a
material is included in the collection if the more recent spectrum is better.
A central committee evaluates, correlates, and edits the spectra to ensure
publication of the best spectra.

The source of each spectrum is indicated. Four indexes are available: alphabetical, molecular formula, chemical classes, and numerical. The Chemical Classes Index annually includes a numerical listing of functional groups, an alphabetical listing of the functional groups, and a tabular coded listing of all the spectra in the set.

Publications

Coblentz Society Infrared Spectra, Volumes I—V, set of 5000 spectra, 1968, US $ 100.00 per volume (plus US $ 15.00 for the indexes and US $ 5.00 each for binders), available from the Sadtler Research Laboratories, Inc., 3316 Spring Garden Street, Philadelphia, Pa. 19104.

3.2.19. Documentation of Molecular Spectroscopy

Organization

Documentation of Molecular Spectroscopy (DMS), established in 1956, is a card system used for publishing infrared spectra plus supporting information. This card system is published jointly by Butterworth & Co. Ltd., London, U.K., and Verlag Chemie, GmbH, Weinheim, Germany. The data are prepared by experts working under the direction of the British DMS Advisory Board, London, and the German Institut für Spektrochemie und Angewandte Spektroskopie, Dortmund, Germany. The British Board is headed by H. W. THOMPSON, Oxford University, and the group at the German institute by H. KAISER.

In addition to the infrared spectral data cards, there are two "current literature" services. One covers infrared, Raman, and microwave literature; the other covers nuclear magnetic resonance, electron paramagnetic resonance, and nuclear quadrupole resonance literature. Another important data compilation is the *UV Atlas of Organic Compounds (UV — Atlas organischer Verbindungen*, see 3.2.34.).

Coverage

Before 1960, organic substances — pure compounds and naturally occurring substances for which the composition had not been established, technical products and mixtures — were given; since 1960, both organic and inorganic substances have been included.

Infrared absorption spectra within the range 4000 to 200 cm^{-1} (2.5 to 50 microns) are plotted against percent transmittance and percent absorption. Frequencies of the chief bands and their approximate intensities and peak absorption positions are indicated. Physical properties (melting or boiling point, density, and index of refraction), and molecular and structural formulas are also given. Between 4000 and 2000 cm^{-1}, the scale is reduced by one fourth, thus allowing sufficient space for the clear presentation of the shorter wavelength range.

Sources of data include the current literature and previously unpublished spectral data from industrial, governmental, and academic laboratories throughout the world.

Analysis

Publication of spectra is under the advice and control of an advisory committee consisting of leading spectroscopists. Each spectrum is chosen critically as the best available. The author, source of the spectrum, the purity of the substance, and the conditions under which the spectrum was measured are given. Errors are called to the attention of subscribers by means of a newsletter sent out at intervals.

The spectral cards are issued quarterly, approximately 400 cards per set. DMS spectral traces for organic compounds are reproduced on 15×21 cm pink edge-notched cards. The frequencies of the chief bands are listed beside the spectra. A coded classification is notched at the top and at one end of the card; it is based on three structural features: (1) the number of carbon atoms, (2) the basic skeleton, and (3) the substituent groups. Spectral traces for inorganic compounds are reproduced on blue cards similar to the pink cards except that the coding is essentially stoichiometric.

English and German editions of the spectral cards are issued giving identical information.

An index to the DMS Card System, the DMS-I-Cards, consists of 15×21 cm optical coincidence cards with a coordination system for 5000 possible hole spaces in 50 squares subdivided into 100 smaller squares. These cards make it possible to sort out rapidly all the spectral cards that have a given property.

Yellow literature cards similar to the spectral cards were issued with Volumes 1 through 6 (24 issues). The cards indicated the author, reference, and an abstract of each article from which a spectrum had been reproduced. Often, other articles of interest were also included. The cards usually were coded with sufficient data so that reference to the original article is unnecessary.

Beginning with the 25th issue (Volume 7, 1963), the literature cards have been replaced by a comprehensive list of papers on infrared, Raman, and microspectroscopy; and since 1965 on nuclear magnetic resonance. This list, printed on punched sheets for insertion in a ring binder, is accompanied by a set of IBM-sized optical coincidence cards known as the DMS Junior Index. These smaller cards are replaced by a consolidated set of large punched cards every two years. An author index is published yearly.

Publications

The DMS card service is obtained by subscription from Butterworth & Co. Ltd., 88 Kingsway, London, W.C. 2, England, from Plenum Press, 227 West 17th Street, New York, N.Y. 10011, U.S.A., or from Verlag-Chemie, G.m.b.H., 694 Weinheim/Bergstr., Pappelallee 3, Germany. A subscription covers one volume of four issues. Each one contains about 400 spectral cards (pink) and 100 literature cards (yellow). From issue 17, spectral cards for inorganic compounds (blue) are included and from issue 25, the literature cards were replaced by literature lists.

Users may subscribe either to a slotted or unslotted edition, i.e., the user can decide either to cut the slots himself or to obtain the pack ready for use.

Price — *Unslotted* Subscription:

	£	US $	DM
Vol. 1, Issues 1 to 4	67.0	187.50	750
Vol. 2, Issues 5 to 8	67.0	187.50	750
Vol. 3, Issues 9 to 12	67.0	187.50	750
Vol. 4, Issues 13 to 16	67.0	187.50	750
Vol. 5 onwards, per volume	70.0	210.00	840

Price — *Slotted* Subscription:

Vol. 1, Issues 1 to 4	80.5	225.00	900
Vol. 2, Issues 5 to 8	80.5	225.00	900
Vol. 3, Issues 9 to 12	80.5	225.00	900
Vol. 4, Issues 13 to 16	80.5	225.00	900
Vol. 5 onwards, per volume	88.0	247.00	988

In addition to the cards, subscriptions cover:

1 Code for the literature lists
1 Instruction and Coding Manual (for spectral cards)
1 Formula list for each issue
DMS Newsletters

Prices for the Index Cards are as follows:
First issue (S—1)

	£	US $	DM
One set	22.5	62.50	250
For second and further sets	18.0	50.00	200
Second issue (S—2)			
One set	26.5	73.50	295
For second and further sets	21.0	59.00	236

Accessories such as hand punches for slotting, hand sorting apparatus, sorting needles, blank cards may be purchased from DMS.

3.2.20. The Infrared Data Committee of Japan

Organization

The Infrared Data Committee of Japan (IRDC) is a part of the Infrared and Raman Discussion Group, Tokyo, jointly formed in 1955 by the Chemical Society of Japan, the Spectroscopical Society of Japan, the Japan Society for Analytical Chemistry, the Pharmaceutical Society of Japan, and the Society of Polymer Science, Japan. IRDC was organized to re-examine existing infrared data in Japan and to publish an authoritative standard collection of infrared spectra. The chairman is TAKEHIKO SHIMANOUCHI; Vice-chairmen are YO-ICHIRO MASHIKO and KOJI NAKANISHI; four additional members of the committee, YOSHIO KITAHARA, ICHIRO NAKAGAWA, SHIN-NOSUKE SAEKI, and NOBUYUKI TANAKA, comprise the executive committee.

Coverage

Organic compounds are covered with emphasis on newly synthesized substances.

Properties include the infrared spectra in the range 4000 to 600 cm^{-1} (2.5 to 16.0 microns). For each substance the following are given: name of sample, empirical and semistructural formula, molecular weight, physical constants (melting point, boiling point, or refractive index), classification of the substance (e.g., steroid, alkaloid, hydrate), and the type of skeleton (acyclic or type of cyclic).

Analysis

Spectra are measured using carefully calibrated modern spectrophotometers in three laboratories under the direction of members of the executive committee. All spectra are examined and evaluated by members of the committee to insure the publication of authoritative graphs. The compounds used are obtained from cooperating laboratories, mostly those of universities. Care is taken to control the purity of the substances for which spectra are determined. When possible the compounds are purified by gas chromatography.

Spectra are recorded on 13×21 cm specially prepared, slotted, edge-notched cards. By a special device the original spectrograms are reduced to card size without distortion. Percent transmittance is plotted against both wavelength in microns and frequency in reciprocal centimeters. Wave numbers of absorption bands of greatest intensity are recorded on the spectrogram or marked for punching on the cards. In addition to the spectral data, the date and temperature of measurement, type of spectrophotometer used, serial number, and reference source are given.

Currently, approximately 1200 cards are issued per year. As of September 1968, 9000 cards were available. From Vol. 9 (card no. 9601, to be published in March 1969) the spectrum covers the range 4000 to 400 cm^{-1}. The cards are included in the ASTM Infrared Spectral Index (see 3.2.51.).

Publications

Infrared Data Committee Cards, The Infrared Data Committee of Japan, published by Nankodo Co., Ltd., Tokyo, Japan; 9000 cards available as of 1968, sold on subscription basis at US $ 238.00 for 1200 cards (postage included). In the United States, the cards are available from the Preston Technical Abstracts Co., 909 Pitner Avenue, Evanston, Illinois 60202; and in Europe from Heyden & Son Ltd., Spectrum House, Alderton Crescent, Hendon, London, N. W. 4, England.

3.2.21. Infrared Spectra, Sadtler Research Laboratories, Inc.

Organization

Sadtler Research Laboratories, Inc., was established in 1874. It is a private commercial enterprise based on consulting services. In 1947, the company expanded its activities to include the production and sale of infrared spectra used for analytical purposes. The spectra now compiled and published include infrared, ultraviolet (3.2.32.), and nuclear magnetic resonance (3.2.41.). Sadtler publishes spectra in two categories; one on pure compounds and the other on commercial materials. The two categories are given the copyrighted designations "Standard" and "Reference" respectively. In addition to distributing spectra produced in the Sadtler Laboratories, the company serves as the agent for distributing spectra prepared by the Coblentz Society (see 3.2.18.) and the Japan Electron Optics Laboratory Company, Ltd. (JEOL, see 3.2.43.).

Recently the company initiated a computerized searching service for locating or identifying infrared spectra, and it now offers for rent magnetic tape compilations of digitized infrared spectra. Sadtler Research Laboratories, Inc., is located at 3316 Spring Garden Street, Philadelphia, Pennsylvania 19104.

Coverage

Sadtler offers nine categories of infrared spectra. Two of these categories have been given, by the Sadtler organization, the copyrighted designations "Standard Spectra" (infrared prism) and "Standard Grating Spectra". These two categories include organic compounds which are stated to be at least 98% pure. The other seven categories are: commercial infrared prism spectra, commercial infrared grating spectra, inorganic grating spectra, organometallic grating spectra, pharmaceutical infrared spectra, steroid grating and prism spectra, and biochemical infrared prism spectra. For a group of some 600 substances that cannot conveniently be studied by the transmission method (e.g., films, coatings, and adhesives), attenuated total reflectance (ATR) spectra have been measured. In addition to these spectral compilations, a card system called "IRSCOT", Infrared Structural Correlation Tables, is also available.

Sadtler infrared prism "Standard Spectra" include simple and complex molecules representing most functional groups such as aliphatic, aromatic, alicyclic, and heterocyclic. All prism spectra were measured in the spectral region of 2 to 15 microns, and are presented in linear wavelength format, with microns (and cm^{-1}) plotted against percent transmittance.

The Sadtler "Standard Grating Spectra" are a recent addition. These spectra are scanned in the region from 4000 to 250 cm^{-1} (2.5 to 40 microns), using a linear frequency representation. Frequency in cm^{-1} (and microns) is plotted against absorbance. Standard techniques are used to insure reliable results. This compilation is published in addition to the "Standard Spectra" (prism); the same samples are used for both collections.

Other information given on the spectrograms: name of compound (according to *Chemical Abstracts*), molecular formula, molecular weight, melting/boiling point, reference, source, instrument used, method, spectrum number, and structural formula.

The files are being continually updated and added to; additions to the collection are issued each year. Industrial and research organizations and educational institutions contribute the compounds used for determining the spectra.

Analysis

Spectra are determined in the Sadtler laboratories and are reviewed by consultants. In recent years a noticeable effort has been made to upgrade the quality of the collections. However, these collections of standard spectra, like many other spectroscopic collections, suffer from the lack of sources of compounds of certified high purity. Because of this, Sadtler requests that users submit results of measurements made on different preparations of compounds found in the Sadtler standard spectra collections. If the spectra disagree, they are redetermined, and lists of verified spectra are then sent to subscribers. The primary use of the spectra is for analytical purposes.

Two volumes of 1000 spectra each in the IR prism — "Standard Spectra" — are now being issued yearly. In 1968, the collection included 35,000 spectra. Sadtler "Standard Spectra" are published on 22×29 cm sheets, three spectra to a page. The total number of "Standard Grating Spectra" issued to date is 13,000. These spectra appear two to a page. For both types of spectra, indices (alphabetical, molecular formula, chemical class, and numerical), and the Spec Finder, a book method of locating infrared spectra by the bands, are also available.

Sadtler Commercial Spectra, a collection of infrared spectrograms of several thousand commercial preparations that are not easily characterized as to composition, and the other IR collections listed under Coverage are each published separately.

Digitized infrared spectral data are also available on magnetic (computer) tapes, which are updated every year. The magnetic tape file contains some 40,000 infrared prism spectra.

Publications

All publications listed below and further information are available from: Sadtler Research Laboratories, Inc., 3316 Spring Garden Street, Philadelphia, Pennsylvania 19104.

Collections of "Standard Spectra"

Collection	No. Spectra	US $/ 1000 (Vol)	Total Price US $	Annual Subscription
"Standard Spectra" IR prism	35,000	137.50	4812.50	US $ 385.00/ 2000 spectra
Indices			55.00	
Spec-Finder			55.00	
"Standard Grating Spectra" IR	13,000	192.50	2502.50	US $ 687.00/ 3000 spectra US $ 495.00/ 2000 spectra
Indices			55.00	
Spec-Finder			55.00	
Other Collections of Spectra				
Commercial Infrared Prism — 18 categories	17,330		5719.00	
Commercial Grating — 9 categories	6,500		2502.50	
Inorganic Grating Spectra and Indices	1,000		260.00	
Organometallic Grating Spectra	400		140.00	
Pharmaceutical Infrared Spectra	850		280.00	
Steroid Grating and Prism Spectra	750		287.50	
Biochemical Infrared Prism Spectra	2,000		500.00	
IRSCOT System	8 tables	31.25/table	250.00	

3.2.22.

Other Publications, Output

Magnetic tapes: 40,000 infrared prism spectra. Initial rental fee for installation of system is US $ 475.00; annual updating and maintenance fee (addition of approximately 4,000 spectra per year) is US $ 175.00.

Coblentz Society Spectra, published by Sadtler Research Laboratories for the Coblentz Society (see 3.2.18.), 5000 spectra, US $ 105.00/1000 spectra or US $ 525.00 for the whole collection.

Microfilm: All Sadtler spectra are available on microfilm for the same price.

3.2.22. Berkeley Analyses of Molecular Spectra

Organization

This project at the University of California, Berkeley, California 94720, has been funded by the U. S. National Science Foundation since 1959. Its purpose is the systematic laboratory analysis of the spectra of selected diatomic molecules important to astrophysicists. The project is under the joint direction of SUMNER P. DAVIS, Professor of Physics, and JOHN G. PHILLIPS, Professor of Astronomy.

The production of spectra and plates to be measured and analyzed is carried out in the Physics Department; the reduction, analyses, and preparation of the tabular material are performed in the Astronomy Department of the University.

Coverage

A survey of the following substances was planned: CN, C_2, TiO, AlH, NH, BH, MgH, SiH, HgH, SiF, BO, and ZrO. Studies have been completed and published for the CN (red system) (1963); and for HgH, and C_2 (Swan system) (1968).

Properties compiled for the CN molecule are wavelengths, wavenumbers, intensities, and rotational quantum numbers of various branches for the identification of 11000 lines in 39 bands between λ 4832 and 11382 Å.

The second volume covers the Swan System of the C_2 molecule and the spectrum of the HgH molecule. For the C_2 molecule, information includes light source, wavelength standards and reduction, band analysis and assignment of quantum numbers, and the band line tabulations. Information on HgH includes light sources, band spectrum, and band line tabulations.

Analysis

Results recorded for the CN molecule are based upon the measurement of each band on at least two plates. All measurements are combined into tables.

An average is used for wavelengths, wavenumbers, and intensities. A discussion of accuracies and uncertainties, equations used, and the details of the procedure are given in the introduction. Possible inaccuracies resulting from a line being wider than a sharp single line or being blended with a line of the same or a neighboring band are indicated in the tables. Successful computer programs have been developed to assist in the search for bands in extremely complex as well as simpler spectral regions. Although many of the routine computations were performed by computer, the more difficult and complex operations, such as the assignment of quantum numbers, were done by hand.

Treatment of material in Vol. 2 parallels that of Vol. 1. The methods of observation and analysis of each of the two molecules are discussed, and background discussions are presented in the introduction.

Publications

The Red System ($A^2\Pi$—$X^2\Sigma$) of the CN Molecule, S. P. Davis and J. G. Phillips, University of California Press, Berkeley and Los Angeles, 1963, X, 214 pp, US $ 9.50.

The Swan System of the C_2 Molecule, and the Spectrum of the HgH Molecule, Berkeley Analysis of Molecular Spectra, Vol. 2, J. G. Phillips and S. P. Davis, University of California Press, Berkeley, Calif. 94720, 1968, VIII, 260 pp, US $ 10.00.

3.2.23. Spectral Data and Physical Constants of Alkaloids

Organization

This compilation brings together physical and optical data useful in the identification of alkaloids. Volumes I and II were prepared under the combined editorship of Jiří Holubek and Oldřich Štrouf. Starting with Volume III, Jiří Holubek is the sole editor. The project is located at the Research Institute for Pharmacy and Biochemistry, Prague, Czechoslovakia.

Coverage

Infrared and ultraviolet spectra of alkaloids are included. The infrared spectra are plotted with frequencies in the ranges 2000 to 700 cm^{-1} (NaCl prism) and 3800 to 2600 cm^{-1} (LiF prism) as abscissa, and percent transmission as ordinate. The frequencies of the peaks are tabulated. The ultraviolet spectra have wavelengths in millimicrons as abscissa and log ϵ as ordinate (ϵ is the extinction coefficient).

79

3.2.23.

Molecular and semistructural formulas, melting point, optical rotation, and apparent dissociation constants (in 80 percent aqueous methylcellosolve) expressed as pK are given.

The spectra were recorded in the laboratory of the Research Institute; the samples were supplied by many workers in the field of alkaloid chemistry. In most cases, physical constants (melting point and optical rotation) are those supplied by the donors of the samples or from the literature. The pK values have been determined by the authors.

Analysis

Because the spectral data are recorded on instruments at the Institute, the quality is consistent. The ultraviolet spectra of the alkaloids in methanol were measured using a Zeiss-Jena VSU Universal spectrophotometer (NaCl prism). The infrared spectra of purified samples submitted by collaborators were recorded on a calibrated Zeiss-Jena model UR spectrophotometer, using either a mineral oil suspension, or a chloroform solution. Leading references from the literature regarding the botanical source of individual alkaloids are cited. Synonyms of the alkaloids are cross-referenced in the index.

Volume I of the compilation contains data on 300 alkaloids. Supplements containing spectra of 100 alkaloids each are expected to keep the compilation up-to-date.

The data are issued on 22×29 cm cards in post binders. A descriptive introduction, subject index, and bibliography — 29 pages in Volume I and 17 pages in Volume II — are provided. A five-page addendum to Volume I is included in the introductory material for Volume II.

Publications

Spectral Data and Physical Constants of Alkaloids, published by Heyden & Sons, Ltd., London, in cooperation with The Publishing House of the Czechoslovak Academy of Sciences, Prague. Available in Western Europe and Western Hemisphere from Heyden & Sons, Ltd.

Vol. I, Jiří Holubek and Oldřich Štrouf, Eds., 1965, spectral cards 1—300 issued with two binders to hold Vols. I and II, £ 23.0.0. (US $ 69.00).

Vol. II, Jiří Holubek and Oldřich Štrouf, Eds., 1966, spectral cards 301—400, £ 7.0.0. (US $ 21.00).

Vol. III, Jiří Holubek, Ed., 1968, spectral cards 401—500, US $ 25.00.

Vol. IV, Jiří Holubek, Ed., spectral cards 501—600, in press.

Vol. V, Jiří Holubek, Ed., spectral cards 601—700, to be published in 1970.

Vol. VI, Jiří Holubek, Ed., spectral cards 701—800, to be published in 1971.

3.2.24. Tables of Wavenumbers for the Calibration of Infra-red Spectrometers

E. K. PLYLER, R. N. JONES, and R. C. LORD, Eds., Butterworths, London, 1961, 699 pp, US $ 6.00, distributed in U.S.A. by Plenum Press, New York. Also published in *Pure Appl. Chem.* **1**, 537—699 (1961).

Organization

The preparation of these tables was sponsored by the Commission on Molecular Structure and Spectroscopy, Physical Chemistry Section, International Union of Pure and Applied Chemistry (IUPAC). A subcommittee, composed of members of the Commission and with R. C. LORD (U.S.A.) as Chairman, was constituted to investigate the requirement for an authoritative set of wavenumbers for the calibration of infrared spectrometers. Drs. E. K. PLYLER (U.S.A.), R. N. JONES (Canada), and R. C. LORD prepared the "Tables of Wavenumbers". The Commission presented these as provisional wavenumber standards, which were approved by the Triple Commission on Spectroscopy (now the Joint ICSU Commission on Spectroscopy) of the International Unions of Chemistry, Physics, and Astronomy. Work on the lower mid- and far-infrared ranges is in progress.

Coverage

The tables cover the region 4000 to 600 cm^{-1} and are in two parts. Part I is for use with grating spectrometers of resolution 0.1 to 1 cm^{-1}, and Part II applies to instruments of lower resolution, 0.5 to 10 cm^{-1}. Tables of atomic emission lines listing both wavelength in air and their calculated wavenumber in vacuo of neon, argon, krypton, xenon, and mercury-198, as well as wavelength-to-wavenumber conversion tables and refractive index of standard air are given in the first section. The second section of Part I deals with infrared absorption lines in the spectra of gaseous molecules: CO, C_2H_2, CO_2, HCN, CH_4, HCl, DCl, HBr, DBr, $^{13}CO_2$, NH_3, N_2O, H_2O. These molecular data are presented as wavenumbers in vacuo. Part II, "Wavenumbers for the Calibration of Prism and Small Grating Spectrometers (Resolution 0.5 to 10 cm^{-1}) in the Range 3950 to 600 cm^{-1}", presents tables for the same molecular species listed for Part I, with the addition of DCN. Calibration lines also found in Part I are marked. Data are recorded as wavenumbers in vacuo.

Presentation of data for molecular species follows the same general format in both Parts I and II. Spectra are represented by charts with increasing absorption plotted against decreasing wavenumbers. The identified lines are numbered sequentially on the chart and the precise wavenumbers in vacuo of the identified lines are tabulated on the facing page.

3.2.25.

In Part II, Charts 1 to 34 cover vapor phase spectra for the range 3950 to 590 cm^{-1}, each chart covering 100 cm^{-1}. Charts 35 to 39 present spectra of liquid indene and of a polystyrene film which are suitable for the calibration of the smaller types of prism spectrometers. A series of compressed charts, 1 A to 34 A, are presented for use when measurements at lower resolutions are made. Charts 1 A to 34 A retain the lines found in Charts 1 to 34 which are least influenced by increasing slit widths.

The introduction to Part I states that the tables of wavenumbers were prepared by evaluating existing data including supplementary values determined for this investigation. The tables of data are provided with references which are with few exceptions from the primary literature current to mid-1960. Part II introductory remarks state only that the wavenumber calibration tables were prepared by the Commission, and several references are given in context in the introductory section.

Analysis

The tables were presented as provisional wavenumbers and are not considered standard because tests required of standard wavelengths in the visible region have not been met, and because it is anticipated that the accuracy of the molecular data will be considerably bettered with improvements in spectrometers. However, the Commission emphasized that the tables in Part I especially are the best that can be compiled with existing data. Part I: wavelengths of atomic emission spectra are necessary to determine wavenumber values of molecular absorption lines. The lines in the molecular species spectra in Part I were chosen as accurate wavenumber standards reliable to $\pm$ 0.03 cm^{-1} or better. Calibration lines in Part II, although covering the same region were selected with additional factors under consideration, notably instrumentation, experimental methods, and use for condensed phases. Absolute accuracy in Part II was judged adequate between 0.1 and 0.5 cm^{-1} for work in condensed phases, and as a result, accuracies are rounded to the nearest 0.05 cm^{-1}.

Use of wavenumbers rather than wavelengths is preferred. The introductions to both Parts discuss the considerations used in preparing the Tables: the regions covered, instrumentation, quality of existing data, experimental factors, errors, and assessment of the data.

3.2.25. Microwave Spectral Tables

Organization

From 1952 to 1966, these tables were compiled in the Radio Standards Physics Division, Radio Standards Laboratory, U.S. National Bureau of Standards (NBS), Boulder, Colorado. The project was then transferred to the Atomic

Physics Division, Institute for Basic Standards, NBS, Washington, D.C., where it is presently located. The tables being issued as NBS Monograph 70 are a revision and extension of NBS Circular 518, "Molecular Microwave Spectra Tables", by P. KISLIUK and C. H. TOWNES, published in 1952 and no longer available. The project is now part of the National Standard Reference Data Program of NBS (see 1.1.1.); W. H. KIRCHHOFF is director. Monograph 70 is being published in five volumes; Vol. I, II, IV, and V have been issued.

Coverage

Although emphasis has been on the publication of Monograph 70, another objective is to provide a continuing data center for the collection, critical evaluation, and dissemination of data on the microwave spectra of gases. In general, species to be investigated are limited only by experimental restrictions which usually require that the species be studied in the gas phase and have a permanent dipole moment. Included are the frequencies of transitions between the energy levels of molecules falling in the microwave and millimeter regions, typically from 300 MHz to 300,000 MHz.

Monograph 70 covers microwave spectra of molecules and the physical properties derived from these. The data are published as tabulations of evaluated absorption lines. The five volumes of this series will present a comprehensive compilation of microwave spectral data. Distribution of material in the five volumes will be:

Vol. I: Diatomic Molecules; Vol. II: Line Strengths of Asymmetric Rotors; Vol. III: Polyatomic Molecules With Internal Rotation; Vol. IV: Polyatomic Molecules Without Internal Rotation; and Vol. V: Spectral Line Listing.

In Vol. I, the following properties are tabulated for some 1500 spectral lines: measured frequencies, assigned molecular species, assigned quantum numbers, and intensities computed for 300 K and 195 K. For each molecule, a table of molecular constants including line widths, rotational constants, dipole moments, and various coupling constants are given. A separate table lists values of Casimir's function and hyperfine intensities.

Vol. II includes tabulations of line strengths of asymmetric rotors as a function of Ray's asymmetry parameter $\varkappa$ for rotational quantum numbers J from 0 to 35. Line strengths were computed for $\varkappa$ equal to 0, ± 0.3, ± 0.6, ± 0.8, ± 0.95, and ± 1.0.

Vol. V is a listing of the spectral lines reported in Vols I, III (in press), and IV of Monograph 70. The lines are tabulated according to ascending magnitude of frequency. For each spectral line, the following information is given: the formula for the molecular isotopic species, the number of the

83

3.2.25.

volume of this series in which the line was originally tabulated (1, 3, or 4), the identification number used in that volume for ready reference, rotational quantum number, the vibrational state, the hyperfine quantum numbers, and the frequency and its accuracy.

Data are obtained from the primary literature; other compilations of molecular constants are also used.

Analysis

In general, microwave frequencies are evaluated with regard both to accuracy and correctness of interpretation. In Vol. I, "Diatomic Molecules", frequencies and uncertainties given are those considered most accurate, but ambiguous definitions in the original papers prevented reduction of uncertainties to a common basis. When several values of comparable accuracy are used, an average is given. The molecular constants are given as reported in the originlaraticles. Intensities computed with insufficient data are marked. Computations were carried out on a digital computer; approximations used to simplify the calculations are explained and the constants used are recorded.

The Introduction to Volume II defines and discusses line strengths, methods of computation, and accuracy of results; describes the tables; and gives the procedures for tabulation and interpolation as a function of $\varkappa$, and extrapolation to higher J values.

The spectra and molecular data in Volume I are ordered alphabetically according to nomenclature recommended by the International Union of Pure and Applied Chemistry. The listing is divided first by isotopic molecular species and then by major quantum numbers for the transitions. There is an extensive bibliography.

Publications

Microwave Spectral Tables, NBS Monograph 70, U.S. Government Printing Office, Washington, D.C. 20402.

Vol. I: Diatomic Molecules, P. F. WACKER, MASATAKA MIZUSHIMA, J. D. PETERSON, and J. R. BALLARD, 1964, XVIII, 146 pp, US $ 2.00.

Vol. II: Line Strengths of Asymmetric Rotors, P. F. WACKER and M. R. PRATTO, 1964, XII, 340 pp, US $ 3.00.

Vol. III: Polyatomic Molecules Capable of Internal Rotation (in press).

Vol. IV: Polyatomic Molecules Without Internal Rotation, M. S. CORD, J. D. PETERSON, M. S. LOJKO, and R. H. HAAS, 1968, XII, 418 pp, US $ 5.50.

Vol. V: Spectral Line Listing, M. S. CORD, M. S. LOJKO, and J. D. PETERSON, 1968, V, 533 pp, US $ 4.75.

3.2.26. Landolt-Börnstein, Volume 4, Group II

Molecular Constants from Microwave Spectroscopy by BARBARA STARCK, edited by K.-H. HELLWEGE and A. M. HELLWEGE. Volume 4 of Group II, Atomic and Molecular Physics, of LANDOLT-BÖRNSTEIN, Numerical Data and Functional Relationships in Science and Technology, New Series, Springer-Verlag, Berlin-Heidelberg, 1967, IX, 225 pp, DM 110 (US $ 27.50).

Organization

This compilation was published under the auspices of "LANDOLT-BÖRNSTEIN", described in 2.1.; and prepared by BARBARA STARCK of the Mikrowellenspektroskopische Arbeitsgruppe im Physikalischen Institut der Universität Freiburg, Freiburg, Germany.

Coverage

This volume presents values of molecular constants determined by microwave spectroscopy for the following types of molecules: diatomic, linear, symmetric top, and asymmetric top, with sub-groupings of the latter two types. Data for molecules made asymmetric by isotopic substitution are included with their symmetric analogs. The constants given include: rotational, centrifugal distortion, and rotation-vibration interaction constants; isotopic masses or mass ratios; l-type doubling constants; Fermi interaction constants; Coriolis coupling constants; dipole moments; quadrupole coupling constants; and constants of hindered rotation.

Analysis

All significant information — table of contents, introduction, explanatory matter, and table headings — are given in both German and English. A brief but clear introduction discusses the relationships between observed quantities and derived constants, and explains both the system used by the author in presenting data, and the principles of arrangement used. If several references exist relating to a given measurement criticality is exercised in selecting a value, the source of which is indicated. For most of the numerical data a value of the uncertainty is given. All symbols are defined. The indexing is good. The literature cut-off date is 1965. To fill in gaps values from dissertations and conference reports have been used to a limited extent.

A supplement to this volume is in preparation.

3.2.27.

Raman Spectra

3.2.27. Selected Raman Spectral Data: American Petroleum Institute Research Project 44

Organization

The American Petroleum Institute (API) Research Project 44 (see 2.3.1.), began to publish Raman spectral data in 1948. BRUNO J. ZWOLINSKI, director of the Thermodynamics Research Center (TRC, discussed in 2.3.), Texas A & M University, College Station, Texas 77843, is in charge of the program which is closely associated with the TRC Data Project for Raman spectral data (see 3.2.28.).

Coverage

Substances included are compounds of interest to the petroleum industry: hydrocarbons; related organic compounds containing oxygen, halogens, sulfur, and nitrogen; and selected organometallic compounds.

Raman spectra are presented both as photographic, and photoelectric chart recordings. Intensities for Raman shift frequencies are given graphically by wave number (in vacuum) in the range 4000 to 0 cm^{-1}. Photoelectrically recorded charts are supplemented by tabular presentations of standard intensities for peak values. For spectra measured before development of intensity standardization methods, relative intensities are given numerically. Polarization data and line appearance (broad, diffuse, symmetrical, etc.) may be given for photographically recorded spectra. Approximate refractive indexes are included.

Spectra measured in 12 contributing laboratories are used; TRC staff also measure some. Laboratories interested in cooperating in this project may consult the director.

Analysis

Spectra are selected on the basis of the competence of the investigator, the quality of instrumentation, and the purity of the compounds. Many recent spectral data sheets give the source and purity (in mole percent) of the compound, the precision of measurement, the exciting line, and operating conditions. To standardize the quality of the spectra, detailed instructions are supplied to contributing laboratories.

Spectra are replaced as better ones become available; revisions and additions are made semiannually when warranted by the accumulation of new spectra.

86

The form of publication is the 22×29 cm loose-leaf sheet for which special post binders are available. Before October 1959, spectra were presented in the bar type of chart, with abscissa corresponding to the Raman shifts, and heights indicating the relative intensity. More recent photoelectric recordings are in the form of continuous or semicontinuous curves, with breaks for changes in amplifier sensitivity indicated on the graph. Auxiliary information is given in a legend on the sheets, which are arranged according to serial number. Two indexes are provided, one arranged by type of compound and the other by serial number. The contributing laboratory is identified in the indexes by code letters.

Publications

Catalog of Selected Raman Spectral Data, American Petroleum Institute Research Project 44, B. J. Zwolinski, Dir., Thermodynamics Research Center, Texas A & M University, College Station, Texas 77843; 501 loose-leaf data sheets, comprising 2 volumes, sold initially in complete sets only for US $ 165.50 (with binders), approximate cost of supplements per year is US $ 20.40. Discount prices are available to some educational and non-profit research institutions. Order from the TRC Data Distribution Office, Texas A & M Research Foundation, F. E. Box 130, College Station, Texas 77843.

3.2.28. Selected Raman Spectral Data: Thermodynamics Research Center Data Project

Organization

The Thermodynamics Research Center Data Project, formerly the Manufacturing Chemists Association (MCA) Research Project (see 2.3.2.), began to publish Raman spectral data in 1965. Bruno J. Zwolinski, director of the Thermodynamics Research Center (TRC, discussed in 2.3.), Texas A & M University, College Station, Texas 77843, is in charge of this project which is closely associated with the API RP 44 project on Raman spectral data (see 3.2.27.).

Coverage

Nonhydrocarbon compounds such as organic oxygen, halogen, and nitrogen compounds are covered.

Raman spectra are presented in the form of photographic or photoelectric chart records. Intensity is plotted versus reciprocal centimeters to record the Raman shift, usually in the range 4000 to 0 cm^{-1}. A tabulation of Raman shifts in cm^{-1}, including depolarization ratios in some cases, is included with each spectrum. Other information given on the spectrograms includes the name of the compound, molecular and structural formulas, the source and purity of the compound when available, the contributing laboratory, and the date.

The spectra are generated primarily in the spectral program of TRC, with contributions from government and academic laboratories. Laboratories interested in cooperating in this project may consult the director.

Analysis

The spectral data published to date are all mercury-excited spectra. In the future, laser-excited spectra will be included in the compilation. Spectra are selected on the basis of the competence of the investigator, the quality of instrumentation, and the purity of the compound. Detailed instructions are supplied to laboratories contributing data.

The spectra are published on 22×29 cm loose-leaf sheets for which special post binders are available. Photoelectric recordings are in the form of continuous or semicontinuous curves, with breaks for changes in amplifier sensitivity indicated on the graph. Two indexes are provided, one arranged by type of compound and the other by serial number. The contributing laboratory is identified in the indexes by code letters.

Publications

Catalog of Selected Raman Spectral Data, Thermodynamics Research Center Data Project, B. J. Zwolinski, Director, Thermodynamics Research Center, Texas A & M University, College Station, Texas 77843; 81 loose-leaf data sheets extant December 1967, sold initially in complete sets only for US $ 28.80 (with binders), approximate cost of supplements per year is US $ 19.00. Discount prices are available to some educational and non-profit research institutions. Order from the TRC Data Distribution Office, Texas A & M Research Foundation, F. E. Box 130, College Station, Texas 77843.

Electronic Spectra — Ultraviolet (UV) and Visible

3.2.29. Selected Ultraviolet Spectral Data: American Petroleum Institute Research Project 44

Organization

The American Petroleum Institute (API) Research Project 44 (see 2.3.1.) began publishing ultraviolet spectral data in 1945. Bruno J. Zwolinski, director, Thermodynamics Research Center (TRC, discussed in 2.3.), Texas A & M University, College Station, Texas 77843, is in charge of the program which is closely associated with the TRC Data Project in UV (see 3.2.30.).

Coverage

Substances considered are mainly hydrocarbons; oxygen, halogen, sulfur, and nitrogen derivatives of the hydrocarbons are also included, as well as a few organometallic compounds (particularly etioporphyrins).

The ultraviolet absorption spectral curves are recorded as absorbance (sometimes labeled optical density) versus wavelength in angstrom units or millimicrons; and frequency in reciprocal centimeters, generally in the range 47,000 to 19,000 cm^{-1}. Nominal bandwidths in angstroms are indicated on the charts. Other data given include molecular and structural formula of the compound, source and purity, solvent, concentration, cell length, and instrument used.

Spectra in the catalog have been obtained from 38 selected industrial, academic, governmental, and private laboratories. Laboratories interested in submitting spectra may consult the project director.

Analysis

Spectra are chosen on the basis of the competence of the investigator, the quality of instrumentation employed, and the purity of the compounds used. The source and, when available, the purity of the sample, as well as some supplemental information, are given in the legend. To up-grade quality, the project supplies contributors with detailed instructions. Operating characteristics are given such as temperature, cell length, and concentration and solvent if the substance is in solution, or pressures if in the gaseous state.

Spectra are replaced as better ones become available; revisions and additions are issued when warranted by the accumulation of new spectra.

The form of publication is the 22×29 cm loose-leaf sheet for which special post binders are available. Most of the spectra issued since 1950 are reduced reproductions of original chart recordings. The spectrograms vary in method of presentation, notations, and conventions, such as range of frequencies, with contributor and instrument used. Two indexes are provided, one by type of compound, the other by serial number. Contributing laboratories are identified in the indexes by code letters.

Publications

Catalog of Selected Ultraviolet Spectral Data, American Petroleum Institute Research Project 44, B. J. ZWOLINSKI, Director, Thermodynamics Research Center, Texas A & M University, College Station, Texas 77843; 1154 loose-leaf data sheets extant December 1968, comprising 3 volumes, sold initially in complete sets only for US $ 368.00 (with binders), approximate cost of yearly supplements is US $ 18.00. Discount prices are available to some educational and non-profit research institutions. Order from the TRC Data Distribution Office, Texas A & M Research Foundation, F. E. Box 130, College Station, Texas 77843.

3.2.30. Selected Ultraviolet Spectral Data: Thermodynamics Research Center Data Project

Organization

The Thermodynamics Research Center (TRC) Data Project, formerly the Manufacturing Chemists Association (MCA) Research Project, described in 2.3.2., began to publish ultraviolet spectral data in 1959. BRUNO J. ZWO-LINSKI, director of the Thermodynamics Research Center (discussed in 2.3.), Texas A & M University, College Station, Texas 77843, is in charge of the project which is closely associated with the API RP 44 UV project (see 3.2.29.).

Coverage

Emphasis is placed upon inorganic and nonhydrocarbon compounds important to the chemical industry. Spectra have been published for organic compounds containing oxygen, nitrogen, sulfur, chlorine, and boron, and for diborane and a number of hydrocarbon derivatives.

The ultraviolet absorption spectral curves give absorbance versus wavelength in millimicrons (occasionally in angstrom units) and frequency in reciprocal centimeters, generally in the range 54,000 to 15,000 cm^{-1}.

Spectra published are generated by the Thermodynamics Research Center staff, and also are contributed by cooperating industrial, governmental, and academic laboratories. Laboratories interested in cooperating in this project may consult the director.

Analysis

Spectra are selected on the basis of the competence of the investigator, the quality of instrumentation, and the purity of the compound. The source, purity of the sample, temperature, cell length, and concentration and solvent if in solution, are stated in the legend. The project supplies contributors with recommendations for calibrations, sample techniques, for obtaining and recording spectra.

Spectra are replaced as better ones become available; revisions and additions are issued when warranted by the accumulation of spectra.

Publication is in the form of 22 × 29 cm loose-leaf sheets for which special post binders are available. The first issue of sheets contains smooth hand-drawn curves whereas the later data sheets are reproductions of chart recordings. The concentrations for various sections of the spectrogram are indicated on the spectrogram. The sheets are arranged by serial number. Two indexes are provided, one arranged by type of compound and the other by serial number. Spectrograms vary slightly in presentation with instrument used, spectral region, and contributor. Contributing laboratories are identified in the indexes by code letters.

Publications

Catalog of Selected Ultraviolet Spectral Data, Thermodynamics Research Center Data Project, B. J. ZWOLINSKI, Director, Thermodynamics Research Center, Texas A & M University, College Station, Texas 77843; 126 loose-leaf data sheets extant December 1967, sold initially in complete sets only for US $ 42.30 (with binders), approximate cost of supplements per year is US $ 30.00. Discount prices are available to some educational and non-profit research institutions. Order from the TRC Data Distribution Office, Texas A & M Research Foundation, F. E. Box 130, College Station, Texas 77843.

3.2.31. Organic Electronic Spectral Data

Organization

Organic Electronic Spectral Data, Inc., is a nonprofit organization established in 1957 by a group of physical-organic chemists interested in ultraviolet data. Chemists from government, industry, and universities searched and abstracted the literature on a volunteer basis.

Early support came from the publisher, and the U.S. National Science Foundation. Some support has come from industry, particularly instrument manufacturers. Processing of data for Volumes I, II, and III was carried out at Hebrew University, Israel, and for Volume IV at the University of Louisville in the U.S. The Treasurer is Dr. J. P. PHILLIPS, Department of Chemistry, University of Louisville, Louisville, Kentucky.

Coverage

Spectral data from the ultraviolet and visible regions are compiled.

Properties included are wavelength values in millimicrons for maxima, shoulders, and inflections, also the logarithms of the corresponding molar absorptivities. Additional information provided is name and formula of compound, solvent used, and reference.

The primary literature is searched for pertinent data; for Volumes I and II approximately 65 journals were scanned, for Volume III, more than 70, and for Volume IV, approximately 90 journals.

Analysis

The primary purpose of this collection is to aid in compound identification. Data must meet minimum requirements. The compound must be pure enough for satisfactory analysis and must be definable by a molecular formula. In general, the solvent or the phase is given. The spectral data must be complete enough so that the wavelengths of maximal absorption and molar absorptivities may be calculated if they are not given in the original reference. Wavelength values are given to 0.1 millimicron when reported numerically by the author; otherwise to the nearest millimicron. Molar absorptivity values are given to the nearest 0.01 unit of log ε when reported numerically by the author. Data read from curves are underlined, and the logarithm values are given to 0.1 unit. Fine structure at a given maximum is indicated as are inflections or shoulders. References are given for all data.

The entries are arranged according to the Chemical Abstracts molecular formula index system. Considerable effort has been made to ensure that the compound names conform with the Chemical Abstracts system of nomenclature. No index is needed because the compounds are arranged according to molecular formula.

Publications

Organic Electronic Spectral Data, Wiley Interscience, New York, London, and Sydney.

> Vol. I, 1946 to 1952, M. J. Kamlet, Ed., 1960, XIV, 1208 pp, US $ 25.00.
> Vol. II, 1953 to 1955, H. E. Ungnade, Ed., 1960, X, 919 pp, US $ 17.50.
> Vol. III, 1956 to 1957, O. H. Wheeler and L. A. Kaplan, Eds., 1966, XII, 1210 pp, US $ 25.00.
> Vol. IV, 1958 to 1959, J. P. Phillips, F. C. Nachod, Eds., 1963, IX, 1179 pp, US $ 20.00.
> Vol. V, 1960 to 1961, R. E. Lyle and P. R. Jones, Eds., in press.
> Vol. VI, 1962 to 1963, L. D. Freedman and J. Cymerman Craig, Eds., in press.
> Vol. VII, 1964 to 1965, J. C. Dacons and R. G. Rice, Eds., in press.

3.2.32. Ultraviolet Spectra, Sadtler Research Laboratories, Inc.

Organization

The Sadtler Research Laboratories, discussed in 3.2.21., introduced their "Standard Ultraviolet Spectra" in 1960. This is a copyrighted designation given by Sadtler to a class of spectra to distinguish it from the commercial classes.

Coverage

The "Sadtler Standard Ultraviolet Spectra" is a compendium of spectra in the ultraviolet and visible regions. Most compounds included have conjugated unsaturated systems.

Ultraviolet absorption spectra were recorded in the range 200 to 350 mμ until 1968 when the range was extended to 800 mμ. Information given on each spectrogram includes: the molecular and semistructural formula, molecular weight, melting or boiling point, name and source of chemical, solvent used, UV spectrum number, and the compound's corresponding IR spectrum number. As of 1968, there were some 24,000 spectra of over 1300 compounds. The second type of spectra is the commercial which includes agricultural chemicals, and dyes, pigments, and stains.

Spectra are determined in the Sadtler laboratories using compounds contributed by industrial and research organizations, and educational institutions.

Analysis

For the "Standard Ultraviolet Spectra", Sadtler makes use of five solvents in an order based on laboratory tests that showed minimum loss of energy with optimum solvent action. The spectra are scanned in acid, base, and neutral media to show the effects of pH. As many as four absorbancy curves for solutions of various concentrations appear on each chart. The quality of an individual spectrum depends in part on the purity of the compound. Sadtler advertising literature states only that samples at least 98 percent pure are used. No criteria of purity are presented. Each spectrum measured is reviewed by consultants before publication.

The method of preparation for scanning, cell thickness, concentration, wavelength of maximum absorbance, slit opening at this wavelength for each curve, and the instrument used are indicated for each spectrum.

Photographic copies of the spectra are published, one chart lengthwise on 22×29 cm loose-leaf sheets. Special binders are available. The indexes to the Sadtler Infrared Spectra are applicable to the ultraviolet reference spectra, but ultraviolet alphabetical and numerical indexes are also published.

Publications

Orders and inquiries should be sent to Sadtler Research Laboratories, Inc., 3316 Spring Garden St., Philadelphia, Pa. 19104.

Collection	Total No.	US $/ 1000 (Vol.)	Total Price US $	Annual Subscription
"Ultraviolet Standard Spectra"	24000	132.00	3168.00	US $ 363.00/ 2000 spectra, indices and Locator
Indices			55.00	
Locator			44.00	

3.2.33.

Other Collections

Pharmaceutical Ultraviolet	1500	—	475.00	—
Biochemical Ultraviolet	650	—	165.00	—

Other Publications and Output
All spectra are available on microfilm for the same price.

3.2.33. Absorption Spectra in the Ultraviolet and Visible Region

Organization

The compilation *Absorption Spectra in the Ultraviolet and Visible Region* is edited by L. Láng (Hungary) with the collaboration of A. Bartecki (Poland), J. Szöke, G. Varsányi, and M. Vizesy who comprise the Editorial Board. The program is sponsored by the Hungarian Academy of Sciences. The original purpose was to add the results of Hungarian research to foreign collections and to make available unpublished spectra obtained in Hungary. The publications have taken on an international aspect with spectra contributed by workers in Austria, Czechoslovakia, Germany, the Netherlands, Poland, Rumania, U.K., U.S.A., and U.S.S.R. Volume 9 had 48 contributors.

Coverage

The compilation covers both inorganic and organic complex compounds together with single- and multi-cyclic aromatic systems, hetero-aromatic compounds, and Si-organic compounds. A large number of spectra of pharmaceutical basic materials or of active agents and a wide variety of organic compounds are included. Emphasis is, however, on publishing spectra of recently synthesized compounds, and those spectra not available in other collections. Most of the spectra for organic compounds apply to solutions but a few are for the solid or vapor phase. With Volume 9, some 1677 compounds are covered.

Spectra are represented by graphs of log ε (ε = extinction coefficient) versus wavelength in millimicrons in ranges varying from 200 to 350 mμ, 200 to 600 mμ, to 200 to 800 mμ. Observed values of log I_0/I from which log ε is obtained are tabulated. Data are often given for the same substance in several different media, and in different concentrations in the same medium (solvent). In addition, associated data are given: structural and molecular formulas, molecular weights, concentration and solvent if in solution, melting and boiling points, the instrument used, and the cell length. Supplementary notes are sometimes provided.

Most spectra are obtained from contributors. The Editorial Board welcomes contributions of spectra of new compounds; these may be sent to Dr. L. LÁNG, Budapest, XI., Budafoki ut 16—18, Hungary.

Analysis

The Editorial Board evaluates all spectra and original measurements or records. Spectra that have been previously published are included if substantial additional information is given.

Because this compilation is a continuing series, no effort is made to group the spectra according to a particular system. Subject (compound), formula, author, and figure (i.e. diagram number) indexes are provided. The author index includes the name of the institution with which the author is associated. The books are in English but the titles of each index are also in German and Russian. "Theoretical and Technical Introduction" accompanies the first volume, and includes several conversion tables (e.g., wavelengths — wavenumbers, wavelengths — fresnels, and a spectroscopical conversion table for energies), and a list of symbols and formulas used in the compilation.

To date, this compilation consists of 9 volumes issued as 17×24 cm loose-leaf sheets in ring binders. Although each volume begins on page 1, the spectra are numbered continuously through the volumes — to 1677 in Volume 9. Cumulative indexes for Volumes 1 to 5 are included in Volume 5; a cumulative index for Volumes 6 to 10 will be issued with Volume 10, scheduled for publication in 1968.

Publications

Absorption Spectra in the Ultraviolet and Visible Region, L. LÁNG, Ed., coproduction of the Academic Press, New York and London, and the Publishing House of the Hungarian Academy of Sciences, Budapest. Printed in English in Hungary. Available in North and South America from Academic Press, New York.

Vol. 1, A Theoretical and Technical Introduction, and Substances, 170; 1959, 518 pp, 2nd ed, 1961, 3rd ed, 1963, US $ 18.00.

Vol. 2, Substances, 179; 1961, 439 pp, 2nd ed, 1964, US $ 18.00.

Vol. 3, Substances, 172; 1962, 448 pp, US $ 20.00.

Vol. 4, Substances, 185; 1963, 438 pp, US $ 20.00.

Vol. 5, Substances, 192; 1965, 556 pp (including a cumulative Index for Vols. 1 to 5), US $ 23.00.

Vol. 6, Substances, 197; 1966, 442 pp, US $ 22.00.

Vol. 7, Substances, 190; 1967, 442 pp, US $ 23.00.

Vol. 8, Substances, 197; 1967, 440 pp, US $ 23.00.

Vol. 9, Substances, 195; 1967, 416 pp, Index pamphlet, US $ 23.50.

Vol. 10, In preparation; Cumulative Index, Vols. 6 to 10.

Vol. 11, In preparation.

3.2.34. The UV Atlas of Organic Compounds/UV-Atlas organischer Verbindungen

Organization

The *UV Atlas of Organic Compounds* is produced within DMS (see 3.2.19.) under the joint auspices of the Photoelectric Spectrometry Group, London, England, and the Institut für Spektrochemie und Angewandte Spektroskopie, Dortmund, Germany, the latter directed by H. KAISER. The editors of the Atlas are H.-H. PERKAMPUS, Brunswick, and I. SANDEMAN, London.

Two groups of experts assist in the selection of spectra and the preparation. The British group includes G. H. BEAVEN, London, S. F. MASON, Norwich, E. M. F. ROE, London, and C. J. TIMMONS, Nottingham. The German experts are B. HAMPEL, Darmstadt, G. HOHLNEICHER, Munich, G. KRESZE, Munich, H.-H. PERKAMPUS, Brunswick, and M. PESTEMER, Leverkusen. Workers in various laboratories contribute spectra.

Coverage

The Atlas presents selected ultraviolet absorption spectra of about 1000 organic reference compounds containing the most important organic chromophores. Among these are compounds containing multiplybonded C-atoms, $C = O$ and $C = S$ functional groups, C multiply-bonded to N, benzene and derivatives, condensed aromatics and heterocyclics, aromatic compounds containing non-benzenoid rings, monocyclic and polycyclic heterocyclics, and derivatives of saturated organic compounds. Also included are selected compounds of biochemical and clinical interest, and spectrophotometric standard substances and solvents.

In the spectrograms, the molar absorptivity (log ε) is plotted against the wavenumber (in cm^{-1}) and the wavelength (in mμ). For most of the spectra, the molar absorptivity runs from $\varepsilon = 10$ to $\varepsilon = 10^5$ and the wavenumbers run either from 55,000 to 20,000 cm^{-1}, or 45,000 to 10,000 cm^{-1} (182 to 500 mμ, or 222 to 1000 mμ) depending on the spectrum.

Analysis

The UV Atlas will consist of five volumes (loose-leaf binders), each holding some 200 spectra; Volumes I, II, III, and IV have been published. It represents a carefully and critically selected collection of solution spectra of organic compounds containing typical chromophoric groups. Many spectra were measured for the Atlas by new and improved techniques. Particular attention was given to important organic compounds for which reliable spectra had not been published.

The spectra are supplemented by tables showing the effects of substituents and solvents, by explanatory text in English and German, and by formula indexes.

The spectra are arranged in thirteen sections based on the above mentioned chromophoric groups. Each main section is divided into appropriate subgroups. In addition a ten-digit code number is given for each spectrum based on a new classification system of those organic structures which are of interest in UV spectroscopy (see Angewandte Chemie, Internat. Edit. **4**, 516 (1965).

Each spectrum is printed singly on a page (format 21×30 cm) of translucent paper, so that the spectra can be compared (up to five at a time) when placed against an illuminated background. Information concerning the purity of the compound and the conditions (spectral resolution, cell length, solvent and concentration) under which the spectrum was measured is included.

Publications

UV Atlas of Organic Compounds, edited by Photoelectric Spectrometry Group, London, and Institut für Spektrochemie und Angewandte Spektroskopie, Dortmund. Published within "Documentation of Molecular Spectroscopy" by Verlag Chemie, Weinheim/Bergstr. and Butterworths & Co., London. £ 7.2.6. or DM 80.00 (US $ 20.00) per volume and £ 35.10.0. or DM 400.00 (US $ 100.00) per set. Available from Plenum Press, New York, in the U.S.A., Central and South America at the price of US $ 27.50 per volume, or US $ 115.00 per set.

Vol. I, 1966, 239 pp, 14 pp molecular formula index.

Vol. II, 1966, 288 pp.

Vol. III, 1967, 290 pp, 20 pp molecular formula index.

Vol. IV, 1968, 288 pp, 28 pp molecular formula index.

Vol. V, scheduled for 1969.

Mass Spectra

3.2.35. Selected Mass Spectral Data: American Petroleum Institute Research Project 44

Organization

The American Petroleum Institute (API) Research Project 44, discussed in 2.3.1., began to publish mass spectral data in 1947. A matrix, or grid, format for mass spectral data of hydrocarbons of high molecular weight was introduced in 1961. The only comparable program for the compilation and distribution of mass spectral data is the complementary program of the

3.2.35.

Thermodynamics Research Center Data Project, described in 3.2.36. BRUNO J. ZWOLINSKI, director of the Thermodynamics Research Center (discussed in 2.3.), Texas A & M University, College Station, Texas 77843, is in charge of both programs.

Coverage

Substances covered are principally hydrocarbons; elemental oxygen, hydrogen, neon, argon, and nitrogen; a few hydrides, oxides, and chlorides; and selected groups of organic compounds, especially those containing oxygen, halogens, sulfur, and nitrogen of interest to the petroleum and petrochemical industries.

The mass spectral data are presented in tabular form. For each observed mass-to-charge ratio, the relative intensity of the peak and the operating conditions — magnetic field and the ionizing voltage — are given. The type of peak is sometimes indicated. The base peak (with relative intensity of 100), the parent peak and corresponding entries are underscored. The molecular weight, molecular and semistructural formulas, and approximate boiling point are also given.

A matrix format for mass spectral data for hydrocarbons of high molecular weight provides a grid of whole-number mass-to-charge ratios for entry of relative intensities of observed peaks. This emphasizes the relation between peaks that differ in mass units by one CH_2 group. Relative intensities for fractional ratios and other data are given in the conventional tabular form.

Spectra are obtained from 35 cooperating laboratories. Laboratories interested in cooperating in this project should contact the project director.

Analysis

Spectra are selected on the basis of the competence of the investigator, the quality of instrumentation employed, and the purity of the compounds used. The importance of high purity of samples and calibrating gases, including information on isotopic purity, is emphasized. Information concerning the instrument used (make, model, and operating conditions) and the relative intensities and sensitivities for the standards used (e.g., *n*-butane and *n*-hexadecane) give an indication of the quality of the measurements. To ensure high quality of submitted spectra recommendations for calibration and techniques are provided by the project.

Revision and additions are issued when warranted by the accumulation of new spectra.

The spectra are published on 22×29 cm loose-leaf sheets for which special post binders are available. Two indexes are provided, one arranged by type of compound and the other by serial number. Spectra in the matrix format are indexed in separate supplements. The name of the contributing laboratory is given on the spectral sheet and identified in the indexes by code letters.

Publications

Catalog of Selected Mass Spectral Data, American Petroleum Institute Research Project 44, B. J. ZWOLINSKI, Director, Thermodynamics Research Center, Texas A & M University, College Station, Texas 77843; 2528 loose-leaf data sheets extant December 1968, comprising 6 volumes, sold initially in complete sets only for US $ 800.60 (with binders), approximate cost of yearly supplements is US $ 54.00. Discount prices are available to some educational and nonprofit research institutions. Order from the TRC Data Distribution Office, Texas A & M Research Foundation, F. E. Box 130, College Station, Texas 77843.

3.2.36. Selected Mass Spectral Data: Thermodynamics Research Center Data Project

Organization

The Thermodynamics Research Center (TRC) Data Project, formerly the Manufacturing Chemists Association (MCA) Research Project, is described in 2.3.2. Mass spectral data were first published in 1959; a matrix format was introduced in 1961. BRUNO J. ZWOLINSKI, director of the Thermodynamics Research Center (discussed in 2.3.), Texas A & M University, College Station, Texas 77843, is in charge of the program, which is closely associated with the API RP44 mass spectral data program (see 3.2.35.).

Coverage

In general, substances include classes of organic nonhydrocarbon compounds containing oxygen, halogens, sulfur, nitrogen, silicon, and boron; and certain inorganic substances including hydrides of boron, bromine, and silicon. High-quality mass spectral data of any compound not included in the American Petroleum Institute catalog are accepted. Duplication in the two catalogs is avoided.

The mass spectral data are presented in either the classical standard tabular form with relative intensities or more recently in the convenient matrix format with absolute intensities given. The two kinds of mass spectral data loose-leaf sheets are usually prepared and distributed in separate semiannual supplements with unique numbering codes. For the standard format, the mass-to-charge ratio, the relative intensities and the operating conditions — magnetic field, ionizing voltage, etc. — are given. The base peak (with relative intensity of 100) and the parent peak are underscored and often corresponding peaks of interest are defined. In the matrix or grid format, particularly convenient in analytical studies, the ten principal intensities are delineated in a bold face type. In addition to the usual information regarding molecular weight, IUPAC or Chemical Abstracts nomenclature, and structural formula of the substance, information on the simple physical properties is often included.

Spectral data are obtained from 6 cooperating laboratories. Laboratories interested in contributing data may consult the director.

Analysis

Spectral data are selected on the basis of the competence of the investigator, the quality of instrumentation employed, and the purity of the compounds. The importance of high purity of samples and calibrating gases, including information on isotopic purity, is emphasized by the project. Information concerning the instrument used (make, model, and operating conditions) and the relative intensities and sensitivities for the standards (*n*-butane and *n*-hexadecane) give an indication of the quality of the measurements. To ensure high quality of submitted spectra, instructions including recommendations for calibration and techniques to be used in the measurements are provided by the project on request. Corrections and instrument modification or conditions that affect the quality of the data are often recorded.

Data sheets are replaced as better ones become available; revisions and additions are issued when warranted by the accumulation of spectra.

Mass spectral data are presented in either the standard or matrix format (for hydrocarbons of high molecular weight). Publication is in the form of 22×29 cm loose-leaf sheets for which special post binders are available. Two indexes are provided, one arranged by type of compound and the other by serial number. The name of the contributing laboratory is given on the spectral sheet and identified in the index by code letters.

Publications

Catalog of Selected Mass Spectral Data, Thermodynamics Research Center Data Project, B. J. ZWOLINSKI, Director, Thermodynamics Research Center, Texas A & M University, College Station, Texas 77843; 253 loose-leaf data sheets extant June 1968, sold initially in complete sets only for US $ 80.85 (with binders), approximate cost of supplements per year is US $ 25.00. Discount prices are available to some educational and non-profit research institutions. Order from the TRC Data Distribution Office, Texas A & M Research Foundation, F. E. Box 130, College Station, Texas 77843.

3.2.37. Compilation of Mass Spectral Data (Index de Spectres de Masse)

Organization

Compilation of Mass Spectral Data was first prepared by A. Cornu and R. Massot in 1964; the second edition was published in 1966; and a third edition is in preparation. This compilation together with its first supplement serves as a four-part index to some 6,000 spectra collected by the Laboratory of Mass Spectrometry, Centre d'Etudes Nucléaires de Grenoble, Département de Physico-Chimie, B. P. No. 269, 38 Grenoble, France, under the Commissariat à l'Énergie Atomique, where the authors are members of the staff.

Coverage

Most of the compounds covered are organic gases or vaporizable compounds. The spectra are obtained from existing spectral collections, such as the API RP 44 (see 3.2.35.), those in French laboratories, and the literature. Each of the four parts of the index lists the name of the element or compound, the molecular weight, a number for calculating absolute peak heights from that of a standard, the ten highest peaks and their relative abundances (or intensities), the formula, and the reference. The four parts are essentially four indexes, and the compounds are arranged as follows: in Part A by reference numbers to a list of mass spectral compilations, in Part B by molecular weight, in Part C by molecular formula, and in Part D by fragment ion values. Part D comprises half the book; it is 323 pages.

Analysis

This publication is more than an index and, consequently is described briefly here. The compilation provides information so that many organic unknowns may be identified; the references may be utilized if further data are required.

Publications

Compilation of Mass Spectral Data (Index de Spectres de Masse), 2nd ed, A. Cornu and R. Massot, published by Heyden & Son Ltd., London, in cooperation with Presses Universitaires de France, Paris, 1966, XV, 617 pp, US $ 42.00.

First Supplement, A. Cornu and R. Massot, published by Heyden & Son, Ltd., London, in cooperation with Presses Universitaires de France, Paris, 1967, 160 pp, 70 s.

3.2.38. Mass Spectrometry Data Centre

Organization

The center is located at the Atomic Weapons Research Establishment (AWRE) in Aldermaston, United Kingdom. It was established in 1965, based on an existing mass spectrometry group. The director is R. G. RIDLEY; support is provided by the Office for Scientific and Technical Information (OSTI, see 1.1.2.).

Coverage

The primary function of the center is to provide an international data service. It also acts as a depository for critically evaluated mass spectra and for data on closely allied subject fields. The center maintains close contact with other groups with similar interests, such as the Data Center for Atomic and Molecular Ionization Processes (see 3.2.12.). Assembly of a mass spectral computer file is in progress. Closely associated with this activity are projects to develop an information retrieval service, and computer-generated indexes.

In addition to the development of a data information service in the area of mass spectrometry, the center also works on mass spectroscopy applications, exemplified by a study to develop methods for compound identification using low resolution mass spectra.

At present, the center issues a monthly "Mass Spectrometry Bulletin" which provides references, based on a comprehensive literature survey, on research and other activities in the mass spectral area. The "Bulletin" is prepared from a computer file and computer-ordered indexes.

Analysis

The center is utilizing computers to develop a comprehensive and up-to-date file of critically evaluated mass spectral data. Once established, the center's tape files will also be used to answer inquiries from the public. Low resolution Mass Spectral Data is being distributed in Tabular Form on Data Sheets and copies of the tapes are available.

Publications

"Mass Spectrometry Bulletin", Mass Spectrometry Data Centre, available through Her Majesty's Stationery Office, P. O. Box 569, London, S. E. 1.

"MSDC Mass Spectral Data Sheets", available from the Mass Spectrometry Data Center, AWRE, Aldermaston, Berkshire, England.

Nuclear Magnetic Resonance (NMR) Spectra

3.2.39.   Selected Nuclear Magnetic Resonance Spectral Data: American Petroleum Institute Research Project 44

Organization

The American Petroleum Institute (API) Research Project 44, discussed in 2.3.1., began to publish nuclear magnetic resonance (NMR) spectra in October 1959. BRUNO J. ZWOLINSKI, director of the Thermodynamics Research Center (described in 2.3.), Texas A & M University, College Station, Texas 77843, is in charge of the program which is closely associated with the TRC Data Project in NMR (see 3.2.40.).

Coverage

Substances are mostly hydrocarbons and related organic compounds containing oxygen, nitrogen, and sulfur; a few organometallic compounds of interest to the petroleum industry are also included.

NMR spectral data are presented as reduced reproductions of instrument tracings. The standard abscissa scale is frequency separation (in cycles per second) from the external reference standard, although secondary scales are frequently employed, such as the shielding numbers, N for external references, and δ and τ for internal TMS references. The abscissa scale for the more recent sheets is in parts per million, δ and τ. The height of each resonance peak is normally shown without scale, and the exact frequencies of prominent resonances are usually identified on the spectrum.

Spectra are obtained from 15 cooperating laboratories. Laboratories interested in cooperating in this project should consult the director.

Analysis

Spectra are selected on the basis of the laboratory, the competence of the investigator, the quality of instrumentation, and the purity of the compounds. API Standard or Research Samples are used in many of the measurements. Generally, information is given concerning purity, source of compound, identification of external reference standard, instrument, and operating conditions. The project supplies contributors with instructions that encourage the use of both internal and external reference standards, describe standardization methods, and provide useful suggestions on experimental techniques.

Spectra are replaced ꞏs better ones become available; revisions and additions are issued when the accumulation of new spectra warrant it.

3.2.40.

Publication is in the form of 22 × 29 cm loose-leaf sheets for which special post binders are available. The spectra, sometimes including multiple curves at different scanning rates, are shown graphically. Methods of presenting tracings, and notation conventions vary slightly with contributing laboratory, frequently because of the different instruments used. The format for tabular data is standard for all spectra: this includes data on the compound, and instrument and operation. Supplementary information is given in a legend. Sheets are arranged according to serial number. Indexes include a numerical listing by serial number, a formula index subdivided by chemical classes of compounds, and a functional group index arranged alphabetically. The Functional Group Index lists 253 NMR (40 MHz) spectral data sheets contributed by the Humble Oil and Refining Company.

Publications

Catalog of Selected Nuclear Magnetic Resonance Spectral Data, American Petroleum Institute Research Project 44, B. J. Zwolinski, Director, Thermodynamics Research Center, Texas A & M University, College Station, Texas 77843; 714 loose-leaf data sheets in 3 volumes, sold initially in complete sets only for US $ 236.00 (with binders), approximate cost of supplements per year is US $ 36.00. Discount prices are available to some educational and non-profit research institutions. Order from the TRC Data Distribution Office, Texas A & M Research Foundation, F. E. Box 130, College Station, Texas 77843.

3.2.40. Selected Nuclear Magnetic Resonance Spectral Data: Thermodynamics Research Center Data Project

Organization

The Thermodynamics Research Center Data Project, formerly known as the Manufacturing Chemists Association (MCA) Research Project, is described in 2.3.2. It began to publish nuclear magnetic resonance (NMR) spectra in 1960. Bruno J. Zwolinski, director of the Thermodynamics Research Center (discussed in 2.3.), Texas A & M University, College Station, Texas 77843, is in charge of the program which is closely associated with the API RP 44 NMR program (see 3.2.39.).

Coverage

The current compilation includes 40, 60, and 100 MHz NMR spectral data on closely related groups of organic substances including oxygen, halogen, sulfur, nitrogen, and phosphorus compounds.

NMR spectral data are presented as reduced reproductions of instrument tracings. The standard abscissa scale is frequency separation (in cycles per second) from benzene, the external reference standard; for a few, it is parts per million, and for some both units are given. The shielding number is usually given as a secondary horizontal scale. The height of resonance peaks is normally shown without scale. Exact frequencies of prominent resonances are identified on the spectrum in many instances.

The spectra contained in the current compilation were generated by the staff of the Thermodynamics Research Center spectral program, and contributed by eight cooperating industrial laboratories. Laboratories interested in cooperating in this project may consult the director.

Analysis

Spectra are selected on the basis of the competence of the investigator, the quality of instrumentation employed, and the purity of the compounds. When available, the source and purity of the material are given. On request, the project supplies contributors with information on the use of both internal and external reference standards, standardization methods, and experimental techniques.

Spectra are replaced as better ones become available; revisions and additions are issued when warranted.

Publication is in the form of 22×29 cm loose-leaf sheets for which special post binders are available. The spectra, sometimes including multiple curves at different scanning rates, are shown graphically, usually with two abscissa scales. Presentation of the spectra varies slightly with contributor and instrument used. Sheets are arranged according to serial number. Indexes include a numerical listing by serial number, a formula index subdivided by chemical classes of compounds, and a functional group index arranged alphabetically. The Functional Group Index includes 253 NMR (40 MHz) spectral data sheets contributed by the Humble Oil and Refining Company.

Publications

Catalog of Selected Nuclear Magnetic Resonance Spectral Data, Thermodynamics Research Center Data Project, B. J. ZWOLINSKI, Director, Thermodynamics Research Center, Texas A & M University, College Station, Texas 77843; 683 loose-leaf data sheets extant June 1968, sold initially in complete sets only for US $ 209.85 (with binders), approximate cost of supplements per year is US $ 30.00. Discount prices are available to some educational and non-profit research institutions. Order from the TRC Data Distribution Office, Texas A & M Research Foundation, F. E. Box 130, College Station, Texas 77843.

3.2.41. Nuclear Magnetic Resonance Spectra, Sadtler Research Laboratories, Inc.

Organization

The Sadtler Research Laboratories, discussed in 3.2.21., began to issue nuclear magnetic resonance (NMR) spectra in 1964.

Coverage

Sadtler has given one class of NMR spectra the copyrighted designation "Standard Nuclear Magnetic Resonance High Resolution Spectra". These NMR spectra are presented as reproductions of instrument tracings with the abscissa as a dual scale in parts per million and cycles per second. Information given includes: name *(Chemical Abstracts)*, molecular formula, structural formula with the assignments indicated, molecular weight, melting and boiling points (when known), source of compound, Sadtler IR number (when applicable), solvent and concentration, and any available physical data. Also included on the same page is a tabulation of assignments and pertinent instrument operating information, and comments when needed.

A second class of NMR spectra, commercial spectra, includes solvents and surface active agents. All spectra are determined in the Sadtler laboratories.

Analysis

The high resolution spectra are scanned with a Varian A-60 High Resolution NMR spectrometer. Appropriate solvents such as deuterated chloroform and carbon tetrachloride are used. Tetramethylsilane (TMS) is used as an internal reference. Variables such as temperature and scanning techniques have been standardized. The sweep offset, frequency response, sweep time, spectrum amplitude, weight of sample per volume of $CDCl_3$, and assignments are recorded. When applicable the number of the corresponding Sadtler infrared spectrum is given so that identification of an unknown sample may be made more easily. Alphabetical, numerical, and molecular formula indexes are provided to make the spectra easily accessible.

Spectra are issued annually; as of 1968, 6000 were available.

Publications

Orders and inquiries should be sent to Sadtler Research Laboratories, Inc., 3316 Spring Garden St., Philadelphia, Pa. 19104.

Collection	Total No.	Total Price US $	Annual Subscription
NMR	6000	1200.00	US $ 400.00/2000 spectra, Indices, Spec-Finder, and Chemical-Shift Index
NMR Commercials			

Substance	No. of spectra	List price
Solvents	300	US $ 75.00
Surface Active Agents	300	US $ 75.00

Other Publications or Output

Japan Electron Optics Laboratory, Ltd. (JEOL) High Resolution NMR Spectra (see 3.2.43.) are published by Sadtler Research Laboratories, Inc., 225 spectra, US $ 7.00.

3.2.42. High Resolution NMR Spectra Catalog

Varian Associates, Analytical Instrument Division, Palo Alto, California 94303.

Vol. I, N. S. BHACCA, L. F. JOHNSON, and J. N. SHOOLERY, 1962, 43 pp + 368 spectra, US $ 6.00 (soft cover).

Vol. II, N. S. BHACCA, D. P. HOLLIS, L. F. JOHNSON, and E. A. PIER, 1963, X, 62 pp, US $ 6.00 (soft cover).

Vols. I and II, combined hardback edition, US $ 20.00.

Organization

Varian Associates is a commercial organization which produces analytical instruments. The Analytical Instrument Division carries out research in the area of applied spectroscopy, and has prepared a number of technical publications.

Coverage

Compounds which meet the following criteria are included: (1) a spectrum with several interpretable chemical shift positions characteristic of functional groups frequently encountered in organic structure problems, (2) presence of more than a single line with interpretable fine structure illustrating either a

107

chemical shift or spin-spin coupling pattern, and (3) availability of a sufficiently pure sample. Among the substances included are alkaloids, monomers, peroxides, steroids, terpenes, and vitamins. These volumes do not attempt to cover all spectra recorded in the literature.

NMR spectra are presented as reproductions of instrument tracings with the abscissa as a dual scale in parts per million and cycles per second. Semistructural formulas are given with the assignments indicated on the formulas and their values tabulated.

All spectra were obtained in the Applications Laboratory of the Instrument Division of Varian Associates on the Varian A-60 High-Resolution NMR Spectrometer.

Analysis

All data should be within 1 cps or 0.02 ppm. The sweep offset, sweep time, frequency response, specific instrument amplitude setting, and unusual operating conditions are given. An alphanumeric system of coding proton chemical environments was set up to permit a search of the functional group contents of the spectra in the collection. The system is fully described, and examples of the coding are given. Three indexes — name, functional group, and chemical shift — are provided.

The preface to Volume I appears in both Volumes I and II and describes the compilation and its use. A second preface in Volume II calls attention to the differences in the two volumes. Indexes in Volume II are cumulative for Volumes I and II. A foldout chart of the main and functional groups is included in each volume.

3.2.43. JEOL High Resolution NMR Spectra

Prepared in the Japan Electron Optics Laboratory Company, Ltd., published and distributed by Sadtler Research Laboratories, 3316 Spring Garden Street, Philadelphia, Pa. 19104, 1967, 225 spectra, US $ 7.00.

Organization

The Japan Electron Optics Laboratory Company, Ltd. (JEOL) is an instrument company located in Tokyo. Spectroscopists in the JEOL laboratories have assembled high resolution NMR spectra produced in their own laboratories or contributed from other laboratories in Japan. By special arrangement, this collection of spectra was published and is being distributed by Sadtler Research Laboratories, Inc. (see 3.2.41.).

Coverage

A variety of compounds is included: alkanes, alkylbenzenes, cyclohexane and its derivatives, heterocyclic compounds, ferrocenes, steroids, and polymers and their model compounds. Most of the polymer spectra were run at elevated temperatures. The spectra are divided into three main groups: 60 Mc, 100 Mc, and Fluorine-19, and are presented as chart reproductions with the abscissa marked both in ppm and cps. Information on the chart includes: frequency, instrument sweep width, sweep time, response, solvent, concentration, reference (generally TMS for non-fluorine compounds), temperature, name of compound (as assigned by JEOL), structural formula, source of data, and remarks. A tabulation of chemical shifts is given for each spectrum. Sadtler has provided varied indexes to this collection: alphabetical, molecular formula, chemical classes, chemical shift, and numeric sequence.

Analysis

All spectra were determined by JEOL on instruments produced by the company. Various academic, industrial, and governmental groups contributed samples and data. The Introduction includes a description of the instruments, the indexes, and explanations of their use. Sadtler has renamed compounds by *Chemical Abstracts* rules when the names used on the spectra do not comply. The indexes give the *Chemical Abstracts* names, and frequently include other names for the compound. However, the compound name given on the graphical representation is not always included in the index, nor are the *Chemical Abstracts* and other names listed in the indexes noted on the graph when they differ.

The collection includes 225 spectra, 125 at 60 Mc, 65 at 100 Mc, and 35 at F-19; but somewhat fewer compounds since some appear in two of the groups. The compounds are presented as models, generally grouped according to structural characteristics being considered. The indexes are useful, but must be used with discretion. For example, the fluorine compound category lists only four compounds, but some 35 fluorine-containing compounds comprise the third group of spectra. JEOL uses Tau (τ) values, while Sadtler uses the more prevalent Delta (δ), and indexes the compounds accordingly.

Other Atomic and Molecular Projects

3.2.44. Interatomic Distances and Configurations in Molecules and Ions

Organization

This publication is the outgrowth of an initial 26-page compilation by P. W. ALLEN and L. E. SUTTON in *Acta Crystallographica* 3, 46, 1949. The need for a more comprehensive work resulted in the preparation of a book of tables by Dr. SUTTON and a number of cooperating specialists. The work was sponsored by the Chemical Society, London, and issued as their Special Publication No. 11 in 1958. A supplementary volume appeared as Special Publication No. 18 in 1965. L. E. SUTTON was the editor of both volumes. The future plan for compilation of interatomic distances is to include it in the program of the International Data Centre for Work on Crystallography at Cambridge (see 3.3.7.).

Coverage

Most molecules and ions for which interatomic distances and bond angles have been measured are included: gaseous molecules or radicals, molecules in the solid state, complex ions occurring in a solid, crystals for which pairs of ions have been reported as molecules or ion-pairs in the vapor state, and adamantine lattices. The emphasis is on molecules, no attempt having been made to cover minerals, salts, or alloys. Both inorganic and organic compounds are included.

Properties presented are interatomic distances, bond angles, crystal structure, molecular formulas with perspective diagrams showing spatial arrangement when needed, and crystal symmetry in both the Hermann-Maugium and Schoenflies notations. Both volumes have a main table in which the first half is devoted to inorganic compounds arranged according to the Mendeleeff classification of elements, and the second half, devoted to organic compounds following the Chemical Abstracts system of arrangement. Pagination of both volumes is by sections.

Sources of data are mostly journal articles, and some books. For data from papers published in Japanese, the compilers had to rely upon abstracts (provided by the authors or published in *Chemical Abstracts*).

Analysis

Data were obtained from spectroscopic, electron diffraction, neutron diffraction, and X-ray diffraction measurements. For vapor-phase measurements, preliminary results are included unless they have been superseded by later work. References for electron diffraction data are more comprehensive than for other subjects. For early crystallographic work other compilations are cited. In the supplementary volume, values for data published in final form since 1955 are recorded only if a change has been made in those values reported in the main volume; references to both values are given with the notation that the later supersedes the earlier one. Thus, it is often necessary to consult both the main volume and the supplement. In both volumes, coded references, which include date and method of measurement, often make possible a quick guess as to the reliability of the values quoted.

Bond lengths and angles obtained from crystalline structure are presented as top grade, considered reliable within ± 0.02 Å or better; middle grade, reliable within ± 0.05 Å; and third grade, marked "errors uncertain". However, the errors are unlikely to exceed ± 0.1 Å. Preliminary or doubtful results, comments, or values recalculated by the compilers are indicated.

Notations, formulas, diagrams, and symmetry symbols are fully explained in the introductions. All symbols are adequately explained. Values for bond lengths are given in ångström units; angles, in degrees of arc.

For the 1958 edition, the literature was searched through 1955. The supplement covers the period 1956 through 1959 and includes a few later data. It also includes lists of errata in and addenda to the main volume. The work is continuing at the International Data Centre for Work on Crystallography, Cambridge, with the expectation of publishing a second edition or supplement.

Publications

Tables of Interatomic Distances and Configurations in Molecules and Ions, L. E. SUTTON, Ed., Special Publication No. 11, The Chemical Society, London, 1958, 390 pp, £ 2.2.0. (US $ 6.00).

Tables of Interatomic Distances and Configurations in Molecules and Ions, Supplement, 1956 to 1959, L. E. SUTTON, Ed., Special Publication No. 18, The Chemical Society, London, 1965, 296 pp, £ 4.4.0. (US $ 12.00).

Both publications are also available from Polycrystal Book Service, P. O. Box 11567, Pittsburgh, Pa. 15238.

3.2.45. Bond Energies, Ionization Potentials, and Electron Affinities

By V. I. VEDENEYEV, L. V. GURVICH, V. N. KONDRAT'YEV, V. A. MEDVEDEV, and YE. L. FRANKEVICH. St. Martin's Press, New York, 1966, XIV, 202 pp, US $ 8.50.

First published under the title *Energiya razryva khimicheskikh svyazei*: *Potentsialy ionizatsii i srodstvo k elektronu* by the Academy of Sciences, Moscow, U.S.S.R., 1962.

Coverage

This volume is a source book of information on the energetics of atoms, molecules, and ions in their ground electronic states. It presents selected numerical values of bond energies of inorganic and organic molecules; of heats of formation of atoms from the elements in their standard states and of heats of formation of organic and inorganic radicals from specified reactants; of ionization potentials of atoms, and various categories of molecules and radicals; and electron and proton affinities of atoms, molecules and radicals.

Analysis

Most of the physical parameters included in this volume may be determined by a diversity of experimental methods, and to some extent by theoretical and empirical correlations. Interpretation of the experimental data is frequently difficult. The authors have given careful definitions of the quantities presented, and have briefly described the various methods of determination.

In the tables, for each property value, there is given the process or reaction of interest, the experimental value with associated uncertainty, the method used, and the literature reference. Most reliable values are given in bold face type. Each chapter has its own introduction and bibliography. Most chapters are followed by explanatory notes on controversial or uncertain values and on the authors' basis of selection. The literature is covered to the beginning of 1962, the year of original publication.

3.2.46. Bond Dissociation Energies in Simple Molecules

Organization

This project is directed by B. DE B. DARWENT, The Catholic University of America, Washington, D.C. 20017. It was initiated in 1966. Support is provided by the Office of Standard Reference Data of the National Bureau of Standards (NBS, see 1.1.1.).

Coverage

Bond dissociation energies at 0 K and 298 K for simple inorganic compounds and organic compounds containing not more than one carbon atom, except that the groups $> C = O$ and $—C \equiv N$ are not regarded as being "organic", are compiled. The literature between 1956 and 1966, with special attention to 1962 to 1966, is covered.

Analysis

A compilation is in press. All values are included, but preferred values are indicated, when possible, with assigned probable errors.

It is estimated that revision and updating of the compilation will be needed every two or three years.

Publications

Bond Dissociation Energies in Simple Molecules, B. DE B. DARWENT, in press.

3.2.47. X-Ray Attenuation Coefficient Information Center

Organization

The center is located in the Radiation Theory Section, Center for Radiation Research of the National Bureau of Standards (NBS) in Washington, D. C. It was established in 1952, and is currently supported by the Office of Standard Reference Data, NBS (see 1.1.1.). The director is J. H. HUBBELL.

Coverage

Substances covered include 26 elements from $_1$H to $_{92}$U, and H_2O, NaI, and concrete — in the energy range 10 keV to 100 MeV. Plans include extending coverage to all elements and additional substances.

Properties covered are: photon (X-ray and gamma-ray) attenuation coefficients, i.e., total probability or cross section for interaction of a photon with material; cross sections for the most frequent types of interactions: photoelectric absorption, Compton (incoherent) scattering, Rayleigh (coherent) scattering, and creation of electron-positron pairs; and derived properties such as the energy absorption and energy transfer coefficients.

Analysis

The center was set up to generate and periodically update standard reference tables of photon and related electromagnetic cross sections over the energy range of about 0.1 keV to beyond 10 GeV. In this capacity, it collects and evaluates experimental and theoretical data taken from the literature, and utilizes evaluated data from such sources as the Photonuclear Data Center

3.2.48.

(see 3.1.16.). In addition, the center calculates and tabulates electromagnetic cross sections in cases where accuracy is inadequate, collaborates with and encourages other programs in theoretical and experimental work in this area, and serves as an information center and coordinator for other programs in photon cross section measurements.

A number of publications have resulted from these activities. Several are journal papers discussing theoretical calculations; however, some numerical data compilations are published or in the process of being published as parts of larger works.

Publications

"Tables of Attenuation and Energy Absorption Coefficients", in Ch. 3: "X-Ray and Gamma-Ray Interactions", by R. D. EVANS, in *Radiation Dosimetry*, 2nd ed., Vol. 1 (Fundamentals), F. H. ATTIX and W. C. ROESCH, Eds., Academic Press, New York, 1968.

"Photon Attenuation and Energy Absorption Coefficients. Tabulations and Discussion", J. H. HUBBELL and M. J. BERGER, in *Engineering Compendium on Radiation Shielding*, Vol. 1 (Shielding Fundamentals and Methods), (International Atomic Energy Agency, Vienna), R. G. JAEGER, Ed., Springer-Verlag, Berlin-Heidelberg-New York, in press. (NBS Report 8681, Sept. 28, 1696).

3.2.48. Tables de Constantes Sélectionnées, Volume 15

Data relative to Sesquiterpenoids by G. OURISSON, S. MUNAVALLI, and C. EHRET. Volume 15 of International Tables of Selected Constants, Pergamon Press, Paris, 1966, 70 pp, 28 pp structural formulas, F 63.

Organization

This volume was published under the auspices of "Tables de Constantes et Données Numériques", described in 2.2., and prepared by G. OURISSON, Faculté des Sciences de Strasbourg, S. MUNAVALLI, Université de Karnatak, and C. EHRET, Stagiaire de Recherches au CNRS (Centre National de la Recherche Scientifique).

Coverage

The table lists for each of almost 500 naturally occurring sesquiterpenoids the boiling point, density, refractive index, specific rotation, wavelength and log ε of the UV absorption maximums.

The values of the boiling points are accompanied by the pressure, the density, and refractive index at the temperature of the measurements, and

114

the specific rotation of the solvent. The concentration, and temperature of the measurement of optical rotation, have usually only a slight influence on values of the optical properties and therefore are mentioned only when they were outside the usual range.

In addition to the numerical property values, bibliographic references are given when possible to UV, IR, Raman, mass, and NMR spectra, to rotatory dispersion or circular dichroism data, and to the X-ray structure.

Tables are faced by pages with the corresponding structural formulas and references to the structure mentioned, to the method of synthesis, and to the melting point.

Analysis

The authors have had to deal with widely conflicting values in the literature, particularly for specific rotation. They have chosen, when possible, the publication describing the apparently most exhaustive purification and have extracted from that article the best constants.

In the Introduction the user is warned that the constants are to be taken as indicative only.

No completely systematic classification and nomenclature systems were available and the authors have therefore had to be arbitrary in these matters. Trivial names have been used extensively. However, the user is greatly helped by an alphabetical substance index. The extensive bibliography and author index are valuable features of the book. As usual in this series explanatory text is given in French and English. Data were compiled from the primary literature.

3.2.49. Landolt-Börnstein, Volume 3, Group II

Luminescence of Organic Substances by A. SCHMILLEN and R. LEGLER, edited by K.-H. HELLWEGE and A. M. HELLWEGE. Volume 3 of Group II, Atomic and Molecular Physics of LANDOLT-BÖRNSTEIN, Numerical Data and Functional Relationships in Science and Technology, New Series, Springer-Verlag, Berlin-Heidelberg, 1967, VII, 416 pp, DM 196 (US $ 49.00).

Organization

This compilation was published under the auspices of "Landolt-Börnstein", described in 2.1., and prepared by A. SCHMILLEN and R. LEGLER, both of the University of Giessen, Germany (B.R.D.).

3.2.49.

Coverage

The most important data on the luminescence of more than 1000 organic compounds are given (190 pages). The compounds are arranged according to increasing number of C-atoms. However, tables include special groups of compounds such as carbonium ions, natural substances, p-oligophenylenes, substituted oxazoles, chelates, molecular compounds, and compounds with uncertain structural formulas.

The properties included are absorption wavenumbers of greatest wavelength, wavenumbers of fluorescence and phosphorescence emission, decay time, and quantum efficiency. The values are given for the condensed state (liquid or solid) of the substances, and for solutions in several solvents as well.

In supplementary tables (187 pages), values of additional properties on luminescence, fluorescence and phosphorescence are presented. These tables include diagrams of typical luminescence spectra, spectra of standard substances, special data on the luminescence center (vibrational structure of selected spectra, relationship between absorption and emission spectra, triplet-singlet transitions, degree of polarization), intermolecular processes in the excited state (dipole moments, reactions in the excited state, quenching of fluorescence, energy transfer, sensitized fluorescence, dimer or excimer fluorescence), application of luminescent organic substances in the scintillation technique (ratios of pulse heights at alpha- and beta-excitation, absolute energy efficiency, Kallmann parameter, relative pulse heights), and reduction of luminescence by radiation damage.

Analysis

The authors have critically evaluated the collected data and discarded values of doubtful reliability, e.g., owing to insufficient purity of the substances investigated or to the application of theories which have become obsolete.

The supplementary tables contain only the most important substances as well as characteristic examples selected by the authors. Complete coverage was not intended in these tables.

Explanations and arrangements of the tables are described bilingually (German and English) in detail in the introduction. All symbols and abbreviations are tabulated. An alphabetical index of substances for main and complementary tables is given.

The literature is covered from 1949 through 1964. Almost 900 references are cited including monographs and review articles on the luminescence of organic substances. For earlier publications and data the authors refer to the monographs of P. PRINGSHEIM: Fluorescence and Phosphorescence, J. Wiley, New York, 1949, and T. FÖRSTER: Fluoreszenz Organischer Ver-

116

bindungen, Vandenhoek und Ruprecht, Göttingen, 1951, which have extensive bibliographies.

The authors state that the time available prevented completely exhaustive compilation. Some papers in Slavic languages were omitted.

3.2.50. Landolt-Börnstein, Volume 1, Group II

Magnetic Properties of Free Radicals by H. F. FISCHER, edited by K.-H. HELLWEGE and A. M. HELLWEGE, Volume 1 of Group II, Atomic and Molecular Physics of LANDOLT-BÖRNSTEIN, Numerical Data and Functional Relationships in Science and Technology, New Series, Springer-Verlag, Berlin-Heidelberg, 1965, IX, 154 pp, DM 68 (US $ 17.00).

Organization

This compilation was published under the auspices of "Landolt-Börnstein", described in 2.1., and prepared by H. FISCHER, Deutsches Kunststoff Institut, Darmstadt, Germany (B.R.D.).

Coverage

Property values are given for about 660 free radicals of known structure. These include inorganic free radicals and radical ions, uncharged organic free radicals, organic negative and positive radical ions, and organic biradical and donor-acceptor-complexes. The substances are characterized by their name and/or structural formulas, the methods of generation of the free radical, and the matrix or solvent in which the free radicals were studied.

The magnetic properties given are the splitting or coupling parameters and the *g*-factor. The temperature and frequency of measurement, and references are also listed.

Magnetic properties of free radicals, especially of free atoms, may also be derived from optical spectra. Results of such studies are not included in this volume but are found in: W. KLEMM: Magnetic moments of atoms and atom ions: Landolt-Börnstein-Tables, 6th Ed., Vol. 1, part 1, table 1325; P. BRIX, H. KOPFERMANN: Hyperfine structure of atomic levels and atomic lines: Landolt-Börnstein-Tables, 6th Ed., Vol. 1, part 5, table 1612.

Analysis

The Introduction gives a detailed description of the arrangements of tables, and of the symbols and abbreviations used.

Often, only one value for an individual substance and property was available in the primary literature. If more than one value was available the critically evaluated best one was listed. The literature was considered up to March 1964 and ca. 750 references are cited.

Besides the tables and the corresponding references, the book contains a bibliography of ca. 540 papers in which only the presence of free radicals in a sample is noted but the detailed structure is not given, e.g., references on free radicals in irradiated low molecular weight compounds, in irradiated polymers, during polymerization, in biological systems, etc. Also listed are 120 references on the theory of free radicals, and monographs, review, and survey articles in this area of science. A supplement to this volume is in preparation.

Indexes to Compilations

The American Society for Testing and Materials (ASTM) has prepared indexes to specific data in the major catalogs of spectra. These indexes are listed below. Further details may be obtained by writing to ASTM, 1916 Race Street, Philadelphia, Pennsylvania 19103. Those indexes prepared by a program for their own publications are described in the entry discussing the program.

3.2.51. Indexes to Infrared Spectral Data Compilations

Infrared Spectral Index Cards, ASTM-AMD 30: 92,000 standard IBM cards, including some cards for the far-infrared region. Complete set of cards, US $ 5400.00; less 20% to ASTM members.

Molecular Formula List of Compounds, Names, and References to Published Infrared Spectra, ASTM-AMD 31: source of references to the published literature of the 92,000 infrared spectra noted above. To be published in 1969.

Serial Number List of Compound Names and References to Published Infrared Spectra, ASTM-AMD 32: indexes 92,000 spectra by serial number with the compound names for all spectra included in the Infrared Spectral Index Cards noted above. To be published in 1969.

SIRCH: ASTM/DOW Infrared File Searching System: a computerized file search system. It includes a complete data file coded from the 92,000 spectra noted above. The data file plus SIRCH program are available for an initial fee of US $ 500.00 plus a lease price per year of US $ 1080.00 (US $ 90.00 per month).

3.2.52. Indexes to Ultraviolet-Visible Spectral Data Compilations

Ultraviolet-Visible Spectral Absorption Index Cards, ASTM-AMD 40: 25,000 standard IBM cards, including 2200 cards relating to spectra in the visible light range. Complete set of cards, US $ 1500.00; less 20% to ASTM members.

Molecular Formula List of Compounds, Names, and References to Published Ultraviolet and Visible Spectra, ASTM-AMD 41: source of references to the published literature of the 25,000 spectra noted above. To be published in 1969.

Serial Number List of Compound Names and References to Published Ultraviolet and Visible Spectra, ASTM-AMD 42: indexes 25,000 spectra by serial number with the compound names for all spectra included in the spectral index cards noted above. To be published in 1969.

3.2.53. Indexes to Mass Spectral Data Compilations

Mass Spectral Data — Punched Card Index: ASTM-AMD 10a, Mass Spectral Data-Structure, 3200 cards, US $ 192.00; ASTM-AMD 10b, Mass Spectral Data-Name, 3400 cards, US $ 204.00; ASTM-AMD 10c, Name-Formula, 3500 cards, US $ 210.00; Unpunched Cards, 2000, US $ 6.50. Less 20% to members.

First Supplement to Mass Spectral Cards: supplemental punched cards of uncertified spectra. ASTM-AMD 10a—S1, Mass Spectral Data-Structure, 172 cards, US $ 10.00; ASTM-AMD 10b—S1, Mass Spectral Data-Name, 211 cards, US $ 12.00; ASTM-AMD 10c—S1, Name-Formula, 211 cards, US $ 12.00. Less 20% to members.

Mass Spectral Data, Index of ASTM-AMD 11 A: 3200 spectra. To be published in 1969.

3.3. Solid State, Including Crystallographic, Mineralogical, Electrical and Magnetic, and Related Properties

Crystallographic Properties

3.3.1. Crystal Data

Organization

The first edition of *Crystal Data* was published in 1954 as Memoir 60 of the Geological Society of America, with the subtitle "Classification of Substances by Space Groups and Their Identification from Cell Dimensions". It consisted of two parts: Part I: Systematic Tables — Classification of Crystalline Substances by Space Groups, by WERNER NOWACKI, University of Berne, Switzerland; and Part II: Determinative Tables — Identification of Crystalline Substances from Cell Dimensions, by J. D. H. DONNAY, The Johns Hopkins University, Baltimore, Maryland, with the collaboration of GABRIELLE DONNAY, U.S. Geological Survey, Washington, D.C.

The second edition of "Systematic Tables", by WERNER NOWACKI, was published in 1967 as Monograph No. 6 of the American Crystallographic Association (ACA). Support was provided by the Schweizerischer National-fonds.

3.3.1.

"Determinative Tables", second edition, had previously appeared in 1963 as ACA Monograph No. 5, with J. D. H. DONNAY as general editor and GABRIELLE DONNAY as assistant editor. Co-editors were E. G. COX, University of Leeds, and Agricultural Research Council, London, for inorganic compounds; OLGA KENNARD, National Institute for Medical Research, London, and the University Chemical Laboratory, Cambridge, England, for organic compounds; and MURRAY VERNON KING, Massachusetts General Hospital, Boston, Mass., for proteins (Appendix I). Cooperation and encouragement for the work were given by the International Union of Crystallography, its Commission on Crystallographic Data, related national commissions in Japan and the Soviet Union, and ACA, particularly its Crystal Data and Publication committees. The National Science Foundation (U.S.A.) and the Institute of Physics (U.K.) provided financial support.

The third edition of *Crystal Data : Determinative Tables* is being prepared by the Crystal Data Center of the Institute for Materials Research of the National Bureau of Standards (NBS), Washington, D.C. 20234, under the sponsorship of the National Standard Reference Data System (NSRDS, see 1.1.1.) of NBS. The scientific staff are: Chief Editor — J. D. H. DONNAY, The Johns Hopkins University; Assistant Editor — H. M. ONDIK, NBS; Organic Editor — O. KENNARD, International Data Centre for Work on Crystallography (see 3.3.7.), Cambridge University; Inorganic Editors — H. M. ONDIK, NBS, and G. WOLTEN, Aerospace Corporation; Mineral Editor — M. MROSE, U.S. Geological Survey; Intermetallic Editors — S. SAMSON, California Institute of Technology, M. H. MUELLER, Argonne National Laboratory, Q. JOHNSON, Lawrence Radiation Laboratory, and E. RYBA, Pennsylvania State University; and Protein Editor — M. V. KING, Massachusetts General Hospital.

Coverage

The original purpose of Crystal Data was to present, in a single volume, a critical compilation of crystallographic data, obtained mainly by X-ray or electron diffraction. The first edition contained Part I: Systematic Tables, and Part II: Determinative Tables in a single volume. Subsequently, however, revised editions of Parts I and II appeared as separate volumes.

Part I (Systematic Tables) is divided into two main sections. The first, "Main Table", lists the space groups, and under each space group, the (crystalline) compounds assigned to that group. The compounds are subdivided by composition into 7 categories and include elements, alloys, and inorganic and organic compounds. Some 3800 compounds were included in the first edition; 8800 in the second. The second section consists of statistical tables giving the absolute number and percentage of compounds found in the 219 distinguishable space groups; the 14 Bravais lattices (the 1st edition used the Delaunay-reduced cell for triclinic compounds); the 32 crystal classes; the 7 crystal systems; symmorphic, hemisymmorphic, and asymmorphic space groups; the most frequent space groups; and the centric and acentric space groups (not included in 1st edition).

Part II (Determinative Tables) consists of tables for the identification of crystalline substances by means of cell constants and auxiliary properties. These include axial ratios (determinative numbers), space group, the number of formula units per cell, and measured and calculated specific gravities. Additional properties include melting point, color, pleochroism, twinning, cleavage, and crystal habit. Some optical properties, such as indexes of refraction, optic axial angle, and optical orientation, are given for a number of compounds. Space-group criteria are included in Appendix II of the second edition. The Bravais-reduced cell (defined by the shortest three translations) is used in the second edition, replacing the Delaunay-reduced cell, which had been used in the first edition.

The first edition of Determinative Tables included some 6000 entries; the second edition, 13000; and it is anticipated that the third edition will contain approximately 30000. The third edition will include the same categories of data as previous editions.

Data are obtained from the scientific literature. For the second edition, abstracting journals and pertinent major journals were searched, and the original papers checked. The primary literature is practically the only source of data for the third edition of Determinative Tables. Some pre-publication data are included.

Analysis

Parts I and II of the first edition of Crystal Data were prepared independently, and conventions for presentation of data differ in the two parts. However, formula and name indexes are given, cumulative for Parts I and II.

The second edition (1967) of Part I: Systematic Tables used the second edition (1963) of Part II: Determinative Tables as the basis for statistical work. In some cases, additional space-group determinations found in the literature are given. Complete references are given; those compounds found in Determinative Tables (2nd ed) include the page number in the data line. The introduction covers the use of the tables and includes background information.

For the second edition of Determinative Tables, all new data (1951 and later) were processed and checked. Many crystallographers provided corrections to errors in the first edition. The data sheets were further checked by the editors in the Baltimore office. Data from more than one source are often given. The Introduction to Determinative Tables adequately describes the methods of compilation and presentation of the data. The data for the third edition are first processed and checked by the section editors, then by the general editors, then further processed and rechecked by computer. In order to reduce typographical errors and maintain good typographical style, the third edition will be printed from computer controlled phototypesetting copy.

In the first edition, Part I covers the literature to mid-1948, and Part II to the end of 1951. The second edition (1963 and 1967) includes data to January 1961. The cut-off date for data in the third edition is January 1967.

Publications

Crystal Data, Classification of Substances by Space Groups and their Identification from Cell Dimensions, Parts I and II, J. D. H. DONNAY and WERNER NOWACKI, Memoir 60 of the Geological Society of America, Geological Society of America, New York, N.Y. 10027, 1954, IX, 719 pp (out of print).

Crystal Data, Determinative Tables, Part II, 2nd ed, J. D. H. DONNAY, General Editor; GABRIELLE DONNAY, Assistant Editor; E. G. Cox, Inorganic Compounds; OLGA KENNARD, Organic Compounds; MURRAY VERNON KING, Proteins; Monograph 5 of the American Crystallographic Association, Williams and Heintz, Washington, D.C., 1963, X, 1,302 pp, US $ 10.00. Available from Polycrystal Book Service, P. O. Box 11567, Pittsburgh, Pa. 15238.

Crystal Data, Systematic Tables, Part I, 2nd ed, WERNER NOWACKI, with A. EDENHARTER and T. MATSUMOTO, Monograph 6 of the American Crystallographic Association, Williams and Heintz, Washington, D.C., 1967, US $ 5.00. Available from Polycrystal Book Service, P. O. Box 11567, Pittsburgh, Pa. 15238.

3.3.2. Crystal Structures

Organization

The author of *Crystal Structures* is RALPH W. G. WYCKOFF, University of Arizona, Tucson, Arizona 85721. The first edition appeared in loose-leaf form between 1948 and 1960. The second edition, an amplified and updated version of the original work, is being published in book form. Crystal Structures is in effect a continuation of the author's *Structure of Crystals*, begun some forty years previously, in which abbreviated statements of atomic arrangements in crystalline solids were presented.

Coverage

Substances covered in the *second* edition are: Vol. 1, the elements, and compounds RX and RX_2; Vol. 2, complex binary compounds R_nX_m and compounds $R(MX_2)_n$ and $R_n(MX_3)_p$; Vol. 3, inorganic compounds $R_x(MX_4)_y$ and $R_x(M_nX_p)_y$, hydrates, and ammoniates; Vol. 4, miscellaneous inorganic compounds, silicates, and basic structural information; and Vol. 5, aliphatic compounds — methane, ethane, ethylene, and acetylene derivates, longer-chain compounds, and amino acids and related compounds. Volumes 6 and 7 will deal with benzene derivatives.

All essential structure parameters are included, such as cell dimensions, atomic parameters, bond lengths and angles, and typical intermolecular distances. The crystalline form and space groups are covered. There is extensive use of illustrations for all important structures. These illustrations are usually accurate projections and shaded drawings in which molecules take on a three-dimensional effect.

The primary literature is searched for data.

Analysis

The second edition is self-contained and does not require any reference to the author's previous tabulations. It is limited to determinations which define the positions of most, if not all, the atoms in a crystal; and contrary to the first edition, does not include the numerous studies by X-rays which have led only to unit cells and possible space groups.

Because of the enormous volume of data used in crystal analysis, no estimate is given of the accuracy of spacing measurements. The cell dimensions given are considered the best currently available, and the structures included are those considered correct, or having a reasonable chance of being correct.

Volume 5 initiates an important change. Contrary to previous use of left-handed axes in illustrations, the right-handed axes have been adopted to conform to universal practice. Because of this, the axial sequence is noted in the legends for each illustration. Also in Volume 5, a statement of accuracy is included for new data. This accuracy is based on the original author's evaluation; the compiler exercises judgement when more than one set of data is available. Therefore, a complete description of the structure of an organic crystal presents not only atomic parameters, but an estimate of accuracy. This is done only with the latest determinations.

The second edition uses the space group symbols of Schoenflies together with those symbols preferred in the International Tables (see 3.3.6.).

Each chapter includes a dictionary-type listing of each substance with a description of the crystal structure, and comments; a table listing each substance with its references; and a complete bibliography.

Volume 1 is current through 1961; Volume 2 through 1962; Volume 3 through 1963; Volume 4 through 1966; and Volume 5 through 1964.

3.3.3.

Publications

Crystal Structures, first ed, R. W. G. WYCKOFF, Wiley Interscience, New York-London-Sydney, loose-leaf.

Section I: Chapters I to VIII, 1948, 378 pp, US $ 13.50.

Section II: Chapters VIII to X, XIII, 1951, 509 pp, US $ 17.00.
Supplement I: Additions to Chapters II to VII, 1951, 143 pp, US $ 5.00.

Section III: Chapters XIV, XV, Organic Index, 1953, 465 pp, US $ 25.00.
Supplement II: Additions to Chapter XIII, 1953, 85 pp, US $ 8.50.

Section IV: Chapters XI and XII, 1957, 261 pp, US $ 8.00.
Supplement III: Additions to Chapters II to VIII, 1958, 311 pp, US $ 20.00.
Supplement IV: Additions to Chapters IX, X, XIII to XV, 1959, 509 pp, US $ 22.00.
Supplement V: Additions to Chapters II to XV, Indexes, 1960, 513 pp, US $ 26.50.

Complete set with necessary binders, US $ 153.50.

Note: Sections and Supplements are integrated to form Volumes (5). Complete information for purchase should be requested from publisher.

Crystal Structures, 2nd ed, R. W. G. WYCKOFF, Wiley Interscience, New York-London-Sydney, hardback (see "Coverage" for contents).

Vol. 1: 1963, 467 pp, US $ 17.50.

Vol. 2: 1964, 588 pp, US $ 24.00.

Vol. 3: 1965, 981 pp, US $ 27.50.

Vol. 4: 1968, 566 pp, US $ 22.50.

Vol. 5: 1966, 785 pp, US $ 25.00.

3.3.3. Powder Diffraction File: Joint Committee on Powder Diffraction Standards

Organization

This activity is carried out under the auspices of the American Society for Testing and Materials (ASTM), the American Crystallographic Association, the National Association of Corrosion Engineers, and the British Institute of Physics. It is administered by ASTM, who with the National Academy of Sciences-National Research Council started the project in 1941. The Joint Committee on Powder Diffraction Standards is composed of representatives of the sponsoring organizations and invited research scientists. Its aims are to collect, edit, and publish powder diffraction data and to advance the techniques by which these diffraction data can be used for chemical identification.

The present chairman of the Committee is WILLIAM L. FINK. The current editor is J. V. SMITH, Department of Geophysical Sciences, The University of Chicago. Associate editors are: L. G. BERRY, Queen's University, Ontario, Canada, for minerals; BENJAMIN POST, Polytechnic Institute of Brooklyn, Brooklyn, N.Y., for inorganic and organic substances; SIGMUND WEISS-MANN, Rutgers — The State University, New Brunswick, N.J., for metals and alloys. The Committee finances research associateships at the U.S. National Bureau of Standards (NBS) where needed measurements are made in the Constitution and Microstructure Section.

Coverage

Data on crystalline materials, organic and inorganic, of interest to science and industry are compiled. These include inorganic compounds, metals, alloys, minerals, and organic and organo-metallic compounds.

Powder patterns in terms of interplanar spacings, relative intensities, and Miller indices are recorded. The interplanar spacings corresponding to the three strongest lines in the diffraction pattern are given special prominence. Also given are crystallographic systems, space groups, lattice parameters, interaxial angles, indices of refraction, density, melting point and color, number of formula units per structural unit, molecular and semistructural formulas, and operating characteristics such as wavelength of X-rays used and type of filter.

Patterns are submitted by groups in the United States, Great Britain, the Netherlands, Norway, Israel, and Japan. Data from the literature and from individual investigators are also included.

Analysis

The quality of data is continually being upgraded as the result of elimination of errors and careful editing of new patterns by the associate editors. In 1957, the data in sets 1 to 5 (see below) were critically reviewed and new cards were marked to indicate corrections and data reliability. A critical review of the data in sets 6 to 10 was begun in 1965. Comments on and reported errors in the File have been given in supplements to the File since 1964.

Each year a new set of data consisting of new patterns and revisions is added to the File. The indexes also are brought up-to-date annually. Set 18 (1968) contains 1500 inorganic patterns and 500 organic-organo-metallic patterns.

The X-ray powder diffraction patterns are available on 8×13 cm cards, 10×15 cm Keysort cards, or magnetic tape. After critical review, revised sets 1 to 5 and 6 to 10 were issued as clothbound books, one for inorganic and one for organic substances.

There are now four types of cumulative indexes, two in book form and one on optical coincidence cards. The "Index to the Powder Diffraction File" is issued in two volumes, Organic and Inorganic, which list eight "d" values with intensities. The three most intense lines are permuted and arranged in Hanawalt Groups. The Inorganic volume includes an alphabetical list of compounds and an alphabetical list of minerals. The Organic volume includes organic and organo-metallic compounds arranged as in the Inorganic volume, plus a convenient formula listing.

The "Fink Inorganic Index" was introduced in 1963. It uses the "d" values of the eight strongest lines to characterize each pattern in the Inorganic section of the File. Each substance is listed eight times in the Index by cyclically permuting the eight "d" values. No relative intensities are listed or used for listing; the Fink Index is suited to the identification of electron diffraction patterns.

The Matthews Coordinate Index (Termatrex cards) includes standard, supplementary, and negative element cards. Negative Line cards became available in 1964.

The "KWIC Guide to the Powder Diffraction File (Inorganic)" is a fourth type of index. The KWIC (Key-Word-in-Context) Guide is based on chemical fragments. It consists of three sections: the dictionary, the KWIC listing, and the alphabetical mineral listing. The KWIC Guide allows a search for a compound with a specified chemical content.

Data obtained from patterns measured at NBS are published at the Bureau in separate booklets.

Publications

Eighteen sets of the Powder Diffraction File (formerly known as the X-Ray Powder Data File) have been published by ASTM. They may be purchased in any of the following card forms. Some separate sets and combinations of sets are also available; write to ASTM for details.

Powder Diffraction File, 18 sets

(1) *Cards*

		Plain (US $)	Keysort (US $)	IBM Index (US $)
Sets 1 to 17	Organic	1025	1250	
	Inorganic	1675	1900	
	Both	2425	2875	800
Set 17 only	Organic	100	125	
	Inorganic	175	200	
	Both	250	300	80
Set 18 only	Organic	125	150	
	Inorganic	225	250	
	Both	325	375	

(2) *Book form*

			US $
Inorganic	Vol. Sets 1 to 5	PDiS—5iRB	75.00
Organic	Vol. Sets 1 to 5	PDiS—5oRB	50.00
Inorganic	Vol. Sets 6 to 10	PDiS—10iRB	75.00
Organic	Vol. Sets 6 to 10	PDiS—10oRB	50.00

(3) Magnetic tape available on lease only. The tape contains all "d" values, relative intensities, chemical names, formulas and file numbers of patterns in Sets 1 to 17. Write to ASTM for details and prices.

Powder Diffraction File, Indexes
*Index to the Powder Diffraction File, 1968 Edition**

		US $
Inorganic	PDIS—18i	100.00
Organic	PDIS—18o	75.00

Fink Inorganic Index, 1968 Edition

PDIS—18F	75.00

KWIC Guide to the Powder Diffraction File (Inorganic)
1968 Edition PDIS—18K   50.00

Matthews Coordinate Index, Sets 1 to 17

Deck A, B, C	825.00
Deck D (Negative Line)	250.00
Both	1,000.00

Related Publications

Standard X-ray Diffraction Powder Patterns, NBS Circular 539, U.S. Government Printing Office, Washington, D.C. 20402.

Vol. I,   H. E. Swanson and E. Tatge, 1953, 95 pp, US $ 0.45.

Vol. II,   H. E. Swanson and R. K. Fuyat, 1953, 65 pp, US $ 0.45.

Vol. III, H. E. Swanson, R. K. Fuyat, and G. M. Ugrinic, 1954, 73 pp, US $ 0.45.

Vol. IV, H. E. Swanson, R. K. Fuyat, and G. M. Ugrinic, 1955, 75 pp, US $ 0.45.

Vol. V,   H. E. Swanson, N. T. Gilfrich, and G. M. Ugrinic, 1955, 75 pp, US $ 0.45.

Vol. 6,   H. E. Swanson, N. T. Gilfrich, and M. I. Cook, 1956, 62 pp, US $ 0.40.

Vol. 7,   H. E. Swanson, N. T. Gilfrich, and M. I. Cook, 1957, 70 pp, US $ 0.40.

Vol. 8,   H. E. Swanson, N. T. Gilfrich, M. I. Cook, R. Stinchfield, and P. C. Parks, 1959, 76 pp, US $ 0.45.

*) The respective Index Book (Organic and/or Inorganic) is supplied free of charge with the purchase of Plain or Keysort cards of Sets 11 to 17.
Order from: American Society for Testing and Materials, Diffraction Data Sales, 1916 Race Street, Philadelphia, Pa. 19103.

Vol. 9, H. E. SWANSON, M. I. COOK, T. ISAACS, and E. H. EVANS, 1960, 64 pp, US $ 0.40.

Vol. 10, H. E. SWANSON, M. I. COOK, E. H. EVANS, and J. H. DE GROOT, 1960, 61 pp, US $ 0.40.

Standard X-ray Diffraction Powder Patterns, NBS Monograph 25, U.S. Government Printing Office, Washington, D.C. 20402.

Section 1, H. E. SWANSON, M. C. MORRIS, R. P. STINCHFIELD, and E. H. EVANS, 1962, 56 pp, US $ 0.40.

Section 2, H. E. SWANSON, M. C. MORRIS, R. P. STINCHFIELD, and E. H. EVANS, 1963, 46 pp, US $ 0.35.

Section 3, H. E. SWANSON, M. C. MORRIS, E. H. EVANS, and L. ULMER, 1964, 64 pp, US $ 0.40.

Section 4, H. E. SWANSON, M. C. MORRIS, and E. H. EVANS, 1966, 83 pp, US $ 0.55.

Section 5, H. E. SWANSON, H. F. McMURDIE, M. C. MORRIS, and E. H. EVANS, 1967, 90 pp, US $ 0.55.

Section 6, H. E. SWANSON, H. F. McMURDIE, M. C. MORRIS, and E. H. EVANS, 1968, IV, 97 pp, US $ 0.60.

3.3.4. Structure Reports

Organization

Structure Reports is an annual collection of abstracts of a special type. It continues and replaces *Strukturbericht*, which was published in seven volumes between 1913 and 1939. Work on *Structure Reports* began in 1949 under the guidance of the Commission on Structure Reports of the International Union of Crystallography. In 1960, W. B. PEARSON, National Research Council, Ottawa, Canada, became general editor. The project is on a self-sustaining basis.

Coverage

Metals, and inorganic and organic crystalline compounds are included.

Unit cell dimensions, space groups, atomic positions and parameters, and interatomic and intermolecular distances are given. The data presented are derived primarily from X-ray diffraction measurements. Only material of structural interest is extracted from the literature. Papers containing data obtained by electron diffraction, neutron diffraction, and nuclear magnetic resonance studies are reported when of structural interest. Data from such papers published in Russian, Japanese, and in journals not readily available have been included more freely than data from easily accessible sources.

Data are collected by reporters in several countries from research papers in the open literature.

Analysis

This publication attempts to provide a source of precise information on all determinations of crystal structures, presenting critical reports rather than abstracts. It aims at giving complete structural information from the papers reported so that no further reference to the papers themselves is necessary. The minimum criterion for a report is generally that the paper contain the determination of a unit cell or a more accurate determination of a unit cell previously reported. Detailed assessments of each structure are made and critical comments are inserted by the reporters and editors when necessary. Limits of error and very doubtful last digits are often indicated. Interatomic distances or other information calculated by the reporters from the data in the paper may be added to the structural report.

Structure Reports covers the period from 1940 (Volume 8) onward and thus forms a continuous series with the last volume of Strukturbericht (Volume VII). The latest volume, published in 1968 (Volume 24), covers the literature until 1960. The currency is still imperfect, despite the fact that there are now teams of editors working on all years up to 1965. It is estimated that a publication lag of three to four years is the best that can be expected. The field covered is now somewhat restricted in order to limit the large size of the yearly volumes caused by the increase in the number of papers being published.

Structure Reports is published in book form. The volumes are divided into three main sections: Metals, Inorganic Compounds, and Organic Compounds. In each volume there are subject, formula, and author indexes, and, since 1955, an index of carbon compounds. Volume 14 contains a few supplementary reports for the period 1940 to 1950, but it is mainly a cumulative index for Volumes 8 through 13. Most volumes have a corrigenda for previous volumes.

Publications

Structure Reports, Vols. 8 to 16 and Vol. 18, A. J. C. Wilson, General Editor; Vol. 17 and Vols. 19 to 24, W. B. Pearson, General Editor; published for the International Union of Crystallography by N. V. A. Oosthoek's Uitgevers, Mij, Utrecht, The Netherlands. Agent in the U. S. — Polycrystal Book Service, P. O. B. 11567, Pittsburgh, Pa. 15238.

3.3.5.

The years covered, year published, and price of each volume are as follows:

Volume	Years Covered	Year Published	Price Dutch florins	US $
8	1940 to 1941	1956	80	22.50
9	1942 to 1944	1955	70	19.50
10	1945 to 1946	1953	55	15.50
11	1947 to 1948	1951	100	28.00
12	1949	1952	70	19.50
13	1950	1954	100	28.00
14 (index)	1940 to 1950	1959	35	10.00
15	1951	1957	110	31.00
16	1952	1959	120	33.50
17	1953	1963	125	35.00
18	1954	1961	120	33.50
19	1955	1963	100	28.00
20	1956	1963	100	28.00
21	1957	1964	100	28.00
22	1958	In preparation	***	**.**
23	1959	1965	120	33.50
24	1960	1968	140	39.00

Note: A new reprint of "Strukturbericht", Supplement to "Zeitschrift für Kristallographie", forerunner to "Structure Reports", was published in 1965 by the Johnson Reprint Corporation, New York, and Johnson Reprint Company, Ltd., London.

Vols. 1 to 7, Leipzig, 1913/1928 to 1939, clothbound, US $ 140.00 per set; paperbound, US $ 120.00 per set.

Vols. 1 to 3, 1913/1928 to 1935, paperbound, US $ 20.00 per volume; clothbound, US $ 23.00 per volume.

Vols. 4 to 7, 1936 to 1939, paperbound, US $ 15.00 per volume; clothbound, US $ 18.00 per volume.

3.3.5. A Handbook of Lattice Spacings and Structures of Metals and Alloys

Organization

This handbook was compiled by WILLIAM BURTON PEARSON, National Research Council, Ottawa. Volume I was published in 1958; Volume II, in 1967. The object of the publication is to provide an up-to-date summary of knowledge on the structures of metals and alloys. The National Research Council (NRC) of Canada has supported the work continuously. Volume I was issued as NRC No. 4303 and Volume II as NRC No. 8752.

Coverage

Substances covered are metals, and binary, ternary, and a few more complex alloys, including intermetallic phases of borides, carbides, hydrides, nitrides, and oxides.

Included are structural details, crystallographic data for Strukturbericht types (Vol. 1), atomic lattice parameters and their variations with composition in solid solution ranges and with temperature, densities, and expansion coefficients. The second volume includes a classification of structures of elements and alloy phases according to the Bravais lattice and number of atoms per unit cell. From the data given, known structures of any alloy phase can be drawn up and interatomic distances calculated. In some cases it may be necessary to obtain the coordinates of the appropriate point-sets from Volume I of "International Tables for X-ray Crystallography" (see 3.3.6.).

Research papers in the open literature are the sources of data.

Analysis

In both Volumes I and II, a critical selection is made in order to present only the most accurate data. In making the selection, consideration is given to alloy purity, knowledge of composition and equilibrium temperature, and reliability of the X-ray methods or other means of investigation. Each system is discussed to the extent justified by available data. Complete references are included.

In Volume I, most crystal settings for orthorhombic and monoclinic classes were transformed to the Standard Settings given in the International Tables for X-Ray Crystallography. The particular author's use of kX or ångström units was generally maintained. In Volume II, all data are in ångström units.

Volume I is divided into two parts. Part I (75 pages), is a general introduction to X-ray investigation of metals and alloys. Part II includes the compilation and assessment of data, presented in text, tables, and diagrams. The systems are arranged alphabetically by chemical symbols. The content of Volume II (1,446 pages) corresponds to that of Part II of Volume I.

Volume I covers all available structural work on metals and alloys through 1955 and some through 1956. Volume II covers the interval between 1955 and 1965, although the tabular listing (414 pp) is cumulative, including all data up to 1965. The relationship between Volumes I and II is:

(1) Vol. II, the index of work on metals and alloys (Chapter V) and the index of work on borides, carbides, hydrides, and nitrides (Chapter VI) update the same material in Vol. I (Chapter XI and XII). Vol. I and II must therefore be used together.

(2) Vol. II, tabulated lattice parameters and data on elemental metals and metalloids (Chapter II), intermediate phases in alloy systems (Chapter III), and borides, carbides, hydrides, nitrides, and binary oxides (Chapter IV), contain data both from Vol. I and from work published since Vol. I. These chapters of Vol. II are therefore independent.

(3) Vol. II includes a table of crystallographic data on binary oxides, whereas Vol. I described the work.

Publications

A Handbook of Lattice Spacings and Structures of Metals and Alloys, W. B. PEARSON,
Vol. I, (International Series of Monographs on Metal Physics and Physical
Metallurgy, Vol. 4), Pergamon Press, Ltd., Oxford-London-Edinburgh-
New York-Paris, and Frankfurt, 1958, X, 1044 pp, US $ 38.00.

Vol. II, (International Series of Monographs on Metal Physics and Physical
Metallurgy, Vol. 8), Pergamon Press, Ltd., Oxford-London, and New
York, 1967, VIII, 1456 pp, 500 s. net. (US $ 75.00).

3.3.6. International Tables for X-Ray Crystallography

Organization

This series was planned by the International Union of Crystallography (IUCr) to bring up-to-date the former Internationale Tabellen zur Bestimmung von Kristallstrukturen (International Tables for the Determination of Crystal Structures) published in 1935. The present "Tables" were prepared under the direction of an editorial committee of the IUCr with Dame KATHLEEN LONSDALE as general editor. The present chairman of the Commission on International Tables is N. F. M. HENRY, Department of Mineralogy, Downing Street, Cambridge, England. Crystallographers from many countries have contributed to the compilation. Financial help was provided by UNESCO and the National Academy of Sciences-National Research Council (U. S. A.). The Netherlands Organization for Pure Research (ZWA), the N. V. Philips' Gloeilampenfabrieken, Eindhoven, the Netherlands, and the University College, London, provided secretarial and editorial assistance, as well as staff time for work on Volume III.

Coverage

Volume I, Symmetry Groups, presents tables, explanations, and diagrams for crystal lattices, point-group symmetry, and space-group symmetry. Volume II, Mathematical Tables, contains tables of functions, formulas, and general relationships between physical quantities.

Volume III, Physical and Chemical Tables, deals with the processes involved in the X-ray study of crystals. In Volume III tables of properties are included in each of the following sections: X-Rays and Their Interaction with Crystals (wavelength, intensities, and scattering of X-rays); Measurement and Interpretation of Intensities (absorption, and atomic scattering factors); and Interatomic and Interionic Distances (inorganic, organic, and metallic crystals).

Analysis

Volumes I and II do not contain data for substances but are concerned with the mathematical and geometrical background required by serious workers in crystallography. Volume III, however, in addition to descriptive material on experimental methodology, contains a wealth of critically evaluated numerical property values in tabular form. Recognized experts from many countries have contributed to the many sections and subsections of the volume. The extensive bibliographies reveal selective use of both the primary literature and existing compilations.

Methods of calculating tabulated values are discussed, and references are cited when possible. Necessary symbols are explained, and the difficulty of maintaining complete consistency is admitted. Terms other than strictly crystallographic ones are also defined if necessary. Although the main text is in English, a Dictionary of Crystallographic Terms for each volume is given in English, French, German, Russian, and Spanish.

Volume I of the present Tables appeared in 1952, Volume II in 1959 and Volume III in 1962. All three Volumes have been reprinted with corrections.

The bound volumes are 21.8×28.2 cm. Each Volume has a detailed table of contents, and Volume III has a cumulative general subject index. The layout of tables and the printing are of exceptional quality.

The Commission on International Tables is at present compiling a "pilot-issue" in line with the planning of a completely new edition. It is expected that this future edition will be divided into two series: A — Symmetry Tables and B — Diffraction Tables. In the meantime a Supplement to the existing Volumes II and III is expected to appear late in 1969; this will contain new material in the field covered by these two volumes.

Publications

International Tables for X-Ray Crystallography, KATHLEEN LONSDALE, General Editor, published for the International Union of Crystallography by the Kynoch Press, Birmingham, England. Also available from Polycrystal Book Service, P. O. Box 11567, Pittsburgh, Pa. 15238 (Special prices are offered to members of the American Crystallographic Association).

3.3.7.

Vol. I: Symmetry Groups, N. F. M. HENRY and KATHLEEN LONSDALE, Eds., 1952, XII, 558 pp, £ 5.5.0. (US $ 14.70).

Vol. II: Mathematical Tables, J. S. KASPER and KATHLEEN LONSDALE, Eds., 1959, XVIII, 444 pp, £ 5.15.0. (US $ 16.10).

Vol. III: Physical and Chemical Tables, C. H. MacGILLAVRY and G. D. RIECK, Eds., 1962, XVI, 362 pp, £ 5.15.0. (US $ 16.10).

3.3.7. International Data Centre for Work on Crystallography

Organization

This center was set up in 1965 in the University Chemical Laboratory, Cambridge, England, with the financial support of the Office for Scientific and Technical Information (OSTI, see 1.1.2.), and as part of the British contribution to international collaboration on critical data compilations. As a data center, it is anticipated that it will contribute to many crystallographic projects. At present it is responsible for the organic (carbon-containing) volume of the third edition of *Crystal Data* (see 3.3.1.), and for references for the inorganic volume. The Centre is providing numerical data for the 1962, 1963, 1964 volumes of *Structure Reports* (see 3.3.4.) and it is planning a revision of the *Interatomic Distance Tables* (see 3.2.44.). Basic structural research of chemical or biological interest is also carried out. The Centre is manned with a staff of six; the Honorary Directors are J. D. BERNAL and Mrs. OLGA KENNARD.

Coverage

The Centre works closely with all groups involved in crystallographic documentation and data evaluation. The main project of the Centre is to assemble a computer-oriented file, The Structural Library, containing published data relevant to molecular and crystal structures as obtained by X-ray and neutron diffraction methods. At present only carbon-containing structures are compiled excluding polymers and substances with molecular weight greater than 2,000 and also inorganic carbides, carbonates, carbonyls, cyanides, cyanates, etc.

Forty-three different types of information are recorded including unit cell constants and atomic coordinates with standard deviations and isotopic thermal parameters.

Sources of data include the scientific literature, private communications, and structures determined or refined by the Crystallography Group. The files are maintained up-to-date; publications before 1960 will be scanned.

134

Analysis

All data and other information are critically examined, and many of the data are recalculated. These include constants and structural information relating to bond distances, bond angles, and molecular geometry, which are recalculated from the coordinates. There is also a critical descriptive text prepared for each structure. All information is maintained on punched cards. The project benefits from the cooperation of crystallographers throughout the world.

Publications

The Centre is playing an essential role in the publication of the third edition of *Crystal Data*. It has published a bibliography of organic structures classified according to chemical types and covering the years 1960 to 1966 inclusive. A supplement for 1967 is in preparation. The bibliography was produced directly from computer printout for private distribution, but commercial publication is planned.

3.3.8. The Barker Index of Crystals

A Method for the Identification of Crystalline Substances, published by W. Heffer & Sons, Ltd., Cambridge, England.

Vol. I: Crystals of the Tetragonal, Hexagonal, Trigonal and Orthorhombic Systems, M. W. PORTER and R. C. SPILLER, 1951, two parts, £ 6.0.0. (US $ 16.80).
Part 1: Introduction and Tables, IX, 350 pp, £ 1.10.0. (US $ 4.20).
Part 2: Crystal Description, X, 1086 pp, £ 4.10.0. (US $ 12.60).

Vol. II: Crystals of the Monoclinic System, M. W. PORTER and R. C. SPILLER, 1956, three parts, £ 10.0.0. (US $ 28.00).
Part 1: Introduction and Tables, V, 383 pp.
Part 2: Crystal Descriptions, M. 1 to M. 1800, VIII, 760 pp.
Part 3: Crystal Descriptions, M. 1801 to M. 3572, VIII, 688 pp.

Vol. III: Crystals of the Anorthic System, M. W. PORTER and L. W. CODD, 1964, two parts, £ 12.0.0. (US $ 33.60).
Part 1: Introduction and Tables, VI, 50 pp, and unpaginated tables.
Part 2: Crystal Descriptions, A. 1 to A. 831 and Atlas of Configurations, VII pp, unpaginated descriptions.

Organization

Measured values of interfacial angles of crystals are used to classify and identify chemical substances. This classification-angle system was developed

3.3.8.

by T. V. BARKER. The compilation work was undertaken in the 1930's by interested crystallographers in the Department of Mineralogy of the University Museum at Oxford; and numerous individuals in Great Britain, the Netherlands, the United States, and Belgium also contributed. Further support was given by the Barker Index Committee, composed of representatives of scientific societies and of academic, governmental, and industrial organizations in the United Kingdom and the Netherlands, and financial aid is acknowledged from the Department of Scientific and Industrial Research, from Imperial Chemical Industries in Great Britain, and from the Organisation for Pure Research (ZWA) in the Netherlands. Present chairman of the committee is J. WREN-LEWIS, Imperial Chemical Industries Ltd. Editors for Volumes I and II were MARY W. PORTER and the late R. C. SPILLER, both of Oxford University, and for Volume III, Dr. PORTER, and L. W. CODD of Imperial Chemical Industries. Although there are no plans to continue this publication as such, work in this area will be continued at the International Data Centre for Work on Crystallography, described in 3.3.7.

Coverage

Volume I gives crystal descriptions of 2991 compounds belonging to the hexagonal, tetragonal, trigonal, and orthorhombic systems; Volume II gives descriptions of 3572 monoclinic substances and Volume III, descriptions of 831 substances in the anorthic system. Most of the substances included are those described in GROTH's five-volume "Chemische Krystallographie" (1906 to 1919, see 4.3.4.).

The Barker System is based on the use of a small number of interfacial angles chosen for indexing purposes: a single angle for hexagonal, tetragonal, and trigonal crystals; three angles for orthorhombic crystals; five for monoclinic; and six for anorthic. In addition to the classification angles, axial ratios, symmetry, forms, habit, physical properties (cleavage, color, specific gravity, melting point, etc.), optical properties (including refractive indexes), transformations, and in some cases the strongest three lines in the X-ray powder diffraction pattern are given.

The Index is essentially a new treatment of previously compiled morphological data which facilitates the identification of listed substances from their measured angles.

Analysis

Calculations for Volumes I and II were made independently by two workers and checked by one of the editors. For Volume III, so many errors existed in the source material that individual notes and corrections could not be

136

made. Corrected calculated values for the axial ratios and axial angles were obtained by use of a computer; however, errors in experimental data remain. Adaptation of the Barker method to anorthic crystals in Vol. III required considerable extension of the original Barker rules. The final, but lengthy, rules are made easy to apply by use of an atlas of configurations developed by M. H. HEY of the British Museum of Natural History, and a table of configurations developed by P. TERPSTRA and coworkers at the University of Groningen (the Netherlands).

Accepted crystallographic symbolism has been used; technical terms, particularly those peculiar to the Barker technique, are explained.

The publication covers essentially data reported by GROTH, corrected where necessary, with few references to later data, but it should be noted that GROTH is now out of print and that the present work makes the large bulk of information which it contained available to many who could not otherwise obtain it.

3.3.9. Landolt-Börnstein, Volume 1, Group III

Elastic, Piezoelectric, Piezooptic, and Electrooptic Constants of Crystals by R. BECHMANN and R. F. S. HEARMON, edited by K.-H. HELLWEGE and A. M. HELLWEGE. Volume 1 of Group III, Crystal and Solid State Physics, of Landolt-Börnstein, Numerical Data and Functional Relationships in Science and Technology, New Series, Springer-Verlag, Berlin-Heidelberg, 1966, X, 160 pp, DM 68 (US $ 17.00).

Organization

This compilation was published under the auspices of "Landolt-Börnstein", described in 2.1. Chapter 1 was prepared by R. F. S. HEARMON, Princes Risborough, Bucks., England; Chapters 2 and 3 were prepared by R. BECHMANN, Shrewsbury, N. J., U. S. A.

Coverage

This volume consists of three chapters. Chapter 1 (39 pages) by R. F. S. HEARMON treats elastic constants (i.e., the components of elastic stiffnesses and compliances) of non-piezoelectric crystals including temperature and pressure coefficients of these quantities, and their variation over a wide temperature range, generally from 0 K to the melting point, in graphical form. A few organic substances are included but the primary content is data for elements, inorganic compounds, alloys, and minerals. Chapter 2

(84 pages) by R. Bechmann covers elastic, piezoelectric and dielectric constants of piezoelectric crystals and gives elastic compliances and stiffnesses, piezoelectric strain and stress constants, dielectric permittivities, and the temperature coefficients of these quantities. Electromechanical coupling factors are given for the few substances for which they are known. Substances discussed include a wide range of inorganic compounds, double salts and mixtures of varied composition such as mixed titanates, niobates, tartrates as well as simpler compounds. Grouping is by crystal class. This chapter is an updated revision of a chapter with the same title and author in Landolt-Börnstein, 6th edition, Vol. 2, Part 6. I, p. 414—448 (1959). Chapter 3 (37 pages), also by R. Bechmann, is on the piezooptic, elastooptic, and the three electrooptic constants of 56 inorganic and a few organic crystalline compounds.

Analysis

Each chapter begins with discussion and explanation of the tables. Quantities are clearly defined, the symbols and units are given, and statements are made about the treatment of data. In general the authors have tried to treat the data critically. In Chapter 1, a "coefficient of variation" is given when sufficient data are available. In separate sections of chapters 2 and 3, detailed comments, explanatory notes, and graphs are included that outline the principles applied for the critical evaluation of data in the corresponding tables. Complete references, some as recent as 1965, are given after each chapter. A useful alphabetically arranged substance index is included. A supplement to this volume is in preparation.

Mineralogical Properties

3.3.10. Dana's System of Mineralogy

Organization

Five editions of *The System of Mineralogy* were compiled by James Dwight Dana and published between 1837 and 1868. The author's son, Edward Salisbury Dana, compiled the sixth edition, published in 1892.

Three volumes of the seventh edition, a complete revision and updating, have been published. A number of persons in the United States and Great Britain contributed data and worked on the compilation. Clifford Frondel, Harvard University, Cambridge, Massachusetts, was co-author of Volumes I and II, sole author of Volume III, and is presently working on Volumes IV and V.

Financial aid for the first two volumes was provided by the Sterling Fund of Yale University, the Penrose Funds of the Geological Society of America and the American Philosophical Society, the publishers (John Wiley & Sons, Inc.), Mr. H. S. HOLDEN, and Harvard University.

Coverage

All minerals are included. Volume I contains elements, sulfides, sulfosalts, and oxides; Volume II contains halides, carbonates, nitrates, iodates, borates, sulfates, selenates, tellurates, selenites, tellurites, chromates, phosphates, arsenates, vanadates, antimonates, antimonites, arsenites, vanadium oxysalts, and salts of organic acids; and Volume III contains silica minerals with the major part devoted to quartz. The silicates will be covered in future volumes.

Crystallographic, physical, optical, and chemical properties are compiled. The crystallographic data include interaxial angles and unit cell dimensions. Volumes I and II contain few X-ray data, but Volume III includes X-ray powder diffraction data for each substance. The physical and optical properties include color, transparency, index of refraction, hardness, melting point, cleavage, fracture, tenacity, and specific gravity. Chemical formulas, if known, and analyses are also given. Synthesis and phase relations, type of occurrence and association in nature, and the more important localities are cited.

Primary journals are the major source of data. Abstracts and other secondary sources are used only when original papers are not available.

Analysis

Throughout its history, "Dana's System" has been an authoritative reference source for mineralogists. All information was carefully appraised and uncertain facts were so designated. An authentic experimental diffraction pattern was obtained for each substance and optical properties were frequently checked.

Recommendations of international authorities such as the International Union of Crystallography and the International Mineralogical Association are followed. There is a complete list of synonyms — the different names found for each substance — at the beginning of each species description. References are given for each mineral description, and a general index is included in each volume.

Every effort is made to keep the compilation current. Work on Volume II was completed in the winter of 1949/1950 and some of the references are as late as 1950. The cut-off date for the literature examined for Volume III was 1960, but a few more recent papers are cited. A revision of Volume I (the beginning of an eighth edition) is planned following the completion of the remaining two volumes of the seventh edition.

Publications

The System of Mineralogy of JAMES DWIGHT DANA and EDWARD SALISBURY DANA, 7th ed, John Wiley and Sons, Inc., New York-London.

> Vol. I: Elements, Sulfides, Sulfosalts, Oxides; CHARLES PALACHE, HARRY BERMAN, and CLIFFORD FRONDEL, 1944, XIII, 834 pp, US $ 14.00.

> Vol. II: Halides, Nitrates, Borates, Carbonates, Sulfates, Phosphates, Arsenates, Tungstates, Molybdates, etc.; CHARLES PALACHE, HARRY BERMAN, and CLIFFORD FRONDEL, 1951, XI, 1124 pp, US $ 16.00.

> Vol. III: Silica Minerals, CLIFFORD FRONDEL, 1962, XII, 334 pp, US $ 7.95.

3.3.11. Rock-Forming Minerals

Organization

Rock-Forming Minerals by W. A. DEER, Cambridge University, Cambridge, England, R. A. HOWIE, King's College, Strand, London, W. C. 2, England, and J. ZUSSMAN, The University of Manchester, Manchester 13, England, is a series of five volumes designed as a reference work for advanced students and research workers in the geological sciences, but also useful to workers in other fields, particularly ceramic technologists. Though not primarily a compilation of property values, crystallographic and optical data needed for identification of rock-forming minerals are given. The work was performed at The University of Manchester where the authors were members of the Department of Geology.

Coverage

Rock-forming minerals are, in the authors' words, "those which by their presence, or absence, serve to determine or modify the name of a rock". The subtitles of the five volumes indicate the types of minerals included: (1) Ortho- and Ring Silicates, (2) Chain Silicates, (3) Sheet Silicates, (4) Framework Silicates, and (5) Non-Silicates.

A condensed table of properties including refractive indexes, dispersion, cleavage, twinning, color, cell dimensions, and solubilities precedes discussions that give additional property values under the following headings: Structure, Chemistry, Optical and Physical Properties, Distinguishing Features, and Paragenesis. Structural and phase diagrams as well as diagrams relating optical and chemical data are often given.

Analysis

The books are largely descriptive; textual material is interspersed with property values. The chemistry sections include tables of analyses. The relation of crystal structure to physical and chemical properties is exceptionally well presented. Data on synthetic systems, especially phase diagrams, form the basis of interpreting the composition of complex minerals. In Volume III, Sheet Silicates, the wide variability of the materials and the attendant difficulty of clear-cut definitions are well presented. This volume should be of particular interest to ceramists.

Where points of nomenclature are debatable, the authors give alternative names in parentheses. Extensive references at the end of each section are an excellent guide to the literature. Abbreviations and symbols used are defined. An index is included.

The literature through 1959 was well covered, coverage for some sections extended through 1961, and a few references extend to 1962.

Publications

Rock-Forming Minerals, W. A. DEER, R. A. HOWIE, and J. ZUSSMAN, published by Longmans, Green and Co., Ltd., London. Rights in U.S.A., Philippines, and Central America — John Wiley & Sons, Inc., New York.

Vol. I: Ortho- and Ring Silicates, 1962, 333 pp, US $ 16.50.

Vol. II: Chain Silicates, 1963, 379 pp, US $ 19.50.

Vol. III: Sheet Silicates, 1962, 270 pp, US $ 16.50.

Vol. IV: Framework Silicates, 1963, 435 pp, US $ 17.95.

Vol. V: Non-Silicates, 1962, 371 pp, US $ 17.95.

Electrical and Magnetic Properties

3.3.12. Electrical Resistivity of Metals at Low Temperatures

Organization

This project, established in 1966, is carried out by L. A. HALL and H. M. RODER at the Cryogenic Data Center (described in detail in 3.4.21.), Cryogenics Division, Institute for Materials Research, National Bureau of Standards (NBS), Boulder, Colorado. Support is provided by NASA and the Office of Standard Reference Data, NBS (see 1.1.1.).

Coverage

Electrical resistivity, sample preparation, purity, and crystal structure of 16 metals (Al, Be, Co, Cu, Au, In, Fe, Pb, Mg, Mo, Ni, Nb, Pt, Ag, Ta, and Sn) at low temperatures have been covered. Work on additional metals has been started.

Data are obtained from the primary literature.

Analysis

The first stage of this project is the collection of data and the publication of a non-critical compilation of data.

The first such publication, *Survey of Electrical Resistivity of 16 Pure Metals in the Temperature Range 0 to 273 °K* has been published as NBS Technical Note 365. The critical evaluation of these data will be performed as a later stage of the project.

Publications

Survey of Electrical Resistivity Measurements on 16 Pure Metals In the Temperature Range 0 to 273 °K, NBS Technical Note 365, L. A. HALL, U.S. Government Printing Office, Washington, D.C. 20402, 1968, III, 111 pp, US $ 0.60.

3.3.13. Tables de Constantes Sélectionnées, Volume 12

Selected Constants relative to Semi-Conductors by P. AIGRAIN and M. BALKANSKI. Volume 12 of Tables of Constants and Numerical Data, Selected Constants, Pergamon Press, Paris, 1961, 65 pp, F 27 (US $ 6.50).

Organization

This volume was published under the auspices of "Tables de Constantes et Données Numériques", described in 2.2., and prepared under the direction of P. AIGRAIN and M. BALKANSKI, both of the Faculté des Sciences de Paris, with a staff of five scientific workers.

Coverage

The tables give numerical data and other information for 78 inorganic semiconductors of current interest. Included are the elements Ge, Si, Te, Se and diamond; and compounds of the types I—V, II—IV, II—V, II—VI, III—V, III—VI, IV—IV, IV—VI, V—VI, and VI—VIII.

Among the numerical quantities included are energies of valence and conduction bands, and their variations with temperature and pressure, electron and hole mobilities, and effective masses. In addition twenty other useful properties of a more general physical character related to the subject are included, i.e., lattice constants, dielectric constants, magnetic susceptibility, thermal conductivity, work function, elastic coefficients, phonon temperature, linear expansion coefficient, fusion and sublimation temperatures and heats, and density. The selection of parameters was intended to be useful for band theory considerations.

Analysis

In the Introduction, given in both French and English, the authors state that they "have evaluated the data in the manner in which a specialist in the field would do so" and that the data presented for properties "represent the best possible values in view of phenomenological and theoretical indications presently available".

The Introduction defines terms when necessary and lists all symbols used. All source references are given at the end of each section and also other relevant references under the heading "Voir aussi". A complete bibliography of 1600 references, ranging from the year 1832 to 1961, is at the end of the volume. Data were compiled from the primary literature.

3.3.14. Landolt-Börnstein, Volume 2, Group II

Magnetic Properties of Coordination and Organo-Metallic Transition Metal Compounds by E. König, edited by K.-H. Hellwege and A. M. Hellwege. Volume 2 of Group II, Atomic and Molecular Physics, of Landolt-Börnstein, Numerical Data and Functional Relationships in Science and Technology, New Series, Springer-Verlag, Berlin-Heidelberg, 1966, XII, 578 pp, DM 232 (US $ 58.00).

Organization

This volume was published under the auspices of "Landolt-Börnstein", described in 2.1., and prepared by E. König, Institut für Physikalische Chemie der Universität Erlangen-Nürnberg, Germany (B.R.D.).

Coverage

This volume deals with coordination and organo-metallic compounds of transition metals in the broadest sense of the word. More than 5000 compounds are listed. Hydrated and anhydrous simple and double salts are included for comparison purposes also if they do not belong to this class of compounds. Compounds with filled shell configurations of transition metals are listed for completeness. Not included are most of the mixed oxides of transition elements, especially those of variable composition. The magnetic data on such mixed oxides may be found in the relevant chapters on ferrospinels, magnet garnets, perovskites, and hexagonal ferrites contained in Landolt-Börnstein, 6th ed, Vol. 2, part 9, and in Vol. III/2 of the New Series, which will be published soon.

The results of susceptibility measurements (susceptibilities per gram and per mole, Curie-constants, magnetic moments, and Curie or Néel temperatures) are arranged in one table. The results of electron spin resonance measurements (g-factors and other parameters, i.e., hyperfine splitting and fine structure parameters, etc., of the applied spin Hamiltonian) are given in another.

Most of the susceptibilities were measured over a limited range of temperatures, frequently between room temperature and the temperature of liquid nitrogen (77 K), or, more often, at room temperature only. For a limited number of compounds, data are available down to liquid helium temperature and sometimes lower.

Analysis

The volume contains several introductory chapters on the arrangement of tables, presentation of experimental results, selection and accuracy of data, abbreviations and list of symbols, and order of arrangement of substances. Tables of diamagnetic ionic susceptibilities and correction constants are added.

The author has attempted to include and sift critically the very voluminous literature material as completely as possible. In cases where several measurements were reported in the literature the evaluation was made in terms of the chemical purity of the substances (as given by the results of the chemical analysis and the absence of a field-dependence for non-ferromagnetic substances), the accuracy of the measurements (established by the precision of the method used, the reliability of the calibration, definition of the field, and the constancy of the temperature during the time of the measurements), and the presentation of the results (where it is important that the actually measured quantities be reported in addition to derived quantities). When only a single measurement of the magnetic susceptibility of a certain substance is available, this datum is included in the table even if its accuracy is questionable.

The literature covered, if published prior to 1955, has been taken from G. Foëx, C. J. Gorter, and L. J. Smits, Tables de Constantes et Données Numériques, Vol. 7, Masson & Cie, Éditeurs, Paris, 1957 (see 3.3.15.) and checked against the original literature. Additional references were added where necessary. The literature from 1955 until the end of 1964 has been compiled mainly from Chemical Abstracts. Altogether more than 2600 references are cited.

3.3.15. Tables de Constantes Sélectionnées, Volume 7

Diamagnétisme et Paramagnétisme by G. Foëx, and *Relaxation Paramagnetique* by C. J. Gorter and L. J. Smits, Volume 7 of Tables de Constantes et Données Numériques, Constantes Sélectionées, Masson et Cie, Paris, 1957, 317 pp, 97 F (US $ 29.00).

Organization

This volume was published under the auspices of "Tables de Constantes et Données Numériques", described in 2.2., and prepared by G. Foëx, Université de Strasbourg, C. J. Gorter, Université de Leyde, and L. J. Smits.

Coverage

In the first part of this volume are given: (1) 217 pages of tables of magnetic susceptibility data for a variety of categories of inorganic and organic compounds (elements, inorganic compounds, alloys, minerals, organic compounds including cyclic compounds, sugars, mixtures, free radicals, etc.), and (2) 49 pages of magnetic moments and Curie points for elements, single atoms, alloys, inorganic compounds (solid and in solution), solid solutions and free radicals. In the second part are given six pages of paramagnetic relaxation data for double and other complex salts, mostly sulfates of Cr, Cu, Fe, Gd, Mn, Ni and V.

Analysis

In a short introduction the authors define their terms, explain the arrangement of tables, and tabulate symbols, definitions and abbreviations. They are also meticulous in pointing out the sensitivity of the data to traces of impurities and for proper reduction of temperature at the time of measurement to a standard value. Values agreed on to 1% by two *independent* workers are marked with an asterisk. Two asterisks indicates that several workers agree to within 1% or two authors to better than 5 parts in a thousand.

3.3.16. Tables de Constantes Sélectionnées, Volume 3

Pouvoir Rotatoire Magnétique (Effet Faraday) by R. DE MALLEMANN, and *Effet Magnéto-Optique de Kerr* by F. SUHNER, Volume 3 of Tables de Constantes et Données Numériques, Constantes Sélectionnées, Hermann et Cie, Paris, 1951, 138 pp, 15 F (US $ 4.50).

Organization

R. DE MALLEMANN and F. SUHNER are both attached to the University of Nancy. For a description of the organization of "Tables de Constantes et Données Numériques", see 2.2.

Coverage

In the first section of the book Faraday Effect data are given for gaseous elements, gaseous inorganic and organic compounds, for a few inorganic and a large number of organic liquids, and for solutions of electrolytes. The tables give empirical formula and name, temperature and wavelength of the measurement, Verdet Constants, specific magnetic rotatory power, molar magnetic rotatory power and related constants. In the second section of the book Kerr effect data are given for iron, iron compounds as appropriate, cobalt, nickel, and a number of alloys having magnetic properties.

Analysis

All text is in French but the method of arrangement of compounds makes it relatively easy to locate the numerical data. Literature referencing is adequate.

Other Solid State

3.3.17. Superconductive Materials Data Center

Organization

The center was established in 1965 at its present location, the General Electric Research and Development Center, Schenectady, New York. Support is provided by the Office of Standard Reference Data of the National Bureau of Standards (see 1.1.1.). The director is B. W. ROBERTS. The work of the data center is mainly literature searching, compilation, and dissemination of information and numerical data.

Coverage

Properties of superconductive materials are covered, i.e., critical temperatures, critical magnetic fields, crystallographic parameters, critical magnetic fields of high field superconductors, and some thermodynamic data.

In late 1966, the center issued a compilation on superconductive materials and some of their properties. Covered were composition, critical temperature, critical field crystallographic data, and lowest temperature tested for superconductivity. Substances included were superconductive elements, and alloys, mostly two-component. The publication supplements superconductive materials data presented in *Progress in Cryogenics* (Vol. 4, 1964, pp 160 to 231). (Also published in *New Materials and Methods of Investigating Metals and Alloys*, I. I. KORNILOV, Editor, Moscow, 1966).

Analysis

Standard values of important parameters of superconductive materials are to be developed. As yet, the main work is in literature search and data collection.

Superconductive Materials and Some of Their Properties is described as a "noncritical" compilation. However, it is noted that data were selected from recent studies in which sample purity and perfection appear to have been considered.

As a supplement to *Progress in Cryogenics*, this publication covers the period 1963 to 1965. A supplement to Superconductive Materials and Some of Their Properties is in progress. Most references in this publication are to the primary literature.

Publications

Superconductive Materials and Some of Their Properties, NBS Technical Note 408, B. W. ROBERTS, U.S. Government Printing Office, Washington, D.C. 20402, 1966, IV, 76 pp, US $ 0.45.

3.4. Thermodynamic and Transport Properties, Including Solution Properties

Thermodynamic Properties

3.4.1. Selected Values of Chemical Thermodynamic Properties

Organization

Selected Values of Chemical Thermodynamic Properties (NBS Circular 500) was issued in 1952. The Chemical Thermodynamics Data Group, Thermochemistry Section, Physical Chemistry Division of the Institute for Basic Standards of the National Bureau of Standards (NBS), Washington, D.C. 20234, is continuing the data compilation program which produced NBS Circular 500. The Group is now revising Series I of this compilation which is a part of a continuing program of the NBS Thermochemistry Section. This project is an important part of the National Standard Reference Data System (NSRDS, see 1.1.1.). Started and first directed by FREDERICK D. ROSSINI, it is now the responsibility of DONALD D. WAGMAN and WILLIAM H. EVANS. The staff numbers about eight technical people plus supporting personnel. Most recent financial support has come from the Office of Standard Reference Data.

Coverage

The program includes all elements, inorganic compounds, C_1 and C_2 organic compounds, aqueous solutions of important acids, bases, and salts, and some gaseous and aqueous ions. Data in NBS Circular 500 are grouped in two series. Series I includes standard state values at 25 °C for heat (enthalpy), Gibbs energy and logarithm of equilibrium constant of formation, entropy, and heat capacity, and for a few substances, values for heat of formation at 0 K. For solutions of important salts, thermodynamic properties are given at concentrations from near saturation to infinite dilution. Series II gives change-of-phase values, i.e., temperature, heat and entropy of transition, fusion, vaporization, or sublimation, and heat capacity, and some vapor pressure values.

Revisions of Series I are being issued in sections as NBS Technical Notes until the whole series has been revised. These publications include values of the enthalpy and Gibbs energy of formation, enthalpy, entropy and heat capacity at 298.15 K (25 °C), and the enthalpy of formation at 0 K, for all inorganic substances, organic molecules containing not more than two carbon atoms, and some metal-organic compounds and complexes. To date, tables for the first thirty-four elements in the Standard Order of Arrangement have been issued.

As part of the planned total review of the available chemical thermodynamic data, a systematic review of the heat capacity, heat of solution, and heat of dilution data on simple uni-univalent electrolytes has been made. Tables of selected values of apparent heat capacities, and heats of dilution are given, as well as selected values of the heats of solution to infinite dilution. A publication covering the aqueous uni-univalent electrolytes was issued as NSRDS-NBS 2.

Analysis

The objective of the program is to provide self-consistent tables of selected values of enthalpy and Gibbs energy of formation, the entropy, heat capacity, and change of phase properties for chemical compounds. NBS Circular 500 and the revisions are designed to provide key property values for use in thermodynamic calculations. Values given have been selected or calculated after evaluation of all experimental data, using consistent values for all subsidiary quantitites. The values selected have been adjusted so that the relations existing among different thermodynamic properties of a substance, or the same property for different substances, are satisfied by the tabulated values.

No complete index is given because the tables are arranged according to the Standard Order System, explained in the introduction to the Circular. An alphabetical list of elements with their table numbers is provided. Tables giving specific references for each entry, and a complete general list of references are included.

Usages for nomenclature, symbols, and basic physical constants prescribed by international committees and bodies such as the International Union of Pure and Applied Chemistry (IUPAC) are followed. In the revision of Circular 500, use is being made of the 1963 fundamental constants and of the IUPAC "Table of Relative Atomic Weights 1961"* based on the atomic mass of $^{12}C = 12$ exactly. Values of energy units and fundamental constants are given, symbols and abbreviations are defined, and conventions regarding standard states are explained in the introduction.

Publications

Selected Values of Chemical Thermodynamic Properties, Circular of the National Bureau of Standards 500, F. D. ROSSINI, D. D. WAGMAN, W. H. EVANS, S. LEVINE, and I. JAFFE, U.S. Government Printing Office (GPO), Washington, D.C. 20402, 1952, IV, 1268 pp, US $ 7.25 (out of print). Paperback reprint issued in two parts: I. Tables; and II. References; GPO, Washington, D.C. 20402, 1961 (out of print).

Revisions to Circular 500 published as NBS Technical Note 270 with the same title: *Selected Values of Chemical Thermodynamic Properties*:

270—1. "Tables for the First Twenty-three Elements in the Standard Order of Arrangement", D. D. WAGMAN, W. H. EVANS, I. HALOW, V. B. PARKER, S. M. BAILEY, and R. H. SCHUMM, GPO, Washington, D.C. 20402, 1965, IV, 124 pp, US $ 0.65. Superseded by 270—3.

270—2. "Tables for the Elements Twenty-four through Thirty-two in the Standard Order of Arrangement", D. D. WAGMAN, W. H. EVANS, I. HALOW, V. B. PARKER, S. M. BAILEY, and R. H. SCHUMM, GPO, Washington, D.C. 20402, 1966, IV, 62 pp, US $ 0.40. Superseded by 270—3.

* *Pure and Applied Chemistry 5*, 255 (1962).

270—3. "Tables for the First Thirty-four Elements in the Standard Order of Arrangement", D. D. WAGMAN, W. H. EVANS, V. B. PARKER, I. HALOW, S. M. BAILEY, and R. H. SCHUMM, GPO, Washington, D.C. 20402, 1968, IV, 264 pp, US $ 1.25. Supersedes Technical Notes 270—1 and 270—2.

Thermal Properties of Aqueous Uni-univalent Electrolytes, NSRDS-NBS 2, V. B. PARKER, GPO, Washington, D.C. 20402, 1965, V, 66 pp, US $ 0.45.

Note: As a related activity the group assists in preparation of the IUPAC "Bulletin of Thermodynamics and Thermochemistry" which contains a complete annual bibliography indexed by substance and property. The Bulletin is available through Prof. EDGAR F. WESTRUM, JR., Department of Chemistry, University of Michigan, Ann Arbor, Michigan 48104.

3.4.2. Selected Values of Properties of Hydrocarbons and Related Compounds

Organization

This project was established in 1942 at the U.S. National Bureau of Standards (NBS) in Washington, D.C. It is presently located in the Thermodynamics Research Center (discussed in 2.3.), Texas A & M University, College Station, Texas 77843. FREDERICK D. ROSSINI directed the project until 1960 when BRUNO J. ZWOLINSKI, director of the Thermodynamics Research Center, succeeded him. Until 1966, when it was put on a self-sustaining basis, the American Petroleum Institute (API) sponsored and financed the project. A complete discussion of the organization of this project and its associated programs may be fund in Entry 2.3.1. This program is closely associated with the Thermodynamics Research Center Data Project in physicochemical and thermodynamic properties (see 3.4.3.).

Coverage

The following substances are included: aliphatic, alicyclic, and aromatic hydrocarbons; oxygen-containing compounds such as alcohols, aldehydes, ketones, ethers, and alkanoic acids; sulfur derivatives such as thiaalkanes, thiols, and alkyl thiophenes; certain classes of nitrogen compounds, and a few important simple substances, e.g., O_2, N_2, CO ,CO_2, and H_2O.

For each substance listed, values are given for the following physicochemical and thermodynamic properties: boiling point; dt/dp; freezing point; refractive index; molal and specific refraction; refractivity intercept; density; specific gravity; vapor pressure; specific dispersion; surface tension; absolute and kinematic viscosity; isothermal compressibility coefficient; compressibility factor and activity coefficient of gases; critical temperature, pressure, density, volume, and compressibility factor; Gibbs energy (free

150

energy); Gibbs energy function; enthalpy, entropy, and temperature of phase changes; heat of combustion; enthalpy, Gibbs energy and logarithm of the equilibrium constant of formation; standard entropy; enthalpy; enthalpy function; heat capacity; enthalpy, entropy, and Gibbs energy deviations from ideal or standard state values for gases. Property values are presented at standard reference points, or at selected even intervals of the variables (temperature, pressure, etc.) over ranges dictated by probable use of the data and reliability of the extrapolation methods.

The major source of data is the open literature. Selected unpublished data from contributing industrial, academic, and governmental laboratories are also used. Property values are calculated by tested methods in inaccessible temperature ranges or when experimental data are not available.

Analysis

Evaluation of all available data and use of tested correlation methods provide reliable values, frequently better than source data. The introduction to the publication includes a discussion of criteria applied in making selections, and equations employed to obtain computed values. Computational techniques are: extrapolation and interpolation, calculation of derived thermodynamic functions from spectroscopic and molecular structure data, and extension of experimental values by way of molecular structure similarities. A table gives the magnitudes of estimated uncertainties in the values. Internal consistency is maintained.

Recommendations of national and international committees on nomenclature and symbols are followed. The introductory material includes rigorous definitions of properties, values of fundamental and derived constants, and unit conversion factors. Data are carefully conformed to consistent units. Newly recommended values for constants and atomic weights are introduced into revisions when internal consistency can be maintained. For the benefit of engineers, separate tables are given in English units when appropriate.

The physicochemical and thermodynamic property values are published on 21×27 cm loose-leaf sheets for which special post binders are available. Each sheet gives the names and molecular formulas of the compounds, the names and units of property values, and the dates of original issue and revisions. The properties are grouped in tables designated a, b, c, etc.; in each group pages are arranged in an order based on the Standard Order System and when necessary on structure. No references are given on the data sheets, but two types of reference sheets are provided, specific and general, for identification of sources of background data. A cumulative "General List of References", with 7351 entries, was issued in 1963.

3.4.3.

Revisions and additions are issued semiannually. The loose-leaf format permits regular updating so that the information includes the most recent values. Often, unpublished data are made available in less time than through regular channels.

Publications

Selected Values of Properties of Hydrocarbons and Related Compounds, American Petroleum Institute Research Project 44, B. J. ZWOLINSKI, Director, Thermodynamics Research Center, Texas A & M University, College Station, Texas 77843; 2427 loose-leaf datas heets extant June 1968, sold initially in complete sets of seven volumes for US $ 749.10 (with binders), approximate cost of supplements per year is US $ 75.00. Discount prices are available to some educational and non-profit research institutions. Order from the TRC Data Distribution Office, Texas A & M Research Foundation, F. E. Box 130, College Station, Texas 77843.

Selected Values of Physical and Thermodynamic Properties of Hydrocarbons and Related Compounds, F. D. ROSSINI, K. S. PITZER, R. L. ARNETT, R. M. BRAUN, and G. C. PIMENTEL, published for the American Petroleum Institute by Carnegie Press, Pittsburgh, 1953, IX, 1050 pp, US $ 7.00 (out of print). Cumulative to December 31, 1952.

Selected Values of Properties of Hydrocarbons, National Bureau of Standards Circular 461, F. D. ROSSINI, K. S. PITZER, W. J. TAYLOR, J. P. EBERT, J. E. KILPATRICK, C. W. BECKETT, M. G. WILLIAMS, and H. G. WERNER, U.S. Government Printing Office, Washington, D.C. 20402, 1947, XIII, 483 pp, US $ 3.75 (out of print). Cumulative to May 31, 1947.

3.4.3. Selected Values of Properties of Chemical Compounds

Organization

This project was established in 1955 at the Carnegie Institute of Technology (now the Carnegie-Mellon University) in Pittsburgh, Pennsylvania. Since 1961, it has been located in the Thermodynamics Research Center (discussed in 2.3.), Texas A & M University, College Station, Texas 77843. FREDERICK D. ROSSINI directed the project until 1960 when he was succeeded by BRUNO J. ZWOLINSKI, director of the Thermodynamics Research Center (TRC). The Office of Standard Reference Data of the U.S. National Bureau of Standards (see 1.1.1.) provides some financial support. Other support is realized from the sale of data sheets. For a complete discussion of the organization of this program and associated projects, see 2.3.2. This program is closely associated with the American Petroleum Institute Research Project 44 in physicochemical and thermodynamic properties (see 3.4.2.).

Coverage

TRC covers inorganic and organic compounds of importance to the chemical industry and science in general. Included to date are nonmetallic elements and their inorganic compounds, oxygen-containing organic compounds (alkanols, glycols, phenols, aldehydes, ketones, alkanoic acids, and esters), halogen-substituted acyclic compounds, and nitrogen-containing compounds such as amines and nitriles. The project is complementary to API Research Project 44; hydrocarbons and certain related nitrogen and sulfur compounds covered by that project are excluded.

The plan has been to cover the same properties as those covered by API Research Project 44. To date, numerical values have been published for the following properties: refractive index, density, boiling point, dt/dp, and freezing point; density at temperatures in °C; refractive index at wavelengths in Å; critical temperature, pressure, density, volume, and compressibility factor; vapor pressures and boiling points; for transitions, the temperature, change in enthalpy, entropy, ΔC_p, and cryoscopic constant; and enthalpy and Gibbs energy function, entropy, enthalpy, heat capacity, heat and Gibbs energy of formation, and logarithm of equilibrium constant of formation, all at temperatures in K.

The primary sources of data are the open literature, and selected unpublished data from contributing laboratories. Tested correlating and computational methods are used to derive property values when experimental data are not available, and to extend the temperature range.

Analysis

Careful evaluation of available data and the use of tested correlation methods ensure that tabulated values are as reliable as possible, frequently better than source data. Internal consistency within related bodies of information is maintained. The selection of a value for a given compound may be done in the context of data for a group of structurally related compounds. The reliability of the individual values is enhanced through correlation with molecular structure.

Recommendations of national and international committees on nomenclature, symbols, and constants are followed. The introduction to the compilation contains a summary statement of the units in which property values are given.

The data in *Selected Values of Properties of Chemical Compounds* are presented in tables on 21×27 cm loose-leaf sheets. Within a given section, sheets are arranged according to the Standard Order System, based on the periodic table. No references are given on the data sheets, but two types of reference sheets are provided, specific and general, for identification of sources of

153

background data. Unpublished values created by the project by calculation and correlation are referenced as TRC Data Project values.

Revisions and additions are issued periodically, with the goal of semi-annual supplements. The loose-leaf format permits regular updating so that the information always includes the most recent values. Data for families of compounds are first brought up-to-date and then kept current. New groups of properties and series of compounds are added as needs arise and data become available.

Publications

Selected Values of Properties of Chemical Compounds, Thermodynamics Research Center Data Project, B. J. Zwolinski, Director, Thermodynamics Research Center, Texas A & M University, College Station, Texas 77843; 886 loose-leaf data sheets extant June 1968, sold initially in complete sets only for US $265.80 (with binders), approximate cost of supplements per year is US $ 60.00. Discount prices are available to some educational and non-profit research institutions. Order from the TRC Data Distribution Office, Texas A & M Research Foundation, F. E. Box 130, College Station, Texas 77843.

3.4.4. JANAF Thermochemical Tables

Organization

The Joint Army-Navy-Air Force (JANAF) Thermochemical Tables project was established in late 1959 at the Dow Thermal Research Laboratory, Midland, Michigan. D. R. Stull is the project director. Technical advice and guidance have been provided by a group of consultants. The purpose of the project is to compile and publish consistent tables of thermodynamic data required for propellant performance calculations. A related experimental program, carried on in a number of laboratories, has provided missing data and the redetermination of questionable values.

Coverage

The project covers thermodynamic properties in the solid, liquid, and/or ideal gaseous state. *JANAF Thermochemical Tables* includes the following elements: Al, B, Be, Br, C, Cl, Co, Cu, F, Fe, H, Hg, I, K, Li, Mg, Mo, N, Na, O, P, Pb, S, Si, Ti, W, Zr, and e^- and their simple compounds. These compounds are principally those with the halogens, oxygen, and hydrogen.

The properties given are heat capacity, entropy, Gibbs energy function, heat content (enthalpy), heat of formation, and Gibbs energy of formation for the ideal gas, liquid or solid state as appropriate. The logarithm of equilibrium constant of formation of each compound from the elements in their standard reference states is also given. The foregoing properties are given at 100-degree intervals from 0 K to 1000 to 6000 K. Other pertinent properties are presented, such as molecular weight, point group, ground state configuration or quantum weight, vibrational frequencies and degeneracies, bond distances and angles, and product of the moments of inertia.

Sources of data consist of the open literature, and to some extent private communications. Empirical or quasi-theoretical computations, and estimates obtained by various means are used to supply data not available from other sources.

Analysis

Property values for each element and compound are evaluated from all relevant data. An effort is made to maintain internal consistency. Some of the values, particularly early ones, were estimates based on inadequate supporting data. Revised tables of values are issued as better data become available. Pertinent references, a brief analysis of available data, and the basis for the selections made are also given. The introduction includes explanations of and equations for methods used to compute values needed to fill gaps in the experimental data. Values are reviewed before incorporation into the collection.

All symbols used are defined; values and units are given for basic, derived, and defined constants. However, units used are not in complete agreement with international recommendations. In 1966, beginning with the first addendum to the JANAF Thermochemical Tables (see Publications), the fundamental constants used are those recommended by the National Academy of Sciences-National Research Council and adopted by international bodies.

The publication consists of 22×28 cm loose-leaf sheets. The formulas of compounds are written according to the modified Hill (Chemical Abstracts) System; the chemical symbols in the formulas are arranged alphabetically, except for carbon compounds, when C is placed first, followed by H if hydrogen is present. Pages are ordered alphabetically according to the Hill formula of the compounds. No page numbers are required, and revisions and additions are easily accommodated.

In August 1965, the existing tables, with data up to July 1965, were made available to the public. The first addendum was issued in 1966, and incorporated Supplements 18, 19, 20, and 21; the second addendum, published in 1967, incorporated Supplements 22, 23, 24 and 25. Third addendum (Supplements 26, 27, 28, and 29) was issued in 1968.

Publications

JANAF Thermochemical Tables, PB 168370, D. R. Stull, project director, and
staff, Dow Chemical Co., Midland, Michigan for the U.S. Air Force, 1965,
V, 945 pp, US $ 10.00, microfiche US $ 3.50, available from the Clearinghouse
for Federal Scientific and Technical Information, U.S. Department of Commerce (CFSTI), Springfield, Virginia 22151.

JANAF Thermochemical Tables: First Addendum, PB 168 370—1, D. R. Stull,
project director, J. Chao, A. T. Hu, G. C. Karris, E. W. Phillips, H. Prophet, G. C. Sinke, A. N. Syverud, and S. K. Wollert, 1966, VII, 197 pp,
US $ 3.00 (Supplements 18, 19, 20, and 21). CFSTI, Springfield, Virginia 22151.

JANAF Thermochemical Tables: Second Addendum, PB 168 370—2, D. R. Stull,
project director, J. Chao, A. T. Hu, G. C. Karris, H. Prophet, and A. N.
Syverud, 1967, VII, 193 pp, US $ 3.00 (Supplements 22, 23, 24, and 25).
CFSTI, Springfield, Virginia 22151.

JANAF Thermochemical Tables: Third Addendum, PB 168 370—3, D. R. Stull,
project director, J. Chao, A. T. Hu, G. C. Karris, H. Prophet, A. N.
Syverud, D. U. Webb, 1968, IX, tables (unpaginated), US $ 3.00 (Supple-
ments 26, 27, 28, and 29). CFSTI, Springfield, Virginia 22151.

All tables are available on magnetic tape; consult Dr. Harold Prophet, Thermal
Research Laboratory, 1707 Building, The Dow Chemical Company, Midland,
Michigan 48640.

3.4.5. Contributions to the Data on Theoretical Metallurgy

Organization

The Bureau of Mines of the U.S. Department of the Interior supported a
thermodynamics project at the Berkeley Thermodynamics Laboratory,
University of California, Berkeley, Calif., from the early 1920's until 1967.
From 1930, when compilation of data was started, until 1964, it was directed
by K. K. Kelley. Since mid-1967, the thermodynamics laboratory has been
located at the Albany Metallurgy Research Center, Albany, Oregon; E. G.
King is project director. An integrated program of precision thermodynamic
measurements is associated with the compilation activity, thus providing
the staff with experience valuable in the critical evaluation of data.

Coverage

The elements and their inorganic compounds of interest in metallurgical and
ceramic operations are covered. Included are oxides, halides, carbides, carbonates, sulfides, sulfates, nitrates, nitrides, and some intermetallic and interoxidic compounds.

Properties given include Gibbs energy, entropy, heat content (enthalpy), high and low temperature heat capacity, heat and free energy of formation and phase change, and vapor pressure. In some cases, properties of substances in their standard states are given. The values compiled are those needed for the thermodynamic evaluation of metallurgical processes.

Data for evaluation are taken from the open literature and to some extent from measurements made at the Laboratory.

Analysis

Specific thermodynamic property values are selected after a critical evaluation, by consistent methods, of all available experimental and calculated values. Complete references are cited, and those given the greatest weight are indicated. Uncertainties are assigned when possible. A critical discussion of source data and of equations used for calculations is often given. Usage of nomenclature, symbols, units, and physical constants follows with a few exceptions the recommendations of authoritative national and international committees.

In the publications, elements and their compounds are arranged alphabetically by name; the bibliographies are also alphabetical, arranged by author. Bulletins on important topics such as low and high temperature heat capacities and entropies for oxides are revised periodically. However, the pattern of publication, i.e., bulletins at intervals of several years, provides a periodic updating of important topics included in the program.

Publications

Many early Bulletins are out-of-print or have been superseded. A complete current set of data consists of Bulletins 542, 584, 592, and 601:

Contributions to the Data on Theoretical Metallurgy, Bureau of Mines, U. S. Government Printing Office, Washington, D. C. 20402.

> XII. Bulletin 542, Heats and Free Energies of Formation of Inorganic Oxides, J. P. COUGHLIN, 1954, 80 pp, out of print.

> XIII. Bulletin 584, High-Temperature Heat-Content, Heat Capacity, and Entropy Data for the Elements and Inorganic Compounds, K. K. KELLEY, 1960, 232 pp, US $ 1.25.

> XIV. Bulletin 592, Entropies of Elements and Inorganic Compounds, K. K. KELLEY and E. G. KING, 1961, 149 pp, US $ 0.75.

> XV. Bulletin 601: a reprint of Bulletins 383, 384, 393, 406 (III, IV, V, and VII), 1962, 525 pp:

>> III. Bulletin 383, The Free Energies of Vaporization and Vapor Pressures of Inorganic Substances, K. K. KELLEY, 1935, 132 pp.

157

IV. Bulletin 384, Metal Carbonates, Correlation and Applications of Thermodynamic Data, K. K. KELLEY, and C. T. ANDERSON, 1935, 73 pp.

V. Bulletin 393, Heats of Fusion of Inorganic Substances, K. K. KELLEY, 1936, 166 pp.

VII. Bulletin 406, The Thermodynamic Properties of Sulphur and Its Inorganic Compounds, K. K. KELLEY, 1937, 154 pp.

Other Publications

Related publications of considerable interest appear as Bureau of Mines "Report of Investigations". Each publication in this group presents critically evaluated properties of one element and its inorganic compounds. Recent issues include:

Report of Investigations, U.S. Bureau of Mines, Pittsburgh, Pa. 15213:

R. I. 5600, Thermodynamic Properties of Manganese and Its Compounds, A. D. MAH, 1960, 35 pp, US $ 0.30.

R. I. 6727, Thermodynamic Properties of Vanadium and Its Compounds, A. D. MAH, 1966, 84 pp, no charge.

3.4.6. Thermodynamic Properties of Chemical Substances

Organization

The first edition of this compilation appeared in 1956 under the title *Thermodynamic Properties of Combustion Product Components*. Its purpose was to aid in thermodynamic calculations of processes occurring at high temperatures. The second edition, described here, was published in 1962 under the new title *Thermodynamic Properties of Chemical Substances*. The values were compiled over a period of 10 years by collaborators in the Institute of Mineral Fuels (IGI) of the U.S.S.R. Academy of Sciences and the U.S.S.R. State Institute of Applied Chemistry (GIPKh). V. P. GLUSHKO, chief editor, and L. V. GURVICH direct the work, which is sponsored by the U.S.S.R. Academy of Sciences. This program is related to "Thermodynamic Constants of Substances" (see 3.4.7.).

Coverage

This program covers the thermodynamic properties of elements and simple inorganic compounds in their standard reference states over a wide range of temperatures. Thermodynamic properties are given for the following elements and isotopes: O, H, D, T, He, Ne, Ar, Kr, Xe, F, Br, I, S, N, P, C, Si, Pb, Hg, Zr, B, Al, Be, Mg, Ca, Sr, Ba, Li, Na, K, Rb, and Cs; also for their oxides, hydrides, fluorides, chlorides, and nitrides in the solid

(45 substances), liquid (44 substances), and gaseous (335 substances) phases, including monatomic and diatomic ionized gases and electron gas. The first and second supplements will cover compounds of alkaline and alkaline earth metals and revision of the data included in the second edition. The first supplement will be published in 1969 to 1970. Arrangement of the material is according to the Standard Order (see 3.4.1.).

The following thermodynamic property values are given at selected temperatures for gases in the ideal state at 1 atmosphere pressure:

Gibbs energy function $(G° — H_0°)/T$ or Φ_T^*, entropy $S_T°$, relative enthalpy $H_T° — H_0°$, heat of formation $\Delta Hf°$ or $I_T°$, and equilibrium constant K_p and log K_p where K_p is the constant of dissociation or ionization. Values are given between 400 and 6000 K at 100 K intervals and also at 293.15 and 298.15 K. For 22 substances, values up to 10000 K are given at 200 K intervals, and then to 20000 K at 500 K intervals. For compounds in the condensed phase, values for heat capacity $C_p°$ and vapor pressure P are also given from 293.15 K to appropriate temperatures. Methods of calculation (polynomial equations) are given for the tabulated thermodynamic properties.

Data are compiled from world literature sources. An associated research program by a number of institutions within the Soviet Union provided data not in the literature.

Analysis

Literature articles were carefully examined, and many experimental values were re-evaluated, providing corrected values for the compilation. Some recalculations were made to provide a system of self-consistent values. Estimates were made when experimental data were lacking. Volume I includes discussion of the properties tabulated, calculation methods, critical analyses and evaluation of the data found in the literature, the bases for selection of the values and their uncertainty limits. Limits of error in the Gibbs energy function Φ_T^*, caused by uncertainties in values of molecular constants and the method of evaluation, are given for each gas. More than 4000 references are cited.

Complete references, an author index with English equivalents of names, and a formula index to Volumes I and II are included. Symbols, terminology, and values of constants are those recommended by international organizations except when the recommendations differ materially from Soviet usage. All symbols, designations, and constants are explained or defined. The values of all thermodynamic functions are expressed in calories per mole and calories per mole degree, and those of equilibrium constants and vapor pressures are expressed in atmospheres.

159

3.4.7.

The compilation consists of two bound volumes, 21×27 cm. Volume I is largely descriptive, with a number of short tables. Volume II consists entirely of tables: 380 tables present the thermodynamic properties of 335 substances.

Publications

Thermodynamic Properties of Chemical Substances, V. P. GLUSHKO, Chief Ed., Vol. I, 1164 pp, Vol. II, 916 pp, U.S.S.R. Academy of Sciences, Moscow (1962), approximately US $ 16.00. First supplement, in late 1969 or early 1970, also will be published by the U.S.S.R. Academy of Sciences.

3.4.7. Thermodynamic Constants of Substances

Organization

The compilation and publication of *Thermodynamic Constants of Substances* are directed by V. P. GLUSHKO, chief editor, and V. A. MEDVEDEV. Specialists in several institutes are assisting in the project. Three parts of a planned series of ten have appeared. Upon completion of the ten parts, the entire work incorporating new values and corrections will be issued in two volumes. The work is sponsored by the U.S.S.R. Academy of Sciences, and is related to "Thermodynamic Properties of Chemical Substances" (see 3.4.6.).

Coverage

This program is concerned with the thermodynamic properties at 298.15 K of elements and inorganic, simple organic, and metallo-organic compounds. In Part I thermal constants are given at 298.15 K for O, H, D, T, F, Cl, Br, I, At, ^{3}He, He, Ne, Ar, Kr, Xe, Rn, and their compounds; in Part II for S, Se, Te, Po; and in Part III for N, P, As, Sb, Bi, and their compounds. The Standard Order of Arrangement is used. The completed compilation will cover inorganic compounds of all elements, organic compounds containing not more than two carbon atoms, and metallo-organic compounds in which each organic group contains only one or two carbon atoms (cf. NBS Circular 500, see 3.4.1.).

Data covered include the following thermodynamic property values: Heat capacity $C_{p\,298.15\,K}$; enthalpy $H^{\circ}_{298.15\,K} - H^{\circ}_0$; entropy $S^{\circ}_{298.15\,K}$; dissociation energy D_0; enthalpy of formation $\Delta H f^{\circ}_{298.15\,K}$ and $\Delta H f^{\circ}_0$; Gibbs energy of formation $\Delta G f^{\circ}_{298.15\,K}$; enthalpy and entropy of polymorphic transformations, fusion, vaporization, and sublimation; and temperature and vapor pressure at phase transformations. Symmetry, structural type, ionization potentials, and critical temperatures, pressures, volume, and density are given in the appendixes.

Data are compiled from the world literature.

Analysis

All values are stated to be self-consistent, and an indication of the uncertainty is generally given. When necessary, values lacking in the literature were estimated. In some cases special experimental investigations were carried out in Soviet institutions to supply needed data. A separate set of tables identifies the specific references for each value. There are 3809 references in the first three Parts.

In general, the symbols, terminology, and units are those recommended by international organizations modified in part to accord with Soviet usage. The values of thermodynamic constants are expressed in calories per mole or calories per mole degree, and vapor pressure is expressed in atmospheres. The symbols and abbreviations used are explained in the introduction. A long list of abbreviations for references cited is given in Part I and a short addendum to the list is given in Part II and in Part III. The books, 21 × 27 cm, have hard covers. They consist almost entirely of tables.

Part I of the series was published in 1965, Part II early in 1966 and Part III in 1968. The schedule for publication of the other parts called for Part IV in 1969.

Publications

Thermodynamic Constants of Substances, Handbook in 10 Parts, V. P. Glushko, Ed., U.S.S.R. Academy of Sciences, All-Union Institute of Scientific and Technological Information, Moscow; Part I, 1965, 146 pp, 72 kopecks (US $ 1.75); Part II, 1966, 96 pp, 52 kopecks (US $ 1.40); Part III, 1968, 222 pp, 1 ruble 21 kopecks; available in the United States from Victor Kamkin, Inc., Bookstore, 1410 Columbia Rd., N.W., Washington, D.C. 20009.

3.4.8. Chemical Thermodynamics in Nonferrous Metallurgy

Organization

Chemical Thermodynamics in Nonferrous Metallurgy is a series of handbooks compiled by J. I. Gerassimov, A. N. Krestovnikov, and A. S. Shakhov. This series is the outgrowth of two earlier publications, *Chemical Thermodynamics of Nonferrous Metallurgy* by Gerassimov and Krestovnikov in 1933, and *Thermodynamics and Physicochemical Properties of Rare Metals* by Krestovnikov and Shakhov in 1943. Eight volumes are planned to cover thermodynamic and physicochemical properties of industrially important nonferrous and rare metals. Four volumes have been published. The authors plan to present thermodynamic methods and the calculations for pyrometallurgical processes, as well as methods of calculation for thermodynamic properties of important nonferrous and rare metals. They will also examine and compare existing literature of numerical data for the thermodynamics of nonferrous metallurgy and consider the problems involved.

Coverage

Substances included are important gaseous elements and compounds involved in nonferrous metallurgy: zinc, copper, lead, tin, silver, tungsten, molybdenum, titanium, zirconium, niobium, tantalum, aluminum, antimony, magnesium, nickel, bismuth, and cadmium, and their compounds to date.

Property values given include those for atomic volume, density, melting and boiling point, vapor pressure, specific and atomic heat capacity, enthalpy and entropy of formation and phase changes, Gibbs energy of formation, and enthalpy and Gibbs energy functions.

Data are compiled from the world literature.

Analysis

Values reported are both experimental and calculated. When possible, recommended values are given. Lists of references for each chapter are given in Roman characters, except for references to Russian publications which are given in Russian. A number of the references are to well-known compilations. Although the text is in Russian, international symbols are used for properties and for chemical elements and compounds. Equations and tables are therefore independent of language.

In general, the symbols, terminology, and units are those recommended by international organizations, modified in part to accord with Soviet usage. Volume I has a two-and-a-half-page table (in Russian) explaining symbols. The books are hardbound, an English translation of Volume III is paperbound.

Although the data references in the early publications are quite old, there are numerous references for data in the 1950's and some for data as late as 1962. The four volumes were published in 1960, 1961, 1963, and 1966, respectively. Volumes V and VI are in preparation.

Publications

Chemical Thermodynamics in Nonferrous Metallurgy, J. I. GERASSIMOV, A. N. KRESTOV-NIKOV, and A. S. SHAKHOV, Metallurgical Publishing House, Moscow.

Vol. I: Theoretical Introduction, Thermodynamic Properties of Important Gases, Thermodynamics of Zinc and Its Important Compounds, 1960, 231 pp.

Vol. II: Thermodynamics of Copper, Lead, Tin, Silver, and Their Important Compounds, 1961, 263 pp.

Vol. III: Thermodynamics of Tungsten, Molybdenum, Titanium, Zirconium, Niobium, Tantalum, and Their Important Compounds, 1963, 284 pp. English translation published for the National Aeronautics and Space Administration and the National Science Foundation, Washington, D.C., by the Israel Program for Scientific Translations, available as NASA-TT-F-285 for US $ 6.00, or N66-14133 for US $ 3.00, from the Clearinghouse for Federal Scientific and Technical Information, Springfield, Va. 22151.

Vol. IV: Thermodynamics of Aluminum, Antimony, Magnesium, Nickel, Bismuth, Cadmium, and Their Important Compounds, 1966, 428 pp.

3.4.9. Selected Values for the Thermodynamic Properties of Metals and Alloys

Organization

This compilation project, started in 1955, is under the direction of RALPH R. HULTGREN, University of California, Berkeley, California. *Selected Values for the Thermodynamic Properties of Metals and Alloys* was published in 1963; supplements have been issued since 1964. The work is carried out within the Inorganic Materials Research Division of the Lawrence Radiation Laboratory and the Department of Mineral Technology of the University. The sponsor is the U.S. Atomic Energy Commission, with assistance from the American Iron and Steel Institute and the International Copper Research Association. The project is associated with the National Standard Reference Data Program of the U.S. National Bureau of Standards (see 1.1.1.). The compilation work is supplemented by experimental investigation conducted as graduate thesis topics.

Coverage

All metallic elements and binary alloy systems for which published thermodynamic data have been found are covered, and included in the published data when evaluation is completed.

Selected Values for the Thermodynamic Properties of Metals and Alloys includes complete thermodynamic data for both elements and alloys. For the elements, the following functions relative to the standard states for both the condensed and gas phases at selected temperature intervals are tabulated: heat capacity, enthalpy (heat), entropy, Gibbs energy (free energy). Values for enthalpy

3.4.9.

and entropy of phase changes, for Gibbs energy and enthalpy of vaporization, and for vapor pressure are also given.

For alloys, the integral quantities presented are enthalpy, Gibbs energy, entropy, excess Gibbs energy, and excess entropy of formation. Values for activities and activity coefficients, and for partial molar thermodynamic quantities over a range of compositions are given. Phase diagrams for most of the alloys are also included.

Sources of data include journals or compilations of critically evaluated data. Some values are obtained by extrapolation or by calculation.

Analysis

A detailed introduction to Selected Values of Thermodynamic Properties of Metals and Alloys presents the methodology and guidelines followed in the evaluation of data. Graphical and analytic methods used to develop consistent and reliable values are discussed. All surveys of the literature and evaluations of data were conducted by members of the staff under the supervision of one of the authors. Each final evaluation was then reviewed and checked by at least three of the four authors. The evaluation of each system is discussed; and the source and basis of selection of data are given. Uncertainties in tabulated values are often recorded or they may be estimated from information given in the discussion of the system.

In Selected Values for the Thermodynamic Properties of Metals and Alloys (1963), the tables were based on the values of the fundamental constants in LEWIS, RANDALL, PITZER, and BREWER, Thermodynamics (2nd ed, McGraw-Hill, N.Y., 1961); and on O (Oxygen) = 16.000. After October 1964, the values used were those recommended by IUPAC and IUPAP, and the Committee on Fundamental Constants of the U.S. National Academy of Sciences; and those of the atomic weight scale $^{12}C = 12.000$.

In 1963, data evaluated (and previously issued in loose-leaf form) to about 1961 to 1962 were published in book form. Included are 63 elements and 168 alloy systems. Each system is discussed separately and tables (data and graphs) are provided. Data sources and complete references are given. A systems index by formula and an alphabetical author index for references to original data are provided.

New and revised data sheets issued at intervals as supplements to the text keep the compilation up-to-date. As of January 1968, data on 42 elements, nine of these new, and 65 binary alloy systems, 56 of these new, had been issued as supplementary data sheets. Work is progressing on the revision and expansion of the 1963 text.

Publications

Selected Values for the Thermodynamic Properties of Metals and Alloys, R. R. HULTGREN,
L. ORR, P. D. ANDERSON, and K. K. KELLEY, John Wiley and Sons, Inc.,
New York, 1963, XI, 963 pp, US $ 12.50.

Requests for new supplementary data sheets, having the same title as the book,
should be sent to Professor RALPH R. HULTGREN, Department of Mineral
Technology, University of California, Berkeley, Calif. 94720.

3.4.10. Thermochemistry* for Steelmaking

Organization

The object of this program is to collate, consolidate, and summarize in
handbook form all available thermodynamic and physicochemical data for
substances and systems involved in steelmaking. This material is also relevant to the chemistry of many metallurgical systems at elevated temperatures. This program was established some eight years ago with the support
of the American Iron and Steel Institute. It is directed by J. F. ELLIOTT,
Department of Metallurgy, Massachusetts Institute of Technology, Cambridge, Massachusetts 02139.

Volumes I and II have been published. Compilation of related data is
being continued under the sponsorship of the U.S. National Bureau of
Standards, Office of Standard Reference Data (see 1.1.1.).

Coverage

Selected elements and compounds that are involved in the chemistry and
technology of steelmaking are treated in Volume I. The compounds include
carbides, nitrides, oxides, phosphides, silicides, and sulfides. Volume II, in
addition to elements and compounds, specifically treats binary and ternary
iron alloys and solutions, complex oxide systems, and slags.

Thermodynamic properties are given for elements and compounds in
their various states and phases, and for solutions. The properties include
heat (enthalpy) and temperature of phase changes; heat capacity; enthalpy,
entropy, and Gibbs energy function at 100-degree intervals; and enthalpy,
Gibbs energy, and log K_p of formation as appropriate. When available, the
following properties are also given: density, thermal conductivity, electrical

---

* The word "thermochemistry" is usually used in a restrictive sense to refer
to the thermodynamics of chemically reacting systems. Here it is used to include
properties of both reacting and nonreacting systems for which the term "thermodynamics" or "chemical thermodynamics" is usually used.

resistivity, total and spectral emissivity, viscosity, surface tension, vapor pressure, solubility (including that of gases), diffusion, activity, and activity coefficients. Phase diagrams, which take up approximately 30 percent of Volume II, include binary diagrams for elements, oxides, and iron solutions, and show the effect of the addition of a second metallic element upon the solubility of graphite in iron.

For Volume I, data sources include reviews, books, papers in primary journals, some unpublished data, and also compilations of critically evaluated data published elsewhere, such as those of the U. S. Bureau of Mines (see 3.4.5.) and of NBS (see 3.4.1.), "Thermodynamic Properties of the Elements" by D. R. STULL and G. C. SINKE (American Chemical Society, Washington, D. C., 1956, see 5.3.38.), and "Metallurgical Thermochemistry" by O. KUBASCHEWSKI and E. L. EVANS (3rd ed, Pergamon Press, Inc., London, 1958, see 5.3.43.). For source material, Volume II depends much more on the primary literature.

Analysis

The aim is to present up-to-date information mutually consistent with regard to base and reference states, in forms useful in both the laboratory and plant. Some material has appeared elsewhere, but much new information from the literature is evaluated. How revised values are selected is not always indicated but references used are given, and short discussions precede the data for most systems. Calculated or estimated values are identified. Facts from major sources were brought up-to-date when new information became available.

This compilation is unique in that it includes useful thermodynamic properties of slag and metal solutions, interaction coefficients, and diffusion coefficients in melts.

Most symbols and their units are given in the introduction to Volume I. Others are explained in the sections in which they appear.

The authors referenced their sources of data meticulously. The preface to Volume II is dated July 1963, but there are few references later than 1960.

The compilation consists of two bound volumes. Each volume has a short introduction, a detailed table of contents, and a comprehensive index. The index of Volume I lists the elements and compounds under the properties recorded rather than under their own names, that of Volume II is cumulative for the two volumes and lists topics, titles of tables, substances, and systems of substances with properties covered under each section.

Publications

Thermochemistry for Steelmaking, Addison-Wesley Publishing Company, Inc., Reading (Massachusetts), and London.

Vol. I, J. F. ELLIOT and M. GLEISER, 1960, VIII, 296 pp, US $ 17.50.

Vol. II, J. F. ELLIOT, M. GLEISER, and V. RAMAKRISHNA, 1963, XVI, 550 pp, US $ 25.00.

3.4.11. Binary Metal and Metalloid Constitution Data Center

Organization

Constitution of Binary Alloys by MAX HANSEN and KURT ANDERKO was published in 1958 as a revised edition of HANSEN's *Der Aufbau der Zweistofflegierungen*, published in 1936. The 1958 edition and the subsequent *Constitution of Binary Alloys, First Supplement*, 1965, and *Constitution of Binary Alloys, Second Supplement*, to be published (1969), were compiled at the Illinois Institute of Technology (IIT) Research Institute under the sponsorship of the U. S. Air Force. RODNEY P. ELLIOTT and FRANCIS A. SHUNK, respectively, directed the work on the First and Second Supplement. Since June 1967, the work has been carried on at the Binary Metal and Metalloid Constitution Data Center, Illinois Institute of Technology Research Institute, Chicago, Illinois 60616, under the direction of F. A. SHUNK. The program is linked to the National Standard Reference Data System of the National Bureau of Standards (NBS, see 1.1.1.), and is sponsored by the U. S. Atomic Energy Commission, Aerospace Research Laboratories, National Aeronautics and Space Administration, and National Bureau of Standards.

Coverage

Data for more than 1700 binary systems are included in the 1969 volume and for more than 2300 in the combined 1958, 1965, and 1969 volumes. The systems are mostly alloys; some borides, hydrides, oxides, chalcogenides, and phosphides are included.

Phase diagrams are given for many systems. Values for solubilities, eutectic points, melting points, and other constitutional features as well as crystal structures and cell dimensions are given.

All available literature has been searched for sources of data. For the 1965 and 1969 volumes, references were found principally in Chemical Abstracts, Metallurgical Abstracts, and Review of Metal Literature. Specialized abstract bulletins, bibliographies, reviews, and monographs were also used.

3.4.12.

The 1958 edition covers the literature through 1955 with limited coverage of the 1956 and 1957 literature; the 1965 volume reviews literature published between 1955 and December 1961; and the second supplement covers the literature published from 1962 through 1964.

Analysis

The authors analyzed and evaluated all relevant data. In most cases their conclusions are incorporated in composite diagrams based upon their evaluation of the data. Uncertainties are indicated.

The table of contents to the Second Supplement is a cumulative listing of systems contained in the three volumes. Diagrams cannot be used without the text, nor the material in the Supplements without reference to a previous review in earlier volumes if such exists. Factors for use in the interconversion of atomic and weight percent for each system are given in the three volumes, but the directions and tables needed to use them are in the 1958 volume only. Thus, the 1958 edition is a necessity for full use of the Supplements.

The systems are arranged in alphabetical order by chemical symbols. Tables of some physical properties and structural data of the elements are included in the appendixes to both the 1958 volume and the 1965 Supplement. A table on crystal-structure types according to "Strukturbericht", and conversion tables for temperatures and for atomic and weight percentages are in the 1958 volume. The 1969 volume is to contain a table of crystal-structure types ordered according to the composition of representative compounds.

Publications

Constitution of Binary Alloys, 2nd ed, M. Hansen and K. Anderko, McGraw-Hill Book Co., New York, 1958, XIX, 1305 pp, US $ 39.50.

Constitution of Binary Alloys, First Supplement, R. P. Elliott, McGraw-Hill Book Co., New York, 1965, XXXII, 877 pp, US $ 35.00.

Constitution of Binary Alloys, Second Supplement, F. A. Shunk, McGraw-Hill Book Co., New York, to be published (1969).

3.4.12. Phase Diagrams for Ceramists

Organization

The American Ceramic Society and the U.S. National Bureau of Standards (NBS) sponsor this compilation activity which is located at NBS. Searching of the literature, editing for presentation, and critical decisions are made at NBS, while the Society provides editorial assistance, drafting, printing and distribution. Compilations are now financed from a revolving fund acquired from sales of previous issues.

Coverage

Systems included are of special interest to ceramists — metal-oxygen and metal oxide systems (including Si), systems with oxygen-containing radicals, systems containing halides, sulfides, cyanides, alone and with other substances, systems of water with metal oxides and miscellaneous substances. Borides, carbides, and silicides are not included.

Simple and complex phase diagrams for one-, two-, three-, and multicomponent systems are given. For some systems, multidiagrams show isothermal and isoplethal sections of phase relations; for others, isofracts, temperature-composition projections, compatibility relations, and base systems of tetrahedra are given. Melting points of metallic oxides, molecular weights of oxides, and 1961 atomic weights of the elements are presented in separate tables.

Data are compiled from the literature.

Analysis

The first compilation of this project appeared in the *Journal of the American Ceramic Society* in 1933. The 1964 edition is the seventh compilation in this series and supersedes previous publications of the series. The literature has been covered up to 1962. A supplement containing 2083 new diagrams is in press (1969 Part II edition).

The authors were more critical in the 1964 edition than in previous ones and in general only include a selected "best" diagram for a system. Occasionally several diagrams representative of current interpretation or composite diagrams constructed from the work of several investigators have been included. Many diagrams are too small to permit values to be read with accuracy. Diagrams of partial systems, such as a high corner of a ternary system or an enlargement of a complicated portion of a system and some figure reproductions, increase the legibility.

The introductory material includes: selected and annotated bibliography that covers theory, interpretation, methods and techniques, mathematical treatment, thermodynamic calculations, silicate chemistry, special collections of phase diagrams, and phase diagrams in related fields. The phase rule, the diagrams, and some experimental methods are also discussed.

Diagrams are sometimes accompanied by explanatory notes, and complete references are given below each diagram. An author index and a system index are included. Temperatures are in degrees Celsius, but it is not always apparent whether the scale is the Geophysical Laboratory Temperature Scale of 1914 or the International Temperature Scale of 1927 or that of 1948.

3.4.13.

Publications

Phase Diagrams for Ceramists, E. M. LEVIN, H. F. McMURDIE, and F. P. HALL, American Ceramic Society, Columbus, Ohio 43214, 1956, 286 pp, 811 phase diagrams, US $ 10.00.

Phase Diagrams for Ceramists, Part II, E. M. LEVIN and H. F. McMURDIE, American Ceramic Society, Columbus, Ohio 43214, 1959, 153 pp, 462 phase diagrams, US $ 8.00.

Phase Diagrams for Ceramists, E. M. LEVIN, C. R. ROBBINS, and H. F. McMURDIE (7th compilation), American Ceramic Society, Columbus, Ohio 43214, 1964, 601 pp, 2064 phase diagrams, US $ 18.00. (Supersedes previous volumes.)

Phase Equilibrium Diagrams of Oxide Systems, revised and redrawn by E. F. OSBORN and A. MUAN, American Ceramic Society, Columbus, Ohio 43214, 1960. Ten 49×59 cm plates for three-oxide systems containing SiO_2, four of them for oxide phases in equilibrium with metallic iron. Diagrams are US $ 2.00 each, US $ 15.00 for the set of 10. (Reproductions of these plates appear in the 1964 compilation.)

3.4.13. High Temperature Behavior of Inorganic Salts

Organization

The Information Center on High Temperature Behavior of Inorganic Salts was established in 1963 in the Electrochemistry Section of the Institute for Basic Standards of the U. S. National Bureau of Standards (NBS) in Washington, D. C. It was moved to the Electrochemistry Branch, Naval Research Laboratory, Washington, D. C. 20390, in August 1968. KURT H. STERN is the director of the Center, which is supported by the Office of Standard Reference Data of NBS (see 1.1.1.).

Coverage

The purpose of this program is to evaluate and publish in concise form existing thermodynamic and kinetic data relevant to the high temperature behavior of important classes of inorganic salts. The Center is investigating three types of information for each salt: 1) the reactions by which salts decompose in various temperature ranges; 2) thermodynamic functions for these reactions: Gibbs energies, free-energy functions, equilibrium constants, and partial pressures; and 3) kinetic parameters such as rate constants, activation energies, and mechanisms.

A series of publications is planned to cover anhydrous salts which contain monatomic cations, and oxyanions with one element besides oxygen, such as sulfates, carbonates, nitrogen-oxygen, and halogen-oxygen anions. Each volume will cover one anion. The first, on sulfates, was published recently; the second, on carbonates, is in progress; a third, on nitrates, is being planned.

The first volume, on sulfates, was published in October 1966. Sixty cations are covered. The properties are: phase transition temperatures above 298.15 K, standard heat of formation and standard entropy values of reactants and products at 298.15 K, densities at 298.15 K, and information on the kinetics of thermal decomposition. Some supplementary material is also provided. The literature was searched through 1964. Half the references are pre-1954.

Analysis

Data are lacking for many salts which fit into the categories covered by the program. In many cases, thermodynamic functions cannot be calculated because information needed on reactants and products over a wide temperature range is not available. Information on the kinetics of thermal decomposition is often too poor for use as reference data. However, qualitative or semi-quantitative kinetic information is given when deemed useful. Thermodynamic information has been stressed because of its importance to stability problems.

In the introductory part of *High Temperature Properties and Decomposition of Inorganic Salts: Part 1. Sulfates*, the properties covered are discussed. Experimental methods and theory are briefly outlined and the quality and treatment of the data reviewed. Pertinent equations are provided. A table of units, symbols, and abbreviations is also included. The compilation is arranged in dictionary format; all data about a compound appear together and critical commentaries introduce each compound. Most data are given in tables. All data and critical commentaries are referenced. Densities are listed in the units given by the original authors. The procedures used for the evaluation are not described. It is also stated that thermodynamic data already critically evaluated are used whenever possible, but that qualitative and semi-quantitative information is also included. There are specific warnings concerning some data; uncertainties frequently are not indicated.

Publications

High Temperature Properties and Decomposition of Inorganic Salts, Part 1. Sulfates, NSRDS-NBS 7, K. H. STERN and E. L. WEISE, U.S. Government Printing Office, Washington, D.C. 20402, 1966, V, 38 pp, US $ 0.35.

3.4.14. Low Temperature Specific Heats Data Center

Organization

This program was initiated in 1963. It is located in the Institute for Basic Standards, U.S. National Bureau of Standards (NBS), Washington, D.C. 20234. The principal investigator is GEORGE T. FURUKAWA. The Data Center functions as part of the National Standard Reference Data System (NSRDS) of NBS (see 1.1.1.).

Coverage

The center's primary concern is the determination and presentation of critically evaluated values for specific heat and derived thermodynamic properties (entropy, Gibbs energy, and enthalpy) of pure substances in the range from 0 to 300 K. Emphasis at present is on the lower temperature ranges. High temperature relative enthalpy data are also examined to determine the best values of specific heat around 300 K. Substances covered include the elemental species, and oxides, halides, and others.

The center has issued *Critical Analysis of the Heat Capacity Data of the Literature and Evaluation of Thermodynamic Properties of Copper, Silver, and Gold from 0 to 300°K*. Properties covered are heat capacity, enthalpy, entropy, Gibbs energy, enthalpy function, and Gibbs energy function. Supplementary information such as the electronic coefficient of heat capacity, experimental method, and purity of substances are given.

The critically evaluated, selected values for the thermodynamic properties are presented in a table. Other data are presented in tables and graphs. Discussion of the sources of data and general assessment are in text. The introduction provides good background information. References include a number from 1967.

Analysis

The center compiles heat capacity data from the literature and critically evaluates these data to obtain selected "best values". These values are then used to calculate the derived thermodynamic properties enumerated above.

Critical Analysis of the Heat Capacity Data of the Literature and Evaluation of Thermodynamic Properties of Copper, Silver, and Gold from 0 to 300°K includes tables of the selected "best values", deviation plots, and other supporting information used to document the selected values. For each of the elements, a comprehensive assessment of the data sources is included.

This publication is the first of several planned, which will appear in the NSRDS-NBS numbered series.

Publications

*Critical Analysis of the Heat Capacity Data of the Literature and Evaluation of Thermo-
dynamic Properties of Copper, Silver, and Gold from 0 to 300 °K,* NSRDS-NBS 18,
G. T. FURUKAWA, W. G. SABA, and M. L. REILLY, U.S. Government Printing
Office, Washington, D.C. 20402, 1968, V, 49 pp, US $ 0.40.

3.4.15. The Thermodynamic Tables Project of the International Union of Pure and Applied Chemistry

Organization

The Thermodynamic Tables Project was established by the Commission
on Thermodynamics and Thermochemistry of the IUPAC Division of
Physical Chemistry in 1964. Its mission is to prepare agreed tables of
thermodynamic and transport properties of simple fluids of interest to
science and industry. A Project Office, with salaried staff, is located at
Imperial College, London; the scientific director is SELBY ANGUS. Financial
support has been received from France, Germany, Sweden, the U.K., the
U.S.A., and the U.S.S.R., with the Office for Scientific and Technical
Information (described in 1.1.2.) of the U.K. acting as a guarantor of the
financial stability of this program. Policy guidance is provided by the
IUPAC Commission on Thermodynamics and Thermochemistry. The
scientific work is organized under working panels, one panel for each fluid
or group of fluids. The following countries are represented on panels by
one or more members: France, Germany/B.R.D., India, Japan, the Netherlands, the U.K., the U.S.A., and the U.S.S.R.

Coverage

Individual panels have been established for the following single gases or
groups of gases: (1) Carbon dioxide (CO_2); (2) Atmospheric gases (O_2, N_2,
and air); (3) Quantum fluids (H_2, D_2 and He); (4) Inert fluids (Ne, Ar, Kr,
Xe); (5) Aliphatic hydrocarbons (CH_4, C_2H_6, C_2H_4, etc.); (6) Halogenated
hydrocarbons (all); (7) Multicomponent systems (to be selected); and (8)
Ammonia (NH_3). In addition, a Panel on Correlating Functions has been
established which will have the task of selecting or developing mathematical
correlating functions for representing the data within agreed tolerances.
For each gas the objective will be to publish thermodynamically consistent
tables of data such as pressure, temperature, enthalpy, and entropy over the
widest possible range of the variables.

3.4.16.

Analysis

The IUPAC Centre on Thermodynamic Tables Project is in a real sense following in the footsteps of the International Conference on the Properties of Steam (see 3.4.16.). That is, its purpose is to prepare, for each fluid under review, tables of such high quality that they can be accepted as the "best possible" by workers in the field and also can lend themselves to use as "International Standards" if their position in science and industry warrants the assignment of "standard" status. Basic to the whole program is the idea that all available literature data will be examined for each fluid. Experts of the highest competence in each narrow area will evaluate the data, and the presentation of the best values will be done in a consistent way with due regard to proper selection of units, constants and precise mathematical formulation of the results.

Fruition of the project may take 10 years. A comprehensive publication of the properties of carbon dioxide is anticipated in 1969.

Information on the Project and its Working Panels can be supplied by Dr. SELBY ANGUS, Scientific Director, IUPAC Thermodynamic Tables Project Centre, Dept. of Chemical Engineering, Imperial College of Science and Technology, Prince Consort Road, London S. W. 7, England.

Publications

Several documents have been produced for use by members of the Project, and of these the following may be of interest to others, and are available free of charge from the Project Centre:

"An Account of the IUPAC Thermodynamic Tables Project", by S. ANGUS, IUPAC Thermodynamic Tables Project Centre, London, 1968, 8 pp (Reference PC/D 5.5.).

"Guide to Working Panel Procedures", by S. ANGUS, IUPAC Thermodynamic Tables Project Centre, London, 1965, 14 pp (Reference PC/D 1.2.).

"Guide to Procedures in the Reporting of Experimental Data", by S. ANGUS, IUPAC Thermodynamic Tables Project Centre, London, 1966, 5 pp (Reference PC/D 2.3.).

3.4.16. International Conference on the Properties of Steam

Organization

The First International Conference on the Properties of Steam (ICPS) met in London in 1929, and the Seventh in Tokyo in 1968. Its aim is to produce skeleton tables of thermodynamic and transport properties of steam agreed on by experts from participating countries. The skeleton tables are tables of reference points, with assigned tolerances, which can serve as the basis for expanded reliable tabulations for use, particularly by the electrical industry, in all countries. The expanded tables, although not produced by the ICPS, present values within the ICPS tolerances and thus assure international compatibility. Over the years, successive conferences have increased the reliability and range of the skeleton tables to meet the demands of advancing technology. The Conference is a relatively informal body for which the American Society of Mechanical Engineers, 345 East 47th Street, New York, N.Y. 10017, is acting as the Secretariat. Czechoslovakia, Germany, Japan, the U.K., the U.S.A., and the U.S.S.R., each have National Committees on the Properties of Steam, either of governmental status (Czechoslovakia, U.K. and U.S.S.R.) or belonging to the appropriate national engineering institute (Germany, Japan, U.S.A.). Members of the National Committees continue the work of the ICPS between its meetings, and send formal delegations to business sessions of the ICPS. Other nations are represented at Conferences on an ad hoc basis, and any scientist in the field may attend the scientific sessions of ICPS.

In 1963, at the Sixth International Conference on the Properties of Steam, held in New York City, "The International Skeleton Tables of 1963", covering the temperature range 0 to 800°C, and the pressure range to 1000 bars, were adopted by the 16 member nations of the Conference. Also, as a result of the Conference, an International Formulation Committee (IFC) was established to develop correlating equations for the 1963 skeleton table, suitable for computer use, which would ensure that computed values would be within assigned tolerances, and would be thermodynamically consistent. The IFC has since drawn up, ratified, and promulgated "The 1967 IFC Formulation for Industrial Use: A Formulation of the Thermodynamic Properties of Ordinary Water Substance" and "The 1968 IFC Formulation for Scientific and General Use". Another panel formulated tables for transport properties which have been published by the Secretariat of the Conference as "International Skeleton Tables of the Transport Properties of Water Substance, 1964".

Coverage and Analysis

The International Conference on the Properties of Steam is an example of fruitful, long-term international cooperation which has produced critically evaluated numerical property values in an area both scientifically difficult and industrially important.

The properties covered by the 1963 International Conference include thermodynamic properties of saturated water and saturated steam (entropy, enthalpy, and specific heat); specific volume, specific enthalpy, and viscosity of compressed water and superheated steam; and thermal conductivity of water and superheated steam, all given with assigned tolerances. For viscosity and thermal conductivity, equations for interpolation and other calculations are an integral part of the skeleton tables. For all properties, formulations (equations) for computer use were subsequently established. An important feature of the 1963 tables was the pushing upward of the temperature and pressure limits to 800° C and 1000 bars respectively in response to industrial needs for these data.

Publications

Publications based on the work of the ICPS are in two categories: (1) Books containing comprehensive tables obtained by suitable expansion of the skeleton tables published on the initiative of individuals or groups, in various countries, for use by scientists and engineers; and (2) reports and proceedings issued directly by the Secretariat of ICPS and given skeleton tables and other pertinent results of the Conferences. The publications described below are grouped in these two classifications.

(1) Tables of Thermodynamic and Transport Properties:
  (a) Most recent; conform with *1963 International Skeleton Tables*
    Steam Tables 1964: Physical Properties of Water and Steam, 0 to 800 °C and 0 to 1000 bars, R. W. BAIN (National Engineering Laboratory), Her Majesty's Stationery Office, Edinburgh, 1964, V, 147 pp, £ 1.15.0. net. Units used: Temperature: Celsius scale; Pressure: bar; Volume: cm³/g; Energy: kJ/kg.

    Supplement to Steam Tables 1964: International Skeleton Tables of the Transport Properties of Water Substance, 1964, National Engineering Laboratory, Her Majesty's Stationery Office, Edinburgh, 1966, 4 pp, 2 s. Units used: Temperature: Celsius scale; Pressure: bar; Volume: cm³/g; Energy: kJ/kg.

    1967 ASME Steam Tables: Thermodynamic and Transport Properties of Steam, C. A. MEYER, R. B. McCLINTOCK, G. J. SILVESTRI, and R. C. SPENCER, JR., The American Society of Mechanical Engineers, New York, 1967, X, 328 pp, US $ 12.50. Comprises tables and charts for steam and water; calculated using the *1967 IFC Formulation for Industrial Use*. Prepared for the ASME Research Committee on Properties of Steam. Units used: Temperature: Fahrenheit scale; Pressure: lbf/in²; Volume: ft³/lb; Energy: BTU/lb.

    1967 Steam Tables: Thermodynamic Properties of Water and Steam; Viscosity of Water and Steam; Thermal Conductivity of Water and Steam, Electrical Research Association, Edward Arnold and Co., St. Martin's Press, U.K., 1967, 146 pp, US $ 18.50. (An equivalent volume, but in SI units, is forthcoming). Based on smoothing of the 1966 and 1967 IFC Formulations. Units used: Temperature: Fahrenheit scale; Pressure: lbf/in²; Volume: ft³/lb; Energy: BTU/lb.

1967 Steam Charts, Electrical Research Association, Edward Arnold & Co., St. Martin's Press, U.K., 1967, £ 3. A large-scale atlas of the enthalpy/ entropy diagram for steam and water, compatible with 1967 IFC Formulation. Also auxiliary charts for engineering calculations. Units used: Temperature: Fahrenheit scale; Pressure: lbf/in²; Volume: ft³/lb; Energy: BTU/lb.

(b) The following publications are based on older formulations of skeleton tables:

Thermodynamic Properties of Steam, Including Data for the Liquid and Solid Phases, J. H. KEENAN and F. G. KEYES, John Wiley and Sons, Inc., New York, 1939, 80 pp, US $ 5.50. Units used: Temperature: Fahrenheit scale; Pressure: lbf/in²; Volume: ft³/lb; Energy: BTU/lb.

Thermodynamic Properties of Water and Steam, 6th ed, M. P. VUKALOVITCH, published by State Publishing House of Scientific-Technical Literature Concerning Mechanical Engineering "Mashgis", Moscow, and "VEB Verlag Technik", Berlin, 1958, 245 pp plus separate charts. Text in English, French, German, and Russian. Units used: Temperature: Celsius scale; Pressure kgf/cm²; Volume: m³/kg; Energy: kcal$_{IT}$/kg, cf. 5.3.55.

Wasserdampftafel der Allgemeinen Elektricitäts-Gesellschaft, HELMUT HOTES, R. Oldenbourg, München, 1960, 48 pp.

VDI-Steam Tables, Including a Mollier h, s-Diagram for Temperature up to 800 °C and a T, s-Diagram, 6th ed, ERNST SCHMIDT, Springer-Verlag, Berlin-Heidelberg-New York, and R. Oldenbourg, München, 1963, 151 pp. Two parts: Part A (out of print). Superseded by 7th ed. Part B (out of sprint). Superseded by *Properties of Water and Steam in SI-Units*.

VDI-Steam Tables up to 800°C and 1000 at, Including a Mollier h, s-Diagram and a T, s-Diagram, 7th ed, ERNST SCHMIDT, Springer-Verlag, Berlin-Heidelberg-New York, and R. Oldenbourg, München, 1968, 197 pp, US $ 12.00. Text in English, French, German, and Spanish. Units used: Temperature: Celsius scale; Pressure: atmosphere; Volume: m³/kg; Energy: kcal$_{IT}$/kg.

Properties of Water and Steam in SI-Units, 0-800°C and 0-1000 bar, Including a Mollier h, s-Diagram and a T, s-Diagram, ERNST SCHMIDT, Springer-Verlag, Berlin-Heidelberg-New York, 1969, 205 pp, US $ 12.00. Text in English, French, German, and Spanish; foreword and table of contents also in Japanese and Russian. Units used: Temperature: Celsius scale; Pressure: bar; Volume: m³/kg; Energy: kJ/kg.

(c) Tables for steam not directly related to the skeleton tables:

Tables of the Thermodynamic Properties of Heavy Water, J. N. ELLIOTT, Atomic Energy of Canada Limited, Chalk River, Ontario, January 1963, 90 pp.

The Thermodynamic Functions of Dissociating Steam in the Range 1000 to 5000 °K, 0.01 to 100 b, VLADIMIR KMONICEK, Academia, Prague, 1967, 105 pp.

An Equation of State for Water and Steam, Steam Tables in the Critical Region and in the Range from 1000 to 100,000 Bars, JAN JŮZA, Academia, Prague, 1966, 142 pp. Conforms with 1963 International Skeleton Table, within its range.

3.4.17.

(2) Conference Reports:

"International Skeleton Tables of the Thermodynamic Properties of Water Substance, 1963" from *Proceedings of the Sixth International Conference on the Properties of Steam*, R. W. HAYWOOD, Ed. on behalf of the Secretariat, the American Society of Mechanical Engineers, New York, 1963, 57 pp. Units used: Temperature: Celsius scale; Pressure: bar; Volume: cm^3/g; Energy: kJ/kg.

"International Skeleton Tables of the Viscosity and Thermal Conductivity of Water Substance" from *Official Report of the Thermal Conductivity Panel of the Sixth International Conference on the Properties of Steam*, R. W. HAYWOOD, Ed. on behalf of the Secretariat, the American Society of Mechanical Engineers, New York, 1964, 21 pp. Units used: Temperature: Celsius scale; Pressure: bar; Volume: cm^3/g; Energy: kJ/kg.

"The 1967 IFC Formulation for Industrial Use: A Formulation of the Thermodynamic Properties of Ordinary Water Substance", International Formulation Committee of the Sixth International Conference on the Properties of Steam, Düsseldorf, Germany, February 1967, 31 pp.

"Supplement to the 1967 IFC Formulation for Industrial Use: Formulae for the Specific Isobaric Heat Capacity of Ordinary Water Substance", IFC of the Sixth International Conference on the Properties of Steam, Düsseldorf, 1967, 8 pp.

"Thermodynamic Property Values of Ordinary Water Substance Calculated from the 1967 IFC Formulation for Industrial Use", U.S. Delegation for the Secretariat of the International Formulation Committee of the Sixth International Conference on the Properties of Steam, The American Society of Mechanical Engineers, New York, February 1967, 19 pp.

"The 1968 IFC Formulation for Scientific and General Use: A Formulation of the Thermodynamic Properties of Ordinary Water Substance, April 1968", and "Thermodynamic Property Values of Ordinary Water Substance Calculated from the 1968 IFC Formulation for Scientific and General Use, April 1968", IFC of the Sixth International Conference on the Properties of Steam. Available from the Secretariat, The American Society of Mechanical Engineers, New York, April 1968, 67 pp, US $ 12.00.

3.4.17. Thermodynamic Functions of Gases

F. DIN, Ed., Butterworth & Co. Ltd., London (Available in the U.S.A. and dependencies from Plenum Publishing Corporation, New York), US $ 12.50 per volume.

Vol. 1: Ammonia, Carbon Dioxide, Carbon Monoxide, 1956 (reprinted 1962), VIII, 175 pp.

Vol. 2: Air, Acetylene, Ethylene, Propane, and Argon, 1956 (reprinted 1962), VI, 201 pp.

Vol. 3: Methane, Nitrogen, Ethane, 1961, VI, 218 pp.

Other Publications

Temperature-entropy diagrams, available as wall charts, US $ 3.00 each.

Organization

Surveys of the thermodynamic properties of industrially important gases were started in 1948 under the supervision of the Thermodynamics Committee of the Mechanical Engineering Research Board of the Department of Scientific and Industrial Research (now part of the Ministry of Technology) of Great Britain. The late Dr. F. DIN served as general editor of the series and contributed several sections.

Coverage

This compilation provides a comprehensive survey of all data in the open literature for each gas considered. The following industrially important gases are covered: ammonia, carbon dioxide, carbon monoxide, air, acetylene, ethylene, propane, argon, methane, nitrogen, and ethane.

Properties include temperature-entropy diagrams, entropy, enthalpy, and volume for single phases and/or two phases in equilibrium, specific heats at constant pressure and volume, and Joule-Thomson coefficients. Also given are physical properties including density, molecular volume, boiling point, triple point temperature and pressure, and critical constants.

Analysis

The authors give a critical, detailed survey of the existing data; methods of calculation of the thermodynamic functions and of the construction of the temperature-entropy diagrams; an evaluation of the compiled data; a list of references; and tables of the thermodynamic functions. Short tables of the properties under discussion are included in the textual material which is followed by tables of data. Each volume has a table of contents, but no complete index. Some details of treatment were left to individual authors; units are consistent for an individual gas but are not consistent throughout the series. The International Steam Tables calorie (4.1868 absolute joules) is used. Temperature-entropy diagrams, on separate pages, are too small for accurate interpolations. However, they are also available as wall-sized charts.

The first two volumes, with data for eight gases, appeared in 1956; Volume 3 appeared in 1965. This series will not be continued. A program with similar objectives, aiming at higher quality, is being sponsored by the International Union of Pure and Applied Chemistry (see 3.4.15.).

3.4.18. Thermodynamic Properties of Ammonia

Organization

This project is located in the Heat Division, Equation of State Section, Institute for Basic Standards, National Bureau of Standards (NBS), Washington, D.C. 20234, where it was initiated in 1966. The principal investigator is LESTER HAAR. Support is provided by the Office of Standard Reference Data, NBS (see 1.1.1.).

Coverage

The object of this program is to prepare tables of accurate data for the thermodynamic properties of ammonia. This effort will be in effect a revision of *Tables of Thermodynamic Properties of Ammonia*, NBS Circular 142, first issued in 1923.

The first publication, *Thermodynamic Properties of Ammonia as an Ideal Gas*, presents calculated values for Gibbs energy function, enthalpy function, heat capacity at constant pressure, and entropy at closely spaced intervals from 50 to 5000 K in the ground electronic state.

Analysis

Values presented were calculated taking into consideration the contributions of ordinary vibrational anharmonicity and vibrational-rotational coupling together with rotational stretching and rotational quantum effects. The molecular data used to calculate the thermodynamic functions are referenced. In addition to tables of data, a review and discussion are presented.

The values of the thermodynamic functions presented in *Thermodynamic Properties of Ammonia as an Ideal Gas* will be used as a basis for real gas correction to the properties.

Publications

Thermodynamic Properties of Ammonia as an Ideal Gas, NSRDS-NBS 19, LESTER HAAR, U.S. Government Printing Office, Washington, D.C. 20402, 1968, IV, 10 pp, US $ 0.20. Reprinted from the *Journal of Research of the National Bureau of Standards A. Physics and Chemistry 72 A*, No. 2, March-April 1968.

3.4.19. Thermodynamic Functions of Air

Organization

This is a continuing program carried out under the auspices of the G. M. KRZHIZHANOVSKII Power Engineering Institute, Academy of Sciences of the U.S.S.R., and the Department of Physics of the M. V. LOMONOSOV

Moscow State University. The work has been carried out under the general direction of A. S. PREDVODITELEV. This program is part of the work devoted to the study of the properties of gases at high temperatures.

Coverage

The composition of air at normal conditions was used, i.e., N_2, 78.08%; O_2, 20.95%; and Ar, 0.97%. Properties covered include specific enthalpy, internal energy, entropy and heat capacity at constant pressure and constant volume; molecular weight; velocity of sound; density of air and mole fractions of air components at pressures in ranges of interest; and the entropy, internal energy, and specific heat at constant volume for the air components N, O, Ar, N^+, O^+, and Ar^+.

Tables of Thermodynamic Functions of Air (1957) covers the range 6000 to 12000 K and 0.001 to 1000 atm; Tables of Thermodynamic Functions of Air (1959), 12000 to 20000 K and 0.001 to 1000 atm.

Analysis

The values tabulated are calculated by computer. The introductions to the publications include discussion on the theoretical background, equations and mathematical treatments used, fundamental constants, and the reliability of the calculations.

Publications

Tables of Thermodynamic Functions of Air: 6000 to 12000 °K and 0.001 to 1000 ATM, A. S. PREDVODITELEV, E. V. STUPOCHENKO, E. V. SAMUILOV, I. P. STAKHANOV, A. S. PLESHANOV, and I. B. ROZHDESTVENSKII, Infosearch Ltd., London, sole distributors (except U.S.A.), Cleaver-Hume Press Ltd., London, 1958, 301 pp, US $ 9.50. Available in U.S.A. from Associated Technical Services, Inc., Glen Ridge, New Jersey 07028. Published 1962, 302 pp, US $ 21.75. Translated from the Russian, *Tablitsy Termodinamicheskikh Funktsii Vozdukha: dlya temperatur ot 6000° do 12000°K i davlenii ot 0,001 do 1000 atmosfer*, Publishing House of the U.S.S.R. Academy of Sciences, Moscow, 1957, 302 pp, 4 rubles 3 kopecks.

Tables of Thermodynamic Functions of Air: 12,000 to 20,000 °K and 0.001 to 1000 ATM, A. S. PREDVODITELEV, E. V. STUPOCHENKO, A. S. PLESHANOV, E. V. SAMUILOV, and I. B. ROZHDESTVENSKII, Associated Technical Services, Inc., Glen Ridge, New Jersey 07028, 1962, 230 pp, US $ 16.50. Translated from the Russian, *Tablitsy Termodinamicheskikh Funktsii Vozdukha: dlya temperatur ot 12000 do 20000 °K i davlenii ot 0,001 do 1000 atmosfer*, Publishing House of the U.S.S.R. Academy of Sciences, Moscow, 1959, 230 pp, 2 rubles 10 kopecks.

3.4.20.

Tables of Thermodynamic Functions of Air (for Temperatures from 200 to 6000 °K and Pressures from 0.00001 to 100 Atmospheres), [*Tablitsy Termodinamicheskikh Funktsii Vozdukha (dlya temperatur ot 200° do 6000 °K i davlenii ot 0,00001 do 100 atmosfer)*], A. S. PREDVODITELEV, E. B. STUPOCHENKO, A. S. PLESHANOV, E. B. SAMUILOV, and I. B. ROZHDESTVENSKII, Publishing House of the Computer Center of the U.S.S.R. Academy of Sciences, Moscow, 1962, 268 pp, 2 rubles 77 kopecks (in Russian).

Other Publications

Charts of Thermodynamic Functions of Air: 1000 to 12,000 °K and 0.001 to 1000 ATM, A. S. PREDVODITELEV, E. V. STUPOCHENKO, , V. P. IONOV, A. S. PLESHANOV, I. B. ROZHDESTVENSKII, and E. V. SAMUILOV, Associated Technical Services, Inc., Glen Ridge, New Jersey, 1962, 56 pp, 44 figures, US $ 6.50. Translated from the Russian, Termodinamicheskikh Funktsii Vozdukha (dlya temperatur ot 1000 do 12000 °K i davlenii ot 0,001 do 1000 atm) (graphike funktsii). Publishing House of the U.S.S.R. Academy of Sciences, Moscow, 1960, 56 pp, 36 kopecks.

Transport (including Thermophysical) Properties

3.4.20. Thermophysical Properties Research Center

The Thermophysical Properties Research Center (TPRC) is a separate department in the Schools of Engineering, Purdue University, Lafayette, Indiana 47907. TPRC's activities include scientific documentation, generation of data tables, and both theoretical and experimental research. A major aim is the correlation and evaluation of data and the publication of tables. The professional staff of approximately 50 members also carries on an extensive supporting research program. Y. S. TOULOUKIAN has been director of TPRC since its inception. Collaborators include T. MAKITA, University of Kobe, Japan, and L. DEFFET and P. HESTERMANS of the Institut Belge des Hautes Pressions (Brussels, Belgium) where a European Branch of TPRC has been established.

The present primary support for the compilation program is provided by the Office of Standard Reference Data of the U.S. National Bureau of Standards (see 1.1.1.), and other federal agencies.

TPRC has three unique and major publications which will be treated separately within this entry. TPRC itself will be discussed under the major headings of "Coverage" and "Analysis".

Coverage

TPRC's overall interest encompasses 16 properties, designated as thermophysical and which include transport and thermodynamic properties. Thir-

182

teen of these are covered in the *Thermophysical Properties Research Literature : A Retrieval Guide* (Plenum Press, 1967), a product of the TPRC Scientific Documentation Division described under "Publications". Of primary interest to readers of this Compendium is the production of critically evaluated numerical data compilations — the prime activity of the TPRC Data Tables Division. Nine properties are covered: thermal conductivity, specific heat, thermal reflectivity, thermal absorptivity, thermal emissivity, thermal transmissivity, thermal diffusivity, thermal expansion, and viscosity. The publications are discussed separately below.

Analysis

The stated aims of TPRC are (1) to produce, whenever possible, an internally consistent set of "recommended" values of a particular property of a material as of a given date; (2) to supplement experimental data by semi-empirical correlation methods when such methods are justified; and (3) by use of statistical thermodynamics, to generate tables of transport properties when experimental values for such properties are not available. These aims are met by the critical evaluation, analysis, and correlation of existing data and the calculation, when possible, of values to fill gaps in the available data.

TPRC Data Book

Coverage

Until December 1966, the Center issued critically evaluated numerical data compilations as a three volume loose-leaf data book. The *TPRC Data Book* will now be published commercially (Plenum Press) in a standard hardbound format, and will be based on the same underlying philosophy as its predecessor. There will be thirteen volumes, one property (as listed above) per volume or in some cases multiple volumes. Publication of the first ten volumes is scheduled for 1969, with the latter three staggered over the next two years. Complete revisions are anticipated once every five years. The content and titles of the thirteen volumes are:

Vol. 1. Thermal Conductivity of Metallic Elements and Alloys.
Vol. 2. Thermal Conductivity of Nonmetallic Solids.
Vol. 3. Thermal Conductivity of Nonmetallic Liquids and Gases.
Vol. 4. Specific Heat of Metallic Elements and Alloys.
Vol. 5. Specific Heat of Nonmetallic Solids.
Vol. 6. Specific Heat of Nonmetallic Liquids and Gases.
Vol. 7. Thermal Radiative Properties of Metallic Elements and Alloys.
Vol. 8. Thermal Radiative Properties of Nonmetallic Solids.
Vol. 9. Thermal Radiative Properties of Coatings.

Vol. 10. Thermal Diffusivity.

Vol. 11. Viscosity.

Vol. 12. Thermal Expansion of Metallic Elements and Alloys.

Vol. 13. Thermal Expansion of Nonmetallic Solids.

Data are compiled from the primary literature; foreign and English language abstracting services; governmental, academic, and industrial research reports; masters and doctoral theses from universities; and cooperative arrangements with major research laboratories in the United States and abroad.

Analysis

In Volumes I and III of the loose-leaf *Data Book* (no longer available), tables or graphs, or both, of all experimental values recorded were given. Substances for which recommended values had been selected were given on a separate chart and table, and estimated errors in recorded values indicated. In Volume II, only recommended values were tabulated. A "Specification Table" gave for each curve the literature reference number, experimental method used, year of measurement, temperature range, reported errors, specimen designation, and composition of the material in weight percent. The pertinent constants used in the equations for the calculations of thermal conductivity were given above the tabular results for each element. Literature references were listed at the end of each chapter. The introductory material included a table of contents and sections on general information and generation of recommended values, a discussion with explanations of symbols and units used, and an alphabetical directory of materials. Policies concerning symbols, units, and physical constants took into account the dual orientation to engineering and pure science and were those accepted or recommended by international organizations such as the International Organization for Standardization.

NSRDS-NBS Publications:

As a component of the U.S. National Bureau of Standards-National Standard Reference Data Program (NBS-NSRDP), TPRC also prepares a series of more rigorous and critical reports giving recommended values of thermophysical properties of definable substances or systems. The research reports for NSRDP discuss in detail the considerations involved in arriving at the recommended values. The final report will be published in the NSRDS-NBS publication series. At present, two parts (NSRDS-NBS 8 and 16) have been issued of a final volume scheduled for publication in 1969. The volume will contain the critical analysis and recommendations of the thermal conductivity of all the elements.

Thermophysical Properties of High Temperature Solid Materials:

Coverage

TPRC updated and revised the *Handbook of Thermophysical Properties of Solid Materials* published by Macmillan in 1961. The new six-volume reference work (Macmillan, 1967) consists of nine books covering more than 1300 material groups including 14000 samples, and 3000 references. The general contents of the several volumes are as follows:

Volume 1 — Elements; Volume 2 — Nonferrous Alloys, Part I. Binary Alloys, Part II. Multiple Alloys; Volume 3 — Ferrous Alloys; Volume 4 — Oxides and their Solutions and Mixtures, Part I. Simple Oxygen Compounds and their Mixtures, Part II. Solutions and their Mixtures of Simple Oxygen Compounds, including Glasses and Ceramic Materials; Volume 5 — Monoxides and their Solutions and Mixtures, including Miscellaneous Ceramic Materials; Volume 6 — Intermetallics, Cermets, Polymers, and Composite Systems.

The 12 specific properties covered in each volume are: density, melting point, heat of fusion, heat of vaporization, heat of sublimation, electrical resistivity, specific heat at constant pressure, thermal conductivity, thermal diffusivity, thermal linear expansion, thermal radiative properties (absorptance, emittance, reflectance, and transmittance), and vapor pressure. Generally, only materials with melting points above 800 K are included, except for materials within the categories of polymers, plastics, and composites. A detailed discussion of the material classification procedure and a comprehensive Materials Index for the entire work is included at the end of each volume.

Analysis

In the preparation of *Thermophysical Properties of High Temperature Solid Materials*, major additions, corrections, and re-evaluation were extensive. The organization of the material and the index to materials have been redesigned completely for greater ease in locating the information desired.

Whenever possible, an effort was made to suggest recommended values of the properties. In the plots, recommended values are indicated by curves. The designation "recommended values", however, does not imply that a critical analysis has been performed in all cases, nor does it suggest that they represent definitive values. Because most of the materials covered are not well-defined engineering materials, and because there is often a lack of information, any critical evaluation of these data is difficult — if not impossible.

Publications

Thermophysical Properties Research Center Data Book. Issued semi-annually as loose-leaf sheets; Thermophysical Properties Research Center, Purdue University, Research Park, 2595 Yeager Road, West Lafayette, Indiana 47906. No longer available; is being superseded by "TPRC Series on Thermophysical Properties of Matter". Covered the following properties in each volume: thermal conductivity, viscosity, radiative properties, thermal diffusivity, and specific heat.

Vol. I: Metallic Elements and Their Alloys (In Solid, Liquid, or Gaseous State).

Vol. II: Nonmetallic Elements, Compounds and Mixtures (In Liquid or Gaseous State at Normal Temperature and Pressure).

Vol. III: Nonmetallic Elements, Compounds and Mixtures (in Solid State at Normal Temperature and Pressure).

TPRC Reports in the Standard Reference Data Series:

Thermal Conductivity of Selected Materials, R. W. POWELL, C. Y. HO, and P. E. LILEY, U.S. Government Printing Office, Washington, D.C. 20402,

Part 1, NSRDS-NBS 8, 1966, VIII, 168 pp, US $ 1.00.

Part 2, NSRDS-NBS 16, 1968, IX, 146 pp, US $ 2.00.

Thermophysical Properties of High Temperature Solid Materials, Y. S. TOULOUKIAN, Ed., Six Volumes (9 book set), The Macmillan Co., New York, Collier-Macmillan Ltd., London, 1967, 8500 pp, US $ 250.00 per set (also available by individual volumes). This work supersedes an earlier compilation (1960), by the Armour Research Foundation entitled *Handbook of Thermophysical Properties of Solid Materials,* published first as WADC TR 58-476 and as a hard bound set by the Macmillan Co.

Other publications

Thermophysical Properties Research Literature: A Retrieval Guide, 2nd ed, Y. S. TOULOUKIAN, J. K. GARRITSEN, and N. Y. MOORE, Eds., Plenum Press, New York, 1967, 2759 pp, US $ 275.00. This three-book volume provides access to the literature on the following 13 thermophysical properties: thermal conductivity (including accommodation coefficient and contact resistance), thermal diffusivity, diffusion coefficient, specific heat at constant pressure, viscosity, thermal radiative properties (including emissivity, reflectivity, absorptivity, transmissivity, optical constants) and Prandtl number.

This volume completes the coverage of the literature from 1920 (in some cases earlier) to July 1964. It is a consolidation of the material contained in two earlier volumes (*Retrieval Guide to Thermophysical Properties Research Literature,* Y. S. TOULOUKIAN, Ed., Vol. I, 1960, and Vol. II, 1964, McGraw-Hill Book Co., New York, each US $ 150.00) together with the material of a third volume which was not published separately.

3.4.21. Cryogenic Data Center

Organization

The Cryogenic Data Center was established in 1958 in the Cryogenics Division of the National Bureau of Standards (NBS), in Boulder, Colorado 80302. It is directed by VICTOR J. JOHNSON. The Data Center is primarily concerned with thermophysical property values of materials used in low temperature applications. It has two major types of activity: documentation, and data evaluation — including the correlation and publication of data. Related experimental work is carried on in the Cryogenics Division. The Data Compilation Unit is supervised by HANS M. RODER. The Center is a charter member of the Office of Standard Reference Data of NBS (see 1.1.1.) with the principal support for the data compilation effort being provided by the National Aeronautics and Space Administration.

Coverage

Data on cryogenic fluids and selected solids are compiled by the Center. Compilations are published in various ways, as journal articles, papers, charts, monographs, and technical notes. The fluids include helium, hydrogen in its various forms, neon, nitrogen, oxygen, air, carbon monoxide, fluorine, argon, methane, xenon, krypton, and mixtures of these fluids. Solids include metallic elements, selected alloys, and element dielectrics (solid state materials). Emphasis is on properties useful in engineering applications to cryogenic systems. The compilation program covers a number of thermodynamic, transport, and physicochemical properties (sometimes loosely referred to as thermophysical) in the temperature range from near absolute zero to 110 K, and when desirable and practical to 300 K (room temperature). Properties of fluids include pressure-volume-temperature relations, vapor pressure, saturation densities, isothermal compressibility, volume expansivity, entropy, enthalpy, internal energy, specific heats (C_p, C_v, C_{sat}), velocity of sound, thermal conductivity, viscosity, Prandtl Number, diffusion coefficients, thermal diffusion coefficients, dielectric constant, refractive index, dielectric breakdown, electrical resistivity, surface tension, magnetic properties, and optical properties. For solids, properties include: electrical resistivity, dielectric constant, thermal conductivity, thermal expansion, specific heat, and enthalpy.

In addition to data obtained from the primary literature, available unpublished data and original calculations are used. The literature is monitored on a continuing basis and a weekly bibliography, "Current Awareness Service", is produced. The Center's automated storage and retrieval system is also used to prepare specific bibliographies on request.

3.4.21.

One of the Center's first publications was the *Compendium of the Properties of Materials at Low Temperatures*, issued in 1960 to 1961. It covered the cryogenic fluids (see above) and pure metals, nonferrous and ferrous alloys, and inorganic and organic compounds. Many of the properties listed above were covered. Subsequent publications have expanded and refined the material and property coverage within the general scope of the initial compendium.

Analysis

The objectives are to present critically evaluated and internally consistent sets of data over wide ranges of temperature and pressure, and in particular for the cryogenic engineering ranges. Data are compared and evaluated by theoretical and statistical means. "Best values" thus selected are presented in tables and graphs. Sources of data, comments, and additional references are provided.

The metric system is used for the primary coordinates of graphs, but "English" or engineering units may be also shown as alternate coordinates. The symbols and terminology used for physical quantities are, in general, compatible with proposed international standards.

The various journal articles, papers, NBS Monographs and Technical Notes, and other publications are prepared in this manner. The Compendium of the Properties of Materials at Low Temperatures, however, was prepared to fill a specific and urgent need for cryogenic engineering data, and was directed primarily to the design engineer. There are no plans to update or revise the Compendium, and since its publication, new or revised data on one or several substances have been issued — mainly as NBS Technical Notes and journal articles. Plans include publication of more comprehensive compilations as NBS Monographs.

Publications

The Cryogenic Data Center has issued a large number of publications; the major data compilations, and examples of other publications are listed here. Information on services (such as literature searches) and publications such as NBS Technical Notes, Monographs, papers, journal articles, and thermodynamic charts is available from the Cryogenic Data Center, NBS, Boulder, Colorado 80302.

A Compendium of the Properties of Materials at Low Temperatures, standard size looseleaf sheets. Available from the Clearinghouse for Federal Scientific and Technical Information, U.S. Dept. of Commerce, Springfield, Virginia 22151, as follows:

Phase I, Part I, Properties of Fluids, V. J. Johnson, Ed., July 1960, 489 pp, WADD Technical Report 60-56, Part I (PB-171-618), US $ 6.00.

Phase I, Part II, Properties of Solids, V. J. Johnson, Ed., Oct. 1960, 330 pp, WADD Technical Report 60-56, Part II (PB-171-619), US $ 4.00.

Phase I, Part III, Bibliography of References (cross-indexed), V. J. Johnson, Ed., Oct. 1960, 161 pp, WADD Technical Report 60-56, Part III (PB-171-620), US $ 3.00.

Phase II, Part IV, R. B. Stewart and V. J. Johnson, Eds., Dec. 1961, 501 pp, WADD Technical Report 60-56, Part IV (AD-272-769), US $ 8.10.

NBS Technical Notes and Monographs

The Thermodynamic Properties of Nitrogen From 64 to 300 °K Between 0.1 and 200 Atmospheres, NBS Technical Note 129, (PB-161-630), T. R. Strobridge, Jan. 1962, 85 pp, US $ 2.25. Available from the Clearinghouse for Federal Scientific and Technical Information, Springfield, Virginia 22151.

The Thermodynamic Properties of Helium From 3 to 300 °K Between 0.5 and 100 Atmospheres, NBS Technical Note 154, D. B. Mann, U.S. Government Printing Office (GPO*), Washington, D.C. 20402, 1962, 95 pp, US $ 0.50.

Thermodynamic Property Values for Gaseous and Liquid Carbon Monoxide From 70 to 300 °K With Pressures to 300 Atmospheres, NBS Technical Note 202, J. G. Hust and R. B. Stewart, GPO*, Washington, D.C. 20402, Nov. 1963, 105 pp, US $ 0.60.

Thermodynamic and Related Properties of Parahydrogen From the Triple Point to 100 °K at Pressures to 340 Atmospheres, NBS Monograph 94, H. M. Roder, L. A. Weber, and R. D. Goodwin, GPO*, Washington, D.C. 20402, Aug. 1965, 112 pp, US $ 0.75.

Thermodynamic Properties of Argon from the Triple Point to 300 °K at Pressures to 1000 Atmospheres, NSRDS-NBS 27, A. L. Gosman, in press.

Other Publications

Cryogenic Data Center Current Awareness Service, Cryogenic Data Center, National Bureau of Standards, Boulder, Colorado 80302. Weekly, subscription price: US $ 15.00 U.S. and Canada, US $ 20.00 elsewhere (includes airmail).

3.4.22. Molten Salts Data Center

Organization

The Molten Salts Data Center was formally established in 1961 by George J. Janz in the Department of Chemistry of the School of Science at Rensselaer Polytechnic Institute, Troy, New York 12181. Pre-doctoral and post-doctoral researchers in molten salts at Rensselaer have aided Professor Janz in maintaining a cumulative data file on this subject. Support has been provided by several government agencies. The Office of Standard Reference Data, National Bureau of Standards (see 1.1.1.) has been a supporter since 1965.

3.4.22.

Coverage

Inorganic compounds in the molten state are covered. Properties included are: electrical conductance, viscosity, density, surface tension, and emf (formation cells). Additional physical properties will be considered.

The compilation of numerical data concerning molten salts is the primary function of the center. Auxiliary activities include literature searching and information retrieval, and upgrading of available data. Computerized information storage and retrieval is being implemented.

Publications ranging from bibliographies to critically evaluated numerical data compilations have been issued.

Analysis

The Molten Salts Data Center produces bibliographies, and both non-critically and critically evaluated data compilations. The work being done for the NSRDS emphasizes the critical evaluation of data, with some effort also devoted to upgrading present data.

NSRDS work is exemplified by *Molten Salts: Volume 1, Electrical Conductance, Density, and Viscosity Data*, the result of a critical assessment made of data compiled from the literature up to Dec. 1966. The choice of recommended values, uncertainties, symbols and units, and work done on the compounds included are well covered in the introductory sections.

The Bibliography on Molten Salts covered both the field of molten salts and high temperature chemistry. Published in early 1961, the edition covered the literature through 1960.

The Molten Salts Handbook is in general a compilation of numerical data taken directly from the source material, without much editing. It is divided into six sections: physical properties, thermodynamic properties, electrochemical properties, spectroscopy and structure, practical features, and experimental techniques. Because of the present state of molten salt work, this policy has the virtue of focusing attention on problem areas. Data in the handbook critically evaluated by the Center include the properties of density, viscosity, surface tension, refractive index, and electrical conductance for various compounds as single salt melts. References follow individual tables; those references given most weight are indicated.

A compilation of critically evaluated surface tension data is in press. This publication will include some 106 compounds and will be issued in the National Standard Reference Data Program publication series (NSRDS).

190

Publications

Bibliography on Molten Salts, 2nd ed, G. J. JANZ, Rensselaer Polytechnic Institute, Troy, New York, 1961, IV, 173 pp.

Survey of Non-Aqueous Conductance Data, G. J. JANZ, F. J. KELLY, and H. V. VEN-KATASETTY, Rensselaer Polytechnic Institute, Troy, New York, 1962, III, 51 pp.

Molten Salt Data: Electrical Conductance, Density, and Viscosity, G. J. JANZ, A. T. WARD, and R. D. REEVES, Rensselaer Polytechnic Institute, Troy, New York, 1964, III, 180 pp.

Molten Salts Handbook, G. J. JANZ, Academic Press, New York-London, 1967, XII, 588 pp, US $ 25.00.

Molten Salts: Volume 1, Electrical Conductance, Density, and Viscosity Data, NSRDS-NBS 15, G. J. JANZ, F. W. DAMPIER, G. R. LAKSHMINARAYANAN, P. K. LORENZ, and R. P. T. TOMKINS, U.S. Government Printing Office, Washington, D.C. 20402, 1968, VI, 139 pp, US $ 3.00.

Solution Properties

3.4.23. Seidell's Solubilities of Inorganic, Metal-Organic, and Organic Compounds

Organization

ATHERTON SEIDELL's famous compilationseries on solubilities first appeared in 1907. The second edition was published in 1919; and the third, in 1940 and 1941. A supplement to the third edition appeared in 1952. Volume I of the fourth edition, under the authorship of W. F. LINKE, was published in 1958 and Volume II in 1965. Volume III, "Solubilities of Organic Compounds", is in preparation under the authorship of ALAN F. CLIFFORD and GERALD W. DULANEY. In 1943 Dr. SEIDELL assigned the copyright to the American Chemical Society (ACS), which assumed responsibility for publication of later volumes.

Coverage

Substances include elements and inorganic, metal-organic, and organic compounds for which solubility data are found in the literature. Volume I of the fourth edition covers the elements and their inorganic compounds from argon (Ar) through iridium (Ir); Volume II covers the solubilities of the elements and compounds from potassium (K) through zirconium (Zr).

Properties include solubilities in water, acids, bases, salts, aqueous solvents, non-aqueous solvents, and fused salts. Phase diagrams are given for some systems. References, but no values, are given for the solubility of gases in metals. Solubility products sometimes are given.

191

3.4.23.

For the earlier editions, the primary journals were scanned. For the fourth edition, Chemical Abstracts was used for locating new data which were then extracted from the primary publications.

Analysis

The tables of data were compiled and evaluated from the results of various authors. Closely agreeing results sometimes were averaged; unreliable results were omitted. If there was no clear choice between conflicting sets of data, both sets were included. Remarks accompanying most entries provide further information and some evaluation of the data. Because of the diversity of sources, investigators, and methodology, the presentation and quality of data vary. The source of the data is generally indicated, and an author index gives complete references by year.

Volume I of the fourth edition was published in 1958 and covers the literature through 1956. Volume II was released in February 1965 and covers the literature through the early 1960's. Publication of the organic volume is expected in 1970, or soon thereafter, and will be followed as soon as practical by a fifth edition.

The offset printing is clear but in the indexes suffers from overreduction. Elements are listed alphabetically by their chemical symbols, and their compounds are listed alphabetically according to the chemical symbols of their anions or radicals. Volume II of the fourth edition contains cumulative indexes covering Volumes I and II for subjects and literature cited or author index.

Publications

D. Van Nostrand Company, Inc., published this compilation until 1943, when the copyright was assigned to the ACS. The books were then published by the ACS but still distributed by Van Nostrand. Since 1965 they have been both published and distributed by the ACS.

Solubilities of Inorganic and Metal Organic Compounds, A Compilation of Quantitative Solubility Data from the Periodical Literature, 3rd ed, A. SEIDELL, Vol. I, 4th printing, Van Nostrand Co., New York, 1953, IV, 1698 pp (out of print).

Solubilities of Organic Compounds, A Compilation of Quantitative Solubility Data from the Periodical Literature, 3rd ed, A. SEIDELL, Vol. II, 4th printing, Van Nostrand Co., New York, 1941, VI, 926 pp (out of print).

Solubilities of Inorganic and Organic Compounds, A Compilation of Solubility Data from the Periodical Literature, Supplement to the 3rd ed, A. SEIDELL, W. F. LINKE, with sections by A. W. FRANCIS and R. G. BATES, Van Nostrand Co., New York, 1952, IV, 1254 pp (out of print).

Solubilities of Inorganic and Metal-Organic Compounds, Seidell, A Compilation of Solubility Data from the Periodical Literature, 4th ed, W. F. LINKE, Vol. I, A—Ir, American Chemical Society, 1155 16th St., N.W., Washington, D.C. 20036, 1958, IV, 1487 pp, US $ 32.50.

Solubilities of Inorganic and Metal-Organic Compounds, Seidell, A Compilation of Solubility Data from the Periodical Literature, 4th ed, W. F. LINKE, Vol. II, K—Z, American Chemical Society, 1155 16th St., N.W., Washington, D.C. 20036, 1965, IV, 1914 pp, US $ 32.50.

Solubilities of Organic Compounds, Seidell, A Compilation of Solubility Data from the Periodical Literature, 4th ed, A. F. CLIFFORD, and G. W. DULANEY, Vol. III, American Chemical Society, 1155 16th St., N.W., Washington, D.C. 20036, in preparation.

3.4.24. Stability Constants of Metal-Ion Complexes

Organization

The first edition of *Stability Constants of Metal-Ion Complexes, with Solubility Products of Inorganic Substances*, was compiled by J. BJERRUM of the Københavns Universitet, Copenhagen (Denmark), G. SCHWARZENBACH of Eidgenössische Technische Hochschule, Zürich (Switzerland), and L.G. SILLÉN, Kungliga Tekniska Högskolon, Stockholm (Sweden), under the auspices of the Commission on Equilibrium Data of the International Union of Pure and Applied Chemistry. It was published by The Chemical Society, London. The second edition, published in 1964, was compiled by Professor SILLÉN, and A. E. MARTELL, Texas A & M University, College Station, Texas.

Coverage

Soluble as well as solid complexes of both organic and inorganic ligands are covered. Acid dissociation constants of the ligands are recorded by including the hydrogen ion among the metals as one of the cations with which the ligands associate. Redox equilibria are represented by including the electron as a ligand, and hydrolysis of the metallic ions is described by regarding the hydroxyl ion as one of the ligands.

Equilibrium constants are given, expressed as logarithms to the base 10. They include those for reactions of ligands with "metal" ions, for acidic and basic reactions both stepwise and cumulative, for redox and special reactions, and for solubility constants. The minimum number of constants necessary to represent the author's results is given; as a rule, enthalpy and entropy changes are often recorded. Some equilibrium constants for liquid-liquid distribution are given.

Data are compiled from the primary literature; a few private communications are used.

3.4.25.

Analysis

All available values are recorded; doubtful values are indicated. No attempt was made to select best values. The compilers state that doubtful values could have been indicated more frequently in a critical compilation. The method of measurement, temperature, medium, and coded references are given for each entry with a list of complete references following each table.

The abbreviations and symbols used to describe the media in which the measurements are made are explained in the introductory material and are consistent with IUPAC recommendations.

The 1964 edition includes all available data published to the end of 1960, some that appeared in 1961 to 1963, and a few data omitted in the first edition. A supplement to the 2nd edition is being prepared.

The data are published in book form, 18.6×25.6 cm, in six-column tables, the form and content of which are adequately described in an introductory section, "How to Use the Tables". An index of inorganic ligands and an index of organic ligands are arranged alphabetically by names and an index of metals is arranged alphabetically by symbols.

Publications

Stability Constants of Metal-Ion Complexes, with Solubility Products of Inorganic Substances, JANNIK BJERRUM, GEROLD SCHWARZENBACH, and LARS GUNNAR SILLÉN, The Chemical Society, London.

> Part I: Organic Ligands, Special Publication No. 6, 1957, XVI, 105 pp (out of print).
> Part 2: Inorganic Ligands with Solubility Products of Inorganic Substances, Special Publication No. 7, 1958, XVI, 131 pp (out of print).

Stability Constants of Metal-Ion Complexes, 2nd ed, Section I: Inorganic Ligands, LARS GUNNAR SILLÉN; Section II: Organic Ligands, ARTHUR E. MARTELL; Special Publication No. 17, The Chemical Society, London, 1964, XVIII, 754 pp, US $ 23.00.

3.4.25. Dissociation Constants of Acids and Bases

Organization

The tables of dissociation constants of acids and bases are the results of a program of the Commission on Electroanalytical Chemistry (before 1963: Electrochemical Data), Analytical Chemistry Division, of the International Union of Pure and Applied Chemistry (IUPAC). Two compilations have been published: one on organic acids in aqueous solution in 1961, and a companion volume on organic bases in aqueous solution in 1965. Both volumes were prepared by members of the Commission: GUSTAV KORTÜM,

194

University of Tübingen, Tübingen, Germany, for the work on acids, and D. D. PERRIN, The Australian National University, Canberra, Australia, for the work on bases. A compilation of dissociation constants of inorganic acids and bases in aqueous solution is anticipated in 1969, and further compilations in related areas are under study.

Coverage

The compilation of these tables was a part of the Commission's task of collecting reliable data of general interest, especially analytical, and subsequently of making the data readily accessible.

The first volume, *Dissociation Constants of Organic Acids in Aqueous Solution* covers aliphatic, alicyclic, and aromatic carboxylic acids, and phenolic and sulfonic, phosphoric, phosphonic, and phosphinic acids. *Dissociation Constants of Organic Bases in Aqueous Solution* covers the conjugate acids of organic bases: aliphatic, alicyclic, aromatic, and heterocyclic bases up to five rings with one heteroatom, and also natural products, and a few other types of bases.

Both volumes, including the tables, are arranged in the same format. The tables include the name, chemical formula, thermodynamic dissociation constant, the temperature, range of concentrations, and the method of measurement, evaluation procedure and any corrections used. Also given are the reliability of the value, and a literature reference.

For the work on acids, the literature of the period 1927 through 1956 was searched; for bases, through 1961.

Analysis

The Commission's objective of collecting reliable data has entailed exhaustive literature searching and critical evaluation of the data. All data in these compilations have been critically evaluated and assigned a measure of reliability. For the acids, four grades, and for the bases, three grades are used, based on the estimated uncertainty of the value of the dissociation constant. In the volume on acids, the introduction presents a thorough discussion of dissociation constants, experimental variables, and the methods of measurement and the procedure for evaluating the quality of the measurement. The volume on bases uses the same format and symbols and provides information on using the tables. Although this volume can be used independently, the reader is referred to the volume on acids for a discussion of the methods of measurement and the other considerations noted above. Both volumes have a reference section and an index of compounds arranged alphabetically.

3.4.26.

Publications

Dissociation Constants of Organic Acids in Aqueous Solution, G. KORTÜM, W. VOGEL, and K. ANDRUSSOW, Butterworths, London, 1961, 340 pp, US $ 7.50, distributed in the U.S.A. by Plenum Press, New York. Also published in *Pure Appl. Chem.* **1**, 187-536 (33 pp index), (1961).

Dissociation Constants of Organic Bases in Aqueous Solution, D. D. PERRIN, Butterworths, London, 1965, 515 pp, US $ 28.00, distributed in U.S.A. by Plenum Press, New York.

3.4.26. Tables de Constantes Sélectionnées, Volume 8

Potentiels d'Oxydo-Réduction by G. CHARLOT, D. BÉZIER, and J. COURTOT, Volume 8 of Tables de Constantes et Données Numériques, Constantes Sélectionnées, Pergamon Press, Paris, London, and New York, 1958, 44 pp, 21.60 F (US $ 5.00).

Organization

Professor CHARLOT, the senior author of this small volume is at l'Ecole Supérieure de Physique et de Chimie de Paris. The work was done under the auspices of the Commission on Electrochemical Data (cf 3.4.25.) of the Section of Analytical Chemistry of the International Union of Pure and Applied Chemistry (IUPAC). The program "Tables de Constantes et Données Numériques" is described in 2.2.

Coverage

Electrode potentials are given for a large number of inorganic half-cell reactions in aqueous media. Many of the values given are for unit activity of the concerned species. When activities of one or more of the species involved differ from unity the conditions are specified. The data are arranged in tables which give the cell reaction, potential value, molality, medium, method of measurement or estimation, and references.

Analysis

This volume aims to be a useful tool for the analytical chemist. Some of the values are of the highest precision (indicated by the number of significant figures) but others are of lower accuracy. Some values are not those found in the literature but are averages. The literature references of doubtful value have been eliminated. The authors have been careful to follow IUPAC recommendations regarding signs, symbols, and nomenclature.

Indexes to Compilations

3.4.27. Consolidated Index of Selected Property Values

Physical Chemistry and Thermodynamics, Publication 976, National Academy of Sciences-National Research Council Printing and Publishing Office, 2101 Constitution Avenue, N.W., Washington, D.C. 20418, 1962, XXIII, 274 pp, clothbound, US $ 6.00. Prepared by the Office of Critical Tables, it is a key to the contents of six compilations that present critically evaluated numerical property values. These are 3.4.1., 3.4.2., 3.4.3., 3.4.5., 3.4.9., and 5.3.38.

3.5. Properties Relating to Chemical Reaction Rates

Chemical Kinetics

3.5.1. Chemical Kinetics Information Center

Organization

The Chemical Kinetics Information Center is located in the Institute for Basic Standards of the National Bureau of Standards (NBS), Washington, D.C. 20234. DAVID GARVIN directs the project, staffed by one full-time and four part-time professional staff members, plus supporting clerical personnel. The Chemical Kinetics Information Center was begun in 1963 as the successor to the Chemical Kinetics Data Project, directed by CHARLES H. STAUFFER of St. Lawrence University. The latter project was established in the 1940's at Princeton University under the direction of the late Professor N. THON. The Information Center is a part of the National Standard Reference Data System (NSRDS, see 1.1.1.), NBS, and is supported by the NBS Office of Standard Reference Data and other government agencies.

Coverage

Fields covered by the Information Center are: rates of homogeneous chemical reactions in gaseous, liquid and solid phases, photochemistry, and inelastic scattering. Information sources include journals, title announcements, abstracts, unpublished reports, and bibliographies from NSRDS reviews. An up-to-date file of information will be maintained by the Information Center.

The original Chemical Kinetics Data Project produced several publications. These covered homogeneous inorganic and organic reactions in the gaseous, liquid, and solid phases. Values were included for rate constants, frequency factors, and heats, energies, and entropies of activation.

3.5.2.

Analysis

The Chemical Kinetics Information Center was set up to supply bibliographies on kinetic data to the public, to centralize and coordinate the analysis of kinetic data within NBS, and to provide bibliographies for critical reviews in the NSRDS series. Two such reviews are: *Tables of Bimolecular Gas Reactions*, NSRDS-NBS 9, by A. F. TROTMAN-DICKENSON and G. S. MILNE (see 3.5.2.); and *Gas Phase Reaction Kinetics of Neutral Oxygen Species*, NSRDS-NBS 20, by H. S. JOHNSTON (see 3.5.5.).

The Chemical Kinetics Data Project publications stressed experimentally determined values. When possible, values were selected; otherwise, closely agreeing data were averaged and less concordant data given side by side to indicate the reproducibility of the rate of reactions. Additional information is sometimes given.

Publications

(Chemical Kinetics Data Project)

Tables of Chemical Kinetics, Homogeneous Reactions, NBS Circular 510, N. THON, Ed., U.S. Government Printing Office, Washington, D.C. 20402, 1951, XXIV, 732 pp, US $ 4.00 (out of print).

Tables of Chemical Kinetics, Homogeneous Reactions, Supplement 1 to NBS C 510, C. H. STAUFFER, project director, U.S. Government Printing Office, Washington, D.C. 20402, 1956, XIV, 422 pp, US $ 3.25 (out of print).

Alphabetical Index to Tables of Chemical Kinetics, Homogeneous Reactions, Supplement 2 to NBS C 510, C. H. STAUFFER, project director, U.S. Government Printing Office, Washington, D.C. 20402, 1960, IV, 37 pp, US $ 0.35.

Tables of Chemical Kinetics, Homogeneous Reactions, NBS Monograph 34, Supplementary Tables, C. H. STAUFFER, project director, U.S. Government Printing Office, Washington, D.C. 20402, 1961, VIII, 459 pp, US $ 2.75.

Tables of Chemical Kinetics, Homogeneous Reactions, NBS Monograph 34, Vol. 2, Supplementary Tables, C. H. STAUFFER, project director, U.S. Government Printing Office, Washington, D.C. 20402, 1964, VI, 264 pp, US $ 2.00.

3.5.2. National Standard Reference Data System, NSRDS-NBS 9

Tables of Bimolecular Gas Reactions, NSRDS-NBS 9, A. F. TROTMAN-DICKENSON and G. S. MILNE, U.S. Government Printing Office, Washington, D.C. 20402, 1967, VI, 129 pp, US $ 2.00.

Organization

This compilation was prepared by A. F. TROTMAN-DICKENSON, U.K., and G. S. MILNE, U.K., at the Edward Davies Chemical Laboratory, Aberystwyth, Wales, under the auspices of the Office of Standard Reference Data, National Bureau of Standards (NBS), described in 1.1.1.

Coverage

Bimolecular reactions, defined as "reactions in which two molecules are involved as reactants, that yield two or more molecules as products", are covered. These include atom reactions (H, F, Cl, Br, I, S, Na, and K); radicals with up to four carbon atoms; miscellaneous carbon-containing radicals; inorganic radicals; and radical-radical, as well as molecule-molecule, reactions. A table of termolecular reactions is also given.

Kinetic properties covered are: activation energy, $\log_{10} A$, $\log_{10} k$, temperature range (°C), and ratios of rate constants, including equilibrium constants. Other information given includes reactants, radical source, references, and notes.

The primary literature was searched through December 1965, and, where possible, data published to August 1966 were included. The Chemical Kinetics Information Center (see 3.5.1.) provided bibliographic references. International conventions for symbols and nomenclature were followed.

Analysis

Experimental work in this area has not progressed to the point where critical evaluation of the data is meaningful. This publication is, as a result, a compilation of all data found in the literature. Although, as the authors note, recommended Arrhenius values are given where possible, most indications of quality are provided in the "Notes", and, in relatively fewer cases, by uncertainties printed with the data. Also, cross referencing of the data gives the user sources of further information.

The introductory section includes a brief discussion of the area, the errors involved, and the use of the tables.

3.5.3. National Standard Reference Data System, NSRDS-NBS 13

Hydrogenation of Ethylene on Metallic Catalysts, NSRDS-NBS 13, JURO HORIUTI and KOSHIRO MIYAHARA, U. S. Government Printing Office, Washington, D. C. 20402, 1968, 62 pp, US $ 1.00.

Organization

This publication was prepared at the Research Institute for Catalysis, Hokkaido University, Sapporo, Japan, with the financial support of the Office of Standard Reference Data of the National Bureau of Standards (NBS, see 1.1.1.).

3.5.4.

Coverage

The hydrogenation of ethylene on unsupported metallic catalysts, in particular the evaporated films of pure metals, is examined in detail. Supported catalysts are also considered, but more for comparison purposes.

The major table of numerical data is "Reaction Kinetics of Catalyzed Hydrogenation of Ethylene" in which the following information is given: reaction, metal (Ni, Pt, Pd, Rh, Ru, Cu, Fe, alloys, NaH, LiH, Ta hydride, and CaH_2), form, preparation, pretreatment, reaction temperature (°C), initial pressure of ethylene and hydrogen, modes of measurement, rate law, optimum temperature, and activation heat (kcal · mol^{-1}). The publication includes some 29 graphs and 29 tables of data.

The authors review the state-of-the-art of this reaction by discussing in detail the experimental data reported in the literature, the observed kinetics, and the various attempts to formulate a reaction mechanism.

Most references are to the primary literature; a number are from 1966.

Analysis

This publication is a critical review of the reaction kinetics data of the catalyzed hydrogenation of ethylene. Unsupported metals enhance the possibility of correlating the catalytic activity of the catalyst with its characteristics. On the basis of this evaluation, the authors develop an associative mechanism which satisfies the observed conditions.

There are several major tables, but the greater part is discussion of the experimental methods and data, catalytic activity of various pure metals and alloys, the reaction kinetics, and other fundamental considerations in this field. Some uncertainties are given in the tables of data; discussions of the reliability of data are included in the text.

3.5.4. Tables de Constantes Sélectionnées, Volume 13

Radiolytic Yields by M. HAISSINSKY and M. MAGAT (with 11 collaborators). Volume 13 of Tables of Constants and Numerical Data, Selected Constants, Pergamon Press, Paris, 1963, 217 pp, F 114 (US $ 25.50).

Organization

This volume was published under the auspices of "Tables de Constantes et Données Numériques", described in 2.2. It was prepared by M. HAISSINSKY and M. MAGAT, both of the Faculté des Sciences de Paris, with the aid of a staff of 11 scientific workers.

Coverage

This volume deals with the chemical effects of ionizing radiations. The radiolytic yields are expressed in G units — the number of molecules, ions, or radicals, formed or destroyed per 100 eV of absorbed energy. The substances included are inorganic compounds in the gas, liquid, and solid states and in aqueous solution, and organic compounds including polymers. Results for a number of mixed systems are presented. Each entry gives information on the nature of ionizing radiation, dose rate when available, temperature, pressure, references, and brief remarks.

Analysis

The authors have critically reviewed about 1500 papers ranging from 1905 to 1961. To the extent possible, data from the original papers have been conformed to a uniform mode of presentation. For example, early results expressed in terms for M/N (molecules transformed per pair of ions produced) have been transformed to G units when appropriate, and monomer disappearance rates have been replaced by radical yields $G(R°)$. Single values have been given for particular systems when a critical selection among several values was possible. As with other volumes of this series, introductory and explanatory material is given in French and English. Substances are indexed by formulas and alphabetically by name. The extensive bibliography is supplemented by an alphabetical author index. Data were obtained from the primary literature.

3.5.5. National Standard Reference Data System, NSRDS-NBS 20

Gas Phase Reaction Kinetics of Neutral Oxygen Species, NSRDS-NBS 20, H. S. JOHNSTON, U.S. Government Printing Office, Washington, D.C. 20402, 1968, VI, 49 pp, US $ 0.45.

Organization

This publication was prepared at the University of California, Berkeley, California, with the support of the Office of Standard Reference Data of the National Bureau of Standards (NBS, see 1.1.1.), and other government agencies. The Chemical Kinetics Information Center, NBS (see 3.5.1.), provided an extensive set of reprints.

Coverage

Reactions among neutral oxygen species, oxygen atoms, oxygen molecules, and ozone are covered. The data compiled from the literature were critically evaluated and selected values for rates of reaction are given for:

$$O_2 + M \rightarrow O + O + M \text{ —— } (M = O_2, Ar)$$
$$O + O + M \rightarrow O_2 + M \text{ —— } (M = O_2)$$
$$O_3 + M \rightarrow O + O_2 + M \text{ —— } (M = O_2, O_3, He, Ar, N_2, CO_2)$$
$$O + O_2 + M \rightarrow O_3 + M \text{ —— } (M = O_2 \ O_3, He, Ar, N_2, CO_2)$$
$$O + O_3 \rightarrow O_2 + O_2$$
$$O + O_2 \rightarrow O + O_2 \text{ (isotopic exchange)}$$

Most references are from the primary literature, including some from 1967.

Analysis

This publication is a critical review. Values given for rates of reactions, enumerated above, are the result of a critical analysis. The original data and the recommendations are presented in graphs and tables. The review also includes discussions of the important factors and considerations involved in these reactions.

3.6. Miscellaneous Projects and Their Publications

Gas Chromatographic Data

3.6.1. Gas Chromatographic Data Committee of Japan

Organization

The Gas Chromatographic Data Committee (GCDC) of Japan was organized in 1961 by the Japan Society for Analytical Chemistry. The chairman of the Committee, which comprises fifteen members, is TADAO SHIBA, president of the Tokyo Institute of Technology, Tokyo, Japan. This compilation project is an independent activity, carried out by the members of the Committee.

Coverage

Data covered are gas chromatograms and retention data: retention time, retention volume, and relative retention or retention index. In general, substances covered are volatile organic compounds.

Publication of the data is in the form of edge-notched punched cards. Some 7000 had been issued as of December 1968.

Information on one side of the card includes the literature reference, experimental conditions, classification of stationary phases, group type classification of sample components by chemical and industrial groupings, C-number, temperature, etc. On the reverse side are a tracing of the gas chromatogram and/or retention data, presented as graphs or tables. Most of this information is punched for retrieval by sorting.

The data are obtained through searching the primary literature. Nearly one hundred journals from Japan and other nations are used.

Analysis

The Gas Chromatographic Data Committee was organized to standardize the presentation of gas chromatographic data and to publish an authoritative collection of these data. The Committee itself collects and evaluates the data for publication, as well as conforming them to certain editorial standards.

Publications

Gas Chromatographic Data Cards, Gas Chromatographic Data Committee of Japan, published by Physico-chemical Data Association, Ltd; Agent: Sanyo Shuppan Boeki Co., Inc., Tokyo, Japan, 1968, 7000 cards available at US $ 240.00 per 1000 cards. Available in the U.S.A. from Preston Technical Abstracts Co., 909 Pitner Avenue, Evanston, Illinois 60202; in Europe from Heyden & Son Ltd., London N.W. 4, England.

3.6.2. Gas Chromatographic Data Compilation

Organization

This project was initiated in the early 1960's by the Gas Chromatography Subcommittee of the Tennessee Eastman Company Analytical Committee. Subsequently, the American Society for Testing and Materials (ASTM) became the sponsor through its Committee E-19 on Gas Chromatography. ASTM is a technical society interested in the promotion of knowledge of the materials of engineering, the standardization of specifications, and methods of testing. Its address is 1916 Race Street, Philadelphia, Pennsylvania 19103.

Coverage

Gas chromatographic data are compiled and tabulations published. The first edition of *Compilation of Gas Chromatographic Data* published in 1963 was followed by a second edition in 1967. The first edition included some 2000 compounds with the following information: liquid phase, reference material, solid support, column temperature (°C), and relative retention. This edition is no longer available.

The second edition covers some 3800 compounds, and in addition to the information listed above, gives retention indices and capacity ratios. This edition has nine tables. The two major ones are tables of gas chromatographic data. Others include codes for computer operations, reference materials, and the Coden abbreviations for journal titles.

Most of the data in both editions are from the published literature; some are unpublished results from laboratories of Eastman Kodak Company, Tennessee Eastman Company and Lockheed-California Co. The second edition benefitted from a literature search program being conducted at the University of Rochester. This edition includes references to gas chromatographic literature through 1965.

Analysis

Although gas chromatographic data are not amenable to rigorous critical analysis, the data in the second edition, *Gas Chromatographic Data Compilation*, were examined by computer analysis. As a result, some data were improved and some deleted.

Publications

Gas Chromatographic Data Compilation, O. E. Schupp III and J. S. Lewis, Eds., DS 25 A, American Society for Testing and Materials (ASTM, 1916 Race Street), Philadelphia, 1967, 740 pp, US $ 40.00 (20% discount to ASTM members).

Other Publications

Gas Chromatographic Data-Punched Card Index,

DS25-1a	Name Formula	4610 cards	US $ 276.00
DS25-1b	Data-bibliography	22,940 cards	US $ 1380.00
DS25-1d	Data-name	21,028 cards	US $ 1260.00
Unpunched cards		2,000 cards	US $ 6.50

Optical Properties

3.6.3. Tables de Constantes Sélectionnées, Volume 14

Optical Rotatory Power, I.a — Steroids by J. Jacques, H. Kagan, G. Ourisson, and S. Allard. Volume 14 of Tables of Constants and Numerical Data, Selected Constants, Pergamon Press, Paris, 1965, 1031 pp, F 258.

Organization

This compilation is a revision of Volume I of a series of four on optical rotatory power, published under the auspices of "Tables de Constantes et Données Numériques", described in 2.2. It was prepared by J. JACQUES, Centre National de la Recherche Scientifique, Paris, H. KAGAN, Laboratoire au Collège de France, and G. OURISSON, Faculté des Sciences de Strasbourg. Contributions were received from workers in Australia, Canada, Germany, Japan, Switzerland, the U.K., and the U.S.A.

Coverage

This volume updates and supersedes *Optical Rotatory Power, I. — Steroids* of this series. It covers 20000 compounds compared to 8000 in the 1956 edition. For each compound there are given the empirical formula, systematic chemical name, the melting point, molecular weight, solvent, the concentration and temperature to the extent known, the wavelength of the radiation, and the specific rotation. The source references are also given.

Analysis

All textual material is given in French and English. Particular attention is given to nomenclature which is discussed at some length in the introduction, IUPAC rules being followed when available. Care is taken in indicating structures; early errors of structure assignment pointed out in the literature are noted. The data of this field are in general not highly precise. The authors assign tolerances, sometimes wide, when literature values disagree.

Worthy of special note are: (1) a complete list of references through 1963 arranged by years, and within each year alphabetically by journal and for each journal alphabetically by author; (2) an alphabetical author index; and (3) a complete substance index incorporating both systematic and trivial names.

3.6.4. Tables de Constantes Sélectionnées, Volume 9

Optical Rotatory Power, II. — Triterpenes by J.-P. MATHIEU and G. OURISSON. Volume 9 of Tables of Constants and Numerical Data, Selected Constants, Pergamon Press, Paris, 1958, 302 pp, F 93.60 (US $ 21.00).

Organization

This volume is number II in a series of four on optical rotatory power published under "Tables de Constantes et Données Numériques", described

3.6.5.

in 2.2. The compilation was prepared by J.-P. MATHIEU, the originator of this series, Faculté des Sciences de Paris, and G. OURISSON, Faculté des Sciences de Strasbourg, with nine collaborators.

Coverage

This volume presents specific rotation values, $[\alpha]_D$, for over 3000 triterpenes both naturally occurring and synthetic. In the tables, which have pages ordered by increasing number of carbon atoms in the empirical formula, there are given in addition to $[\alpha]_D$, a systematic name, solvent, concentration, temperature, and a key to references.

Analysis

As is usual for data on natural products, and relatively large molecules in general, the purity factor prevents a high level of agreement among values obtained by different workers. The authors recognize this fact. Another difficulty is the assignment of a correct structure and particularly the correct designation of active centers for each molecule. To minimize this problem the authors have, in the Introduction, explained at length the nomenclature system used and have conformed all names in the tables to this system. Readers are cautioned about the uncertainty of some structural assignments. The user is helped by the 90 page substance index which lists many trivial and outdated names in addition to the systematic names.

The primary literature was searched through 1957. Some 1958 references are included.

3.6.5. Tables de Constantes Sélectionnées, Volume 10

Optical Rotatory Power, III. — Amino-acids by J.-P. MATHIEU, P. DESNUELLE, and J. ROCHE. Volume 10 of Tables of Constants and Numerical Data, Selected Constants, Pergamon Press, Paris, 1959, 61 pp, F 28 (US $ 6.50).

Organization

This volume is number III in a series of four on optical rotatory power published under the auspices of "Tables de Constantes et Données Numériques", described in 2.2. The compilation was prepared by J.-P. MATHIEU, the originator of this series, Faculté des Sciences de Paris, P. DESNUELLE, Faculté des Sciences de Marseille, and J. ROCHE, Collège de France.

Coverage

Specific rotation values are given in tabular form for 167 amino-acids which are those elaborated by nature and occurring frequently in proteins and peptides. For many of the compounds data are given at a number of values of pH. In each entry there are given the nature of the aqueous medium, the concentration and temperature of the measurements, the specific rotation for the wavelength used, and a key to the literature reference.

Analysis

The authors have attempted to be selective in a field in which wide variations exist in reported parameters. Several references given for one value of specific rotation implies agreement among the investigators. References enclosed by double parentheses refer to papers containing questionable data. In the preface it is stated that ". . . the optical rotation of proteins . . . has emerged as a powerful tool for the elucidation of the configuration of peptide chains in proteins . . ." and ". . . determination of the optical rotation is of great value as a criterion of purity of these substances." More definitive data are desirable but this small volume provides a handbook for data generated through 1958. A substance index and extensive bibliography are provided.

3.6.6. Tables de Constantes Sélectionnées, Volume 11

Optical Rotatory Power, IV. — Alkaloids by J.-P. MATHIEU and M.-M. JANOT. Volume 11 of Tables of Constants and Numerical Data, Selected Constants, Pergamon Press, Paris, 1959, 211 pp, F 110.40 (US $ 24.00).

Organization

This volume is number IV in a series of four on optical rotatory power published under the auspices of "Tables de Constantes et Données Numériques", described in 2.2. The compilation was prepared by J.-P. MATHIEU, the originator of this series, Faculté des Sciences de Paris, and M.-M. JANOT, Faculté de Pharmacie de Paris, with six collaborators in countries including Argentina, Australia, Canada, Japan, Spain, and Switzerland.

Coverage

Numerical constants are given in tabular form for more than 1500 naturally occurring alkaloids and their principal salts. In addition to specific rotation $[\alpha]$ the tables include melting points, molecular weights (when known),

3.6.7.

solvent, concentration and temperature of the measurement, the specific rotation for the wavelength used, and a key to references.

Analysis

A useful feature of the volume is that all textual material is given in French and English.

Listed data are taken from primary journals rather than pharmacopoeias which sometimes give a minimum rotation required to meet a legal requirement. Assigned tolerances may seem large to physicists and chemists not familiar with the difficulty of purifying complex natural products.

Some compounds are included which structurally are alkaloids but which have no action on polarized light. Alkaloids having an assigned formula but for which no value of [α] is available are also included. Thus the volume is a dictionary of known alkaloids. In the table, the formula is given in boldface type if the formula seems to be definitive and a good value of the specific rotation is available.

Given at the end of the book are a complete chronological index of references (by year and journal), an author index, and a substance index arranged by number of carbon atoms in the alkaloid molecule. The authors point out the lack of a satisfactory nomenclature system covering all the alkaloids, and hence have used common names throughout. The primary literature was searched for data. References up to and including some from 1959 are given.

Other Properties

3.6.7. Handbook of the Physicochemical Properties of the Elements

By G. V. Samsonov, Ed., IFI/Plenum, New York-Washington, 1968, XII, 941 pp, US $ 40.00. Originally published in Russian as "Fiziko-Khimicheskie Svoistva Elementov" for the Materials Science Institute of the Academy of Sciences of the Ukrainian S.S.R. by Naukova Dumka Pres, Kiev, 1965.

Organization

Professor Samsonov is Director, Laboratory of Metallurgy of Rare Metals and Refractory Compounds, Institute of Cermets and Special Alloys, Academy of Sciences of the Ukrainian S.S.R., Kiev, The handbook was compiled by a large group of authors from the staffs of the Refractory Materials Section of the Institute of Problems in the Study of Materials, Academy of

208

Sciences Ukr. S. S. R., and of the Metal Reduction Laboratory of the Institute of the Physicochemical Principles of Processing of Mineral Raw Materials, Siberian branch of the Academy of Sciences U. S. S. R., as well as consultants from the Geological Institute of the Academy of Sciences Ukr. S. S. R., and the State Institute of Applied Chemistry.

Coverage

All the elements from atomic number 1 to 104 are covered when data are available. Properties and other information included are: "Atomic structure and crystallochemical properties"; "nuclear physical properties"; "thermodynamic and heat properties"; "electrical and magnetic properties"; "optical properties"; "mechanical properties"; "electrochemical properties"; and "chemical properties".

The original Russian text was extensively updated and revised for this edition; there are several references as late as 1967. Compilations and other secondary sources are used in addition to primary references.

Analysis

The preface states data included either agree well with calculated data; or satisfy various correlations, particularly those based on concepts of the distribution of valence electrons of isolated atoms in the formation of a condensed state, as electrons localized at atomic ions in the form of energetically stable configurations, and as nonlocalized electrons. The compilation presents the data judged most reliable, with the degree of reliability determined mainly from the dependability of the method used in obtaining the numerical values, the purity and states of the samples, statistical criteria, and in some cases, from agreement for the measured properties with well-established laws and the logical conclusions from them. Values for which the reliability is doubtful, or for which there are no reliable data, are given in parentheses. Only one numerical value is given for each property. All data are in tables; references for each datum are indicated. Some uncertainties and accuracies are given.

The Introduction provides discussion of the properties covered, the state-of-the-art of certain areas of investigation, and other useful information.

The values are given in the SI (International System) units, except for some units which are not included in the system. In other cases, values are given in other systems (e.g., cgs) in addition to the SI; conversion factors between the systems are provided.

CHAPTER 4

New and Secondary Centers

Chapter 3, the core chapter of this book, is concerned primarily with descriptions of established projects and their available publications. One general criterion for inclusion of a project in Chapter 3 is that data have been published and are available in some form to all who wish to have them. However, there are a number of new activities with definite programs, but which have had insufficient time to make their products available to the public. Some of these will in due course publish tables of data. Others are concerned, at least initially, in preparing complete bibliographies of pertinent papers for various fields.

4.1. Secondary Nuclear Data Centers

In addition to the numerous nuclear data centers described in Chapter 3, there are a number of other national centers that work cooperatively within the general international framework of data activities and either publish through centers described elsewhere in this book or issue occasional publications of their own. Among such centers are the following:

4.1.1. The Nuclear Codes Center

At Ispra, Italy, maintains a file of computer programs of use in both reactor design and shielding applications.

4.1.2. The Central Bureau of Nuclear Measurements

At Geel, Belgium, has sponsored the compilation of certain neutron reactions such as (n, p), (n, d), and (n, 2n). A report of this work has been published by H. Lisskien and A. Paulsen. In addition, other compilations will be undertaken.

4.1.3. The Swedish A. B. Atomenergi and the Research Institute of National Defense

Have sponsored work leading to reports such as (1) Cross Sections for Neutron Inelastic Scattering and n, 2n Processes, A Review of Available Experimental and Theoretical Data, by M. LEIMDORFER, et al., and (2) The Optical Model of the Nucleus, an Index and Abstracted Literature Review, by L. WALLIN, et al.

4.1.4. Mainz—Amsterdam

J. MATTAUCH of the Max Planck Institut for Chemistry in Mainz and A. WAPSTRA of Amsterdam have, for several years, issued a list of atomic masses prepared by a detailed evaluation of the available experimental data for a variety of nuclear reactions in addition to direct mass spectrometric measurements. In addition, Dr. WAPSTRA has compiled energy levels of very heavy nuclei, that is, nuclei heavier than those presently treated in the Nuclear Data Sheets (see 3.1.1.).

4.1.5. Japan Nuclear Data Committee (JNDC)

This center is located in the Japan Atomic Energy Research Institute, Tokai-mura, Ibaraki-ken, Japan. Data compiled on nuclear reactions involving neutrons are submitted as formal reports to ENEA (see 3.1.11.). The work is part of the international program sponsored by IAEA.

4.2. Colloid and Surface Properties

4.2.1. Electrical Properties of Interfaces

This project is directed by J. LYKLEMA of the Coordination Center: Laboratory for Physical and Colloid Chemistry, Agricultural University, De Dreijen 6, Wageningen, Netherlands. It was initiated in 1965, and is supported by the Office of Standard Reference Data of the National Bureau of Standards (see 1.1.1.). Properties covered include the capacitance or charge of the electrical double layer, electrocapillary curves, and electrokinetics, including surface conductance and points of zero charge. Substances covered include

14*

all species that are well defined, and can be reproducibly obtained. The data are critically evaluated. A publication based on the compiled, critically evaluated data is in preparation.

4.2.2. Surface Tension Data of Pure Liquids

The project was originated in 1967 by JOSEPH J. JASPER at Wayne State University in Detroit, Michigan. Support is provided by the National Standard Reference Data Program (NSRDP) of the National Bureau of Standards (see 1.1.1.). Surface tension data of pure liquids, including liquid compounds, are collected and evaluated. Some 1800 compounds have been processed, and the results tabulated.

The older literature was covered by using Chemical Abstracts to locate journal articles which were then examined. Additional information and clarification were obtained by contacting the authors. Most surface tension data of pure liquids have been reported in the literature only once; therefore, comparison of data reported by two or more investigators is infrequent. All surface tension data are, however, subjected to a close scrutiny and evaluated. They are corrected by applying the least squares method to obtain the most probable values over the given temperature range. This process is then further carried out to produce a table giving the surface tension at various temperatures, the method used for measuring the surface tension, the precision measure, and the least squares constants. The evaluated data are presented in tables, each covering a family of compounds, and will be published in the NSRDS series. A table of cryogenic fluids is also included in this survey.

4.2.3. Data for the Field of Critical Micelle Concentrations

This project is being carried out by PASUPATI MUKERJEE at the University of Wisconsin, Madison, Wisconsin 53706, and by KAROL J. MYSELS at the R. J. Reynolds Tobacco Company, Research Division, Winston-Salem, North Carolina 27102. Support of the work being done at the University of Wisconsin is provided by the Office of Standard Reference Data of the National Bureau of Standards (see 1.1.1.). Critical micelle concentration (c.m.c.) data are compiled for amphipathic, surface-active, compounds in aqueous solution. The data are obtained from the literature and from workers in the field. Some c.m.c. data are calculated from high quality solution data. Over 4500 c.m.c. values for more than 700 compounds have been collected. The c.m.c. data have been critically evaluated and their reliability assigned. The analysis included intercomparison and evaluation of experimental methods as well. A computerized compilation based on this work will be published.

4.2.4. Light Scattering Critical Data Center

The center was established in 1965 at Clarkson College of Technology, Potsdam, New York, and is directed by Josip P. Kratohvil. Support is provided by the National Standard Reference Data Program of the National Bureau of Standards (see 1.1.1.). Data in the area of light scattering are collected and evaluated. Properties covered include Rayleigh ratios and depolarization values; refractive index increments; wavelength and temperature dependence of these quantities; calibration and correction factors in measurements of these quantities; and related theoretical aspects. Species covered include gases, liquids, liquid mixtures, solutions, and dispersions. Types of materials under consideration are electrolytes, polymers, detergents, and colloids.

A critically evaluated data compilation of Rayleigh ratio and depolarization values for liquids and liquid mixtures is in press.

Other compilations presently being prepared include the refractive index increments of polymers and other solutes; and scattering by liquids and liquid mixtures.

Data are obtained from the primary literature as well as some secondary sources. The file is maintained up-to-date. The center was established to collect and evaluate data in the area of light scattering. A number of critically evaluated data compilations are either in press or in preparation.

4.3. Other Specialized Centers

4.3.1. High Pressure Data Center (U.S.)

The center is directed by H. Tracy Hall, the Brigham Young University, Provo, Utah 84601. It was started in 1965 and is currently supported by the Office of Standard Reference Data of the National Bureau of Standards (see 1.1.1.). Three main areas of interest to high pressure workers are covered and information from the literature compiled. One is high pressure research, which currently includes equilibrium transition pressures of liquid $\rightleftharpoons$ solid, and solid $\rightleftharpoons$ solid phase transitions up to 100 kbar. Phase diagrams and crystal data on all materials studied at high pressure and temperatures, especially crystal structure data of high pressure polymorphs, comprise a second area. And third, the definition of a pressure scale principally in the range up to 100 kbar is of special concern, and the evaluation of experimental data and equations of state has been undertaken. The primary literature is searched for data.

The primary function of the center is to maintain up-to-date bibliographic and reprint files in the areas of interest. However, evaluations of experimental data, and critical reviews, are underway in all three major areas.

4.3.2. High Pressure Data Center of Japan

The High Pressure Data Center of Japan, established in 1966, is directed by JIRO OOSUGI, Department of Chemistry, Faculty of Science, Kyoto University. Sixty-six high pressure researchers in various centers in Japan cooperate in collecting high pressure data which are compiled on cards and exchanged. No formal publication program has been established. Liaison is maintained with the High Pressure Data Center of Brigham Young University and with similar centers in other countries.

4.3.3. Radiation Chemistry Data Center

The center is located in the Radiation Laboratory of the University of Notre Dame, Notre Dame, Indiana. The director is MILTON BURTON and the supervisor, ALBERTA ROSS. The program was begun in 1965 with the support of the Office of Standard Reference Data of the National Bureau of Standards (see 1.1.1.), and the Atomic Energy Commission. This data center is concerned with the elementary processes that occur in chemical systems exposed to ionizing radiation under a variety of conditions. Numerical data resulting from such investigations are either yields of products, measurements of rates of over-all or individual processes, or changes in properties of the system due to irradiation. Information relating to rates of reactions is covered: specific rates, equilibrium constants, decay time, entropy of activation, cross-section, or probability; activation energy and other Arrhenius parameters; G (yield in molecules/100 eV) or M/N (molecules/ion pair); properties of transients including absorption and emission bands, extinction coefficients, and half-lives; parameters describing interactions of radiation and matter. Species are limited to chemically defined systems, excepting metals, including solid, liquid, gas, and heterogeneous systems made up of organic and inorganic compounds, in the pure state or as mixtures containing two or more components.

214

Publications issued include a "Weekly List" of papers, bibliographies, and preliminary compilations. The data file is complete for all systems since 1966. Literature prior to 1966 has only been covered for ammonia, methanol, water, and aqueous solutions. A computerized system is being set up.

The specific objectives of the center are to compile and critically evaluate numerical data on chemical systems exposed to ionizing radiation. The center also prepares specific bibliographies and compilations of information from the literature upon request. Many of these are used by scientists to prepare critically evaluated data compilations or reviews.

4.3.4. The Groth Institute

The Groth Institute is located at Nova University, Fort Lauderdale, Florida, and is under the direction of RAY PEPINSKY. The Institute derives its name from PAUL VON GROTH's *Chemische Krystallographie*, W. Engelman, Leipzig, a five-volume work that appeared between 1906 and 1919. The Institute was organized to collect physical, chemical, morphological, and structural data for crystals. No publications have appeared since 1960.

4.3.5. Diffusion in Metals and Alloys Data Center

This center was established in 1963. It is located in the Metal Physics Section of the Institute for Materials Research, National Bureau of Standards (NBS), and is supported by the Office of Standard Reference Data, NBS (see 1.1.1.). The director is JOHN R. MANNING. Data concerning diffusion properties of pure metals and binary alloys are compiled: diffusion coefficients and activation energies. Two types of diffusion are of particular interest: tracer diffusion — (radioactive tracer atoms diffuse into a homogeneous crystal) — and chemical interdiffusion — (atoms from bulk specimens in contact intermingle).

A comprehensive literature search has been completed; the data and bibliography file are being maintained on a current basis. The center was set up to critically evaluate data and to prepare compilations of these data. Critical evaluation of the data collected is in progress.

4.3.6. Alloy Data Center

The Center is in the Alloy Physics Section, Metallurgy Division, Institute for Materials Research, National Bureau of Standards (NBS), Washington, D.C., where it was established in 1966. The principal investigators are

4.3.6.

GESINA C. CARTER, project leader, L. H. BENNETT, chief of the Alloy Physics Section, and J. R. CUTHILL, assistant chief of the Alloy Physics Section. Active research carried out by the Alloy Physics Section is of direct benefit to the center. Partial support is provided by the Office of Standard Reference Data, NBS (see 1.1.1.).

Substances covered are metals, semi-metals, intermetallic compounds, and alloys consisting of two, three, and sometimes more components. Nine groups of properties are of interest: electronic transport, magnetic, mechanical (density, internal structure, acoustical), nuclear magnetic resonance (NMR) and other resonances (e.g., electron paramagnetic resonance (EPR), Mössbauer effect, etc.), quantum description of solids (electronic structure of metals), electromagnetic radiation, superconductivity, thermodynamics, and soft X-ray spectroscopy. Complete coverage at this time is being given only to NMR (Knight-or metallic shifts) and soft X-ray data.

References indexed as to properties and substances, as well as author and bibliographic information, are maintained in a computer file. The system contains a complete, up-to-date, annotated file on papers dealing with NMR Knight shift measurements. The soft X-ray spectroscopy bibliography is up-to-date and work is progressing on detailed indexing.

The files are maintained up-to-date by using Current Contents, Physics Abstracts, and other abstracting services to supplement searches of the primary literature.

The Center has published *The NBS Alloy Data Center: Function, Bibliographic System, Related Data Centers, and Reference Books*. Short annotations accompany each entry of the Data Centers and Reference Books — sections providing, in effect, a survey of work in the area described by the nine groups of properties mentioned above.

Critical evaluation of data will be in the areas of NMR, hyperfine fields, soft X-ray spectroscopy, and some magnetic properties. A compilation of critically evaluated NMR Knight shift measurements is nearing completion, and one on soft X-ray spectroscopy is in progress.

The Alloy Data Center will serve both as a coordinating medium for work in this area, and as an information center which will collect, critically evaluate and compile property values for substances of interest. The center presently answers some questions and the automated system is set up to prepare specific bibliographies upon request.

Publications

Annotated Bibliography on Soft X-ray Spectroscopy, NBS Monograph 52, H. YAKO-WITZ and J. R. CUTHILL, U. S. Government Printing Office, Washington, D. C. 20402, 1962, IV, 109 pp, US $ 1.00.

The NBS Alloy Data Center: Function, Bibliographic System, Related Data Centers, and Reference Books, NBS Technical Note 464, G. S. CARTER, L. H. BENNETT, J. R. CUTHILL, and D. J. KAHAN, U.S. Government Printing Office, Washington, D.C. 20402, 1968, IV, 192 pp, US $ 1.25.

4.3.7. Equilibrium Constants of Molten Steel (JAPAN)

This project operates under the aegis of the Japan Society for the Promotion of Science (19th Committee, 3rd Division), Kanda-Hitotsubashi 1-1, Chiyoda-ku, Tokyo, Japan. It is concerned with equilibrium constants of deoxidation reactions in molten steel systems. Pamphlets are issued on each reaction (English language versions are available gratis). The collected results will appear as a monograph.

4.3.8. Molecular Weights of Polymers (JAPAN)

This cooperative venture yields molecular weights and molecular weight distribution of standard samples as determined in different laboratories. The results are published in "Reports on Progress in Polymer Physics in Japan". The Chairman of the responsible committee is A. KOTERA, Department of Chemistry, Tokyo University of Education, Ootsuka, Bunkyo-ku, Tokyo.

4.3.9. Properties of Electrolyte Solutions

This project was established in 1964 at the Institute for Basic Standards of the National Bureau of Standards (NBS), Washington, D.C. 20234. It is supported by the National Aeronautics and Space Administration (NASA) through the Office of Standard Reference Data of NBS (see 1.1.1.). The director is WALTER J. HAMER.

The major fields of interest are the thermodynamic and transport properties of electrolyte solutions, both aqueous and non-aqueous. These properties are: standard electromotive forces, electrode potentials, activity coefficients, electrolytic conductivities, transference numbers, and ionic mobilities.

The publication, *Theoretical Mean Activity Coefficients of Strong Electrolytes in Aqueous Solutions from 0 to 100 °C* presents tables of data for activity coefficients of electrolytes of various valence types from 0 to 100 °C, and for ionic strengths from 0 to 0.1 molal or 0.1 molar, as calculated by different equations based on the theory of interionic attraction.

Publications

Theoretical Mean Activity Coefficients of Strong Electrolytes in Aqueous Solutions from 0 to 100 °C, NSRDS-NBS 24, W. J. HAMER, U.S. Government Printing Office, Washington, D.C. 20402, 1968, V, 271 pp, US $ 4.25.

CHAPTER 5

Handbooks and Other Sources of Useful Tabular Data

The prime reason for assembling this compendium has been to survey the centers of the world that produce critically evaluated numerical data. However, there exist many other sources of useful tabular property values. These sources range from multi-volume encyclopedic handbooks to books literally of pocket size; and from small collections of critically evaluated data assembled by experts, but with no plans for continuity, to small or large compilations, consisting of values selected directly from the literature with no pretense at evaluation.

The titles listed in this section may fall anywhere among the above categories. No judgments are given as to the quality of data presented in these publications. Year of publication, number of pages, etc. are not given for handbooks revised at frequent intervals. The listing is far from complete. It is hoped that future editions of the Compendium will provide better coverage particularly in languages other than English.

5.1. Comprehensive Multi-volume Handbooks

5.1.1. International Critical Tables of Numerical Data, Physics, Chemistry, and Technology, published for the U.S. National Academy of Sciences, by McGraw-Hill Book Co., 330 W. 42nd Street, New York, N.Y. 10036.

Vol. I, 1926, XX, 415 pp.	Vol. V, 1929, IX, 465 pp.
Vol. II, 1927, XVIII, 616 pp.	Vol. VI, 1929, X, 471 pp.
Vol. III, 1928, XIV, 444 pp.	Vol. VII, 1930, IX, 507 pp.
Vol. IV, 1928, VIII, 481 pp.	Index, 1933, VII, 321 pp.

Seven volumes and Index, US $ 250.00; Vols. I-VII and Index, each US $ 35.00.

The ICT contain no data more recent than 1930, so do not meet the test of currency for inclusion in Chapter 3.

5.1.2.   Gmelin's Handbuch der anorganischen Chemie, published by the Gmelin-Institut für anorganische Chemie in the Max-Planck-Gesellschaft zur Förderung der Wissenschaften e. V., in association with the Gesellschaft Deutscher Chemiker (German Chemical Society), Frankfurt/Main. For information on this comprehensive series of volumes write to the publisher, Verlag Chemie, GmbH., Weinheim, Bergstrasse, Germany. (The bulk of the information is descriptive but many data are interspersed throughout the text.)

5.1.3.   Beilsteins Handbuch der Organischen Chemie. Editor Beilstein-Institut für Literatur der Organischen Chemie, 6 Frankfurt am Main W 13, Varrentrapstrasse 40—42, Germany. Publisher, Springer: Berlin-Heidelberg-New York.

Details about this comprehensive encyclopedia of organic compounds may be obtained from the publisher. (Many property values are distributed throughout the text.)

5.2. Desk Handbooks for Broad Fields of Science

Chemistry and Physics

5.2.1.   Handbook of Chemistry and Physics. Editor Robert C. Weast, The Chemical Rubber Company, Cleveland, Ohio.

5.2.2.   Tables of Physical and Chemical Constants and Some Mathematical Functions, G. W. C. Kaye and T. H. Laby, Longmans, Green and Co., London, New York, Toronto.

5.2.3.   Taschenbuch für Chemiker und Physiker, D'Ans Lax, by E. Lax and C. Synowietz, Springer: Berlin-Göttingen-Heidelberg.

5.2.4.   Handbuch des Chemikers, B. P. Nikolski, Vol. I, Allgemeines; Vol. II, Die Chemischen Elements; Vol. III, Chemisches Gleichgewicht und Kinetik, VEB Verlag Technik, Berlin, Germany.

5.2.5.   Handbook of Chemistry, Editor Norbert Adolph Lange, McGraw-Hill, New York.

5.2.6.   Handbook of Chemistry, (Kagaku Binran), Chemical Society of Japan, Maruzen Publishing Co., Tokyo.

5.2.7.   Concise Handbook on Physicochemical Values, Editor, K. P. Mischenko, Khemia Publishing House, Moscow.

5.2.8. Physical Property Values of Substances (Bussei Teisu), Japan Society of Chemical Engineers, Chairman, Editorial Committee, KAZUO SATO, Maruzen Publishing Co., Tokyo. (Annual monographs for chemical engineers, 60 journals abstracted, non-critical).

5.2.9. Handbook of Inorganic Chemistry, (Muki Kagaku Binran), Gihodo Publishing Co., Tokyo.

5.2.10. Handbook of Organic Chemistry, (Yuki Kagaku Binran), Gihodo Publishing Co., Tokyo.

5.2.11. American Institute of Physics Handbook, Editor DWIGHT E. GRAY, McGraw-Hill, New York.

5.2.12. Physikalisches Taschenbuch, HERMANN EBERT, Vieweg & Sohn, Braunschweig, Germany.

5.2.13. Smithsonian Physical Tables, Editor W. E. FORSYTHE, Smithsonian Institution, Washington, D. C.

Biology

5.2.14. Handbook of Biochemistry, Selected Data for Molecular Biology, Editor HERBERT A. SOBER, The Chemical Rubber Co., Cleveland.

5.2.15. Biology Data Book, P. L. ALTMAN and D. S. DITTMER, Federation of American Societies of Experimental Biology, Washington, D. C.

5.2.16. Biochemists' Handbook, Editor CYRIL LONG, D. Van Nostrand Co., Inc., Princeton.

Earth Sciences

5.2.17. Handbook of Physical Constants, Editor SYDNEY P. CLARK, JR., The Geological Society of America, Inc., 231 East 46th Street, New York, N. Y. 10017.
Two chapters of a recent edition were expanded and issued as separate publications by the U. S. Geological Survey. These are (1) "Selected X-ray Crystallographic Data, Molar Volumes, and Densities of Minerals and Related Substances", Geological Survey Bulletin 1248, R. A. ROBIE, P. M. BETHKE, and K. M. BEARDSLEY, U. S. Government Printing Office, Washington, D. C. 20402, 1967, IV, 87 pp, US $ 0.35; and (2) "Thermodynamic Properties of Minerals and Related Substances at 298.15 °K (25.0 °C) and One Atmosphere (1.013 Bars) Pressure and at Higher Temperatures", Geological Survey Bulletin 1259, R. A. ROBIE and D. R. WALDBAUM, U. S. Government Printing Office, Washington, D. C. 20402, 1968, 256 pp, US $ 1.25.

5.2.18. Physical Properties of Rocks under Normal and Standard Temperature and Pressure, by a group of authors of the Institute of the Physicochemical Basis for Treating Raw Materials, Nauka Publishing House, Moscow.

5.2.19. Elastic Properties of Rock-forming Minerals and Rocks, P. B. BELIKOV et al., Nauka Publishing House, Moscow.

5.2.20. Reference Book on Physicochemical Values for Geochemists, G. B. NAUMOV et al., Nauka Publishing House, Moscow.

5.2.21. Smithsonian Meteorological Tables, Editor ROBERT J. LIST, Smithsonian Institution, Washington, D. C.

5.2.22. International Meteorological Tables, Editor S. LETESTU, World Meteorological Organization, Geneva.

5.3. Handbooks for Special Areas of Science

Nuclear Properties

5.3.1. Group Constants for Nuclear Reactor Calculations, L. B. ABAGYAN, N. L. BAZAZYANTS, I. I. BONDARENKO, and M. N. NIKOLAEV, Power Physics Institute, Institute of Atomic Energy, Academy of Sciences of the U. S. S. R., Revised American Edition, Plenum Press, 1964, 151 pp, US $ 17.50.

5.3.2. Compendium of Thermal-Neutron Capture γ Ray Measurements, Part I, $Z \leq 46$, G. A. BARTHOLOMEW, (Atomic Energy of Canada, Ltd., Chalk River, Ont.), A. DOVEIKA, K. M. EASTWOOD, S. MONARO, L. V. GROSHEV, A. M. DEMIDOV, V. I. PELEKHOV, L. L. SOKOLOVSKII, 1967, Nucl. Data, Sect. A, 3: 367—650 (Dec. 1967).

5.3.3. Tables des Isotopes, Vol. II, RAYMOND PANNETIER, Maisonneuve S. A., Moulins, France, 1965, 300 pp.

5.3.4. Concise Handbook for the Engineering Physicist: Nuclear Physics, Atomic Physics, BR-SOV/5425, N. D. FEDEROV, Atomizdat, Publishing House, Moscow, 1961, 507 pp.

5.3.5. Tables of Neutron Resonance Parameters and Neutron Resonance Materials (for structural materials), T. B. GOLASHVILY, YU. P. ELAGIN, Publishing House for State Standards, Moscow.

5.3.6. Systematic Presentation of Isotopes and Reference Diagrams for Nuclides, I. P. SELINOV, Publishing House for State Standards, Moscow, 1968.

5.3.7.—5.3.20.

5.3.7. Album of Gamma Rays, groups of authors of VNIIM, Publishing House for State Standards, Moscow.

5.3.8. Isotopes, Reference Book on Nuclear Physics, I. P. SELINOV, V. A. KREMNEV, Nauka Publishing House, Moscow, 1966.

Spectroscopic Properties

5.3.9. Tables of Spectral Lines of Neutral and Ionized Atoms, A. P. STRIGANOV and N. S. SVETITSKY, Atomizdat, Moscow, 1966.

5.3.10. Tables of Spectral Lines, A. N. ZAIDEL, Nauka Publishing House, Moscow.

5.3.11. Ultraviolet Spectra of Hetero-organic Compounds, G. F. BOLSHAKOV et al., Khemia Publishing House, Moscow.

5.3.12. Handbook of Ultraviolet and Visible Absorption Spectra of Organic Compounds, KENZO HIRAYAMA, Plenum Press Data Division, New York, N. Y., 1967, 642 pp, US $ 40.00.

5.3.13. Ultraviolet Spectra of Elastomers and Rubber Chemicals, V. S. FIKHTENGOLTS, R. V. ZOLOTAREVA, and YU. LVOV, and S. V. LEBEDEV, All-Union Synthetic Rubber Research Institute, Leningrad, Khemia Publishing House, Moscow, English translation, Plenum Press Data Division, New York, 1966, 170 pp, US $ 9.00.

5.3.14. Wavelength Standards in the Infrared, K. N. RAO, C. J. HUMPHREYS, and D. H. RANK, Academic Press, New York and London, 1966, X, 236 pp.

5.3.15. Infrared Spectra and X-ray Spectra of Hetero-organic Compounds, G. F. BOLSHAKOV et al., Khemia Publishing House, Moscow, 1967.

5.3.16. Infrared Spectra and Characteristic Frequencies 700 to 300 cm^{-1}, F. F. BENTLEY, L. D. SMITHSON, and A. L. ROZEK, Interscience Publishers, Division of John Wiley & Sons, New York-London-Sydney, 1968, XI, 779 pp, US $ 35.00.

5.3.17. Infrared Band Handbook, HERMAN A. SZYMANSKI, Plenum Press, New York, 1963, 496 pp, US $ 35.00.

5.3.18. Infrared Band Handbook, Supplements 1 and 2, HERMAN A. SZYMANSKI, Plenum Press, New York, 1964, 259 pp, US $ 15.00.

5.3.19. Infrared Band Handbook, Supplements 3 and 4, HERMAN A. SZYMANSKI, Plenum Press, New York, 1966, 261 pp, US $ 15.00.

5.3.20. Interpreted Infrared Spectra, Vol. III, H. A. SZYMANSKI, Plenum Press, New York, 1967, IX, 275 pp, US $ 12.50.

5.3.21. Absorption Spectra of Minor Bases: Their Nucleosides, Nucleotides, and Selected Oligoribonucleotides, TAT'YANA VLADIMIROVNA VENKSTERN and ALEKSANDR ALEKSANDROVICH BAEV, Institute of Radiation and Physicochemical Biology, Academy of Sciences of the U.S.S.R., English translation, Plenum Press Data Division, 1965, 86 pp, US $ 10.00.

5.3.22. NMR Band Handbook, HERMAN A. SZYMANSKI and ROBERT E. YELIN, Plenum Press Data Division, New York, 1968, approx. 500 pp, US $ 40.00.

5.3.23. Atlas of Electron Spin Resonance Spectra: Theoretically Calculated Multicomponent Symmetrical Spectra, Vol. 2, translated from the Russian, YA. S. LEBEDEV, N. N. TIKHOMIROVA, and Academician V. V. VOEVODSKII, Laboratory of Chemical Radio Spectroscopy, Institute of Chemical Physics, Academy of Sciences of the U.S.S.R., Plenum Press Data Division, 1964, 195 pp, US $ 15.00.

5.3.24. Atlas of ESR Spectra (1200 spectra), B. H. J. BIELSKI, and J. M. GEBICKI, Academic Press, New York, 1967, 665 pp, US $ 27.50.

5.3.25. Tables of Frequencies of Nuclear Quadrupole Resonance, I. P. BIRYUKOV et al., Khemia Publishing House, Moscow, 1968.

Solid State Properties; Including Crystallographic, Mineralogical, and Electrical and Magnetic

5.3.26. Handbook of X-ray Structure Analysis of Polycrystalline Materials, LEV IOSIFOVICH MIRKIN, Institute of Mechanics, Moscow University. English translation, Plenum Press, New York, 1964, 731 pp, US $ 35.00.

5.3.27. Crystallization and Physicochemical Properties of Crystalline Substances, E. V. KHAMSKY, Nauka Publishing House, Moscow, 1968.

5.3.28. Tables of Interplanar Distances, S. S. TOLKACHEV, Khemia Publishing House, Moscow.

5.3.29. Dielectric Properties of Liquids and Solutions, YA. U. AKHADOV, Publishing House for State Standards, Moscow.

5.3.30. Tables of Experimental Dipole Moments, A. L. McCLELLAN, Freeman & Co., San Francisco-London, 1963, 713 pp, US $ 14.00.

5.3.31. Handbook of Thermionic Properties: Electronic Work Functions and Richardson Constants of Elements and Compounds, V. S. FOMENKO and G. V. SAMSONOV. English translation, Plenum Press Data Division, New York, 1966, 151 pp, US $ 12.50.

5.3.32. Basic Data of Plasma Physics, 1966, 2nd ed., Revised, S. C. Brown, Massachusetts Institute of Technology Press, Cambridge, Mass., 1967, 318 pp.

5.3.33. Electronic Properties of Semi-conductor Solid Solutions, A. B. Almazov, Nauka Publishing House, Moscow, 1966.

5.3.34. Electrical Conductivity of Ferroelectric Materials, V. M. Gurevitch, Publishing House for State Standards, Moscow, 1968.

5.3.35. Organic Semi-conductors, group of authors at Toptchiev Institute of Inorganic Synthesis, Nauka Publishing House, 1968.

5.3.36. Electrical and Optical Properties of Semi-conductors, Proceedings of Physics Institute of Academy of Sciences, Nauka Publishing House, Moscow, 1966.

Thermodynamic and Transport Properties; Including Solution Properties

5.3.37. Vapour Pressure of the Elements, A. N. Nesmeyanov, Publishing House of the U.S.S.R. Academy of Sciences, Moscow, 1961, 396 pp, English translation, Academic Press, New York, 1963, VI, 469 pp.

5.3.38. Thermodynamic Properties of the Elements, D. R. Stull and G. C. Sinke, American Chemical Society, Washington, D.C., 1956, 234 pp.

5.3.39. Basic Thermodynamic Constants of Inorganic and Organic Substances, M. Kh. Karapetyants and M. L. Karapetyants, Khemia Publishing House, Moscow. (Covers > 4000 compounds.)

5.3.40. Pressure-Volume-Temperature Relationships of Organic Compounds, 3rd edition, Robert R. Dreisbach, Handbook Publishers, Sandusky, Ohio, 1952, XI, 303 pp.

5.3.41. Tables of Thermal Properties of Gases, Circular 564, National Bureau of Standards, J. Hilsenrath et al., U.S. Government Printing Office, Washington, D.C., 1955, 488 pp, US $ 3.75.

5.3.42. Thermodynamics of Certain Refractory Compounds, Vol. II, Thermodynamic Tables, Bibliography and Property File, Harold L. Schick, Academic Press, Inc., New York, 1966, 792 pp.

5.3.43. Metallurgical Thermochemistry, International Series of Monographs in Metal Physics and Physical Metallurgy, Vol. 1, O. Kubaschewski, E. Ll. Evans, and C. B. Alcock, Pergamon Press, Oxford, London, and New York, 1967, XIX, 495 pp, 75 s.

5.3.44. Properties of Titanium Compounds and Related Substances, FREDER-
ICK D. ROSSINI, PHYLLIS A. COWIE, FRANK O. ELLISON, and
CLARENCE C. BROWNE, U.S. Government Printing Office, Washing-
ton, D.C., 1956, VIII, 448 pp.,

5.3.45. Phase Diagrams of Silicate Systems; Vol. I, Binary Systems; Vol. II,
Metal-oxide Components in Silicate Systems, group of authors at
Grebentschikov Institute for Chemistry of Silicates, Nauka Publish-
ing House, Moscow, 1968.

5.3.46. Constitutional Diagrams of Uranium and Thorium Alloys, F. A.
ROUGH and A. A. BAUER, Addison-Wesley Publishing Co. Inc.,
Reading, Mass., 1959, 153 pp, US $ 5.00.

5.3.47. Handbook of Compositions at Thermodynamic Equilibrium, CHAR-
LES R. NODDINGS and GARY M. MULLET, Interscience Publishers,
Div. of John Wiley & Sons, New York and London, 1965, X,
ca. 450 pp.

5.3.48. Oxidation-Reduction Potentials of Organic Systems, W. M. CLARK,
Williams and Wilkins Co., Baltimore, 1960, XI, 584 pp.

5.3.49. Atlas D'Equilibres Electrochimiques, MARCEL POURBAIX, Gauthier-
Villars & Cie, Paris, 1963, 644 pp. Translation, JAMES A. FRANKLIN
under title "Atlas of Electrochemical Equilibria in Aqueous Solutions", Pergamon Press, London, and New York, 1966.

5.3.50. Electrochemical Data, B. E. CONWAY, Elsevier Publishing Company, Amsterdam, Houston, London, New York, 1952, 374 pp.

5.3.51. Instability Constants of Complex Compounds, K. B. YATSIMIRSKII
and V. P. VASILEV, Pergamon Press, Oxford, 1960, VIII, 218 pp,
42 s. net. Translated from the Russian.

5.3.52. Reference Book on Solubility, Vol. III, Binary and Multiple Systems
Composed of Inorganic Substances, Books 1, 2, 3 and 4, B. V.
KAFAROV, Corresponding Member of U.S.S.R. Academy of Scien-
ces, Nauka Publishing House, Moscow, 1967-1968.

5.3.53. Tables for Activity Properties of Water and Electrolytes in Binary
Water Solutions of Salts, Acids, and Alkalis, G. I. MIKULIN and
I. E. VOZNESENTSKAYA, Publishing House for State Standards,
Moscow, 1968.

5.3.54. Thermophysical Properties of Monatomic Gases and Liquids (2
parts), V. A. RABINOVITCH, Publishing House for State Standards,
Moscow, 1968.

5.3.55.—5.3.66.

5.3.55. Tables of Thermophysical Properties of Water and Water Vapour, M. P. VUKALOVITCH, S. L. RYVKIN, A. A. ALEXANDROV, Publishing House for State Standards, Moscow. (Thermodynamic Properties to 800°C and 1000 bars, cf International Conference on the Properties of Steam, 3.4.16.).

5.3.56. Thermophysical Properties of Water in the Critical Range, S. L. RYVKIN, Publishing House for State Standards, Moscow.

5.3.57. Thermophysical Properties of Carbon Dioxide, M. P. VUKALOVITCH et al., Publishing House for State Standards, Moscow, 1968.

5.3.58. Thermophysical Properties of Mercury (up to 1500°C and 200 bars), M. P. VUKALOVITCH et al., Publishing House for State Standards, Moscow.

5.3.59. Thermophysical Properties of Alkali Metals, group of authors, Editor V. A. KIRILLIN, Publishing House for State Standards, Moscow, 1968.

5.3.60. Thermophysical Properties of Liquid Air and Its Constituents, A. A. VASSERMAN, V. A. RABINOVITCH, Publishing House for State Standards, Moscow, 1968.

5.3.61. Tables for Thermophysical Properties of Gaseous and Liquid Methane, V. A. ZAGORUCHENKO, A. M. ZHURAVLEV, Publishing House for State Standards, Moscow, 1968.

5.3.62. Reference Book on Thermophysical Properties of Gases and Liquids, by N. B. VARGAFTIK, Nauka Publishing House, Moscow.

5.3.63. Thermophysical Properties of Metals and Alloys, R. E. KRYZHIZHANOVSKY, Metallurgia Publishing House, Moscow, 1967.

5.3.64. Heat Conductivity of Gases and Liquids, N. B. VARGAFTIK, L. P. FILIPOV, A. A. TARZIMANOW, R. P. YURCHAK, Publishing House for State Standards, Moscow.

5.3.65. Thermophysical Characteristics of Substances, group of authors, Editor V. A. RABINOVITCH, Publishing House for State Standards, Moscow, 1968.

5.3.66. Thermodynamic Properties of Gases, M. P. VUKALOVICH, V. A. KIRILLIN, C. A. REMIZOV, V. S. SILETSKIY, and V. N. TIMOFEYEV, Sudostroyeniye Publishing House, Moscow, 1953, 375 pp, in Russian.

5.4. Handbooks for Special Substance Categories

5.4.1. Physicochemical Constants of Organo-sulfur Compounds, B. V. AIBAZOV, S. M. PETROV, V. P. KHAIRULLINS, and V. G. YAPRINTSEVA, Publishing House for Chemistry, Moscow, 1964, 280 pp.

5.4.2. Properties of 100 Linear Alkane Thiols, Sulfides, and Symmetrical Disulfides in the Ideal Gas State from 0° to 1000°K, Bulletin 595, U.S. Bureau of Mines, D. W. SCOTT and J. P. McCULLOUGH, Government Printing Office, Washington, D.C.

5.4.3. Metals Handbook, 3rd ed., Vol. 1, Editor TAYLOR LYMAN, prepared under direction of Metals Handbook Committee, American Society for Metals, Novelty, Ohio, 1961, 1300 pp, US $ 30.00.

5.4.4. Plenum Press Handbooks of High Temperature Materials: No. 1, Material Index, PETER T. B. SHAFFER, 785 pp, 1964, US $ 17.50; No. 2, Properties Index, G. V. SAMSONOV, (translated from the Russian), 430 pp, 1964, US $ 22.50; No. 3, Thermal Radiative Properties, W. D. WOOD, H. W. DEEM, and C. F. LUCKS, 476 pp, 1964, US $ 17.50.

5.4.5. Metals Reference Book, 3rd ed., Vols. 1 and 2, C. J. SMITHELLS, Butterworths, London, Washington, 1962.

5.4.6. Rare Metals Handbook, Editor CLIFFORD A. HAMPEL, Reinhold Publishing Co., New York, 1954, XIII, 657 pp.

5.4.7. Plutonium: Physicochemical Properties of its Compounds and Alloys, Editor O. KUBASCHEWSKI, in Atomic Energy Review 4, Special Issue No. 1, International Atomic Energy Agency, Vienna, 1966, 112 pp, US $ 3.00, U.S.A. and Canada, 12 F, France, 10.50 DM, Germany.

5.4.8. Engineering Properties of Selected Ceramic Materials, F. J. LYNCH, C. G. RUDERER, and W. H. DUCKWORTH, American Ceramic Society, Columbus, Ohio 43214, 1966, 674 pp, US $ 16.00.

5.4.9. Oxides of Rare Earth Elements and Their Refractory Compounds, (crystal structures, thermodynamic, and other properties), S. G. TRESVYATSKY, L. M. LOPATO, V. A. DUBOK, Publishing House for State Standards, Moscow, 1968.

5.4.10. High Melting Compounds, G. V. SAMSONOV, Publishing House for State Standards, Moscow, 1968.

5.4.11. Thermodynamic Stability of High Melting Compounds, R. F. VOITOVITCH, Publishing House for State Standards, Moscow, 1968.

5.4.12. Physicochemical Properties of Oxides, Handbook, G. V. SAMSONOV, Publishing House for State Standards, Moscow, 1968.

5.4.13. Metallic and Chemical Properties of Elements of the Periodic System, I. I. KORNILOV et al., Nauka Publishing House, Moscow, 1967.

5.4.14. Materials Data Book, E. R. PARKER, McGraw-Hill, New York, 1957, 398 pp, US $ 8.95.

5.4.15. Handbook of Organometallic Compounds, HERBERT C. KAUFMAN, D. Van Nostrand, Princeton, 1961, 1582 pp, US $ 24.50.

5.4.16. Physical Constants of Linear Homopolymers, O. GRIFFIN LEWIS, No. 12 of Chemie, Physik und Technologie der Kunststoffe in Einzeldarstellungen, Springer-Verlag, New York, Inc. (Springer-Verlag, Berlin-Heidelberg), 1968, 173 pp, US $ 9.75.

5.4.17. Polymer Handbook, Editors J. BRANDRUP and E. H. IMMERGUT, Interscience Publishers, New York, 1966, US $ 19.50.

5.4.18. Hydrocarbon Data Book, American Petroleum Institute, Division of Refining, 1271 Avenue of the Americas, New York.

5.4.19. Properties of Liquid and Solid Hydrogen, B. N. ESELSON, V. G. MANZHELY et al., Publishing House for State Standards, Moscow, 1968.

5.4.20. Standard Alcoholimetric Tables, (in Polish with table headings in Polish, English and Russian), T. PLEBANSKI and B. OGONOWSKA, Scientific-Technical Publications, Warsaw, 1967, 368 pp.

5.5. Handbooks for Analytical Chemistry

5.5.1. Handbook of Analytical Chemistry (Bunseki Kagaku Binran), Japan Society for Analytical Chemistry, Maruzen Publishing Co., Tokyo.

5.5.2. Handbook of Analytical Chemistry, Editor LOUIS MEITES, McGraw-Hill, New York, 1963, 1806 pp.

5.5.3. Handbook of Tables for Organic Compound Identification, 3rd edition, Z. RAPPAPORT, IX, 584 pp. Supplement to Handbook of Chemistry and Physics, published by The Chemical Rubber Co., 2310 Superior Ave., N. E., Cleveland, Ohio.

5.5.4. Melting Point Tables of Organic Compounds, 2nd revision and supplemental edition, WALTHER UTERMARK and WALTER SCHICKE, Interscience Publishers, New York, N. Y., 1963, XXVI, 715 pp.

5.5.5.   Schmelzpunkttabellen zur Organischer Molekularanalyse, R. KEMPF and F. KUTTER, 2nd edition, Vieweg, Braunschweig, Germany, 1928.

5.5.6.   Tables of Spectrophotometric Absorption Data of Compounds Used for the Colorimetric Determination of Elements, (French and English), IUPAC Commission on Spectrochemical and Other Optical Procedures for Analysis, Butterworths, London, 1963, XV, 625 pp.

5.5.7.   Activation Analysis Handbook, R. C. KOCH, Academic Press, New York and London, 1960, X, 219 pp.

Physical Quantities, Units and Symbols; Basic Physical Constants; Nomenclature; and Related Matters

The evaluation of numerical data can be done better if raw data and derived property values reported in primary journals are expressed in precise language. The term language is broadly defined here to include all symbols, constants, units, nomenclature and so on required to transfer scientific knowledge from one individual to another by the printed page. Since science has no national boundaries, it is highly desirable that primary research results and compilations of data derived from the world literature be based on internationally approved nomenclature, symbols for quantities and units, fundamental physical constants including relative atomic masses, temperature scales, and all other factors required in the accurate transmittal of data from one individual to another, from one discipline to another and from one language to another. It is also important that primary articles contain a sufficient revelation of experiment design, of calibration, and of experimental observations so that an independent reader may draw conclusions about the quality of property values presented. In this chapter are listed sources of the foregoing types of information. Their use is commended.

In what follows there is first given a brief description of key international organizations having important standardization functions. Then follow references to publications of these and other international bodies.

6.1. Organizations

6.1.1. Comité International des Poids et Mesures (CIPM)

The International Committee of Weights and Measures is the only regular organization in existence in which government delegates can meet in general conference and decide on a common basis for legal units. The General Conferences of the Committee are meetings of delegates from forty adhering countries who have joined the "Convention du Mètre", a treaty which was signed in Paris in 1875. The Conferences are convened every few years by the Committee which consists of eighteen members. The Committee directs the activities of the International Bureau of Weights and Measures, comprising the Secretariat and the Laboratory, located in the Pavillon de Breteuil, Sèvres, S.-et-O., France. Aided by seven "Consulting Committees" of international experts, it submits proposals for the operation of the Bureau, and drafts the resolutions for action by the General Conference.

In addition to its principal task of defining and/or maintaining the fundamental standards of mass, length, and time, the Bureau carries on research to improve uniformity and precision of physical measurements on selected key standards or measurement procedures on which most others depend.

The Conference has adopted the "International System of Units" — abbreviated *SI* — consisting of six basic units, and a set of derived units plus two supplementary units. The SI is being widely adopted in the recommendations issued by many other international organizations.

6.1.2. International Organization for Standardization (ISO)

The ISO has a membership of fifty-six nations each represented by appropriate national standards organizations. It deals primarily with recommendations for standards of design, measurement and specifications of industrial importance. Its Technical Committee 12 (TC 12) is responsible for recommendations concerning physical quantities, their symbols, the units in which they are expressed, and their symbols and conversion factors. In this work it has liaison representation from all interested unions of ICSU and collaborates with the following specialized international organizations:

(a) Comité International des Poids et Mesures (CIPM); and its Comité Consultatif pour les Etalons de Mesure des Radiations Ionisantes.

(b) International Electrotechnical Commission (IEC); its Technical Committee 24, Electric and Magnetic Magnitudes and Units; and its Technical Committee 25, Letter Symbols and Signs.

(c) International Union of Pure and Applied Chemistry (IUPAC); and its Commission on Symbols, Terminology and Units.

(d) International Union of Pure and Applied Physics (IUPAP); and its Commission for Symbols, Units and Nomenclature (SUN).

(e) International Commission on Illumination (ICI).

(f) Organisation International de Métrologie Legale (OIML).

(g) World Meteorological Organization (WMO).

(h) International Commission on Radiological Units (ICRU).

(i) Comité Consultatif International Télégraphique et Téléphonique (CCITT).

6.1.3. International Unions

The member Unions of the International Council of Scientific Unions (ICSU) play an important role in standardization of nomenclature, definitions, symbols, units and important physical constants. (For a list of such Unions which are Members of CODATA see p. V).

In general, standardization matters are assigned to special Commissions within individual unions although topics of interdisciplinary interest may be handled by joint commissions of two or more unions. The small membership of each Commission is selected on the basis of individual expertise, with due regard to the widest possible geographical representation. Recommendations originating in these Commissions, through solicitation of comments on published tentative rules, obtain authoritative status by final publication sponsored by the parent Union.

Liaison has been established among the working Commissions of CIPM, ISO, IUPAC, and IUPAP. There are also many additional international scientific associations which issue recommendations mainly on nomenclature and terminology covering their specific disciplines. Through mutual consultation, agreement is usually obtained in overlapping areas.

Numerous national professional societies and scientific journals issue recommendations of their own, often in the form of style manuals. Although many adopt internationally agreed recommendations, exceptions dictated by traditional local or discipline oriented usage patterns frequently occur.

The following list of relevant publications is limited mainly to those originating from the three major international organizations mentioned above.

6.2. Physical Quantities, Units, and Symbols; and Basic Physical Constants

6.2.1. Comité International des Poids et Mesures (CIPM)

The decisions reached at the General Conferences of CIPM are recorded in the Proceedings, entitled *Comptes Rendus des Séances de la ... ème Conférence Générale des Poids et Mesures*, published by Gauthiers-Villars & Cie., Paris. Beginning with the Twelfth Conference (1964) summaries appear in "Metrologia", International Journal of Scientific Metrology, Springer, Berlin. (Vol. *1*, 27-29, 1965 for the Twelfth Conference, and Vol. *3*, 87-88 for the Thirteenth Conference held in 1967).

(a) For official definitions of the six Basic SI Units in French, and their translations into English, see Metrologia, International Journal of Scientific Metrology, Vol. 4, No. 3, July 1968.

(b) For a definition of the thermodynamic temperature scale see Comptes Rendus de la Dixième Conférence Générale des Poids et Mesures (1954), p. 79.

(c) For a definition of the International Practical Temperature Scale (IPTS) of 1948, Text Revision of 1960 see Comptes Rendus de l'Onzième Conférénce des Poids et Mesures, 1961, p. 64, and also U.S. National Bureau of Standards Monograph 37, 1961. The IPTS was revised in October 1968 by the International Committee of Weights and Measures. The text of IPTS-68 is expected to be published in Metrologia, April 1969.

6.2.2. International Organization for Standardization Technical Committee 12 (ISO/TC 12)

Quantities, Units, Symbols, Conversion Factors, and Conversion Tables

ISO/TC 12 has a long range project, that began in 1952, to prepare an integrated series of recommendations, in pamphlet form, to cover the main areas of science and engineering. A feature of the program is that the International System of Units is used throughout and coherency of the unit system is stressed. The pamphlets which will be available in English, French and Russian, present information in tabular form. For each physical quantity or concept there is given the name of the quantity, its symbol and an identifying definition; the recommended unit for expressing the quantity, its symbol and a definition; and conversion factors when needed. The series of pamphlets are collectively designated as ISO Recommendation R 31. The following parts have been issued:

a) ISO Recommendation R-31

Issued in English, French, and Russian.

Part I: 1966, 2nd edition, *Basic Quantities and Units of SI.*

Part II: 1958, 1st edition, *Quantities and Units of Periodic and Related Phenomena.*

Part III: 1960, 1st edition, *Quantities and Units of Mechanics.*

Part IV: 1960, 1st edition, *Quantities and Units of Heat.*

Part V: 1965, 1st edition, *Quantities and Units of Electricity and Magnetism.*

Part VII: 1965, 1st edition, *Quantities and Units of Acoustics.*

Part XI: 1961, 1st edition, *Mathematical Signs and Symbols for Use in the Physical Sciences and Technology.*

Copies of the above may be obtained from the national standards organization in each country that adheres to ISO, at prices fixed by these organizations. The following parts are still under development or review by the Committee and have not received final approval:

233

Part VI: Quantities and Units of Radiation and Light.

Part VIII: Quantities and Units of Physical Chemistry and Molecular Physics.

Part IX: Quantities and Units of Atomic and Nuclear Physics.

Part X: Quantities and Units of Nuclear Reactions and Ionizing Radiations.

Part XII: Some Principles for Printing Symbols and Numbers.

Part XIII: Rules for Rounding Numbers.

Part XIV: General Principles Concerning Quantities, Units and Symbols.

Part XV: Dimensionless Parameters.

Part XVI: Procedures for Inter-Conversion of Values from One System of Units to Another.

Part XVII: Rules for the Use of Units of the International System of Units.

Other related available publications:

b) International Electrotechnical Commision (IEC)

Letter Symbols to be used in Electrical Technology, IEC Publication 27, 4th edition, French—English; 1966, US $ 12.00.

Recommendations in the Field of Quantities and Units used in Electricity, IEC Publication 164, French—English, US $ 11.00.

Copies may be obtained from any national standards organization adhering to ISO.

6.2.3. International Unions

a) International Union of Pure and Applied Chemistry (IUPAC)

Values of the Fundamental Constants for Chemistry, IUPAC Commission on Thermodynamics and Thermochemistry and Commission on Physicochemical Data and Standards, F. D. ROSSINI, *Pure Appl. Chem. 9*, No. 3, 453-459, 1964.

Manual of Physico-Chemical Symbols and Terminology — Definitive, IUPAC, Physical Chemistry Section, Commission on Physico-Chemical Symbols and Terminology, 1959, French and English (facing pages), Butterworth and Co. (Publishers) Ltd., London (out of print).

(I) Reprinted in *J. Am. Chem. Soc. 82*, 5,517-5,522 (1960), includes annotation on American usage, available from Chemical Abstracts Service, Box 1378, Columbus, Ohio 43216, US $ 0.50.

(II) Japanese translation published in *Kagaku To Kogyo* (Chemistry and Chemical Industry) in 1964.

(III) Russian translation published in *Zh. Fiz. Khim.* (Journal of Physical Chemistry) *34*, 10, 2,381-2,389 (1960).

(IV) Bulgarian translation may be obtained from Professor Dr. B. KURTEV, Bulgarian Academy of Science, 1, rue du 7-Novembre, Sofia, Bulgaria.

Note: The Commission, now called Commission on Symbols, Terminology, and Units, published a Tentative revision of the Manual in IUPAC Information Bulletin No. 32 in August 1968. The Definitive version will appear in late 1969 or 1970 and will be available from Butterworth Scientific Publications, London.

Table of Relative Atomic Weights

In 1961 both IUPAC and IUPAP agreed to adopt the table of relative atomic weights based on the atomic mass of $^{12}C = 12$ exactly, thus replacing both the previously used physicist's scale based on $^{16}O = 16$ and the chemist's scale based on $O = 16$. Revisions of the tables by adoption of more accurate individual values as they become available are published at intervals. Such revisions, when adopted by the Commission on Atomic Weights of IUPAC, are published officially by IUPAC, and are reprinted in many professional journals. For the latest edition see: IUPAC Comptes Rendus XXIV Conference, Prague, 1967, Butterworths, London, pp. 136 to 141.

b) International Union of Pure and Applied Physics (IUPAP)

(I) *Symbols, Units and Nomenclature in Physics*, IUPAP, SUN Commission, Document U.I.P. 11 (S.U.N. 65-3), 1965, available from Professor J. DE BOER, Secretary, Instituut voor Theoretsche Fysica, Valckenierstraat 65, Amsterdam (c), the Netherlands. A reprint of the previous edition, Document U.I.P. 9 (S.U.N. 61-44), 1961, with comments on AIP usage by H. C. WOLFE, appeared in *Physics Today 15*, 6, 20-36, 1962.

(II) *New Values for the Physical Constants* — Approved 1963 by IUPAP and its Commission on Nuclidic Masses and Related Constants. See NBS News Bull. *47*, No. 10, October 1963, and *Physics Today*, p. 48, Feb. 1964.

c) International Astronomical Union (IAU)

(I) *Astronomer's Handbook:* Transactions of the IAU, Volume XII C (1966), J.-C. PECKER, Editor. Academic Press, New York.

(II) IAU Commission 14 on Fundamental Spectroscopic Values concerns itself with standardization matters of interest to astronomers and laboratory spectroscopists. See Transactions of the International Astronomical Union, 13 A, 229-266, 1967.

d) IAU-IUPAC-IUPAP Joint Commission on Spectroscopy

(I) *Notation for Atomic Spectra*, J. Opt. Soc. Am., v. 43, 422-425 (1953).

(II) *Notation for Spectra of Diatomic Molecules*, J. Opt. Soc. Am. v. 43, 425-426 (1953).

(III) *Notation for the Spectra of Polyatomic Molecules*, J. Phys. Chem. v. 23, 1997-2011 (1955).

Note: The above recommendations are issued by the Commission but may be inconsistent in some details with some recommendations of the parent unions.

e) IAU-IUPAC-IUPAP Joint (formerly Triple) Commission on Spectroscopy

(I) *Nomenclature Problems*, J. Opt. Soc. Am., v. 52, 476 (1962).

(II) *Report on Units and Terminology*, J. Opt. Soc. Am., v. 53, 884-885 (1963).

f) IUPAC Commission on Clinical Chemistry and the International Federation for Clinical Chemistry

Quantities and Units for Clinical Chemistry, 1966 Recommendation, Scandinavian University Books, Munksgaard, Copenhagen.

6.3. Nomenclature

International Unions of ICSU

6.3.1. International Union of Pure and Applied Chemistry (IUPAC)

(a) *Nomenclature of Inorganic Chemistry*, IUPAC 1957 Definitive Rules, French and English on facing pages, Butterworth and Co. (Publishers), Ltd., London (1959), 2nd printing, 1965, US $ 3.00. In U.S., Butterworth, Inc., Washington, D. C. 20014.

(1) English version reprinted in *J. Am. Chem. Soc. 82*, 5,523-5,544 (1960), reprint available from Chemical Abstracts Service, Box 1378, Columbus, Ohio 43216, gratis; also from IUPAC Secretariat, Basle, Switzerland, Swiss F 3.20.

(2) Japanese translation, entitled Muki Kagaku Meimeiho (by K. YAMASAKI, Professor of Chemistry, Nagoya University), available from Nankodo Publishing Co., 23, Harukicho 3-chome, Bunkyoku, Tokyo, 1961, 73 pp, Y 280.

(3) Swedish translation in *Svensk Kem. Tidskr. 72*, 448 (1960); also published by Tekniska Nomenclaturcentralen, P. O. Box 5073, Stockholm 5, Sweden, KR 7.

(4) German translation in *Chem. Ber. 92*, 7 (1959), XLVII-LXXXVI.

(5) Czechoslovakian translation in *Chem. Listy 57*, 494 (1963).

(6) Dutch translations in (1) *Mededel. Vlaam. Chem. Ver. 24*, 108-166 (1962), available from Vlaamse Chemische Vereniging, Maria-Louiza Square 49, Brussels 4, Belgium, Belgian F. 70; (2) *Chem. Weekblad 59*, 149-176 (1963), available from Koninklijke Nederlandse Chemische Vereniging, Burnierstraat 1, The Hague, the Netherlands, HFl.5.

(7) Bulgarian translation may be obtained from Professor Dr. B. KURTEV, Bulgarian Academy of Science, 1, rue du 7-Novembre, Sofia, Bulgaria.

(8) Portuguese translation published in *Rev. Port. Quim. 7*, 32 (1965).

(9) Yugoslav translation in preparation.

(10) Persian translation in preparation.

Extensions to these rules (in English) appear in *Compt. Rend. Conf. Union Intern. Chim. Pure Appl.*, 22nd Conference, July 1963, pp. 207-211, and of the 23rd Conference, July 1965, pp. 183-187.

(b)* *Nomenclature of Organic Chemistry*, IUPAC 1957 Rules. Definitive rules for (I) Section A-Hydrocarbons, (II) Section B-Fundamental Heterocyclic Systems, and (III) Nomenclature of Steroids; and Tentative Rules for Nomenclature in the Vitamin B-12 field, 1st edition, 1953, 2rd edition, 1966. (Includes corrections to 1953 edition and a revised index but omits Tentative Rules for Nomenclature in the Vitamin B-12 Field), Butterworth and Co. (Publishers), Ltd., London.

(1) English version of (I) and (II) with comments, reprinted in *J. Am. Chem. Soc. 82*, 5,545-5,574 (1960), reprint available from Chemical Abstracts Service, Box 1378, Columbus, Ohio 43216, US $ 1.00; also from IUPAC Secretariat, Basle, Switzerland, Swiss F. 4.30. An English reprint also appeared in the "Handbook for The Chemical Society (London) Authors", 1961, pp. 47-131.

(2) French version of (I) and (II) published in the *Bull. Soc. Chim.* France, *1*, January 1957, available from Maison Masson & Cie, 120, boulevard St-Germain, Paris VIᵉ.

(3) Spanish translation of (I), (II), and (III) available from Professor J. Pascual Vila; Facultad de Ciencias, Universidad de Barcelona, Barcelona, Spain.

(4) Japanese translation, Yuki Kagaku Meimeiho, available from Nankado Publ. Co., 23, Harukicho 3-chome, Bunkyoku, Tokyo, Japan, 120 pp. (1959), Y 350.

(5) Czechoslovakian translation of (I) and (II) published in *Chem. Listy*, *56*, 15 and 152 (1962).

(6) Bulgarian translation of (I) and (II) may be obtained from Professor Dr. B. Kurtev, Bulgarian Academy of Science, 1, rue du 7-Novembre, Sofia, Bulgaria.

(7) Italian translation of (I) and (II), "Nomenclatura di Chimica Organica", available from Tipografia Editrice Italia, via del Corse 20—21, Rome, Italy.

(8) Dutch version of (I) and (II) in Chemisch Weekblad, v. 63, 581-595; 601-621 (1967), available from the Koninklijke Chemische Vereniging, Burnierstraat 1, The Hague, The Netherlands.

(c) *Definitive Rules for the Nomenclature of Amino Acids, Steroids, Vitamins and Carotenoids*, IUPAC Commission on the Nomenclature of Biological Chemistry, first printed in *Chem. Eng. News 30*, 4,522-524,526 (1952); *Biochem. J. 42*, 1 (1948), *52*, 1-2 (1952); *J. Biol. Chem. 169*, 237-245 (1947).

(1) Reprinted in *J. Am. Chem. Soc. 82*, 5,575-5,584 (1960), reprint available from Chemical Abstracts Service, Box 1378, Columbus, Ohio 43216, gratis; also from IUPAC Secretariat, Basle, Switzerland, Swiss F. 3.20.

(2) Czechoslovakian translation in *Chem. Listy 57*, 51, 151, 348, 350, 1963.

---

* Many of the publications dealing with nomenclature for specialized areas of organic chemistsry are approved jointly by IUPAC and the International Union of Biochemistry.

(d) *Nomenclature of Organic Chemistry*, Definitive Rules, Section C — Characteristic Groups Containing Carbon, Hydrogen, Oxygen, Nitrogen, Halogen, Sulfur, Selenium and/or Tellurium, issued by IUPAC Commission on the Nomenclature of Organic Chemistry, Butterworth and Co. (Publishers) Ltd., London (1965). (Section C includes changes made in the 2nd editions of Sections A and B).

(e) *Nomenclature of Organosilicon-Compounds — Definitive*. Published in the Comptes Rendus of the XVth Conference of the International Union of Pure and Applied Chemistry, Amsterdam, 1949, pp. 127-132.

(f) *Nomenclature des molécules organiques marquées —- Tentative*. These rules, presented by the French Commission on Nomenclature, were published in French in Information Bulletin 20, pp. 27-29.

(g) *Rules for IUPAC Notation for Organic Compounds — Definitive*. (Issued by the Commission on Codification, Ciphering and Punched Card Techniques). Published in English by Longmans, London (1961). Available from the IUPAC Secretariat, Basle, Price SFr. 15.

(h) *Rules of Carbohydrate Nomenclature — 1962 — Tentative*. Published in English as a supplement to Information Bulletin 17. Copies are available from the IUPAC Secretariat, Basle. These rules are currently being revised.

(i) *Recommendations for Abbreviations of Terms relating to Plastics and Elastomers — Tentative*. Published in English in Information Bulletin 25, p. 41.

(j) *Report on Nomenclature dealing with Steric Regularity in High Polymers*. Published in English in "Pure and Applied Chemistry" *12* (1966), pp. 645-656.

(k) *Abbreviations and Symbols for Chemical Names of Special Interest in Biological Chemistry, 1965 Revision — Tentative*. First published in English in Information Bulletin 20, pp. 13-26. A further revision may be obtained from WALDO E. COHEN, Director, NAS-NRC Office of Biochemical Nomenclature, Oak Ridge National Laboratory, Box Y, Oak Ridge, Tennessee 37831.

(l) *Nomenclature and Symbols for Folic Acid and Related Compounds — Tentative*. Published in English in Information Bulletin 23, pp. 52-54, with *corrigenda* in Information Bulletin 24, p. 35.

(m) *Trivial Names of Miscellaneous Compounds of Importance in Biochemistry — Tentative*. Published in English in Information Bulletin 25, p. 19.

(n) *Nomenclature of Quinones with Isoprenoid Side-Chains — Tentative*. Published in English in Information Bulletin 25, p. 24.

(o) *Abbreviated Designations of Amino Acid Derivatives and Polypeptides — Tentative*. Published in English in Information Bulletin 26, p. 11.

(p) *Rules for the Nomenclature of Corrinoids — Tentative*. Published in English in Information Bulletin 26, p. 19.

(q) *Rules for Naming Synthetic Modifications of Natural Peptides — Tentative*. Published in English in Information Bulletin 27, p. 16.

(r) *Multilingual Dictionary of Important Terms in Molecular Spectroscopy*, Edited by G. HERZBERG with the assistance of R. N. JONES, J. LECOMTE, R. C. LORD, R. MECKE, S. MIZUSHIMA, and A. TERENIN. Published for the Commission on Molecular Structure and Spectroscopy, by the National Research Council of Canada, Ottawa, Canada, 1966.

Note: Rules marked "Tentative" are given for information only.

6.3.2. International Astronomical Union (IAU)

(a) *Astronomer's Handbook*: Transactions of the IAU, Vol. XII C (1966), J.-C. PECKER, Editor, Academic Press, New York.

6.3.3. International Union of Crystallography (IUCr)

(a) *Notes for Authors*, Acta Crystallographica, v. 18, 134-136 (1965).

6.3.4. International Union of Biochemistry (IUB)

(a) *Enzyme Nomenclature*: Recommendations (1964) of the Commission on Enzymes of the IUB on the Nomenclature and Classification of Enzymes, Elsevier, Amsterdam, 1965.

Other Sources of Nomenclature

Outside of ICSU a number of international organizations deal with terminology in specific fields, such as mineralogy, geology, optics, etc. For further information such organizations can be contacted.

6.3.5. Terms in Nuclear Science

In the nuclear field, a glossary of terms is presently being drafted by the International Standardization Committee of the International Atomic Energy Agency. National glossaries in this field are the following:

(a) *Glossary of terms used in nuclear science*, British Standard 3455: 1962, British Standards Institution, 2 Park Street, London, W. 1, 30 s.

(b) *Glossary of atomic terms*, Public Relations Branch, UKAEA, 3rd edition, 1961. London, H. M. Stationery Office, 3 s. 10 d.

(c) *Glossary of Terms in Nuclear Science and Technology*, prepared by the National Research Council, approved by the American Standards Association, and published by The American Society of Mechanical Engineers, New York, N.Y. 10016, US $ 5.00.

6.3.6. International Commission on Illumination (ICI)
International Lighting Vocabulary, 2nd Edition.

(a) Vol. 1 (1957) French-English-German (Terms with definition in 3 languages).

(b) Vol. 2 (1959) French-English-German-Danish-Spanish-Italian, Dutch-Polish-Russian-Swedish (Terms, without definition). Available from Bureau Central CIE, 57 Rue Cuvier, Paris 5ème, France.

6.4. Recommendations on the Publication of Numerical Property Values

In several fields of science concerned groups of experimentalists have prepared and published guidelines for authors of research reports. The purpose is to encourage the inclusion in papers of at least the minimum amount of detail required to permit future evaluation of the results. Such guidelines are of value not only to the author of the paper, but also to editors, referees, and data compilers. They have been observed to have a good effect on the average quality of papers. The three publications cited below were either generated and approved by international groups, or by national groups for possible future endorsement by the appropriate international body.

6.4.1. Primary Crystallographic Data, Acta. Cryst. *22*, 445-449 (1967) prepared and approved by the Commission on Crystallographic Data of the International Union of Crystallography.

6.4.2. Resolution on the Publication of Calorimetric and Thermodynamic Data, *Physics Today*, February 1961, p. 45, prepared by the U.S. Calorimetry Conference, approved at its 15th Annual Conference (1959), and subsequently endorsed by the Commission on Thermodynamics and Thermochemistry of the International Union of Pure and Applied Chemistry.

6.4.3. Specifications for Evaluation of Infrared Reference Data, Anal. Chem., *38*, 27A-38A (1966) prepared by the Coblentz Society and to be submitted to the Commission on Molecular Structure and Spectroscopy of the International Union of Pure and Applied Chemistry for review and possible approval.

Author Index

Abagyan, L. B., 5.3.1.
Abramov, A. I., 3.1.12., 3.1.19.
Aibazov, B. V., 5.4.1.
Aigrain, P., 2.2., 3.3.13.
Ajzenberg-Selove, F., 3.1.1., 3.1.15., 3.1.17.
Akhadov, Y. U., 5.3.29.
Alcock, C. B., 5.3.43.
Alexandrov, A. A., 5.3.55.
Allard, S., 2 2., 3.6.3.
Allen, P. W., 3.2.44.
Almazov, A. B., 5.3.33.
Altman, P. L., 5.2.15.
Anderko, K., 3.4.11.
Anderson, C. T., 3.4.5.
Anderson, P. D., 3.4.9.
Andrussow, K., 3.4.25.
Angus, S., 3.4.15.
Arnett, R. L., 3.4.2.
Attix, F. H., 3.2.47.
Avery, R., 3.1.6.

Baev, A. A., 5.3.21.
Baggett, N. V., 3.1.18.
Bailey, S. M., 3.4.1.
Bain, R. W., 3.4.16.
Balkanski, M., 2.2., 3.3.13.
Ballard, J. R., 3.2.25.
Barker, T. V., 3.3.8.
Barnett, C. F., 3.2.11.
Barrow, R. F., 2.2., 3.2.7., 3.2.8.
Bartecki, A., 3.2.33.
Bartels, J., 2.1.
Bartholomew, G. A., 5.3.2.
Bass, A. M., 3.2.6.
Bates, R. G., 3.4.23.
Bauer, A. A., 5.3.46.
Bazazyants, N. L., 5.3.1.
Bearden, J. A., 3.2.3.
Beardsley, K. M., 5.2.17.

Beaven, G. H., 3.2.34.
Bechmann, R., 3.3.9.
Beckett, C. W., 3.4.2.
Belikov, P. B., 5.2.19.
Bell, V. J., 3.1.11., 3.1.19.
Bennett, L. H., 4.3.6.
Bentley, F. F., 5.3.16.
Berger, M. J., 3.2.47.
Berman, H., 3.3.10.
Bernal, J. D., 3.3.7.
Berry, L. G., 3.3.3.
Bethke, P. M., 5.2.17.
Bézier, D., 2.2., 3.4.26.
Bhacca, N. S., 3.2.42.
Bielski, B. H. J., 5.3.24.
Biryukov, I. P., 5.3.25.
Bjerrum, J., 3.4.24.
Bolshakov, G. F., 5.3.11., 5.3.15.
Bondarenko, I. I., 5.3.1.
Borchers, H., 2.1.
Börnstein, R., 2.1.
Braams, C. M., 3.1.16.
Brady, E. L., 1.1.1.
Brandrup, J., 5.4.17.
Braun, R. M., 3.4.2.
Brix, P., 3.2.50.
Brown, S. C., 5.3.32.
Browne, C. C., 5.3.44.
Brussel, M. K., 3.1.7.
Buckley, F., 3.2.15.
Burr, A. F., 3.2.3.
Burton, M., 4.3.3.

Carter, G. C., 4.3.6.
Carter, R. S., 3.1.7.
Cauchois, Y., 2.2.
Caunt, A. D., 2.2., 3.2.7., 3.2.8.
Chao, J., 3.4.4.
Charlot, G., 2.2., 3.4.26.
Clark, S. P., Jr., 5.2.17.

Clark, W. M., 5.3.48.
Clifford, A. F., 3.4.23.
Codd, L. W., 3.3.8.
Cohen, V. W., 3.1.1.
Cohen, W. E., 6.3.1.
Collard, H. R., 3.1.5.
Collins, T. M., 3.1.18.
Conway, B. E., 5.3.50.
Cook, M. I., 3.3.3.
Cord, M. S., 3.2.25.
Cornu, A., 3.2.37.
Coughlin, J. P., 3.4.5.
Courtot, J., 2.2., 3.4.26.
Cowie, P. A., 5.3.44.
Cox, E. G., 3.3.1.
Craig, J. C., 3.2.31.
Cuthill, J. R., 4.3.6.

Dacons, J. C., 3.2.31.
Dampier, F. W., 3.4.22.
Dana, E. S., 3.3.10.
Dana, J. D., 3.3.10.
Darwent, B. deB., 3.2.46.
Davis, S. P., 3.2.22.
De Boer, J., 6.2.3.
Deem, H. W., 5.4.4.
Deer, W. A., 3.3.11.
Deffet, L., 3.4.20.
De Groot, J. H., 3.3.3.
De Mallemann, R., 2.2., 3.3.16.
Demidov, A. M., 5.3.2.
Desnuelle, P., 2.2., 3.6.5.
Dillard, J. G., 3.2.12.
Din, F., 3.4.17.
Dittmer, D. S., 5.2.15.
Donnay, G., 3.3.1.
Donnay, J. D. H., 3.3.1.
Doveika, A., 5.3.2.
Downie, A. R., 2.2., 3.2.7., 3.2.8.
Draxl, K., 3.2.12.
Dreisbach, R. R., 5.3.40.
Dubok, V. A., 5.4.9.
Duckworth, W. H., 5.4.8.
Dulaney, G. W., 3.4.23.
Dunn, G. H., 3.2.5.
Dutton, J., 3.2.5.
Dzhelepov, B. S., 3.1.14.

Eastwood, K. M., 5.3.2.
Ebert, H., 5.2.12.
Ebert, J. P., 3.4.2.

Edenharter, A., 3.3.1.
Ehret, C., 2.2., 3.2.48.
Elagin, Y. P., 5.3.5.
Elliott, J. F., 3.4.10.
Elliott, J. N., 3.4.16.
Elliott, R. P., 3.4.11.
Ellison, F. O., 5.3.44.
Elton, L. R. B., 3.1.5.
Endt, P. M., 3.1.1., 3.1.16.
Eselson, B. N., 5.4.19.
Eucken, A., 2.1.
Evans, E. H., 3.3.3.
Evans, E. L., 3.4.10., 5.3.43.
Evans, R. D., 3.2.47.
Evans, W. H., 3.4.1.
Everling, F., 3.1.1., 3.1.17.

Fano, L., 3.1.1.
Federov, N. D., 5.3.4.
Field, F. H., 3.2.12.
Fikhtengolts, V. S., 5.3.13.
Filipov, L. P., 5.3.64.
Fink, W. L., 3.3.3.
Fischer, H. F., 3.2.50.
Foëx, G., 2.2., 3.3.14., 3.3.15.
Fomenko, V. S., 5.3.31.
Ford, K. W., 3.1.1.
Förster, T., 3.2.49.
Forsythe, W. E., 5.2.13.
Fowler, W. A., 3.1.15.
Francis, A. W., 3.4.23.
Frankevich, Y. L., 3.2.45.
Franklin, J. A., 5.3.49.
Franklin, J. L., 3.2.12.
Freedman, L. D., 3.2.31.
Frondel, C., 3.3.10.
Fuller, E. G., 3.1.18.
Fuller, G. H., 3.1.1.
Furukawa, G. T., 3.4.14.
Fuyat, R. K., 3.3.3.

Garritsen, J. K., 3.4.20.
Garvin, D., 3.5.1.
Gebicki, J. M., 5.3.24.
Gerassimov, J. I., 3.4.8.
Gilfrich, N. T., 3.3.3.
Gleiser, M., 3.4.10.
Glennon, B. M., 3.2.2.
Glushko, V. P., 3.4.6., 3.4.7.
Golashvili, T. V., 5.3.5.
Goldberg, M. D., 3.1.7.

Goldstein, H., 3.1.19.
Good, W. M., 3.1.8., 3.1.19.
Goodwin, R. D., 3.4.21.
Gorter, C. J., 2.2., 3.3.14., 3.3.15.
Gosman, A. L., 3.4.21.
Gove, N. B., 3.1.1., 3.1.17.
Gray, D. E., 5.2.11.
Grégoire, R., 2.2.
Groshev, L. V., 5.3.2.
Groth, P. von, 3.3.8., 4.3.4.
Gurevitch, V. M., 5.3.34.
Gurvich, L. V., 3.2.45., 3.4.6.

Haar, L., 3.4.18.
Haas, R. H., 3.2.25.
Haïssinsky, M., 2.2., 3.5.4.
Hall, F. P., 3.4.12.
Hall, H. T., 4.3.1.
Hall, L. A., 3.3.12.
Halow, I., 3.4.1.
Hamer, W. J., 4.3.9.
Hampel, B., 3.2.34.
Hampel, C. A., 5.4.6.
Hansen, M., 3.4.11.
Harllee, F. N., 3.2.12.
Harrison, G. R., 3.2.4.
Hart, W., 3.1.10.
Harvey, J. A., 3.1.7.
Hausen, H., 2.1.
Haywood, R. W., 3.4.16.
Hearmon, R. F. S., 3.3.9.
Hellwege, A. M., 3.1.1., 3.1.17., 3.2.26.,
    3.2.49., 3.2.50., 3.3.9., 3.3.14.
Hellwege, K.-H., 2.1., 3.1.1., 3.1.17.,
    3.2.26., 3.2.49., 3.2.50., 3.3.9.,
    3.3.14.
Henry, N. F. M., 3.3.6.
Herman, R., 2.2., 3.2.7., 3.2.8.
Herron, J. T., 3.2.12.
Herzberg, G., 3.2.9., 6.3.1.
Hestermans, P., 3.4.20.
Hey, M. H., 3.3.8.
Hilsenrath, J., 5.3.41.
Hirayama, K., 5.3.12.
Ho, C. Y., 3.4.20.
Hofstadter, R., 3.1.5.
Hohlneicher, G., 3.2.34.
Holden, H. S., 3.3.10.
Holland, J. C., 3.1.18.
Hollander, J. M., 3.1.4.
Hollis, D. P., 3.2.42.

Holubek, J., 3.2.23.
Honeck, H. C., 3.1.7.
Horiuti, J., 3.5.3.
Hornyak, W. F., 3.1.15.
Hotes, H., 3.4.16.
Houtgast, J., 3.2.1.
Howerton, R. J., 3.1.3.
Howie, R. A., 3.3.11.
Hu, A. T., 3.4.4.
Hubbell, J. H., 3.1.18., 3.2.47.
Hughes, D. J., 3.1.7.
Huldt, E., 2.2., 3.2.7., 3.2.8.
Hultgren, R. R., 3.4.9.
Hulubei, H., 2.2.
Humphreys, C. J., 5.3.14.
Hust, J. G., 3.4.21.

Immergut, E. H., 5.4.17.
Ionov, V. P., 3.4.19.
Isaacs, T., 3.3.3.

Jacques, J., 2.2., 3.6.3.
Jaeger, R. G., 3.2.47.
Jaffe, I., 3.4.1.
Janot, M. M., 2.2., 3.6.6.
Janz, G. J., 3.4.22.
Jarmie, N., 3.1.13.
Jasper, J. J., 4.2.2.
Johnson, L. F., 3.2.42.
Johnson, Q., 3.3.1.
Johnson, V. J., 3.4.21.
Johnston, H. S., 3.5.1., 3.5.5.
Joliot-Curie, F., 2.2.
Joliot-Curie, I., 2.2.
Jones, P. R., 3.2.31.
Jones, R. N., 1.2.1., 3.2.24., 6.3.1.
Jůza, J., 3.4.16.

Kafarov, B. V., 5.3.52.
Kagan, H., 2.2., 3.6.3.
Kahan, D. J., 4.3.6.
Kaiser, H., 3.2.19., 3.2.34.
Kamlet, M. J., 3.2.31.
Kaplan, L. A., 3.2.31.
Karapetyants, M. K., 5.3.39.
Karapetyants, M. L., 5.3.39.
Karris, G. C., 3.4.4.
Kasper, J. S., 3.3.6.
Kaufman, A. M., 3.1.1.
Kaufman, H. C., 5.4.15.
Kaye, G. W. C., 5.2.2.

Keenan, J. H., 3.4.16.
Kelley, K. K., 3.4.5., 3.4.9.
Kelly, F. J., 3.4.22.
Kempf, R., 5.5.5.
Kennard, O., 3.3.1., 3.3.7.
Keyes, F. G., 3.4.16.
Khairullins, V. P., 5.4.1.
Khamsky, E. V., 5.3.27.
Khodadad, P., 2.2.
Kieffer, L. J., 3.2.5.
Kilpatrick, J. E., 3.4.2.
Kim, H. J., 3.1.13.
King, E. G., 3.4.5.
King, M. V., 3.3.1.
King, R. W., 3.1.1.
Kirchhoff, W. H., 3.2.25.
Kirillin, V. A., 5.3.59., 5.3.66.
Kisliuk, P., 3.2.25.
Kitahara, Y., 3.2.20.
Klemm, W., 1.2.2., 3.2.50.
Kluyver, J. C., 3.1.16.
Kmonicek, V., 3.4.16.
Koch, R. C., 5.5.7.
Koenig, L. A., 3.1.1., 3.1.17.
Kondrat'yev, V. N., 3.2.45.
König, E., 3.3.14.
Kopfermann, H., 3.2.50.
Kornilov, I. I., 3.3.17., 5.4.13.
Kortüm, G., 3.4.25.
Kotani, M., 1.2.3.
Kotera, A., 4.3.8.
Kratohvil, J. P., 4.2.4.
Krauss, M., 3.2.13.
Kremnev, V. A., 5.3.8.
Krestovnikov, A. N., 3.4.8.
Kresze, G., 3.2.34.
Krupenie, P. H., 3.2.6.
Kryzhizhanovsky, R. E., 5.3.63.
Kubaschewski, O., 3.4.10., 5.3.43.,
  5.4.7.
Kunz, W., 3.1.2.
Kurtev, B., 6.2.3., 6.3.1.
Kutter, F., 5.5.5.

Laby, T. H., 5.2.2.
Lakshminarayanan, G. R., 3.4.22.
Landolt, H., 2.1.
Láng, L., 3.2.33.
Lange, N. A., 5.2.5.
Langner, I., 3.1.9.
Lauritsen, T., 3.1.1., 3.1.15., 3.1.17.

Lax, E., 5.2.3.
Lebedev, S. V., 5.3.13.
Lebedev, Y. S., 5.3.23.
Lecomte, J., 6.3.1.
Lederer, C. M., 3.1.4.
Legler, R., 3.2.49.
Leimdorfer, M., 4.1.3.
Letestu, S., 5.2.22.
Levin, E. M., 3.4.12.
Levine, S., 3.4.1.
Lewis, J. S., 3.6.2.
Lewis, O. G., 5.4.16.
Lide, D. R., Jr., 1.1.1., 3.2.15.
Lidofsky, L., 3.1.1.
Liley, P. E., 3.4.20.
Linke, W. F., 3.4.23.
Lisskien, H., 4.1.2.
List, R. J., 5.2.21.
Livingood, J. J., 3.1.4.
Lojko, M. S., 3.2.25.
Long, C., 5.2.16.
Lonsdale, K., 1.2.4., 3.3.6.
Lopato, L. M., 5.4.9.
Lord, R. C., 3.2.24., 6.3.1.
Lorenz, P. K., 3.4.22.
Lucks, C. F., 5.4.4.
Lvov, Y., 5.3.13.
Lyklema, J., 4.2.1.
Lyle, R. E., 3.2.31.
Lyman, T., 5.4.3.
Lynch, F. J., 5.4.8.

MacGillavry, C. H., 3.3.6.
Magat, M., 2.2., 3.5.4.
Magurno, B. A., 3.1.7.
Mah, A. D., 3.4.5.
Makita, T., 3.4.20.
Mann, D. B., 3.4.21.
Manning, J. R., 4.3.5.
Manzhely, V. G., 5.4.19.
Marie, Ch., 2.2.
Marion, J. B., 3.1.1.
Martell, A. E., 3.4.24.
Maryott, A. A., 3.2.15.
Mashiko, Y., 3.2.20.
Mason, S. F., 3.2.34.
Massot, R., 3.2.37.
Mathieu, J.-P., 2.2., 3.6.4.—3.6.6.
Matsumoto, T., 3.3.1.
Mattauch, J. H. E., 3.1.1., 3.1.17.,
  4.1.4.

May, V. M., 3.1.7.
McClellan, A. L., 5.3.30.
McClintock, R. B., 3.4.16.
McCullough, J. P., 5.4.2.
McGinnis, C. L., 3.1.1., 3.1.17.
McGowan, F. K., 3.1.13.
McKellar, A., 2.2., 3.2.7., 3.2.8.
McKeown, M., 3.1.1.
McMurdie, H. F., 3.3.3., 3.4.12.
Mecke, R., 6.3.1.
Medvedev, V. A., 3.2.45., 3.4.7.
Meites, L., 5.5.2.
Merrill, P. W., 3.2.1.
Meyer, C. A., 3.4.16.
Miescher, E., 2.2., 3.2.7., 3.2.8.
Mikulin, G. I., 5.3.53.
Miles, B. M., 3.2.2.
Milne, G. S., 3.5.1., 3.5.2.
Milner, W. T., 3.1.13.
Minnaert, M. J. G., 3.2.1.
Mirkin, L. I., 5.3.26.
Mischenko, K. P., 5.2.7.
Miyahara, K., 3.5.3.
Mizushima, M., 3.2.25.
Mizushima, S., 6.3.1.
Moiseiwitsch, B. L., 3.2.5.
Monaro, S., 5.3.2.
Moore, N. Y., 3.4.20.
Moore-Sitterly, C. E., 3.2.1.
Mopsik, F. I., 3.2.14.
Morris, M. C., 3.3.3.
Morrison, P., 3.1.15.
Mrose, M., 3.3.1.
Muan, A., 3.4.12.
Mueller, M. H., 3.3.1.
Mughabghab, S. F., 3.1.7.
Mukerjee, P., 4.2.3.
Mullet, G. M., 5.3.47.
Munavalli, S., 2.2., 3.2.48.
Murphy, J. D., 3.1.18.
Mysels, K. J., 4.2.3.

Nachod, F. C., 3.2.31.
Nakagawa, I., 3.2.20.
Nakanishi, K., 3.2.20.
Nakasima, R., 3.1.1., 3.1.17.
Naumov, G. B., 5.2.20.
Nelson, R. D., Jr., 3.2.15.
Nesmeyanov, A. N., 5.3.37.
Nikolaev, M. N., 5.3.1.
Nikolski, B. P., 5.2.4.

Noddings, C. R., 5.3.47.
Norton, D. C., 3.1.10.
Nowacki, W., 3.3.1.

O'Connell, J. S., 3.1.18.
Ogonowska, B., 5.4.20.
Oldenbourg, R., 3.4.16.
Ondik, H. M., 3.3.1.
Oosugi, J., 4.3.2.
Orr, L., 3.4.9.
Osborn, E. F., 3.4.12.
Ourisson, G., 2.2., 3.2.48., 3.6.3., 3.6.4.

Palache, C., 3.3.10.
Pannetier, R., 5.3.3.
Parker, E. R., 5.4.14.
Parker, K., 3.1.10.
Parker, V. B., 3.4.1.
Parks, P. C., 3.3.3.
Paulsen, A., 4.1.2.
Pearlstein, S., 3.1.7.
Pearson, W. B., 3.3.4., 3.3.5.
Pecker, J.-C., 6.2.3., 6.3.2.
Peker, L. K., 3.1.14.
Pelekhov, V. I., 5.3.2.
Pendleburg, E., 3.1.10.
Pepinsky, R., 4.3.4.
Perkampus, H.-H., 3.2.34.
Perlman, I., 3.1.4.
Perrin, D. D., 3.4.25.
Pestemer, M., 3.2.34.
Peterson, J. D., 3.2.25.
Petit, A., 2.2.
Petrov, S. M., 5.4.1.
Phillips, E. W., 3.4.4.
Phillips, J. G., 3.2.22.
Phillips, J. P., 3.2.31.
Pier, E. A., 3.2.42.
Pimentel, G. C., 3.4.2.
Pitzer, K. S., 3.4.2.
Plebanski, T., 5.4.20.
Plechaty, E. F., 3.1.3.
Pleshanov, A. S., 3.4.19.
Plyler, E. K., 3.2.24.
Porter, M. W., 3.3.8.
Post, B., 3.3.3.
Pourbaix, M., 5.3.49.
Powell, R. W., 3.4.20.
Pratto, M. R., 3.2.25.
Predvoditelev, A. S., 3.4.19.

Pringsheim, P., 3.2.49.
Prophet, H., 3.4.4.
Purohit, S. N., 3.1.7.

Rabinovitch, V. A., 5.3.54., 5.3.60., 5.3.65.
Ramakrishna, V., 3.4.10.
Rank, D. H., 5.3.14.
Rao, K. N., 5.3.14.
Rappaport, Z., 5.5.3.
Reeves, R. D., 3.4.22.
Reilly, M. L., 3.4.14.
Remizov, C. A., 5.3.66.
Rice, R. G., 3.2.31.
Ridley, R. G., 3.2.38.
Rieck, G. D., 3.3.6.
Robbins, C. R., 3.4.12.
Roberts, B. W., 3.3.17.
Robie, R. A., 5.2.17.
Roche, J., 2.2., 3.6.5.
Roder, H. M., 3.3.12., 3.4.21.
Roe, E. M. F., 3.2.34.
Roesch, W. C., 3.2.47.
Rosen, B., 2.2., 3.2.7., 3.2.8.
Rosenstock, H. M., 3.2.12.
Ross, A., 4.3.3.
Rossini, F. D., 1.2.5., 2.3., 3.4.1., 3.4.2., 3.4.3., 5.3.44., 6.2.3.
Rough, F. A., 5.3.46.
Rozek, A. L., 5.3.16.
Rozhdestvenskii, I. B., 3.4.19.
Ruderer, C. G., 5.4.8.
Rudge, M. R. H., 3.2.5.
Ryba, E., 3.3.1.
Ryvkin, S. L., 5.3.55., 5.3.56.

Saba, W. G., 3.4.14.
Saeki, S., 3.2.20.
Samson, S., 3.3.1.
Samsonov, G. V., 3.6.7., 5.3.31., 5.4.4., 5.4.10., 5.4.12.
Samuilov, E. V., 3.4.19.
Sandeman, I., 3.2.34.
Sato, K., 5.2.8.
Schäfer, Kl., 2.1.
Scheer, J., 3.1.17.
Schick, H. L., 5.3.42.
Schicke, W., 5.5.4.
Schintlmeister, J., 3.1.2.
Schmidt, E., 2.1., 3.4.16.
Schmidt, J. J., 3.1.9.

Schmillen, A., 3.2.49.
Schopper, H., 3.1.5.
Schumm, R. H., 3.4.1.
Schupp, O. E., 3.6.2.
Schwartz, R. B., 3.1.7.
Schwarzenbach, G., 3.4.24.
Scott, D. W., 5.4.2.
Scott, M. R., 3.1.1.
Seaborg, G. T., 3.1.4.
Seagrave, J. D., 3.1.13.
Seidell, A., 3.4.23.
Selinov, I. P., 5.3.6., 5.3.8.
Sergejev, V. O., 3.1.14.
Shaffer, P. T. B., 5.4.4.
Shafroth, S. M., 3.1.1.
Shakhov, A. S., 3.4.8.
Shiba, T., 3.6.1.
Shimanouchi, T., 3.2.10., 3.2.20.
Shoolery, J. N., 3.2.42.
Shunk, F. A., 3.4.11.
Siletskiy, V. S., 5.3.66.
Sillén, L. G., 3.4.24.
Silvestri, G. J., 3.4.16.
Sinke, G. C., 3.4.4., 3.4.10., 5.3.38.
Slack, L., 3.1.1.
Smith, C. D., 3.2.18.
Smith, D. B., 3.1.13.
Smith, J. V., 3.3.3.
Smith, M. W., 3.2.2.
Smith, S. J., 3.2.5.
Smithells, C. J., 5.4.5.
Smithson, L. D., 5.3.16.
Smits, L. J., 2.2., 3.3.14., 3.3.15.
Snell, A., 3.1.1.
Sober, H. A., 5.2.14.
Sokolovskii, L. L., 5.3.2.
Spencer, R. C., Jr., 3.4.16.
Spiller, R. C., 3.3.8.
Stakhanov, I. P., 3.4.19.
Starck, B., 3.2.26.
Stauffer, C. H., 3.5.1.
Stehn, J. R., 3.1.7.
Stern, K. H., 3.4.13.
Stewart, R. B., 3.4.21.
Stinchfield, R., 3.3.3.
Story, J. S., 3.1.10.
Striganov, A. P., 5.3.9.
Strobridge, T. R., 3.4.21.
Strominger, D., 3.1.4.
Štrouf, O., 3.2.23.
Stull, D. R., 3.4.4., 3.4.10., 5.3.38.

Stupochenko, E. V., 3.4.19.
Styrikovich, M. A., 1.2.6.
Suhner, F., 2.2., 3.3.16.
Sutton, L. E., 3.2.44.
Svetitsky, N. S., 5.3.9.
Swanson, H. E., 3.3.3.
Synowietz, C., 5.2.3.
Syverud, A. N., 3.4.4.
Szöke, J., 3.2.33.
Szymanski, H. A., 5.3.17.—5.3.20., 5.3.22.

Tanaka, N., 3.2.20.
Tarzimanow, A. A., 5.3.64.
Tatge, E., 3.3.3.
Taylor, W. J., 3.4.2.
Terpstra, P., 3.3.8.
Terrall, J. R., 3.1.3.
Thew, K., 3.1.1.
Thompson, H. W., 3.2.19.
Thon, N., 3.5.1.
Tikhomirova, N. N., 5.3.23.
Timmons, C. J., 3.2.34.
Timofeyev, V. N., 5.3.66.
Tolkachev, S. S., 5.3.28.
Tomkins, R. P. T., 3.4.22.
Touloukian, Y. S., 3.4.20.
Townes, C. H., 3.2.25.
Tresvyatsky, S. G., 5.4.9.
Trotman-Dickenson, A. F., 3.5.1., 3.5.2.

Ugrinic, G. M., 3.3.3.
Ulmer, L., 3.3.3.
Ungnade, H. E., 3.2.31.
Utermark, W., 5.5.4.

Van der Leun, C., 3.1.16.
Van Lieshout, R., 3.1.1.
Vargaftik, N. B., 5.3.62., 5.3.64.
Varsányi, G., 3.2.33.
Vasilev, V. P., 5.3.51.
Vasserman, A. A., 5.3.60.
Vedeneyev, V. I., 3.2.45.
Venkatasetty, H. V., 3.4.22.
Venkstern, T. V., 5.3.21.
Vila, J. P., 6.3.1.
Vizesy, M., 3.2.33.
Voevodskii, V. V., 5.3.23.
Vogel, W., 3.4.25.

Voitovitch, R. F., 5.4.11.
Voznesentskaya, I. E., 5.3.53.
Vukalovitch, M. P., 3.4.16., 5.3.55., 5.3.57., 5.3.58., 5.3.66.

Wacker, P. F., 3.2.25.
Wagman, D. D., 3.4.1.
Waldbaum, D. R., 5.2.17.
Wallin, L., 4.1.3.
Wapstra, A. H., 3.1.1., 3.1.17., 4.1.4.
Ward, A. T., 3.4.22.
Way, K., 3.1.1., 3.1.17.
Weast, R. C., 5.2.1.
Webb, D. U., 3.4.4.
Weber, L. A., 3.4.21.
Weise, E. L., 3.4.13.
Weissmann, S., 3.3.3.
Werner, H. G., 3.4.2.
Westrum, E. F., Jr., 3.4.1.
Wheeler, O. H., 3.2.31.
Whitehead, L. T., 3.1.19.
Wieland, K., 2.2., 3.2.7., 3.2.8.
Wiener-Chasman, R., 3.1.7.
Wiese, W. L., 3.2.2.
Williams, M. G., 3.4.2.
Wilson, A. J. C., 3.3.4.
Wolfe, H. C., 6.2.3.
Woll, D., 3.1.9.
Wollert, S. K., 3.4.4.
Wolten, G., 3.3.1.
Wood, W. D., 5.4.4.
Wren-Lewis, J., 3.3.8.
Wyckoff, R. W. G., 3.3.2.

Yakowitz, H., 4.3.6.
Yamasaki, K., 6.3.1.
Yaprintseva, V. G., 5.4.1.
Yatsimirskii, K. B., 5.3.51.
Yelin, R. E., 5.3.22.
Yurchak, R. P., 5.3.64.

Zagoruchenko, V. A., 5.3.61.
Zaidel, A. N., 5.3.10.
Zhuravelev, A. M., 5.3.61.
Zolotareva, R. V., 5.3.13.
Zussman, J., 3.3.11.
Zwolinski, B. J., 2.3., 3.2.16., 3.2.17. 3.2.27.—3.2.30., 3.2.35., 3.2.36., 3.2.39., 3.2.40., 3.4.2., 3.4.3.

Subject Index

.

CAPITAL letters indicate names of data centers and projects, and major property categories; *italic* letters indicate titles of publications. Section numbers in **bold** type refer to description of data center or project.

Absorption coefficient, gamma, X-ray, 3.2.47., *see also* Cross sections
Absorption of X-rays, wavelengths of emission and discontinuities, 2.2.
ABSORPTION SPECTRA IN THE ULTRAVIOLET AND VISIBLE REGION, 3.2.33.
Absorption Spectra of Minor Bases, Their Nucleosides, Nucleotides, and Selected Oligoribonucleotides, 5.3.21.
Absorptivity (absorptance) thermal, *see* Thermal radiative properties
Abundance, relative isotopic, *see* Isotopic abundance, relative
Academy of Sciences of the Ukrainian S.S.R., 3.6.7.
Academy of Sciences of the U.S.S.R., 1.1.3., 1.2.6., 3.1.14., 3.2.45., 3.4.6., 3.4.7., 3.4.19., 5.3.1., 5.3.21., 5.3.23., 5.3.36., 5.3.37., 5.3.52.
Acetylene, physical, thermodynamic properties, 3.4.17.
Acids, activity properties of water, electrolytes in binary water solutions of, 5.3.53.
—, aqueous solutions of, thermodynamic properties, 3.4.1.
—, organic, dissociation constants, 3.4.25.
—, solubilities of elements, inorganic and organic compounds in, 3.4.23.
Acoustic properties, alloys, intermetallic compounds, metals, 4.3.6.
Acoustics, quantities and units (ISO R 31), 6.2.2.
Acta Crystallographica, 3.2.44., 6.4.1.
Actinides, atomic energy levels, 3.2.1.

Activation Analysis Handbook, 5.5.7.
Activation energy, enthalpy, entropy, *see* Energy, Enthalpy, Entropy of activation
Activity coefficient, alloys, 3.4.9.
— —, calculation using interionic attraction theory, 4.3.9.
— —, electrolyte solutions, 4.3.9.
— —, elements, compounds in steelmaking, 3.4.10.
— —, hydrocarbon gases, 3.4.2.
Activity Coefficients, Theoretical Mean, of Strong Electrolytes in Aqueous Solutions, 4.3.9.
Activity properties, water, electrolytes in binary water solutions of salts, acids, alkalis, 5.3.53.
Acyclic compounds, halogen-substituted, thermodynamic properties, 3.4.3.
Advanced Research Projects Agency, Department of Defense, U.S.A. (ARPA), 3.2.5.
Affinity, electron, proton, *see* Electron, Proton affinity
Agricultural University, the Netherlands, 4.2.1.
Air, cryogenic data, 3.4.21.
—, physical properties, 3.4.17.
—, thermodynamic functions, 3.4.19.
—, thermodynamic properties, 3.4.15., 3.4.17.
—, transport properties, 3.4.15.
—, liquid, and constituents, thermophysical properties, 5.3.60.
Albany Metallurgy Research Center, U.S.A., 3.4.5.

Album of Gamma Rays, 5.3.7.

Alcoholimetric Tables, Standard, 5.4.20.

Alcohols, thermodynamic properties, 3.4.2.

Aldehydes, thermodynamic properties, 3.4.2., 3.4.3.

Aliphatic compounds, crystal structures, 3.3.2.

Alkali metals, atomic collision data, low energy, 3.2.5.

— —, thermophysical properties, 5.3.59.

Alkali metal compounds, thermodynamic properties, 3.4.6.

Alkaline earths, transition probability, atomic, 3.2.2.

Alkalis, activity properties of water, electrolytes in binary water solutions of, 5.3.53.

—, transition probability, atomic, 3.2.2.

Alkaloids, infrared spectra, 3.2.20., 3.2.23.

—, NMR spectra, 3.2.42.

—, optical rotatory power, 3.2.22., 3.6.6.

—, physical properties, 3.2.23., 3.6.6.

—, ultraviolet spectra, 3.2.23.

Alkanoic acids, thermodynamic properties, 3.4.2., 3.4.3.

Alkanols, thermodynamic properties, 3.4.3.

Alkyl thiophenes, thermodynamic properties, 3.4.2.

ALLOY DATA CENTER, **4.3.6.**

Alloys, catalysis of ethylene hydrogenation with, 3.5.3.

—, cryogenic data, 3.4.21., 4.3.6.

—, crystallographic properties, 3.3.1.

—, crystal structures, 3.3.1., 3.3.3., 3.3.5., 3.4.11.

—, Curie temperature, 3.3.15.

—, diffusion data, 4.3.5.

—, elastic constants, 3.3.9.

—, lattice parameters, 3.3.5.

—, magnetic moment, susceptibility, 3.3.15.

—, magnetic properties, 4.3.6.

—, NMR spectral data, 4.3.6.

—, optical properties, 3.3.1.

—, phase diagrams, 3.4.9.—3.4.11., 5.3.46.

Alloys, soft X-ray spectral data, 4.3.6.

—, superconductive properties, 3.3.17., 4.3.6.

—, thermodynamic properties, 3.4.9., 3.4.20., 4.3.6.

—, thermophysical properties, 3.4.20., 5.3.63.

—, transport properties, 3.4.20., 4.3.5.

—, X-ray diffraction data, 3.3.3.

—, binary, crystallographic properties, constitution data, 3.4.11.

Alpha decay, disintegration, *see* Radioactive disintegration

Alpha-spectroscopy, angular correlation computations in, numerical tables for, 2.1.

Aluminium and compounds, thermodynamic properties, 3.4.8.

American Ceramic Society, U.S.A., 3.4.12., 5.4.8.

American Chemical Society, U.S.A. (ACS), 3.4.10., 3.4.23., 5.3.38.

American Crystallographic Association, U.S.A. (ACA), 3.3.1., 3.3.3.

American Institute of Physics Handbook, 5.2.11.

American Iron and Steel Institute, U.S.A., 3.4.9., 3.4.10.

American Petroleum Institute, U.S.A. (API), **2.3.,** 3.2.16., 3.2.17., 3.2.27. — 3.2.30., 3.2.35.—3.2.37., 3.2.39., 3.2.40., 3.4.2., 3.4.3., 5.4.18.

AMERICAN PETROLEUM INSTITUTE RESEARCH PROJECT 44 (API RP 44), 2.3., **3.2.16.,** 3.2.17., **3.2.27.,** 3.2.28., **3.2.29.,** 3.2.30., **3.2.35.,** 3.2.36., 3.2.37., **3.2.39.,** 3.2.40., **3.4.2.,** 3.4.3.

American Philosophical Society, U.S.A., 3.3.10.

American Society for Metals, U.S.A., 5.4.3.

American Society for Testing and Materials, U.S.A. (ASTM), 3.2.51. — 3.2.53., 3.3.3., 3.6.2.

American Society of Mechanical Engineers, U.S.A. (ASME), 3.4.16., 6.3.5.

American Standards Association, U.S.A., 6.3.5.

Amines, thermodynamic properties, 3.4.3.

Amino acids, crystal structures, 3.3.2.

— —, nomenclature (IUPAC), 6.3.1.

— —, optical rotatory power, 3.6.5.

Amino acid derivatives, abbreviated designations (IUPAC), 6.3.1.

Ammonia, physical properties, 3.4.17.

—, radiation chemistry data, 4.3.3.

—, thermodynamic properties, 3.4.15., 3.4.17., 3.4.18.

—, transport properties, 3.4.15.

—, (ideal gas), thermodynamic properties, 3.4.18.

Ammoniates, crystal structures, 3.3.2.

Amphipathic, surface-active compounds, aqueous solution, critical micelle concentrations in, 4.2.3.

Analyses, minerals, 3.3.10., 3.3.11.

—, molecular rotational, vibrational spectra, 3.2.22.

—, optical atomic spectra, 3.2.1.

—, silicates, 3.3.11.

Analytical chemistry, handbooks, 5.5.

Angewandte Chemie, 3.2.34.

Angular correlation computations in α-, β- and γ-spectroscopy, numerical tables, 2.1.

Antiferroelectric substances, 2.1.

Antimony and compounds, thermodynamic properties, 3.4.8.

Appearance potential, gaseous positive ions, 3.2.12.

Aqueous solutions, electrochemical equilibria in, 5.3.49.

— —, radiation chemistry data, 4.3.3.

Aqueous solvents, solubility of elements, inorganic and organic compounds in, 3.4.23.

Argon, physical properties, 3.4.17.

—, thermodynamic functions, 3.4.19.

—, thermodynamic properties, 3.4.15., 3.4.17.

—, — —, low temperature, 3.4.21.

—, transport properties, 3.4.15.

Argonne National Laboratory, U.S.A., 3.1.6., 3.3.1.

Aromatic compounds, molecular electronic spectra, 3.2.33., 3.2.34.

Arrhenius values, bimolecular gas reactions, 3.5.2.

ASTM Infrared Spectral Index, 3.2.20.

Astronomer's Handbook (IAU), 6.2.3., 6.3.2.

Astronomical spectra, lines of chemical elements in, 3.2.1.

Astronomie und Geophysik, Landolt-Börnstein, Sixth Edition, 2.1.

Astronomy, Astrophysics and Space Research, Landolt-Börnstein, New Series, 2.1.

Astronomy, 2.1., 3.2.1., 3.2.7., 3.2.8., 3.2.22., 3.2.24., 6.2.3., 6.3.2.

Astrophysics, 2.1., 3.2.1., 3.2.5., 3.2.7., 3.2.22.

Asymmetric rotors, line strengths, 3.2.25.

Atlas d'Equilibres Electrochimiques, 5.3.49.

ATLAS DES LONGUEURS D'ONDE CARACTÉRISTIQUES DES BANDES D'EMISSION ET D'ABSORPTION DES MOLÉCULES DIATOMIQUES, TABLES DE CONSTANTES SÉLECTIONNÉES, 2.2., **3.2.8.**

Atlas of Electrochemical Equilibria in Aqueous Solutions, 5.3.49.

Atlas of ESR Spectra, 5.3.23., 5.3.24.

Atmospheric gases, thermodynamic, transport properties, 3.4.15.

Atom-atom reactions, chemical kinetics data, 3.5.2.

Atomic and Molecular Physics, Landolt-Börnstein, New Series, 2.1.

ATOMIC AND MOLECULAR PROCESSES INFORMATION CENTER, **3.2.11.**

Atomic and nuclear physics, quantities and units (ISO R31), 6.2.2.

Atomic and weight percent, factors for interconversion of, 3.4.11.

Atomic collision data, electron, photon, low energy, 3.2.5.

— — —, heavy particles, 3.2.5., 3.2.11.

ATOMIC COLLISION INFORMATION CENTER, JILA **3.2.5.**

Atomic configurations in molecules, ions, 3.2.44.

Atomic Energy Establishment, Winfrith, U.K., 3.1.10.

ATOMIC ENERGY LEVELS DATA AND INFORMATION CENTER, **3.2.1.**, 3.2.2.

Atomic Energy Levels (from Analyses of Optical Spectra), 3.2.1.

Atomic energy levels, elements, 3.2.1. —3.2.3.

Atomic Energy Research Institute, Japan, 4.1.5.

Atomic mass, 3.1.2., 3.1.15., 3.1.16., 4.1.4.

Atomic mass difference, 3.1.1., 3.1.15., 3.1.16.

ATOMIC PROPERTIES, 1.1.1., **3.2.**

Atomic radius, *see* Nuclear radii

Atomic spectra, elements, 3.2.4.

Atomic Spectra, Notation for, 6.2.3.

Atomic Spectra, Selected Tables, (Si I—IV), 3.2.1.

Atomic Terms, Glossary of, 6.3.5.

ATOMIC TRANSITION PROBABILITIES DATA CENTER, **3.2.2.**

Atomic volume, *see* Volume, atomic

Atomic Weapons Research Establishment, Aldermaston, U. K. (AWRE), 3.1.10., 3.2.38.

Atomic Weights, Table of Relative, 3.4.1., 6.2.3.

Atoms and ions, atomic collision data, low energy, 3.2.5.

— —, magnetic dipole moments, 3.2.50., 3.3.15.

— —, physical constants, 3.2.1., 3.2.45.

— —, rearrangement collisions, 3.2.11.

— —, spectral lines, 5.3.9.

— —, transition probabilities, 3.2.2.

Atoms molecules, radicals; electron, proton affinities, ionization potentials, 3.2.45.

Atom- und Molekularphysik, Landolt-Börnstein, Sixth Edition, 2.1.

Attenuation coefficient, gamma, X-ray, *see* Gamma, X-ray attenuation coefficient

Band Spectrum of Carbon Monoxide, 3.2.6.

Band theory, parameters for, 3.3.13.

BARKER INDEX OF CRYSTALS, **3.3.8.**

Barn Books, 3.1.7.

Bases, solubilities of elements, inorganic and organic compounds in, 3.4.23.

—, aqueous solutions of, thermodynamic properties, 3.4.1.

Bases, minor, absorption spectra, 5.3.21.

—, organic, dissociation constants, 3.4.25.

Basic Data of Plasma Physics, 5.3.32.

Basic Quantities and Units of SI, 6.2.2.

Basic Thermodynamic Constants of Inorganic and Organic Substances, 5.3.39.

Beilsteins Handbuch der Organischen Chemie, 5.1.3.

Bending (stretching) frequency, *see* Vibrational frequency, molecular

Benzene and derivatives, crystal structures, 3.3.2.

— — —, ultraviolet spectral data, 3.2.34.

BERKELEY ANALYSES OF MOLECULAR SPECTRA, **3.2.22.**

Beta decay, disintegration, *see* Radioactive disintegration

Beta-spectroscopy, angular correlation computations in, numerical tables for, 2.1.

BIBLIOGRAPHIES, atomic and molecular processes, 3.2.11.

—, atomic, electron collision data, 3.2.5.

—, chemical kinetics data, 3.5.1.

—, cryogenic data, 3.4.21.

—, crystal structures, organic, 3.3.7.

—, diatomic molecules, spectroscopic data, 3.2.6., 3.2.7.

—, dielectrics, 3.2.14.

—, diffusion data, metals and alloys, 4.3.5.

—, free radicals, 3.2.50.

—, high pressure data, 4.3.1.

—, ion-molecule reactions, 3.2.12.

—, mass spectral data, 3.2.38.

—, microwave spectral data, 3.2.25.

—, molecular spectra, 3.2.9., 3.2.19.

—, molecular structure, 3.2.9.

—, molten salts data, 3.4.22.

—, nuclear data, 3.1.3.

—, nuclear magnetic resonance (NMR) spectral data, 4.3.6.

—, optical atomic spectra, analyses of, 3.2.1.

—, photoabsorption cross section data, 3.2.5.

—, photonuclear data, 3.1.18.

—, radiation chemistry, 4.3.3.

BIBLIOGRAPHIES, sesquiterpenoids, optical, spectral data, 3.2.48.
—, soft X-ray spectroscopy, 4.3.6.
—, thermodynamic properties, 2.3., 3.4.1., 3.4.2.
—, thermophysical properties, 3.4.20.
—, transition probabilities, atomic, 3.2.2.
—, X-ray crystallography, 3.3.6.
Bimolecular gas reactions, chemical kinetics data, 3.5.2.
Binary compounds, crystal structures, 3.3.2.
BINARY METAL AND METALLOID CONSTITUTION DATA CENTER, 3.4.11.
Binding energy, electronic, nuclear, 3.1.14., 3.1.15., 3.1.17.
Biochemistry, handbooks, 5.2.14., 5.2.16.
—, names of important compounds (IUPAC), 6.3.1.
Biochemists' Handbook, 5.2.16.
Biological chemistry, abbreviations, symbols for chemical names of interest in (IUPAC), 6.3.1.
— —, IUPAC Commission on Nomenclature of, 6.3.1.
Biology Data Book, 5.2.15.
Biology, handbooks, 5.2.14.—5.2.16.
Bismuth and compounds, thermodynamic properties, 3.4.8.
Boiling point (temperature), elements, 3.4.1., 3.4.3.
— — —, hydrocarbons, 3.2.35., 3.4.2.
— — —, industrial compounds, 3.2.18., 3.2.21., 3.2.32., 3.2.41., 3.4.17.
— — —, inorganic compounds, 3.2.19., 3.2.21., 3.2.33., 3.4.1., 3.4.3.
— — —, nonferrous metals, 3.4.8.
— — —, organic compounds 3.2.19.—3.2.21., 3.2.32., 3.2.33., 3.2.41., 3.4.1., 3.4.3.
Bond angle, molecules, ions, 3.2.44.
BOND DISSOCIATION ENERGIES IN SIMPLE MOLECULES, 3.2.46.
BOND ENERGIES, IONIZATION POTENTIALS, AND ELECTRON AFFINITIES, 3.2.45.
Bond energy, inorganic, organic molecules, 3.2.45., 3.2.46.

Bond length, *see* Interatomic distance
Borides, crystal structures, phase diagrams, 3.4.11.
Bravais lattice, classification of crystal structures by, 3.3.5.
Brigham Young University, U.S.A., 4.3.1.
British Standards Institution, U.K., 6.3.5.
Brookhaven National Laboratory, U.S.A. (BNL), 3.1.7., 3.1.10.
Bulgarian Academy of Science, 6.2.3., 6.3.1.
Bulletin of Thermodynamics and Thermochemistry, IUPAC, 2.3., 3.4.1.

Cadmium and compounds, thermodynamic properties, 3.4.8.
California Institute of Technology, U.S.A., 3.1.15., 3.1.17., 3.3.1.
Calorimetric data, publication of (IUPAC), 6.4.2.
Canadian National Committee for CODATA, 1.2.1.
Capacity ratio, gas chromatography, 3.6.2.
Carbides, thermodynamic properties, 3.4.5., 3.4.10.
Carbohydrates, nomenclature (IUPAC), 6.3.1.
Carbonates, decomposition reactions, kinetics data, 3.4.13.
—, mineralogical data, 3.3.10.
—, thermodynamic properties, 3.4.5., 3.4.13.
Carbon compounds, crystal structures, 3.3.4.
Carbon-containing compounds, crystallographic properties, crystal structures, 3.3.7.
Carbon dioxide, physical properties, 3.4.17.
— —, thermodynamic properties, 3.4.2., 3.4.15., 3.4.17.
— —, thermophysical properties, 5.3.57.
— —, transport properties, 3.4.15.
Carbon (C_2) molecule, Swan system, 3.2.22.
Carbon monoxide, band spectrum, 3.2.6.

Carbon monoxide, cryogenic data, 3.4.21.
— —, energy levels, spectroscopic data, 3.2.6.
— —, physical properties, 3.4.17.
— —, thermodynamic properties, 3.4.2., 3.4.17.
— —, — —, low temperature, 3.4.21.
Carnegie Institute of Technology, U.S.A., 2.3., 3.4.3.
Carotenoids, nomenclature (IUPAC), 6.3.1.
Catalogue of IAEA Nuclear Data Unit (CINDU), 3.1.8.
Catalysts, metallic, hydrogenation of ethylene on, 3.5.3.
Catholic University of America, U.S.A., 3.2.46.
Cell potential, see Electromotive force (emf)
CENTERS COVERING A NUMBER OF AREAS OF SCIENCE, 2.
CENTRAL BUREAU OF NUCLEAR MEASUREMENTS, 4.1.2.
Ceramics, engineering properties, 5.4.8.
—, phase diagrams, 3.4.12.
—, thermophysical properties, 3.4.20.
Cermets, thermophysical properties, 3.4.20.
Chalcogenides, crystal structures, phase diagrams, 3.4.11.
Characteristic groups containing C, H, O, N, S, Se, Te, and halogens, nomenclature (IUPAC), 6.3.1.
Characteristic Wavelengths for Emission and Absorption Bands of Diatomic Molecules, Atlas of, Tables de Constantes Sélectionnées, 2.2., **3.2.8.**
CHARGED-PARTICLE CROSS SECTIONS, **3.1.13.**
Charged-particle cross sections, 3.1.3., 3.1.13.
Charge Exchange, 3.2.11.
Chemical Abstracts, 3.1.13., 3.2.14., 3.2.21., 3.2.31., 3.2.36., 3.2.41., 3.2.43., 3.2.44., 3.3.14., 3.4.4., 3.4.11., 3.4.23., 4.2.2., 6.2.3., 6.3.1.
CHEMICAL COMPOUNDS, SELECTED VALUES OF PROPERTIES OF, 2.3., **3.4.3.**, *see also* 3.4.2.

CHEMICAL KINETICS, 1.1.1., 3.4.13., 3.5.1.—3.5.5., 5.2.4.
Chemical kinetics data, bimolecular gas reactions, 3.5.2.
— —, decomposition reactions of inorganic salts, 3.4.13.
— — —, homogeneous chemical reactions, 3.5.1.
— — —, hydrogenation of ethylene, catalyzed, 3.5.3.
— — —, neutral oxygen species gas phase reactions, 3.5.5
Chemical Kinetics Data Project, *see* Chemical Kinetics Information Center
CHEMICAL KINETICS INFORMATION CENTER, **3.5.1.**, 3.5.2., 3.5.5.
Chemical properties, crystals, 4.3.4.
— —, elements, 3.6.7., 5.4.13.
— —, minerals, 3.3.10., 3.3.11.
— —, silicates, 3.3.11.
Chemical reactions, homogeneous, kinetics data, 3.5.1.
Chemical Society, U.K., 3.2.44., 3.4.24.
CHEMICAL THERMODYNAMIC PROPERTIES, SELECTED VALUES OF, **3.4.1.**
CHEMICAL THERMODYNAMICS IN NONFERROUS METALLURGY, **3.4.8.**
Chemische Krystallographie, 3.3.8., 4.3.4.
Chemistry and Chemical Industry (Kagaku To Kogyo), 6.2.3.
Chlorides, mass spectia, 3.2.35.
—, thermodynamic properties, 3.4.6.
Chromatographic data, *see* Gas chromatographic data
Chromophoric groups, ultraviolet spectral data for compounds containing, 3.2.34.
CINDA (COMPUTER INDEX OF NEUTRON DATA), 3.1.8., 3.1.11., 3.1.12., **3.1.19.**
—, Division of Technical Information Extension, USAEC, 3.1.19.
—, ENEA Neutron Data Compilation Centre, 3.1.11.
—, IAEA Nuclear Data Unit, 3.1.8.
—, U. S. S. R. Nuclear Data Information Centre, 3.1.12.
Ciphering, IUPAC Commission on, 6.3.1.

CIPM General Conference Proceedings, see Comptes Rendus des Séances de la ... ème Conference Générale des Poids et Mesures

Clarkson College of Technology, U.S.A., 4.2.4.

Classification, crystals, 3.3.1., 3.3.8.

—, gas chromatographic data, 3.6.1.

—, organic structures of interest in ultraviolet spectroscopy, 3.2.34.

Clinical chemistry, International Federation for, 6.2.3.

— —, IUPAC Commission on, 6.2.3.

— —, quantities and units, 6.2.3.

CN molecule, Red system, 3.2.22.

Coatings, thermal radiative properties, 3.4.20.

Coblentz Society, 3.2.18., 3.2.21., 6.4.3.

COBLENTZ SOCIETY INFRARED ABSORPTION SPECTRA, **3.2.18.**

CODATA, *see* Committee on Data for Science and Technology

Codification, IUPAC Commission on, 6.3.1.

COLLOID AND SURFACE PROPERTIES, 1.1.1., **4.2.**

Colloids, light scattering data, 4.2.4.

Colorimetric determination of elements, tables of spectrophotometric absorption data of compounds used for, 5.5.6.

Columbia University, U.S.A., 3.1.19.

Columbium, *see* Niobium

Combustion, enthalpy (heat) of, *see* Enthalpy (heat) of combustion

Combustion product components, thermodynamic properties, 3.4.6.

Comité Consultatif International Télégraphique et Téléphonique(CCITT), 6.1.2.

Comité Consultatif pour les Étalons de Mesure des Radiations Ionisantes, CIPM, 6.1.2.

Comité International des Poids et Mesures (CIPM), 6.1.1.—6.1.3., 6.2.1.

Commissariat à l'Energie Atomique, France, 3.2.37.

Commission Internationale d'Eclairage, *see* International Commission on Illumination (ICI)

Commission for Symbols, Units and Nomenclature, IUPAP (SUN Commission), 3.1.1., 3.1.13., 6.1.2., 6.2.3.

Commission on Atomic Weights, IUPAC, 6.2.3.

Commission on Clinical Chemistry, IUPAC, 6.2.3.

Commission on Codification, Ciphering and Punched Card Techniques, IUPAC, 6.3.1.

Commission on Crystallographic Data, IUCr, 3.3.1., 6.4.1.

Commission on Electroanalytical Chemistry, IUPAC, 3.4.25., 3.4.26.

Commission on Enzymes, IUB, 4.6.3.

Commission on Equilibrium Data, IUPAC, 3.4.24.

Commission 14 on Fundamental Spectroscopic Values, IAU, 6.2.3.

Commission on International Tables, IUCr, 3.3.6.

Commission on Molecular Structure and Spectroscopy, IUPAC, 3.2.24., 6.3.1., 6.4.3.

Commission on Nomenclature of Biological Chemistry, IUPAC, 6.3.1.

Commission on Nomenclature of Organic Chemistry, IUPAC, 6.3.1.

Commission on Nuclidic Masses and Related Constants, IUPAP, 6.2.3.

Commission on Physico-chemical Data and Standards, IUPAC, 6.2.3.

Commission on Physico-chemical Symbols and Terminology, IUPAC, *see* Commission on Symbols, Terminology and Units, IUPAC

Commission on Spectrochemical and Other Optical Procedures for Analysis, IUPAC, 5.5.6.

Commission on Structure Reports, IUCr, 3.3.4.

Commission on Symbols, Terminology and Units, IUPAC, 6.1.2., 6.2.3.

Commission on Thermodynamics and Thermochemistry, IUPAC, 3.4.15., 6.2.3., 6.4.2.

COMMITTEE ON DATA FOR SCIENCE AND TECHNOLOGY (CODATA), 1.1.2., 1.1.3., **1.2.,** 6.1.3.

Committee on Fundamental Constants, NAS, U. S. A., 3.4.9.

COMPENDIUM OF *AB INITIO* CALCULATIONS OF MOLECULAR ENERGIES AND PROPERTIES, **3.2.13.**

Compendium of Properties of Materials at Low Temperatures, 3.4.21.

Compendium of Thermal-Neutron Capture γ-Ray Measurements, 5.3.2.

Compilation of Gas Chromatographic Data, 3.6.2.

Complex compounds, instability constants, 5.3.51.

Complexes, metal-ion, *see* Metal-ion complexes

Composite systems, thermophysical properties, 3.4.20.

Composition at thermodynamic equilibrium, handbook on, 5.3.47.

Composition, superconductive metals, alloys 3.3.17.

COMPREHENSIVE MULTI-VOLUME HANDBOOKS, 5.1.

Compressibility coefficient, factor, cryogenic fluids, 3.4.21.

— —, —, elements, nonmetallic; inorganic, organic compounds, 3.4.3.

— —, —, hydrocarbon gases, 3.4.2.

Comptes Rendus des Séances de la ... ème Conférence Générale des Poids et Mesures, 6.2.1.

Compton (incoherent) scattering cross section, gamma, X-ray, 3.2.47.

Computer Index of Neutron Data, *see* CINDA

Concise Handbook for the Engineering Physicist: Nuclear Physics, Atomic Physics, 5.3.4.

Concise Handbook on Physicochemical Values, 5.2.7.

Conduction, valence band energy, inorganic semiconductors, 3.3.13.

Conductivity (conductance), electrical, *see* Resistivity, electrical

Conductivity thermal, alloys, 3.4.20.

—, —, cryogenic fluids, 3.4.21.

—, —, elements, 3.4.20.

—, —, —, compounds in steelmaking, 3.4.10.

—, —, gases, liquids, 5.3.64.

Conductivity, thermal, nonmetallic solids, liquids, gases, 3.4.20.

—, —, semiconductors, inorganic, 3.3.13.

—, —, steam, water, 3.4.16.

—, —, low temperature, alloys, metals, 3.4.21.

Conference on Electrical Insulation and Dielectric Phenomena, NRC, U. S. A., 3.2.14.

Consolidated Index of Selected Property Values: Physical Chemistry and Thermodynamics, 3.4.27.

Constitutional diagrams, *see* Phase diagrams

Constitution of Binary Alloys, 3.4.11.

CONTRIBUTIONS TO THE DATA ON THEORETICAL METALLURGY, **3.4.5.**

Conversion factors, atomic, weight percent, 3.4.11.

— —, energy, 3.1.4., 3.2.33.

— —, infrared wavelength, wavenumber, 3.2.24.

— —, physical quantities, 6.1.2., 6.2.2.

— —, reciprocal centimeter, electron volt, 3.2.1.

— —, ultraviolet-visible wavelength, wavenumber, 3.2.33.

— —, unit systems, 6.2.2.

Copper, catalysis of ethylene hydrogenation with, 3.5.3.

—, thermodynamic properties, low temperature, 3.4.14.

— and compounds, thermodynamic properties, 3.4.8.

Corrinoids, nomenclature (IUPAC), 6.3.1.

Corrosion, 2.1.

Coupling constants, Coriolis, quadrupole, 3.2.26.

Critical Analysis of the Heat Capacity Data of the Literature and Evaluation of Thermodynamic Properties of Copper, Silver, and Gold from 0 to 300 °K, 3.4.14.

Critical Data in Britain 1966—67, **1.1.2.**

Critical magnetic fields, temperatures, superconductive metals, alloys, 3.3.17.

Critical micelle concentrations for amphipathic, surface active compounds in aqueous solution, 4.2.3.

Critical temperature, pressure, volume, density, elements, 3.4.3., 3.4.7.
— —, —, —, gases, industrial, 3.4.17.
— —, —, —, hydrocarbons, 3.4.2.
— —, —, —, inorganic, organic compounds, 3.4.3., 3.4.7.
— —, —, —, organometallic compounds, 3.4.7.
Cross Section Evaluation Center, *see* National Neutron Cross Section Center (NNCSC), U.S.A.
Cross Section Information Storage and Retrieval System (CSISRS), 3.1.7.
Cross section measurements, neutron, standards for, 3.1.8.
Cross section, charged particle, 3.1.3., 3.1.13.
— —, electron collision, low energy, 3.2.5.
— —, elementary processes, radiation chemistry, 4.3.3.
— —, gamma ray, 3.1.6., 3.1.19.
— —, heavy particle collision, 3.2.11.
— —, neutron, 3.1.3., 3.1.4., 3.1.7.—3.1.12., 3.1.14., 3.1.19., 4.1.3.
— —, nuclear, 3.1.1., 3.1.2., 3.1.13.
— —, photon, 3.1.3., 3.1.10., 3.1.13., 3.1.18., 3.2.5., 3.2.47.
CRYOGENIC DATA CENTER, 3.3.12., **3.4.21.,** *see also* 3.4.14.
Cryogenic fluids, magnetic properties, 3.4.21.
— —, surface tension, 4.2.2.
Cryoscopic constant, elements, nonmetallic; inorganic, organic compounds, 3.4.3.
Crystal and Solid State Physics, Landolt-Börnstein, New Series, 2.1.
CRYSTAL DATA, **3.3.1.,** 3.3.7.
Crystal Data Center, National Bureau of Standards, U.S.A., 3.3.1.
Crystalline materials, physicochemical properties, 5.3.27.
— —, X-ray diffraction data, 3.3.3.
Crystallization and Physiochemical Properties of Crystalline Substances, 5.3.27.
CRYSTALLOGRAPHIC PROPERTIES, 3.2.44., 3.3.1.—3.3.11., 3.3.13., 3.3.17., 3.6.7., 4.3.1., 5.3.26.—5.3.28.
— —, alloys, 3.3.1.

CRYSTALLOGRAPHIC PROPERTIES, carbon-containing compounds, 3.3.7.
— —, elements, 3.3.1., 3.6.7.
— —, handbooks on, 5.3.26.—5.3.28.
— —, inorganic compounds, 3.3.1.
— —, materials at high pressures, temperatures, 4.3.1.
— —, minerals, 3.3.10., 3.3.11., 5.2.17.
— —, organic compounds, 3.3.1.
— —, proteins, 3.3.1.
— —, semiconductors, inorganic, 3.3.13.
— —, silicate minerals, 3.3.11.
— —, superconductive metals, alloys, 3.3.17.
Crystallographic Terms, Dictionary of, 3.3.6.
Crystals, Barker index of, 3.3.8.
—, chemical properties, 4.3.4.
—, classification by space groups, 3.3.1.
—, dielectric properties, 2.1., 3.3.9.
—, elastic, electrooptic constants, 3.3.9.
—, identification, 3.3.1., 3.3.8.
—, interatomic distances, 3.3.6.
—, interfacial angles, 3.3.8.
—, morphology, 3.3.1., 3.3.2., 3.3.8., 4.3.4.
—, optical properties, 3.3.1., 3.3.8.
—, physical properties, 3.3.1., 3.3.3., 3.3.8., 4.3.4.
—, piezoelectric, piezooptic constants, 3.3.9.
—, X-ray diffraction data, 3.3.6., 3.3.8.
CRYSTAL STRUCTURES, **3.3.2.**
Crystal structure, aliphatic compounds, 3.3.2.
— —, alloys, 3.3.1., 3.3.3., 3.3.5., 3.4.11.
— —, amino acids, 3.3.2.
— —, ammoniates, 3.3.2.
— —, binary compounds, 3.3.2.
— —, benzene derivatives, 3.3.2.
— —, borides, 3.4.11.
— —, carbon compounds, 3.3.4.
— —, carbon-containing, compounds, 3.3.7.
— —, chalcogenides, 3.4.11.
— —, classification by Bravais lattice and atoms per unit cell, 3.3.5.

Crystal structure, elements, 3.3.1.,
3.3.2., 3.4.4., 3.4.7., 3.4.11.
— —, halogen compounds, 3.4.4.
— —, hydrates, 3.3.2.
— —, hydrides, 3.4.11.
— —, hydrogen compounds, 3.4.4.
— —, inorganic compounds,
3.2.44., 3.3.1.—3.3.4., 3.4.7.
— —, intermetallic compounds, 3.3.5.
— —, metals, 2.2., 3.3.3.—3.3.5.,
3.3.12.
— —, minerals, 3.3.3., 3.3.10., 3.3.11.
— —, organic compounds, 2.1.,
3.2.44., 3.3.1.—3.3.4., 3.4.7.
— —, organometallic compounds,
3.3.3., 3.4.7.
— —, oxides, 3.4.11., 5.4.9.
— —, oxygen compounds, 3.4.4.
— —, phosphides, 3.4.11.
— —, polymorphs, high pressure,
4.3.1.
— —, refractory compounds, 5.4.9.
— —, sesquiterpenoids, 3.2.48.
— —, silicates, 3.3.2., 3.3.11.
Curie constant, temperature, 3.3.14.,
3.3.15.
Current Contents, 4.3.6.
Cyanides, phase diagrams, 3.4.12.
Czechoslovak Academy of Sciences,
3.2.23.

DANA'S SYSTEM OF MINERALOGY,
3.3.10.
DATA CENTER FOR ATOMIC AND MOLEC-
ULAR IONIZATION PROCESSES,
3.2.12., 3.2.38.
DATA FOR THE FIELD OF CRITICAL
MICELLE CONCENTRATIONS, **4.2.3.**
DATA RELATIVE TO SESQUITERPENOIDS,
TABLES DE CONSTANTES SÉLECTION-
NÉES, 2.2., **3.2.48.**
Data Storage and Retrieval System,
IAEA (DASTAR), 3.1.8.
Decay scheme, light nuclei, 3.1.1.,
3.1.15., 3.1.16.
— —, nuclei, 3.1.2., 3.1.4., 3.1.14.,
3.1.17.
DECAY SCHEMES OF RADIOACTIVE NU-
CLEI, **3.1.14.**
Decomposition reactions, inorganic
salts, sulfates, 3.4.13.

Definitions, International Practical
Temperature Scale (IPTS), 6.2.1.
—, SI Units, 6.2.1.
—, thermodynamic temperature scale,
6.2.1.
Density, air, 3.4.19.
—, alloys, 3.4.20., 4.3.6.
—, elements, 3.4.3., 3.4.20.
—, —, compounds in steelmaking,
3.4.10.
—, gases, industrial, 3.4.17.
—, hydrocarbons, 3.4.2.
—, inorganic compounds, 3.2.19.,
3.4.3.
—, metals, 3.4.8., 4.3.6.
—, minerals, 3.3.10., 5.2.17.
—, molten salts, 3.4.22.
—, nonmetallic solids, 3.4.20.
—, organic compounds, 3.2.19., 3.4.3.
—, semiconductors, inorganic, 3.3.13.
—, sulfates, 3.4.13.
Deoxidation reactions in molten steel,
equilibrium constants, 4.3.7.
Department of Scientific and Industrial
Research, U.K., 3.3.8.
Depolarization ratios, *see* Polarization
data, Raman spectra
Depolarization values, light scattering; colloids, detergents, electrolytes, polymers, 4.2.4.
DESK HANDBOOKS FOR BROAD FIELDS
OF SCIENCE, 5.2.
Detergents, light scattering data,
4.2.4.
Determinative Tables, Crystal Data,
3.3.1.
Deuterium, atomic energy levels, 3.2.1.
—, thermodynamic properties, 3.4.7.,
3.4.15.
—, transport properties, 3.4.15.
Deutsche Akademie der Wissenschaf-
ten, D.D.R., 3.1.2.
Deutsche Forschungsgemeinschaft,
Germany — B.R.D., 1.2.2.
Deutsches KunststoffInstitut,Germany-
B.R.D., 3.2.50
Diamagnetic susceptibility, *see* Magne-
tic susceptibility
DIAMAGNÉTISME ET PARAMAGNÉTISME,
TABLES DE CONSTANTES SÉLECTION-
NÉES, 2.2., 3.3.14., **3.3.15.**

Diamond, semiconducting properties, 3.3.13.

DIATOMIC MOLECULE SPECTRA AND ENERGY LEVELS DATA CENTER, **3.2.6.**

Diatomic molecules, atomic collision data, low energy, 3.2.5.

— —, energy levels, 3.2.6., 3.2.7., 3.2.9., 3.2.13.

— —, microwave spectra, 3.2.25.

— —, notation for spectra of, 6.2.3.

— —, optical spectroscopic data, 3.2.6.

— —, physical constants, 3.2.7., 3.2.13., 3.2.26.

— —, rotational, vibrational spectra, 3.2.9., 3.2.22.

— —, spectroscopic data, 2.2., 3.2.7., 3.2.8.

— —, wavelengths for absorption, emission bands of, 3.2.8.

Dictionary of Crystallographic Terms, 3.3.6.

Dielectric properties, alloys, 3.3.9.

— —, cryogenic fluids, 3.4.21.

— —, crystals, 2.1.

— —, halides, 3.2.15.

— —, inorganic compounds, 3.2.14., 3.2.15., 3.3.9.

— —, liquids, 5.3.29.

— —, minerals, 3.3.9.

— —, organic compounds, 3.2.14., 3.2.15., 3.3.9.

— —, semiconductors, inorganic, 3.3.13.

— —, solutions, 5.3.29.

— —, low temperature, alloys, metals, 3.4.21.

Dielectric Properties of Liquids and Solutions, 5.3.29.

Dielectrics, cryogenic data, 3.4.21.

—, digest of literature on, 3.2.14.

Diffusion coefficient, cryogenic fluids, 3.4.21.

— —, elements, compounds in steel-making, 3.4.10.

— —, metals, alloys, 4.3.5.

— —, metal slags, melts, 3.4.10.

DIFFUSION IN METALS AND ALLOYS, DATA CENTER, **4.3.5.**

DIGEST OF LITERATURE ON DIELECTRICS, **3.2.14.**

Dilution, enthalpy (heat) of, *see* Enthalpy (heat) of dilution

Dimensionless Parameters (ISO), 6.2.2.

Dipole moment, *see* Magnetic dipole moment

Directory to Nuclear Data Tabulations, 3.1.1.

Disintegration energy (Q value), ground state, 3.1.1., 3.1.2., 3.1.15., 3.1.17.

Dispersions, light scattering data, 4.2.4.

DISSOCIATION CONSTANTS OF ACIDS AND BASES, **3.4.25.**

Dissociation constant, alkaloids, 3.2.23.

— —, elements, inorganic compounds, gaseous, 3.4.6.

— —, inorganic, organic acids, bases, 3.4.25.

— —, metal-ion complexes, 3.4.24.

Dissociation energy, diatomic, polyatomic molecules, 3.2.13.

Dissociation enthalpy (heat), entropy of, *see* Enthalpy (heat), Entropy of dissociation

Disulfides, properties, ideal gas state, 5.4.2.

DOCUMENTATION OF MOLECULAR SPECTROSCOPY (DMS), **3.2.19.**, 3.2.34.

DONNÉES SPECTROSCOPIQUES CONCERNANT LES MOLÉCULES DIATOMIQUES, TABLES DE CONSTANTES SÉLECTIONNÉES, 2.2., **3.2.7.**

Dow Thermal Research Laboratory, U.S.A., 3.4.4.

Earth sciences, handbooks, 5.2.17. — 5.2.22.

ECSIL, System for Storage, Retrieval and Display of Experimental Neutron Data, 3.1.3.

Effective mass of conducting band, inorganic semiconductors, 3.3.13.

EFFET MAGNÉTO-OPTIQUE DE KERR, TABLES DE CONSTANTES SÉLECTIONNÉES, 2.2., **3.3.16.**

Eigenschaften der Materie in ihren Aggregatzuständen, Landolt-Börnstein, Sixth Edition, 2.1.

ELASTIC, PIEZOELECTRIC, PIEZOOPTIC AND ELECTROOPTIC CONSTANTS OF CRYSTALS, LANDOLT-BÖRNSTEIN, 2.1 , **3.3.9.**

Elastic properties, *see also* Mechanical properties,

— —, alloys, elements, inorganic compounds, minerals, 3.3.9.

— —, rocks, rock-forming minerals, 5.2.19.

— —, semiconductors, inorganic, 3.3.13.

Elastomers, abbreviation of terms relating to (IUPAC), 6.3.1.

—, ultraviolet spectra, 5.3.13.

Electrical and magnetic properties, handbooks, 5.3.29.—5.3.36.

Electrical and Optical Properties of Semiconductors, 5.3.36.

Electrical conductivity (conductance), *see* Resistivity, electrical

Electrical Conductivity of Ferroelectric Materials, 5.3.34.

Electrical engineering (Elektrotechnik), 2.1.

Electrical instrumentation and measurements, 3.2.14.

ELECTRICAL PROPERTIES OF INTERFACES, **4.2.1.**

Electrical Research Association, U.K., 3.4.16.

ELECTRICAL RESISTIVITY OF METALS AT LOW TEMPERATURES, **3.3.12.**, *see also* 3.4.14., 3.4.21.

Electrical technology, letter symbols used in (IEC 27), 6.2.2.

Electric and Magnetic Magnitudes and Units, Technical Committee 24, IEC, 6.1.2.

Electric charge radius, atomic, *see* Nuclear Radii

ELECTRIC DIPOLE MOMENTS FOR MOLECULES IN THE GAS PHASE, SELECTED VALUES OF, **3.2.15.**

Electricity, quantities and units (IEC 164), (ISO R31), 6.2.2.

Electric quadrupole moment, nuclear, 3.1.14.

Electroanalytical chemistry, IUPAC Commission on, 3.4.25., 3.4.26.

Electrocapillary data, 4.2.1.

Electrochemical Data, 5.3.50.

Electrochemical equilibria in aqueous solutions, 5.3.49.

Electrochemical properties, elements, 3.6.7.

Electrode potential, electrolyte solutions, 4.3.9.

— —, inorganic half-cell reactions, 3.4.26.

Electrokinetic properties, 4.2.1.

Electrolytes, activity properties in binary solutions of salts, acids, alkalis, 5.3.53.

—, light scattering data, 4.2.4.

—, magnetic rotatory power (Faraday Effect), 3.3.16.

—, aqueous uni-univalent, heat capacity, enthalpy of solution, dilution, 3.4.1.

—, aqueous, non-aqueous, properties, 4.3.9.

Electromotive force (emf), electrolyte solutions, 4.3.9.

— — —, formation cells, 3.4.22.

Electron affinity, atoms, ions, 3.2.45.

— —, molecules, 3.2.13., 3.2.45.

Electron capture, numerical tables for, 2.1.

Electron collision, low energy, ionization of atoms, diatomic molecules by, 3.2.5.

Electron gas, thermodynamic properties, 3.4.6.

Electron, hole mobility, inorganic semiconductors, 3.3.13.

Electronic binding energy, *see* Binding energy, electronic

Electronic coefficient of heat capacity, metals, 3.4.14.

Electronic Properties of Semi-conductor Solid Solutions, 5.3.33.

Electronic spectra, molecular, *see* Molecular electronic spectra

Electronic structure, alloys, intermetallic compounds, metals, 4.3.6.

— —, carbon monoxide, 3.2.6.

— —, polyatomic molecules, 3.2.9.

Electronic transport properties, alloys, intermetallic compounds, metals, 4.3.6.

Electronic (thermionic) work function, *see* Work function

Electron paramagnetic resonance (EPR) spectroscopy, alloys, intermetallic compounds, metals, 4.3.6.

Electron paramagnetic resonance (ERP) spectroscopy, documentation of literature, 3.2.19.
Electron spin resonance (ESR) spectra, 3.3.14., 5.3.23., 5.3.24.
Electrooptic constant (Pockels Effect), inorganic compounds, 2.1., 3.3.9.
Elementary processes, radiation chemistry, 4.3.3.
Elements, atomic energy levels, 3.2.1.—3.2.3.
—, atomic spectra, 3.2.1., 3.2.4.
—, chemical properties, 3.6.7., 5.4.13.
—, colorimetric determination of, 5.5.6.
—, crystallographic properties, 3.3.1., 3.6.7.
—, crystal structures, 3.3.1., 3.3.2., 3.4.4., 3.4.7., 3.4.11.
—, Curie temperature, 3.3.15.
—, elastic constants, 3.3.9.
—, electrical properties, 3.6.7.
—, electrochemical properties, 3.6.7.
—, gamma-ray attenuation coefficients, 3.2.47.
—, magnetic moment, susceptibility, 3.3.15.
—, magnetic properties, 2.2., 3.3.15., 3.3.16., 3.6.7.
—, magnetic rotatory power (Faraday Effect), 3.3.16.
—, mass spectra, 3.2.35.
—, mechanical properties, 3.6.7.
—, mineralogical data, 3.3.10.
—, multiplet tables, 3.2.1.
—, nuclear properties, 3.1.1.—3.1.4., 3.6.7.
—, optical properties, 3.3.1., 3.4.3., 3.4.10., 3.6.7.
—, photon cross sections, 3.1.3., 3.2.47.
—, photonuclear data, 3.1.18.
—, physical properties, 3.4.11.
—, physicochemical properties, 3.6.7.
—, radioisotope data, 3.1.4.
—, solubilities, 3.4.10., 3.4.23.
—, specific heat, low temperature, 3.4.14.
—, standard order of arrangement, 3.2.16., 3.4.1.—3.4.3., 3.4.6., 3.4.7.
—, thermionic properties, 5.3.31.
Elements, thermodynamic properties, 2.3., 3.4.1., 3.4.4.—3.4.7., 3.4.10., 3.4.20., 3.6.7., 5.3.38.
—, — —, low temperature, 3.4.14.
—, thermophysical properties, 3.4.20., 5.3.58., 5.3.59., 5.3.63.
—, transition probabilities, atomic, 3.2.2.
—, transport properties, 3.4.20.
—, vapor pressure, 3.4.1., 3.4.3., 3.4.5.—3.4.7., 3.4.10., 3.4.20., 5.3.37.
—, work functions, 5.3.31.
—, X-ray attenuation coefficients, 3.2.47.
—, X-ray spectra, 3.2.3.
—, metallic, cryogenic data, 3.4.21.
—, nonmetallic, thermodynamic properties, 3.4.3.
Emissivity (emittance), thermal, see Thermal radiative properties
ENEA NEUTRON DATA COMPILATION CENTRE, SACLAY, 3.1.8.—3.1.10., 3.1.11., 3.1.12., 3.1.19.
Energy levels, atomic, 3.2.1.—3.2.3.
— —, diatomic molecules, 3.2.6., 3.2.7., 3.2.9., 3.2.13.
— —, heavy nuclei, 4.1.4.
— —, light nuclei, 3.1.1., 3.1.15., 3.1.16.
— —, molecules, 3.2.9., 3.2.13.
— —, nuclei, 3.1.1., 3.1.2., 3.1.4., 3.1.14.—3.1.17., 4.1.4.
— —, radioactive nuclei, 3.1.14.
ENERGY LEVELS OF LIGHT NUCLEI, 3.1.1., 3.1.15., 3.1.16.
ENERGY LEVELS OF NUCLEI: $A = 5$ to $A = 257$, LANDOLT-BÖRNSTEIN, 2.1., 3.1.17.
Energy Levels of Nuclei, $A = 21$ to $A = 212$, 3.1.1.
ENERGY LEVELS OF $Z = 11$—21 NUCLEI, 3.1.1., 3.1.15., 3.1.16.
Energy of activation, bimolecular gas reactions, 3.5.2.
— — —, diffusion in metals, alloys, 4.3.5.
— — —, elementary processes, radiation chemistry, 4.3.3.
— — —, homogeneous chemical reactions, inorganic, organic, 3.5.1.
Engineering Compendium on Radiation Shielding, 3.2.47.

Subject Index

Engineering properties, 1.1.3., 2.1., 3.1.6., 5.4.8.
Engineering Properties of Selected Ceramic Materials, 5.4.8.
Enthalpy (heat content), air, 3.4.19.
— — —, alloys, 3.4.9.
— — —, cryogenic fluids, 3.4.21.
— — —, elements, 3.4.1., 3.4.3.–3.4.7.
— — —, —, compounds in steelmaking, 3.4.10.
— — —, fluids, simple, 3.4.15.
— — —, gases, industrial, 3.4.17.
— — —, halogen, hydrogen, oxygen compounds, 3.4.4.
— — —, hydrocarbon gases, 3.4.2.
— — —, inorganic compounds, 3.4.1., 3.4.3., 3.4.5.—3.4.7.
— — —, metals, 3.4.9., 3.4.14.
— — —, organic compounds, 3.4.1., 3.4.3., 3.4.7.
— — —, organometallic compounds, 3.4.7.
— — —, steam, water, 3.4.16.
— — —, low temperature, alloys, metals, 3.4.21.
Enthalpy function, ammonia (ideal gas), 3.4.18.
— —, hydrocarbon gases, 3.4.2.
— —, metals, 3.4.8., 3.4.14.
Enthalpy function of formation, elements, nonmetallic; inorganic, organic compounds, 3.4.3.
Enthalpy (heat) of activation, catalyzed hydrogenation of ethylene, 3.5.3.
— — — —, homogeneous chemical reactions, inorganic, organic, 3.5.1.
Enthalpy (heat) of combustion, hydrocarbons, 3.4.2.
Enthalpy (heat) of dilution, electrolytes, aqueous uni-univalent, 3.4.1.
Enthalpy (heat) of dissociation, elements, inorganic and organic compounds, 3.4.7.
— — — —, metal-ion complexes, 3.4.24.
Enthalpy (heat) of formation, atoms from elements, 3.2.45.
— — — —, elements, 3.4.1., 3.4.3.—3.4.7.
— — — —, —, compounds in steelmaking, 3.4.10.

Enthalpy (heat) of formation, halogen, hydrogen, oxygen compounds, 3.4.4.
— — — —, hydrocarbons, 3.4.2.
— — — —, inorganic compounds, 3.4.1., 3.4.3., 3.4.5.—3.4.7.
— — — —, metals, nonferrous, 3.4.8.
— — — —, organic compounds, 3.4.1., 3.4.3., 3.4.7.
— — — —, organometallic compounds, 3.4.7.
— — — —, oxides, inorganic, 3.4.5.
— — — —, positive ions, gaseous, 3.2.12.
— — — —, radicals, inorganic, organic, 3.2.45.
— — — —, sulfate decomposition, reactants, products, 3.4.13.
Enthalpy (heat) of mixing, *see* Enthalpy of solution
Enthalpy (heat) of phase change, alloys, 3.4.20.
— — — — —, elements, 3.4.1., 3.4.3., 3.4.5., 3.4.7., 3.4.20.
— — — — —, —, compounds in steelmaking, 3.4.10.
— — — — —, hydrocarbons, 3.4.2.
— — — — —, inorganic compounds, 3.4.1., 3.4.3., 3.4.5., 3.4.7.
— — — — —, metals, nonferrous, 3.4.8., 3.4.9.
— — — — —, nonmetallic solids, 3.4.20.
— — — — —, organic compounds, 3.4.1., 3.4.3., 3.4.7.
— — — — —, organometallic compounds, 3.4.7.
— — — — —, semiconductors, inorganic, 3.3.13.
Enthalpy (heat) of solution, electrolytes, aqueous uni-univalent, 3.4.1.
Enthalpy-entropy diagram for steam, water, 3.4.16.
Entropy, air and components, 3.4.19.
—, alloys, 3.4.9.
—, ammonia (ideal gas), 3.4.18.
—, cryogenic fluids, 3.4.21.
—, elements, 3.4.1., 3.4.3., 3.4.4.—3.4.7.
—, —, compounds in steelmaking, 3.4.10.

Entropy, fluids, simple, 3.4.15.
—, gases, industrial, 3.4.17.
—, halogen, hydrogen, oxygen compounds, 3.4.4.
—, hydrocarbon gases, 3.4.2.
—, inorganic compounds, 3.4.1., 3.4.3., 3.4.5.—3.4.7.
—, metals, 3.4.9., 3.4.14.
—, organic compounds, 3.4.1., 3.4.3., 3.4.7.
—, organometallic compounds, 3.4.7.
—, steam, water, 3.4.16.
Entropy of activation, elementary processes, radiation chemistry, 4.3.3.
— — —, homogeneous chemical reactions, inorganic, organic, 3.5.1.
Entropy of dissociation, metal-ion complexes, 3.4.24.
Entropy of formation, alloys, 3.4.9.
— — —, elements, 3.4.1.
— — —, inorganic, organic compounds, 3.4.1.
— — —, metals, nonferrous, 3.4.8.
— — —, sulfate decomposition, reactants, products, 3.4.13.
Entropy of phase change, elements, 3.4.1., 3.4.3., 3.4.7.
— — — —, hydrocarbons, 3.4.2.
— — — —, inorganic compounds, 3.4.1., 3.4.3., 3.4.7.
— — — —, metals, 3.4.8., 3.4.9.
— — — —, organic compounds, 3.4.1., 3.4.3., 3.4.7.
— — — —, organometallic compounds, 3.4.7.
Enzymes, classification, nomenclature (IUB), 6.3.4.
Equation of state, water and steam, 3.4.16.
Equilibrium constant of dissociation, see Dissociation constant
Equilibrium constant of formation, elements, 3.4.1., 3.4.3.
— — — —, —, compounds in steel-making, 3.4.10.
— — — —, halogen, hydrogen, oxygen compounds, 3.4.4.
— — — —, hydrocarbons, 3.4.2.
— — — —, inorganic compounds, 3.4.1., 3.4.3.

Equilibrium constant of formation, organic compounds, 3.4.1., 3.4.3.
Equilibrium constant of reaction, bimolecular gas reactions, 3.5.2.
— — — —, decomposition, inorganic salts, 3.4.13.
— — — — —, deoxidation, molten steel, 4.3.7.
— — — — —, elementary processes, radiation chemistry, 4.3.3.
— — — —, metal-ion complexes, 3.4.24.
EQUILIBRIUM CONSTANTS OF MOLTEN STEEL, **4.3.7.**
Equilibrium diagrams, see Phase diagrams
Esters, thermodynamic properties, 3.4.3.
Ethane, physical, thermodynamic properties, 3.4.17.
Ethers, thermodynamic properties, 3.4.2.
Ethylene, physical, thermodynamic properties, 3.4.17.
European Nuclear Energy Agency (ENEA), 3.1.7.—3.1.12., 3.1.19.
Eutectics, binary, 3.4.11.
Evaluated Nuclear Data File (ENDF), 3.1.7., 3.1.11.
Evaluation of Infrared Reference Data, Specifications for, 6.4.3.
Excitation, Ionization and Dissociation by Heavy Particles, 3.2.11.
Excitation, ionization of atoms, diatomic molecules, by electron impact, 3.2.5.
Expansion, thermal, alloys, elements, nonmetallic solids, 3.4.20.
—, —, cryogenic fluids, 3.4.21.
—, —, semiconductors, inorganic, 3.3.13.
—, —, low temperature, alloys, metals, 3.4.21.

Faraday Effect, see Magnetic rotatory power
Far infrared spectra, see Infrared, Molecular rotational spectra
Ferrites, magnetic properties, 2.1., 3.3.14.

Ferroelectric materials, 2.1.
— —, resistivity, electrical, 5.3.34.
Ferromagnetic metals, alloys, magneto-optic (Kerr) effect, 3.3.16.
Ferromagnetic transition temperature, *see* Curie temperature
Fink Inorganic Index, *see* Powder Diffraction File
Fluidity, *see* Viscosity
Fluids, simple, thermodynamic, transport properties, 3.4.15.
Fluorescence, *see* Luminescence
Fluorides, thermodynamic properties, 3.4.6.
Fluorine, cryogenic data, 3.4.21.
Folic acid and compounds, nomenclature, symbols (IUPAC), 6.3.1.
Force constant, 3.2.10.
Formation, enthalpy (heat), entropy, equilibrium constant, Gibbs (free) energy of, *see* Enthalpy (heat), Entropy, Equilibrium constant, Gibbs (free) energy of formation
Formulations for Industrial, Scientific and General Use, IFC, 3.4.16.
Free energy, *see* Gibbs energy
Free radicals, magnetic properties, 2.1., 3.2.50., 3.3.15.
Freezing point, *see* Melting point
Frequency factor, homogeneous chemical reactions, inorganic, organic, 3.5.1.
Fugacity coefficient, *see* Activity coefficient for gas
Fundamental constants, 3.1.4., 3.4.1., 3.4.2., 3.4.4., 3.4.9., 3.4.19., 6.2.3.
Fundamental Constants for Chemistry, Values of, 6.2.3.
Fundamental standards, 6.1.1.
Fusion, enthalpy, entropy of, *see* Enthalpy, Entropy of phase change
Fusion temperature, *see* Melting (freezing) point
Fysisch Laboratorium, the Netherlands, 3.1.16.

Gamma-rays,
— —, attenuation, elements, 3.2.47.
— —, —, reactor materials, 3.1.6.
— —, cross section, 3.1.6., 3.1.19.
— —, energy of quanta, 3.1.2.

Gamma-rays, Album of, 5.3.7.
Gamma-spectroscopy, angular correlation computations in, numerical tables for, 2.1.
Gas chromatographic data, computer analysis of, 3.6.2.
— — —, organic compounds, volatile, 3.6.1.
GAS CHROMATOGRAPHIC DATA COMMITTEE OF JAPAN (GCDC), **3.6.1.**
GAS CHROMATOGRAPHIC DATA COMPILATION, **3.6.2.**
Gases, light scattering data, 4.2.4.
—, microwave spectra, 3.2.25.
—, physical properties, 3.4.17.
—, thermal conductivity, 5.3.64.
—, thermal properties, 5.3.41.
—, thermophysical properties, 5.3.54., 5.3.62.
GAS PHASE REACTION KINETICS OF NEUTRAL OXYGEN SPECIES, 3.5.1., **3.5.5.**
General Electric Research and Development Center, U.S.A., 3.3.17.
General Principles Concerning Quantities, Units and Symbols (ISO), 6.2.2.
Geochemistry, 5.2.20.
Geological Society of America, U.S.A., 3.3.1., 3.3.10., 5.2.17.
Geology, 3.3.1., 3.3.10., 3.3.11., 5.2.17.
Geophysical Laboratory Temperature Scale, 3.4.12.
Geophysics and Space Research, Landolt-Börnstein, *New Series*, 2.1.
German Chemical Society, 5.1.2.
German National Committee for CODATA, 1.2.2.
Germanium, semiconducting properties, 3.3.13.
Gibbs (free) energy, alloys, 3.4.9.
— —, elements, 3.4.5.
— —, hydrocarbon gases, 3.4.2.
— —, inorganic compounds, 3.4.5.
— —, metals, 3.4.9., 3.4.14.
Gibbs (free) energy function, ammonia (ideal gas), 3.4.18.
— — — —, elements, 3.4.4., 3.4.6.
— — — —, —, compounds in steelmaking, 3.4.10.
— — — —, halogen, hydrogen, oxygen compounds, 3.4.4.

Gibbs (free) energy function, inorganic compounds, 3.4.6.

— — — —, metals, 3.4.8., 3.4.14.

Gibbs (free) energy function of formation, elements, nonmetallic; inorganic, organic compounds, 3.4.3.

Gibbs (free) energy of formation, alloys, 3.4.9.

— — — — —, elements, 3.4.1., 3.4.3.—3.4.5., 3.4.7.

— — — — —, —, compounds in steelmaking, 3.4.10.

— — — — —, halogen, hydrogen, oxygen compounds, 3.4.4.

— — — — —, hydrocarbons, 3.4.2.

— — — — —, inorganic compounds, 3.4.1., 3.4.3., 3.4.5., 3.4.7.

— — — — — —, metals, nonferrous, 3.4.8.

— — — — —, organic, compounds, 3.4.1., 3.4.3., 3.4.7.

— — — — —, organometallic compounds, 3.4.7.

— — — — —, oxides, inorganic, 3.4.5.

Gibbs (free) energy of phase change, elements, 3.4.5.

— — — — — —, inorganic compounds, 3.4.5.

— — — — — —, metals, 3.4.9.

Gibbs (free) energy of reaction, decomposition, inorganic salts, 3.4.13.

Glasses, thermophysical properties, 3.4.20.

Glycols, thermodynamic properties, 3.4.3.

Gmelin's Handbuch der anorganischen Chemie, 5.1.2.

Gold, thermodynamic properties, low temperature, 3.4.14.

GROTH INSTITUTE, **4.3.4.**

Grotrian Diagrams (Partial) of Astrophysical Interest, 3.2.1.

Group Constants for Nuclear Reactor Calculations, 5.3.1.

G value (quantum yield), *see* Radiolytic yield

Half-cell reactions, inorganic, electrode potentials, 3.4.26.

Half-life, *see* Radioactive disintegration

Halides, dielectric properties, 3.2.15.

—, dipole moments, molecular, 3.2.15.

—, mineralogical data, 3.3.10.

—, phase diagrams, 3.4.12.

—, specific heat, low temperature, 3.4.14.

—, thermodynamic properties, 3.4.5.

—, — —, low temperature, 3.4.14.

Halogens, molecular vibrational frequencies, 3.2.10.

—, thermodynamic properties, 3.4.4., 3.4.7.

Halogen compounds, crystal structures, 3.4.4.

— —, infrared spectra, 3.2.16.

— —, organic, Raman spectra, 3.2.28.

Handbook for The Chemical Society (London) Authors, 6.3.1.

Handbook of Analytical Chemistry, Japan, 5.5.1.

Handbook of Analytical Chemistry, U.S.A., 5.5.2.

Handbook of Biochemistry, Selected Data for Molecular Biology, 5.2.14.

Handbook of Chemistry, Japan, 5.2.6.

Handbook of Chemistry, U.S.A., 5.2.5.

Handbook of Chemistry and Physics, 5.2.1., 5.5.3.

Handbook of Compositions at Thermodynamic Equilibrium, 5.3.47.

Handbook of Inorganic Chemistry, 5.2.9.

HANDBOOK OF LATTICE SPACINGS AND STRUCTURES OF METALS AND ALLOYS, **3.3.5.**

Handbook of Organic Chemistry, 5.2.10.

Handbook of Organometallic Compounds, 5.4.15.

Handbook of Physical Constants, 5.2.17.

Handbook of Tables for Organic Compound Identification, 5.5.3.

HANDBOOK OF THE PHYSICOCHEMICAL PROPERTIES OF THE ELEMENTS, **3.6.7.**

Handbook of Thermionic Properties: Electronic Work Functions and Richardson Constants of Elements and Compounds, 5.3.31.

Handbook of Thermophysical Properties of Solid Materials, 3.4.20.

Handbook of Ultraviolet and Visible Absorption Spectra of Organic Compounds, 5.3.12.

Handbook of X-ray Structure Analysis of Polycrystalline Materials, 5.3.26.

Handbooks, analytical chemistry, 5.5.

—, astronomy, 6.2.3., 6.3.2.

—, biochemistry, 5.2.14., 5.2.16.

—, biology, 5.2.14.—5.2.16.

—, chemistry, physics, 5.2.1.—5.2.13., 6.3.1.

—, crystallographic properties, 5.3.26.—5.3.28.

—, crystal structures, metals, alloys, 3.3.5.

—, earth sciences, 5.2.17.—5.2.22.

—, electrical, magnetic properties, 5.3.29.—5.3.36.

—, molten salts data, 3.4.22.

—, nuclear properties, 5.3.1.—5.3.8.

—, physicochemical properties, elements, 3.6.7.

—, solid state properties, 5.3.26.—5.3.36.

—, special areas of science, 5.3.

—, spectroscopic properties, 5.3.9.—5.3.25.

—, substance categories, 5.4.

—, thermodynamic, transport properties, 5.3.37.—5.3.66.

—, thermophysical properties, solid materials, 3.4.20.

Handbuch des Chemikers, 5.2.4.

Harvard University, U.S.A., 3.3.10.

Haverford College, U.S.A., 3.1.15., 3.1.17.

Heat capacity, *see also* Specific heat

— —, air, 3.4.19.

— —, ammonia (ideal gas), 3.4.18.

— —, elements, 3.4.1., 3.4.3.—3.4.7.

— —, —, compounds in steelmaking, 3.4.10.

— —, halogen, hydrogen, oxygen compounds, 3.4.4.

— —, hydrocarbon gases, 3.4.2.

— —, inorganic compounds, 3.4.1., 3.4.3., 3.4.5.—3.4.7.

— —, metals, 3.4.8., 3.4.9., 3.4.14.

— —, organic compounds, 3.4.1., 3.4.3., 3.4.7.

Heat capacity, organometallic compounds, 3.4.7.

— —, apparent (in solution), electrolytes, aqueous uni-univalent, 3.4.1.

— —, specific isobaric, water, 3.4.16.

Heat Conductivity of Gases and Liquids, 5.3.64.

Heat (content), *see* Enthalpy

Heating engineering (Wärmetechnik), 2.1.

Heavy particle collision, cross sections, 3.2.11.

— — —, low energy, ionization of atoms, diatomic molecules by, 3.2.5.

Heavy particles, dissociation, excitation, ionization by, 3.2.11.

Heavy water, thermodynamic properties, 3.4.16.

Hebrew University, Israel, 3.2.31.

Helium, cryogenic data, 3.4.21.

—, thermodynamic, properties, 3.4.15.

—, — —, low temperature, 3.4.21.

—, transport properties, 3.4.15.

Heterocyclic systems, fundamental, nomenclature (IUPAC), 6.3.1.

HgH molecule, rotational, vibrational spectra, 3.2.22.,

High melting compounds, properties, 5.4.10., 5.4.11., *see also* High temperature materials, Refractory compounds

HIGH PRESSURE DATA CENTER OF JAPAN, 4.3.2.

HIGH PRESSURE DATA CENTER, U.S.A., 4.3.1., 4.3.2.

HIGH RESOLUTION NMR SPECTRA CATALOG, 3.2.42.

HIGH RESOLUTION NMR SPECTRA, JAPAN ELECTRON OPTICS LABORATORY LTD., 3.2.43.

HIGH TEMPERATURE BEHAVIOR OF INORGANIC SALTS, 3.4.13.

High temperature materials, properties, 5.4.4.

High temperature processes, thermodynamic data for, 3.4.6.

Hill System for chemical formulae, 3.4.4.

Hokkaido University, Japan, 3.5.3.

Hole mobility, *see* Electron mobility

Homopolymers, linear, physical constants, 5.4.16.
Hungarian Academy of Sciences, 3.2.33.
Hydrates, crystal structures, 3.3.2.
—, infrared spectra, 3.2.20.
Hydrides, catalysis of ethylene hydrogenation with, 3.5.3.
—, constitution data, crystal structures, 3.4.11.
—, mass spectra, 3.2.35., 3.2.36.
—, phase diagrams, 3.4.11.
—, physical properties, 3.2.36.
—, thermodynamic properties, 3.4.6.
Hydrocarbon Data Book, 5.4.18.
HYDROCARBONS AND RELATED COMPOUNDS, SELECTED VALUES OF PROPERTIES, 2.3., **3.4.2.**, *see also* 3.4.3.
Hydrocarbons, infrared spectra, 3.2.16.
—, mass spectra, 3.2.35.
—, molecular vibrational frequencies, 3.2.10.
—, NMR spectra, 3.2.39.
—, nomenclature (IUPAC), 6.3.1.
—, optical properties, 3.4.2.
—, Raman spectra, 3.2.27.
—, thermodynamic properties, 2.3., 3.4.2., 3.4.15.
—, transport properties, 3.4.2., 3.4.15.
—, ultraviolet spectra, 3.2.29.
Hydrogen, atomic energy levels, 3.2.1.
—, cryogenic data, 3.4.21.
—, mass spectra, 3.2.35.
—, spectroscopic data, 3.2.8.
—, thermodynamic properties, 3.4.7., 3.4.15.
—, transport properties, 3.4.15.
—, atomic, ionic, molecular; atomic collision data, low energy, 3.2.5.
—, liquid, solid; properties, 5.4.19.
Hydrogen compounds, crystal structures, thermodynamic properties, 3.4.4.
HYDROGENATION OF ETHYLENE ON METALLIC CATALYSTS, **3.5.3.**
Hyperfine structure, spectral lines, 3.2.1., 3.2.50.

IAEA NUCLEAR DATA UNIT, **3.1.8.**, 3.1.11., 3.1.12., 3.1.19.

Ideal gases, thermodynamic functions, 3.2.10., 3.4.4., 3.4.18.
Identification, crystals, Barker method for, 3.3.8.
—, rock-forming minerals, crystallographic, optical data for, 3.3.11.
—, substances from cell dimensions, 3.3.1.
Illinois Institute of Technology Research Institute, U.S.A., 3.4.11.
Illumination, International Commission on (ICI), 6.3.6.
Imperial Chemical Industries, U.K., 3.3.8.
Imperial College, U.K., 3.4.15.
INDEXES, API 44 — TRC selected data on thermodynamics and spectroscopy, 2.3.
—, Barker Index of Crystals, 3.3.8.
—, Chemical Kinetics, Tables of, 3.5.1.
—, Consolidated Index of Selected Property Values: Physical Chemistry and Thermodynamics, 3.4.27.
—, infrared spectral data, 2.3., 3.2.51.
—, mass spectral data, 2.3., 3.2.37., 3.2.38., 3.2.53.
—, neutron data, literature (CINDA), 3.1.19.
—, NMR spectral data, 2.3.
—, photonuclear data, 3.1.18.
—, Powder Diffraction File, 3.3.3.
—, Raman spectral data, 2.3.
—, Substance — Property, Bulletin of Thermodynamics and Thermochemistry, 2.3.
—, thermodynamic data, 2.3.
—, ultraviolet-visible spectral data, 2.3., 3.2.52.
Index de Spectres de Mass, *see* Compilation of Mass Spectral Data
Industrial compounds, infrared spectra, 3.2.18., 3.2.19., 3.2.21.
— —, NMR spectra, 3.2.41.
— —, physical properties, 3.2.18., 3.2.32., 3.2.41.
— —, ultraviolet, visible region, spectra, 3.2.32.
— —, nonhydrocarbon, infrared spectra, 3.2.17.
— —, —, ultraviolet spectra, 3.2.30.
Industrial standards, 6.1.2.

Inert fluids (Ne, Ar, Kr, Xe), *see* Rare gases

Inertia, moment, *see* Moment of inertia

Infrared Band Handbook, 5.3.17.—5.3.19.

INFRARED DATA COMMITTEE OF JAPAN (IRDC), 3.2.10., **3.2.20.**

Infrared File Searching System, ASTM (SIRCH), 3.2.51.

Infrared reference data, specifications for evaluation (Coblentz Society), 3.2.18., 6.4.3.

INFRARED SPECTRA, 2.3., 3.2.16.—3.2.24., 5.3.14.—5.3.21., *see also* molecular vibrational spectra

Infrared Spectra and Characteristic Frequencies 700 to 300 cm^{-1}, 5.3.16.

Infrared Spectra and X-ray Spectra of Hetero-organic Compounds, 5.3.15.

INFRARED SPECTRAL DATA, SELECTED, API RP44, 2.3., **3.2.16.**, *see also* 3.2.17.

INFRARED SPECTRAL DATA, SELECTED, TRC, 2.3., **3.2.17.**, *see also* 3.2.16.

Infrared spectral data, alkaloids, 3.2.20., 3.2.23.

— — —, films, coatings, adhesives, 3.2.21.

— — —, halogen compounds, 3.2.16.

— — —, hydrates, 3.2.20.

— — —, hydrocarbons, 3.2.16.

— — —, indexes to, 2.3., 3.2.51.

— — —, industrial compounds, 3.2.18., 3.2.19., 3.2.21.

— — —, industrial nonhydrocarbon compounds, 3.2.17.

— — —, inorganic compounds, 3.2.19., 3.2.21.

— — —, nitrogen compounds, 3.2.16.

— — —, organic compounds, 3.2.16.—3.2.21., 5.3.15.

— — —, oxygen compounds, 3.2.16.

— — —, steroids, 3.2.20., 3.2.21.

— — —, sulfur compounds, 3.2.16.

INFRARED SPECTRA, SADTLER RESEARCH LABORATORIES, INC., **3.2.21.**, 3.2.41.

Infrared spectrometers, calibration of, wavenumber tables for, 3.2.24.

Infrared spectroscopy, wavelength standards, 5.3.14.

Inorganic chemical reactions, homogeneous, chemical kinetics data, 3.5.1.

Inorganic chemistry, nomenclature (IUPAC), 6.3.1.

— —, Gmelin's Handbook, 5.1.2.

Inorganic compounds, boiling, melting (freezing) points, 3.2.19., 3.2.21., 3.2.33., 3.4.1., 3.4.3.

— —, cryogenic data, 3.4.21.

— —, crystallographic properties, 3.3.1.

— —, crystal structures, 3.2.44., 3.3.1.—3.3.4., 3.4.7.

— —, Curie temperature, 3.3.15.

— —, dielectric properties, 3.2.14., 3.2.15., 3.3.9.

— —, elastic, electrooptic constants, 3.3.9.

— —, infrared spectra, 3.2.19., 3.2.21.

— —, interatomic distances, configurations, 3.2.44.

— —, magnetic dipole moments, 3.2.15., 3.3.15.

— —, magnetic rotatory power (Faraday Effect), 2.2., 3.3.16.

— —, magnetic susceptibility, 3.3.15.

— —, mass spectra, 3.2.35., 3.2.36.

— —, molten salts data, 3.4.22.

— —, optical properties, 3.3.1., 3.4.3.

— —, phosphorescence, 2.1.

— —, physical properties, 3.2.19., 3.2.21., 3.2.33., 3.2.36.

— —, piezoelectric, piezooptic constants, 3.3.9.

— —, radiation chemistry data, 4.3.3.

— —, radiolytic yields, 3.5.4.

— —, semiconducting properties, 3.3.13.

— —, solubilities, 3.4.23., 3.4.24., 5.3.52.

— —, thermodynamic constants, 3.4.7., 5.3.39.

— —, thermodynamic properties, 3.4.1., 3.4.3., 3.4.5.—3.4.7.

— —, ultraviolet spectra, 3.2.30., 3.2.33.

— —, visible region spectra, 3.2.33.

— —, X-ray diffraction data, 3.3.3.

Inorganic molecules, bond energies, 3.2.45., 3.2.46.

— —, vibrational frequencies, 3.2.10., 3.4.4.

Inorganic salts, chemical kinetics data, thermodynamic properties, 3.4.13.
Inorganic sulfur compounds, thermodynamic properties, 3.4.5.
Instability constant, *see* Dissociation constant
Instability Constants of Complex Compounds, 5.3.51.
Institut Belge des Hautes Pressions, Belgium, 3.4.20.
Institute of Physics and Energetics, Obninsk, U. S. S. R., 3.1.12.
Institute of Physics, U. K., 3.3.1., 3.3.3.
Institut für Spektrochemie und Angewandte Spektroskopie, Germany-B. R. D., 3.2.19., 3.2.34.
Insulation, electrical, 3.2.14.
Interaction coefficient, metal slags, melts, 3.4.10.
INTERATOMIC DISTANCES AND CONFIGURATIONS IN MOLECULES AND IONS, **3.2.44.**, 3.3.7.
Interatomic distance, calculation of, 3.3.5.
— —, inorganic, organic, metallic crystals, 3.3.6.
Interconversion of unit systems, procedures for (ISO R31), 6.2.2.
Interface phenomena (Grenzflächenerscheinungen), 2.1.
Interfaces, electrical properties, 4.2.1.
Interfacial angle, crystals, 3.3.8.
Intermetallic compounds, crystal structures, 3.3.5.
— —, magnetic properties, 4.3.6.
— —, NMR spectral data, 4.3.6.
— —, soft X-ray spectral data, 4.3.6.
— —, thermodynamic properties, 3.4.5., 4.3.6.
— —, thermophysical properties, 3.4.20.
Internal energy, air and components, 3.4.19.
— —, cryogenic fluids, 3.4.21.
International Atomic Energy Agency (IAEA), 3.1.7., 3.1.8., 3.1.19., 3.2.47., 4.1.5., 5.4.7., 6.3.5.
International Commission on Illumination (ICI), 6.1.2., 6.3.6.
International Commission on Radiological Units (ICRU), 6.1.2.

International Committee on Weights and Measures, *see* Comité International des Poids et Mesures (CIPM)
INTERNATIONAL CONFERENCE ON THE PROPERTIES OF STEAM (ICPS), 3.4.15., **3.4.16.**, 5.3.55.
International Consultative Committee on Telegraphy and Telephony, *see* Comité Consultatif International Télégraphique et Téléphonique (CCITT)
International Copper Research Association, 3.4.9.
International Council of Scientific Unions, *see* International Unions Index
International Critical Tables of Numerical Data, Physics, Chemistry, and Technology, 5.1.1.
INTERNATIONAL DATA CENTRE FOR WORK ON CRYSTALLOGRAPHY, 3.2.44., 3.3.1., **3.3.7.**, 3.3.8., *see also* 3.3.4.
International Electrotechnical Commission (IEC), 6.1.2., 6.2.2.
International Federation for Clinical Chemistry, 6.2.3.
International Formulation Committee, ICPS (IFC), 3.4.16.
International Lighting Vocabulary, 6.3.6.
International Meteorological Tables, 5.2.22.
International Mineralogical Association, 3.3.10.
International Nuclear Data Committee, IAEA, 3.1.8.
International Organization for Standardization (ISO), 3.4.20., 6.1.2., 6.1.3., 6.2.2.
International Organization for Standardization Technical Committee 12 (ISO/TC 12), 6.1.2., 6.2.2.
International Practical Temperature Scale (IPTS), 3.4.12., 6.2.1.
International Projects, *see* International Project Index
International Series of Monographs on Metal Physics and Physical Metallurgy, 3.3.5.
International Skeleton Tables, 3.4.16.
International Standardization Committee, IAEA, 6.3.5.

International System of Units (SI units), 3.4.16., 3.6.7., 6.1.1., 6.2.1., 6.2.2.

— — — — — —, basic quantities and units (ISO R 31), 6.2.2.

— — — — — —, definitions (French, English), 6.2.1.

— — — — — —, rules for use of, 6.2.2.

International Tables for Determination of Crystal Structures, see International Tables for X-ray Crystallography

INTERNATIONAL TABLES FOR X-RAY CRYSTALLOGRAPHY, 3.3.2., 3.3.5., **3.3.6.**

International Unions, *see* International Unions Index

Interoxidic compounds, thermodynamic properties, 3.4.5.

Interplanar distance (spacing), 5.3.28., *see also* Crystal structure

Interpreted Infrared Spectra, 5.3.20.

Ion-Atom Rearrangement Collisions, 3.2.11.

Ionic mobility, electrolyte solutions, 4.3.9.

Ionic radius, *see* Nuclear radii

Ionization potential, atoms, molecules, radicals, 3.2.45.

— —, elements; inorganic, organic, organometallic compounds, 3.4.7,

— —, positive ions, gaseous, 3.2.12.

Ionization processes, atomic and molecular, 3.2.5., 3.2.12.

Ionized gases, energetics, 3.2.12.

— —, ion cross sections, 3.2.5.

— —, thermodynamic properties, 3.4.6.

Ionizing radiation, chemical effects (radiolytic yield), 3.5.4.

— —, elementary processes, interactions in chemical systems, 4.3.3.

— —, quantities and units (ISO R 31), 6.2.2.

Ion-Molecule Reactions, Bibliography on, 3.2.12.

Ions, gaseous, aqueous; thermodynamic properties, 3.4.1.

—, pairs, complex; bond angles, configurations, interatomic distances, 3.2.44.

Iron, catalysis of ethylene hydrogenation with, 3.5.3.

—, solubility of carbon in, 3.4.10.

Iron alloys, solutions; phase diagrams, thermodynamic properties, 3.4.10.

Iron materials (Eisenwerkstoffe), properties, behavior, testing methods, 2.1.

ISO Recommendation 31 (Names, definitions, units, symbols and conversion factors for physical quantities), 6.2.2.

Isotopes, effect upon magnetic dipole moments, 3.2.15.

—, identification and production, 3.1.4.

—, molecular constants, 3.2.7.

—, neutron cross sections for mixtures of, 3.1.7.

—, photonuclear data, 3.1.18.

—, reference book, 5.3.8.

—, relative abundance, 3.1.1., 3.1.2., 3.1.4., 3.1.14., 3.1.16., 3.1.18.

—, systematic presentation, 5.3.6.

—, tables of, 3.1.4., 5.3.3.

—, thermodynamic properties, 3.4.6.

—, fissile, values of parameters of, 3.1.8.

—, radioactive, conventional names, 3.1.14.

Isotopes, Reference Book on Nuclear Physics, 5.3.8.

Isotopic abundance, relative, 3.1.1., 3.1.2., 3.1.4., 3.1.14., 3.1.16., 3.1.18.

Isotopic exchange, oxygen, gas phase reaction kinetics, 3.5.5.

Israel Program for Scientific Translations, 3.4.8.

JANAF THERMOCHEMICAL TABLES, **3.4.4.**

Japan Electron Optics Laboratory, Ltd. (JEOL), 3.2.21., 3.2.41., 3.2.43.

Japanese National Committee for CODATA, 1.2.3.

JAPAN NUCLEAR DATA COMMITTEE (JNDC), **4.1.5.**

Japan Society for the Promotion of Science, 4.3.7.

Johns Hopkins University, U.S.A., 3.2.3., 3.3.1.

Joint Army-Navy-Air Force Thermochemical Tables, *see* JANAF Thermochemical Tables

Joint Committee on Powder Diffraction Standards, ASTM, 3.3.3.
Joint ICSU Commission on Spectroscopy (IAU-IUPAC-IUPAP), 3.2.1., 3.2.6., 3.2.24., 6.2.3.
Joint Institute for Laboratory Astrophysics, U.S.A. (JILA), 3.2.5.
Joule-Thomson coefficient, industrial gases, 3.4.17.
Journal of Physical Chemistry, 6.2.3.
Journal of the American Ceramic Society, 3.4.12.
Journal of the American Chemical Society, 6.2.3., 6.3.1.
Journal of the Optical Society of America, 6.2.3.

Karlsruhe Nuclear Data File (Kerndaten Karlsruhe, KEDAK), 3.1.9., 3.1.11.
Kernforschungszentrum, Karlsruhe, Germany-B.R.D., 3.1.9.
Kerr Effect, *see* Magneto-optic effect
Ketones, thermodynamic properties, 3.4.2., 3.4.3.
Kinetics, *see* Chemical kinetics
Knight shift, *see* Nuclear magnetic resonance (NMR) spectral data
Krypton, thermodynamic, transport properties, 3.4.15.
KWIC (Key-Word-in-Context) Guide to the Powder Diffraction File (Inorganic), 3.3.3.
Kyoto University, Japan, 4.3.2.

Laboratory of Mass Spectrometry, France, 3.2.37.
LANDOLT-BÖRNSTEIN TABELLEN, 2.1., 3.1.1., 3.1.5., 3.1.17., 3.2.26., 3.2.49., 3.2.50., 3.3.9.
Lanthanides, atomic energy levels, 3.2.1.
Lattice parameter, alloys, intermetallic compounds, metals, 3.3.5., *see also* Crystal structure
— —, reactor physics applications, 3.1.6.
— —, variation with composition, temperature, density, expansion coefficients, 3.3.5.

Lawrence Radiation Laboratory, U.S.A. (LRL), 3.1.3., 3.1.4., 3.1.17., 3.3.1., 3.4.9.
Lead and compounds, thermodynamic properties, 3.4.8.
Letter Symbols and Signs, Technical Committee 25, IEC, 6.1.2.
Ligands, inorganic, organic; solution properties, 3.4.24.
Light, quantities and units (ISO R 31), 6.2.2.
Light, heavy metals (Leichtmetalle, Schwermetalle), properties and behavior, 2.1.
Lighting engineering (Lichttechnik), 2.1.
Lighting, International Vocabulary, ICI, 6.3.6.
Light nuclei, decay schemes, energy levels, physical constants, 3.1.1., 3.1.15., 3.1.16., 4.1.5.
LIGHT SCATTERING CRITICAL DATA CENTER, 4.2.4.
Light scattering data, colloids, detergents, electrolytes, polymers, 4.2.4.
Linear molecules, physical constants, 3.2.26.
Line Strengths of Asymmetric Rotors, 3.2.25.
Liquids, dielectric properties, 5.3.29.
—, thermal conductivity, 5.3.64.
—, thermophysical properties, 5.3.54., 5.3.62.
—, mixtures, light scattering data, 4.2.4.
—, pure, surface tension, 4.2.2.
Los Alamos Scientific Laboratory, U.S.A., 3.1.13.
LOW TEMPERATURE SPECIFIC HEATS DATA CENTER, 3.4.14., *see also* 3.3.12., 3.4.21.
LUMINESCENCE OF ORGANIC SUBSTANCES, LANDOLT-BÖRNSTEIN, 2.1., 3.2.49.

Macroscopic and Technical Properties of Matter, Landolt-Börnstein, New Series, 2.1.
Magnesium and compounds, thermodynamic properties, 3.4.8.

Magnetic dipole moment, molecular, 3.2.14., 3.2.15., 3.3.14., 3.3.15., 5.3.30.
— — —, nuclear, 3.1.1., 3.1.5., 3.1.14., 3.1.16., 3.2.50., 3.3.15.
Magnetic properties, alloys, 3.3.15., 4.3.6.
— —, cryogenic fluids, 3.4.21.
— —, elements, 2.2., 3.3.15., 3.3.16., 3.6.7.
— —, ferrites, 2.1., 3.3.14.
— —, free radicals, 3.2.50., 3.3.15.
— —, metals, intermetallic compounds, 2.2., 4.3.6.
— —, oxide systems, transition metal compounds, 2.1., 3.3.14.
MAGNETIC PROPERTIES OF COORDINATION AND ORGANO-METALLIC TRANSITION METAL COMPOUNDS, LANDOLT-BÖRNSTEIN, 2.1., **3.3.14.**
MAGNETIC PROPERTIES OF FREE RADICALS, LANDOLT-BÖRNSTEIN, 2.1., **3.2.50.**
Magnetic radius, atomic, *see* Nuclear radii
Magnetic rotatory power (Faraday Effect), elements, electrolytes; inorganic, organic compounds, 3.3.16.
Magnetic susceptibility, alloys, elements, free radicals, minerals; inorganic, organic compounds, 3.3.15.
— —, semiconductors, inorganic, 3.3.13.
— —, transition metal compounds, 3.3.14.
Magnetism, quantities and units (ISO R31), 6.2.2.
Magneto-optic (Kerr) effect, ferromagnetic metals, alloys, 3.3.16.
Manganese and compounds, thermodynamic properties, 3.4.5.
Manufacturing Chemists Association (MCA) Research Project, *see* Thermodynamics Research Center (TRC)
Massachusetts Institute of Technology, U.S.A. (MIT), 3.2.4., 3.4.10., 5.3.32.
MASS SPECTRA, 2.3., 3.2.12., 3.2.35.—3.2.38.
MASS SPECTRAL DATA, COMPILATION OF (INDEX DE SPECTRES DE MASSE), **3.2.37.**

MASS SPECTRAL DATA, SELECTED, API RP 44, 2.3., **3.2.35.,** *see also* 3.2.36.
MASS SPECTRAL DATA, SELECTED, TRC, 2.3., **3.2.36.,** *see also* 3.2.35.
Mass spectral data, chlorides, 3.2.35.
— — —, elements, 3.2.35.
— — —, gases, organic, 3.2.37.
— — —, hydrides, 3.2.35., 3.2.36.
— — —, hydrocarbons, 3.2.35.
— — —, indexes to, 2.3., 3.2.37., 3.2.38., 3.2.53.
— — —, inorganic compounds, 3.2.35., 3.2.36.
— — —, organic compounds, 3.2.35.—3.2.37.
— — —, organic nonhydrocarbon compounds, 3.2.36.
— — —, oxides, 3.2.35.
— — —, vaporizable compounds, 3.2.37.
— — — for hydrocarbons of high molecular weight, matrix format, 3.2.35., 3.2.36.
Mass Spectrometry Bulletin, 3.2.38.
MASS SPECTROMETRY DATA CENTRE, U.K., **3.2.38.**
Mass Spectrometry Data Center, U.S.A., *see* Data Center for Atomic and Molecular Ionization Processes
Materials Data Book, 5.4.14.
Mathematical functions, 5.2.2.
Mathematical Signs and Symbols for Use in the Physical Sciences and Technology, 6.2.2.
Mathematical Tables for X-ray Crystallography, 3.3.6.
Matthews Coordinate Index, Powder Diffraction File, 3.3.3.
Max-Planck-Institut, Germany-B.R.D., 4.1.4., 5.1.2.
Mechanical properties, 1.1.1., 2.1., 3.3.10., 3.3.11., 3.6.7., 4.3.6., *see also* Elastic properties
— —, alloys, 4.3.6.
— —, elements, 3.6.7.
— —, metals, intermetallic compounds, 4.3.6.
— —, minerals, 3.3.10., 3.3.11.
— —, silicates, 3.3.11.
Mechanics, quantities and units (ISO R31), 6.2.2.

Melting (freezing) point, alkaloids, 3.2.23.

— — —, alloys, 3.4.11., 3.4.20.

— — —, elements, 3.4.1., 3.4.3., 3.4.20.

— — —, hydrocarbons, 3.4.2.

— — —, industrial compounds, 3.2.21., 3.2.32., 3.2.41.

— — —, inorganic compounds, 3.2.19., 3.2.21., 3.2.33., 3.4.1., 3.4.3.

— — —, metals, nonferrous, 3.4.8.

— — —, nonmetallic solids, 3.4.20.

— — —, organic compounds, 3.2.19.—3.2.21., 3.2.32., 3.2.33., 3.2.41., 3.4.1., 3.4.3., 5.5.4., 5.5.5.

— — —, oxides, 3.4.12.

— — —, semiconductors, inorganic, 3.3.13.

Melting Point Tables for Organic Analysis, 5.5.5.

Melting Point Tables of Organic Compounds, 5.5.4.

Mercury, atomic collision data, low energy, 3.2.5.

—, thermophysical properties, 5.3.58.

Metal-ion complexes, stability constants, 3.4.24.

Metallic and Chemical Properties of Elements of the Periodic System, 5.4.13.

Metallo-organic compounds, *see* Organometallic compounds

Metallurgical Abstracts, 3.4.11.

Metallurgical, ceramic operations, thermodynamic data for, 3.4.5.

Metallurgical Thermochemistry, 3.4.10., 5.3.43.

Metallurgy, nonferrous, thermodynamic data for, 3.4.8.

—, physical, 5.3.43.

—, theoretical, thermodynamic data for, 3.4.5.

Metal oxides, phase diagrams, 3.4.12.

Metals, cryogenic data, 3.4.21., 4.3.6.

—, crystal structures, 2.2., 3.3.3.—3.3.5., 3.3.12.

—, diffusion data, 4.3.5.

—, electrical data, 2.1., 2.2.

—, lattice parameters, 3.3.5.

—, magnetic properties, 2.1., 2.2., 4.3.6.

—, NMR spectral data, 4.3.6.

—, phase diagrams, 3.4.10.

Metals, resistivity, electrical, low temperature, 3.3.12.

—, soft X-ray spectral data, 4.3.6.

—, superconductive properties, 3.3.17., 4.3.6.

—, thermodynamic properties, 3.4.9., 4.3.6.

—, thermophysical properties, 5.3.63.

—, transition probabilities, atomic, 3.2.2.

—, X-ray diffraction data, 3.3.3.

—, nonferrous, thermodynamic, physicochemical properties, 3.4.8.

Metals Handbook, 5.4.3.

Metals Reference Book, 5.4.5.

Metals, Thermal and Mechanical Data, Tables de Constantes Sélectionnées, 2.2.

Meteorology, 5.2.21., 5.2.22.

Methane, cryogenic data, 3.4.21.

—, physical, thermodynamic properties, 3.4.17.

—, thermophysical properties, 5.3.61.

Methanol, radiation chemistry data, 4.3.3.

Metrologia, 6.2.1.

Microwave spectra, 3.2.19., 3.2.22., 3.2.25., 3.2.26., *see also* Molecular rotational spectra.

Microwave spectral data, diatomic, polyatomic molecules, 3.2.25.

MICROWAVE SPECTRAL TABLES, **3.2.25.**

Microwave spectroscopy, documentation of literature, 3.2.19.

— —, molecular constants from, 3.2.26.

MINERALOGICAL PROPERTIES, 3.3.10., 3.3.11., 5.2.17.—5.2.19.

Mineralogy, Dana's System, 3.3.10.

Minerals, analyses, 3.3.10., 3.3.11.

—, chemical properties, 3.3.10., 3.3.11.

—, crystallographic properties, 3.3.10., 3.3.11., 5.2.17.

—, crystal structures, 3.3.3., 3.3.10., 3.3.11.

—, density, 3.3.10., 5.2.17.

—, elastic constants, 3.3.9., 5.2.19.

—, magnetic susceptibility, 3.3.15.

—, mechanical properties, 3.3.10., 3.3.11.

—, nomenclature, 3.3.10., 3.3.11.

—, occurrence, 3.3.10.

Minerals, optical properties, 3.3.10., 3.3.11.
—, ortho-, ring, chain, sheet, framework, non-silicates, 3.3.11.
—, physical properties, 3.3.10., 3.3.11.
—, rock-forming, 3.3.11., 5.2.19.
—, thermodynamic properties, 5.2.17.
—, volume, molar, 5.2.17.
—, X-ray diffraction data, 3.3.3., 3.3.10., 5.2.17.
Ministry of Technology, U.K., 3.4.17.
MISCELLANEOUS PROJECTS AND THEIR PUBLICATIONS, 3.6.
M. I. T. WAVELENGTH TABLES, 3.2.4.
Mixing, enthalpy (heat) of, see Enthalpy (heat) of solution
Molar volume, see Volume, molar
Molecular Acoustics, 2.1.
MOLECULAR CONSTANTS FROM MICROWAVE SPECTROSCOPY, 2.1., 3.2.26.
Molecular (magnetic) dipole moment, see Magnetic dipole moment, molecular
Molecular electronic spectra, 2.2., 2.3., 3.2.6.—3.2.9., 3.2.19., 3.2.21., 3.2.23., 3.2.29.—3.2.34., 3.2.48., 3.2.52., 5.3.11.—5.3.13., see also Ultraviolet, Visible region spectra
— — —, diatomic, polyatomic molecules, 3.2.9.
Molecular energies, properties, calculation of, 3.2.13.
Molecular Microwave Spectra Tables, 3.2.25.
Molecular physics, quantities and units (ISO R31), 6.2.2.
MOLECULAR PROPERTIES, 1.1.1., 3.2., 3.4.4.
Molecular rotational spectra, 2.1., 2.3., 3.2.6., 3.2.9., 3.2.10., 3.2.15., 3.2.19., 3.2.22., 3.2.25.—3.2.28. see also Microwave, Far infrared, Raman spectra
— — —, astrophysical interest, 3.2.22.
— — —, diatomic, polyatomic molecules, 3.2.9.
Molecular rotational spectroscopy, documentation of, 3.2.19.
MOLECULAR SPECTRA AND MOLECULAR STRUCTURE, 3.2.9.
Molecular spectra of astrophysical interest, 3.2.22.

Molecular spectroscopy, IUPAC Commission on, 3.2.24., 6.3.1.
— —, multilingual dictionary of important terms, 6.3.1.
Molecular structure, IUPAC Commission on, 3.2.24., 6.3.1.
Molecular vibrational frequency, 3.2.10., 3.2.25., 3.4.4.
Molecular vibrational spectra, 2.2., 2.3., 3.2.7.—3.2.10., 3.2.16.—3.2.24., 3.2.27., 3.2.28., 5.3.14.—5.3.21., see also Infrared, Raman spectra
— — —, astrophysical interest, 3.2.22.
— — —, diatomic, polyatomic molecules, 3.2.9.
Molecular vibrational spectroscopy, documentation of, 3.2.19.
MOLECULAR WEIGHTS OF POLYMERS, 4.3.8.
Molecule-molecule reactions, chemical kinetics data, 3.5.2.
Molecules, atomic configurations, distances, bond angles, 3.2.44.
—, bond energies, 3.2.45., 3.2.46.
—, physical constants, 2.2., 3.2.6., 3.2.7., 3.2.10., 3.2.13.—3.2.15., 3.2.25., 3.2.26., 3.2.35.—3.2.37., 3.2.44.—3.2.46., 3.4.4.
Mollier (h,s)-Diagram, Steam Tables, 3.4.16.
MOLTEN SALTS DATA CENTER, 3.4.22.
Molybdenum and compounds, thermodynamic properties, 3.4.8.
Moment of inertia, molecular, 3.4.4.
Moment, magnetic, see Magnetic dipole moment
Monomers, NMR spectra, 3.2.42.
Morphology, crystals, 3.3.1., 3.3.2., 3.3.8., 4.3.4.
Moscow State University, U.S.S.R., 3.4.19., 5.3.26.
Mössbauer effect, 4.3.6.
Multicomponent systems, thermodynamic, transport properties, 3.4.15.
Multilingual Dictionary of Important Terms in Molecular Spectroscopy, 6.3.1.
Multiplet tables, astrophysical interest, ultraviolet, 3.2.1.

National Academy of Sciences, National Academy of Engineering, National Research Council, U.S.A. (NAS-NAE-NRC), 1.1.1., 1.2.5., 3.1.1., 3.1.15., 3.2.1., 3.2.14., 3.3.3., 3.3.6., 3.4.4., 3.4.27., 5.1., 6.3.1., 6.3.5.

National Aeronautics and Space Administration, U.S.A. (NASA), 3.3.12., 3.4.8., 3.4.11., 3.4.21., 4.3.9.

National Association of Corrosion Engineers, U.S.A., 3.3.3.

National Bureau of Standards, U.S.A. (NBS), 1.1.1., 2.3., 3.1.1., 3.1.18., 3.2.1., 3.2.2., 3.2.3., 3.2.5., 3.2.6., 3.2.10.—3.2.13., 3.2.15., 3.2.18., 3.2.25., 3.2.46., 3.2.47., 3.3.1., 3.3.3., 3.3.12., 3.3.17., 3.4.1.—3.4.3., 3.4.9. —3.4.14., 3.4.18., 3.4.20.—3.4.22., 3.5.1.—3.5.3., 3.5.5., 4.2.1.— 4.2.4., 4.3.1., 4.3.3., 4.3.5., 4.3.6., 4.3.9., 5.3.41., 6.2.1., 6.2.3.

NATIONAL COMMITTEES FOR CODATA, 1.2.

NATIONAL DATA PROGRAMS, 1.1.

National Engineering Laboratory, U.K., 3.4.16.

NATIONAL NEUTRON CROSS SECTION CENTER, U.S.A. (NNCSC), 3.1.7., 3.1.8., 3.1.10.—3.1.12.

National Research Council of Canada, 1.2.1., 3.2.9., 3.3.4., 3.3.5., 6.3.1.

National Science Foundation, U.S.A. (NSF), 3.1.15., 3.2.22., 3.2.31., 3.3.1., 3.4.8.

National Standard Reference Data Series, National Bureau of Standards, U.S.A. (NSRDS-NBS), 1.1.1., 3.1.18., 3.2.1.—3.2.3., 3.2.6., 3.2.10., 3.2.12., 3.2.15., 3.4.1., 3.4.13., 3.4.14., 3.4.18., 3.4.20., 3.4.22., 3.5.1.—3.5.3., 3.5.5., 4.2.2.

NATIONAL STANDARD REFERENCE DATA SYSTEM, U.S.A. (NSRDS), 1.1.1., 2.3., 3.2.1., 3.2.3., 3.2.5., 3.2.15., 3.2.25., 3.3.1., 3.4.1., 3.4.9., 3.4.11., 3.4.14., 3.4.20., 3.5.1.—3.5.3., 3.5.5., 4.2.2., 4.2.4.

Naval Research Laboratory, U.S.A., 3.4.13.

NBS Circular 500, see Selected Values of Chemical Thermodynamic Properties

Neon, thermodynamic, transport properties, 3.4.15.

Netherlands Organization for Pure Scientific Research (ZWA), 3.3.6., 3.3.8.

Neutron cross sections, 3.1.3., 3.1.4., 3.1.7.—3.1.12., 3.1.14., 3.1.19., 4.1.3.

NEUTRON CROSS SECTIONS FOR FAST REACTOR MATERIALS, 3.1.9.

Neutron data, ECSIL System for storage, retrieval, display, 3.1.3.

— —, index to literature (CINDA), 3.1.19.

Neutronics and Photonics Calculational Constants, Integrated System for Production of, 3.1.3.

Neutron resonance parameters and materials, 5.3.5.

NEUTRONS, PROPERTIES OF, 3.1.7.— 3.1.12., 4.1.2., 4.1.5.

NEW AND SECONDARY CENTERS, 4.

New Materials and Methods of Investigating Metals and Alloys, 3.3.17.

New Nuclear Data, Annual Cumulations, 3.1.1.

Nickel, catalysis of ethylene hydrogenation with, 3.5.3.

— and compounds, thermodynamic properties, 3.4.8.

Nitrates, chemical kinetics data, 3.4.13.

—, mineralogical data, 3.3.10.

—, thermodynamic properties, 3.4.5., 3.4.13.

Nitrides, thermodynamic properties, 3.4.5., 3.4.6., 3.4.10.

Nitriles, thermodynamic properties, 3.4.3.

Nitrogen, cryogenic data, 3.4.21.

—, mass spectra, 3.2.35.

—, physical properties, 3.4.17.

—, thermodynamic functions, 3.4.19.

—, thermodynamic properties, 3.4.2., 3.4.7., 3.4.15., 3.4.17.

—, — —, low temperature, 3.4.21.

—, transport properties, 3.4.15.

—, atomic, ionic, molecular; atomic collision data, low energy, 3.2.5.

Nitrogen compounds, infrared spectra, 3.2.16.
— —, thermodynamic properties, 3.4.2.
— —, organic, Raman spectra, 3.2.28.
— —, —, thermodynamic properties, 3.4.3.
Niobium and compounds, thermodynamic properties, 3.4.8.
NMR Band Handbook, 5.3.22.
NOMENCLATURE, 6.3.
—, amino acids, 6.3.1.
—, biological chemistry (biochemistry), 6.3.1.
—, carbohydrates, 6.3.1.
—, carotenoids, 6.3.1.
—, corrinoids, 6.3.1.
—, enzymes, 6.3.4.
—, folic acid, related compounds, 6.3.1.
—, heterocyclic systems, fundamental, 6.3.1.
—, hydrocarbons, 6.3.1.
—, inorganic chemistry, 6.3.1.
—, lighting, 6.3.6.
—, minerals, 3.3.10., 3.3.11.
—, nuclear science, technology, 6.3.5.
—, organic chemistry, 6.3.1.
—, organosilicon compounds, 6.3.1.
—, peptides, natural; synthetic modifications, 6.3.1.
—, physical, 6.1.2., 6.2.3.
—, physico-chemical, 6.2.3.
—, polymers, steric regularity in, 6.3.1.
—, quinones with isoprenoid sidechains, 6.3.1.
—, silicate minerals, 3.3.11.
—, spectroscopic, 6.2.3., 6.3.1.
—, standardization of, 6.1.3.
—, steroids, 6.3.1.
—, vitamins, 6.3.1.
Nomenclature of Amino Acids, Steroids, Vitamins and Carotenoids, IUPAC (English, Czechoslovakian versions), 6.3.1.
Nomenclature of Inorganic Chemistry, IUPAC (English, French, Japanese, Swedish, German, Czechoslovakian, Dutch, Bulgarian, Portuguese, Yugoslavian, Persian versions), 6.3.1.

Nomenclature of Organic Chemistry, IUPAC (English, French, Spanish, Japanese, Czechoslovakian, Bulgarian, Italian, Dutch versions), 6.3.1.
Nomenclature of Organosilicon Compounds, IUPAC, 6.3.1.
Non-Aqueous Conductance Data, Survey of, 3.4.22.
Nonaqueous solvents, solubility of elements, inorganic and organic compounds in, 3.4.23.
Nonferrous metallurgy, thermodynamic data for, 3.4.8.
Nonmetallic solids, liquids, gases; thermodynamic, thermophysical, transport properties, 3.4.20.
Nova University, U.S.A., 4.3.4.
Nuclear charge distribution, 3.1.5.
NUCLEAR CODES CENTER, 4.1.1.
NUCLEAR CONSTANTS GROUP, 3.1.3.
Nuclear Data, 3.1.1., 3.1.13., 5.3.2.
Nuclear Data Cards, 3.1.1.
NUCLEAR DATA PROJECT, 3.1.1., 3.1.13., 3.1.15., 3.1.17.
Nuclear Data Sheets, 3.1.1., 3.1.15., 4.1.4.
Nuclear Data Tables, 3.1.1., 3.1.13.
Nuclear Data Tabulations, Directory to, 3.1.1.
Nuclear (magnetic) dipole moment, *see* Magnetic dipole moment, nuclear
Nuclear engineering, handbook, 5.3.4.
Nuclear Level Properties, Table of Isotopes, 3.1.4.
Nuclear Level Schemes, $A = 40 — A = 92$ (Ca–Zr), 3.1.1.
NUCLEAR MAGNETIC RESONANCE (NMR) SPECTRA, 2.3., 3.2.19., 3.2.39.—3.2.43., 4.3.6., 5.3.22.
NUCLEAR MAGNETIC RESONANCE SPECTRAL DATA, SELECTED, API RP 44, 2.3., 3.2.39., *see also* 3.2.40.
NUCLEAR MAGNETIC RESONANCE SPECTRAL DATA, SELECTED, TRC., 2.3., 3.2.40., *see also* 3.2.39.
Nuclear magnetic resonance (NMR) spectral data, alkaloids, 3.2.42.
— — — — —, alloys, 4.3.6.
— — — — —, hydrocarbons, 3.2.39.
— — — — —, indexes to, 2.3.

Nuclear magnetic resonance (NMR) spectral data, industrial compounds, 3.2.41.

— — — — — —, metals, intermetallic compounds, 4.3.6.

— — — — — —, monomers, 3.2.42.

— — — — — —, organic compounds, 3.2.39.—3.2.43.

— — — — — —, organometallic compounds, 3.2.39.

— — — — — —, peroxides, 3.2.42.

— — — — — —, polymers, 3.2.43.

— — — — — —, steroids, 3.2.42., 3.2.43.

— — — — — —, terpenes, 3.2.42.

— — — — — —, vitamins, 3.2.42.

NUCLEAR MAGNETIC RESONANCE SPECTRA, SADTLER RESEARCH LABORATORIES, INC., **3.2.41.**

Nuclear magnetic resonance (NMR) spectroscopy, documentation of literature, 3.2.19.

Nuclear Physics, 3.1.1., 3.1.15.—3.1.17.

Nuclear Physics and Technology, Landolt-Börnstein, New Series, 2.1.

Nuclear Physics, Tables de Constantes Sélectionnées, 2.2.

NUCLEAR PROPERTIES, 1.1.1., 2.1., **3.1.**, 3.6.7., **4.1.**, 5.3.1.—5.3.8.

— —, general, 3.1.1.—3.1.6.

— —, handbooks, 5.3.1.—5.3.8.

Nuclear Properties, Nuclear Tables, Part I, 3.1.2.

Nuclear quadrupole resonance frequency, 5.3.25.

NUCLEAR RADII, LANDOLT-BÖRNSTEIN, 2.1., **3.1.5.**

Nuclear Reactions, Nuclear Tables, Part II, 3.1.2.

Nuclear reactions, quantities and units (ISO R 31), 6.2.2.

— —, thresholds of, 3.1.3.

Nuclear reactors and instrumentation, 3.1.6.

Nuclear Science Abstracts, 3.1.1., 3.1.13., 3.1.18.

Nuclear Science and Engineering, 3.1.3.

Nuclear science, technology, nomenclature, terms, 6.3.5.

NUCLEAR TABLES (TABELLEN DER ATOMKERNE), **3.1.2.**

Nuclear Theory Index Booklets, Cards, Reference Book, 3.1.1.

Nuclei, decay schemes, 3.1.2., 3.1.4., 3.1.14., 3.1.17.

—, energy levels, 2.1., 3.1.1., 3.1.2., 3.1.4., 3.1.14.—3.1.17., 4.1.4.

—, interactions with electromagnetic radiation, 3.1.18.

—, physical constants, 3.1.1., 3.1.2., 3.1.4., 3.1.5., 3.1.13.—3.1.17., 3.2.1.

—, radii, 3.1.5.

—, heavy, energy levels, 4.1.4.

—, light, energy levels, 3.1.1., 3.1.15., 3.1.16.

—, radioactive, decay schemes, energy levels, physical constants, 3.1.14.

Nucleus, optical model of, 4.1.3.

NUCLIDES, PROPERTIES OF, 3.1.13.—3.1.18.

Nuclides, charged-particle cross sections, 3.1.3., 3.1.13.

—, neutron cross sections, 3.1.3., 3.1.4., 3.1.7.—3.1.12., 3.1.19.

—, photon cross sections, 3.1.3.

—, photonuclear reactions, 3.1.18.

—, physical constants, 3.1.2.

—, reference diagrams, 5.3.6.

—, $A \geq 40$, nuclear data, physical constants, 3.1.1.

Nuclidic masses and related constants, IUPAP Commission on, 6.2.3.

NUMERICAL PROPERTY VALUES, RECOMMENDATIONS ON PUBLICATION OF, 6.4.

N. V. Philips' Gloeilampenfabrieken, Netherlands, 3.3.6.

Oak Ridge National Laboratory, U.S.A. (ORNL), 3.1.1., 3.1.13., 3.1.17., 3.1.19., 3.2.11., 6.3.1.

Occurrence of minerals, 3.3.10.

OFFICE FOR SCIENTIFIC AND TECHNICAL INFORMATION, U.K. (OSTI), **1.1.2.**, 3.2.38., 3.3.7., 3.4.15.

Office of Scientific Research, United States Air Force, 3.1.15.

Office of Standard Reference Data, National Bureau of Standards, U.S.A. (OSRD), 1.1.1., 2.3., 3.1.18., 3.2.3., 3.2.6., 3.2.10.—3.2.12., 3.2.18., 3.2.46., 3.2.47.,

3.3.12., 3.3.17., 3.4.1., 3.4.3., 3.4.10., 3.4.13., 3.4.18., 3.4.20.—3.4.22., 3.5.1.—3.5.3., 3.5.5., 4.2.1., 4.2.3., 4.3.1., 4.3.3., 4.3.5., 4.3.6., 4.3.9.

Optical Atomic Spectra, Bibliography on Analyses of, 3.2.1.

Optical Model of the Nucleus, Index and Abstracted Literature Review, 4.1.3.

OPTICAL PROPERTIES, 2.1., 2.2., 3.6.3.—3.6.6.

— —, alloys, 3.3.1.

— —, cryogenic fluids, 3.4.21.

— —, crystals, 3.3.1., 3.3.8.

— —, elements, 3.3.1., 3.4.3., 3.6.7.

— —, —, compounds in steelmaking, 3.4.10.

— —, hydrocarbons, 3.4.2.

— —, inorganic compounds, 3.3.1., 3.4.3.

— —, minerals, 3.3.10., 3.3.11.

— —, organic compounds, 3.3.1., 3.4.3.

— —, proteins, 3.3.1., 3.6.5.

— —, semiconductors, 5.3.36.

— —, sesquiterpenoids, 3.2.48.

— —, silicate minerals, 3.3.11.

OPTICAL ROTATORY POWER, TABLES DE CONSTANTES SÉLECTIONNÉES, Alkaloids, 2.2., **3.6.6.**

OPTICAL ROTATORY POWER, TABLES DE CONSTANTES SÉLECTIONNÉES, Amino acids, 2.2., **3.6.5.**

OPTICAL ROTATORY POWER, TABLES DE CONSTANTES SÉLECTIONNÉES, Steroids, 2.2., **3.6.3.**

OPTICAL ROTATORY POWER, TABLES DE CONSTANTES SÉLECTIONNÉES, Triterpenes, 2.2., **3.6.4.**

Optical spectroscopic data, diatomic molecules, 3.2.6.

Organic Acids, Bases in Aqueous Solution, Dissociation Constants of, 3.4.25.

Organic chemical reactions, homogeneous, chemical kinetics data, 3.5.1.

Organic chemistry, Beilsteins Handbook, 5.1.3.

— —, nomenclature (IUPAC), 6.3.**1.**

Organic compounds, boiling points, 3.2.19.—3.2.21., 3.2.32., 3.2.33., 3.2.41., 3.4.1., 3.4.3.

— —, cryogenic data, 3.4.**21.**

Organic compounds, crystallographic properties, 3.3.1.

— —, crystal structures, 3.2.44., 3.3.1.—3.3.4., 3.4.7.

— —, dielectric properties, 3.2.14., 3.2.15., 3.3.9.

— —, dipole moments, molecular, 3.2.15.

— —, dissociation constants, 3.4.25.

— —, elastic constants, 3.3.9.

— —, identification, handbook of tables for, 5.5.3.

— —, infrared spectra, 3.2.16.—3.2.21., 5.3.15.

— —, interatomic distances, configurations, 3.2.44.

— —, luminescence, 3.2.49.

— —, magnetic rotatory power (Faraday Effect), 3.3.16.

— —, magnetic susceptibility, 3.3.15.

— —, mass spectra, 3.2.35.—3.2.37.

— —, melting (freezing) points, 3.2.19.—3.2.21., 3.2.32., 3.2.33., 3.2.41., 3.4.1., 3.4.3., 5.5.4., 5.5.5.

— —, NMR spectra, 3.2.39.—3.2.43.

— —, notation, rules for (IUPAC), 6.3.1.

— —, optical properties, 3.3.1., 3.4.3.

— —, physical properties, 3.2.19.—3.2.21., 3.2.32., 3.2.33., 3.2.36., 3.2.41.

— —, pressure-volume-temperature relationships, 5.3.40.

— —, radiation chemistry data, 4.3.3.

— —, radiolytic yields, 3.5.4.

— —, Raman spectra, 3.2.27., 3.2.28.

— —, semiconducting properties, 5.3.35.

— —, solubilities, 3.4.23., 3.4.24.

— —, thermodynamic constants, 3.4.7., 5.3.39.

— —, thermodynamic properties, 2.3., 3.4.1., 3.4.3., 3.4.7.

— —, ultraviolet spectra, 2.3., 3.2.19., 3.2.30.—3.2.34., 5.3.11.—5.3.13.

— —, visible region spectra, 3.2.31.—3.2.33., 5.3.12.

— —, X-ray diffraction data, 3.3.3., 5.3.15.

— —, volatile, gas chromatographic data, 3.6.1.

ORGANIC ELECTRONIC SPECTRAL DATA, **3.2.31.**
Organic gases, mass spectra, 3.2.37.
Organic halogen compounds, NMR spectra, 3.2.40.
Organic molecules, bond energies, 3.2.45., 3.2.46.
— —, vibrational frequencies, 3.2.10.
Organic nitrogen compounds, NMR spectra, 3.2.40.
— — —, thermodynamic properties, 2.3., 3.4.3.
Organic nonhydrocarbon compounds, mass spectra, physical properties, 3.2.36.
Organic oxygen compounds, NMR spectra, 3.2.40.
— — —, Raman spectra, 3.2.28.
— — —, thermodynamic properties, 3.4.3.
Organic phosphorus compounds, NMR spectra, 3.2.40.
Organic sulfur compounds, NMR spectra, 3.2.40.
— — —, physicochemical constants, 5.4.1.
— — —, thermodynamic properties, 2.3., 3.4.2.
Organic Semi-conductors, 5.3.35.
Organic systems, oxidation-reduction potentials, 5.3.48.
Organisation International de Métrologie Légale (OIML), 6.1.2.
Organization for Economic Cooperation and Development (OECD), 3.1.7., 3.1.11., 3.1.19.
Organometallic compounds, crystal structures, 3.3.3., 3.4.7.
— —, handbook of, 5.4.15.
— —, magnetic properties, 3.3.14.
— —, NMR spectra, 3.2.39.
— —, Raman spectra, 3.2.27.
— —, solubilities, 3.4.23.
— —, thermodynamic properties, 2.3., 3.4.1., 3.4.7.
— —, ultraviolet spectra, 2.3., 3.2.29.
— —, X-ray diffraction data, 3.3.3.
Organosilicon compounds, nomenclature, 6.3.1.
Osmotic phenomena (Osmotische Phänomene), 2.1.

Oxford University, U.K., 3.2.19.
Oxidation-reduction potential, 3.4.26., 5.3.48.
Oxidation-Reduction Potentials of Organic Systems, 5.3.48.
Oxides, constitution data, 3.4.11.
—, crystal structures, 3.4.11., 5.4.9.
—, mass spectra, 3.2.35.
—, melting (freezing) points, 3.4.12.
—, mineralogical data, 3.3.10.
—, phase diagrams, 3.4.10.—3.4.12.
—, physicochemical properties, 5.4.12.
—, specific heat, low temperature, 3.4.14.
—, thermodynamic properties, 3.4.5., 3.4.6., 3.4.10.
—, — —, low temperature, 3.4.14.
—, thermophysical properties, 3.4.20.
—, mixed, magnetic properties, 2.1., 3.3.14.
—, rare earth, crystal structures, thermodynamic properties, 5.4.9.
Oxide systems, complex, thermodynamic properties, 3.4.10.
Oxides of Rare Earth Elements and Their Refractory Compounds, 5.4.9.
Oxygen, cryogenic data, 3.4.21.
—, mass spectra, 3.2.35.
—, thermodynamic functions, 3.4.19.
—, thermodynamic properties, 3.4.2., 3.4.7., 3.4.15.
—, transport properties, 3.4.15.
—, atomic, ionic, molecular; atomic collision data, low energy, 3.2.5.
—, —, —, —; gas phase reaction kinetics, 3.5.5.
Oxygen compounds, crystal structure, 3.4.4.
— —, infrared spectra, 3.2.16.
— —, thermodynamic properties, 2.3., 3.4.4.
— —, thermophysical properties, 3.4.20.
Oxygen species, neutral, gas phase reaction kinetics, 3.5.5.
Ozone, gas phase reaction kinetics, 3.5.5.

Palladium, catalysis of ethylene hydrogenation with, 3.5.3.
Parahydrogen, thermodynamic properties, low temperature, 3.4.21.

Paramagnetic relaxation, double, complex salts; metal sulfates, 3.3.15.

Paramagnetic susceptibility, *see* Magnetic susceptibility

Partial molar thermodynamic quantities, alloys, 3.4.9.

Peptide chains in proteins, configurations, 3.6.5.

Peptides, natural, naming of synthetic modifications of (IUPAC), 6.3.1.

Periodic and related phenomena, quantities and units (ISO R 31), 6.2.2.

Peroxides, NMR spectra, 3.2.42.

Pharmaceutical materials, molecular electronic spectra, 3.2.21., 3.2.32., 3.2.33.

Phase change, enthalpy (heat), entropy, Gibbs (free) energy of, *see* Enthalpy (heat), Entropy, Gibbs (free) energy of phase change

Phase (constitutional, equilibrium) diagrams, alloys, 3.4.9.—3.4.11., 5.3.46.

— —, borides, 3.4.11.

— —, ceramics, 3.4.12.

— —, chalcogenides, 3.4.11.

— —, cyanides, 3.4.12.

—, elements, compounds in steelmaking, 3.4.10.

—, —, inorganic and organic compounds in solvents, 3.4.23.

— —, halides, 3.4.12.

— —, hydrides, 3.4.11.

—, materials at high pressures, temperatures, 4.3.1.

— —, multicomponent systems, 3.4.12.

— —, oxides, 3.4.10.—3.4.12.

— —, phosphides, 3.4.11.

— —, silicates, 3.3.11., 5.3.45.

— —, sulfides, 3.4.12.

— —, thorium and uranium alloys, 5.3.46.

PHASE DIAGRAMS FOR CERAMISTS, 3.4.12.

Phase Diagrams of Silicate Systems, 5.3.45.

Phase Equilibrium Diagrams of Oxide Systems, 3.4.12.

Phase transition pressures, high pressure, 4.3.1.

Phenols, thermodynamic properties, 3.4.3.

Phonon temperature, inorganic semiconductors, 3.3.13.

Phosphates, mineralogical data, 3.3.10.

Phosphides, crystallographic properties, 3.4.11.

—, thermodynamic properties, 3.4.10.

Phosphorescence, *see* Luminescence

Photochemistry, 3.5.1.

Photoelectric Spectrometry Group, U.K., 3.2.34.

Photon Attenuation and Energy Absorption Coefficients, 3.2.47.

Photon collision, low energy, ionization of atoms, diatomic molecules by, 3.2.5.

Photon cross sections, 3.1.3., 3.1.10., 3.1.13., 3.1.18., 3.2.5., 3.2.47.

PHOTONUCLEAR DATA CENTER, **3.1.18.,** 3.2.47.

Physical and Chemical Tables for X-ray Crystallography, 3.3.6.

Physical chemistry, consolidated index of selected property values, 3.4.27.

— —, quantities and units (ISO R 31), 6.2.2.

PHYSICAL CONSTANTS, 5.2.2., 5.4.16., 6.1.1., 6.1.3., **6.2.**

Physical Constants of Linear Homopolymers, 5.4.16.

Physical Constants, New Values for, 6.2.3.

Physical properties, alkaloids, 3.2.23.

— —, crystals, 3.3.1., 3.3.3., 3.3.8., 4.3.4.

— —, gases, industrial, 3.4.17.

— —, hydrides, 3.2.36.

— —, industrial compounds, 3.2.18., 3.2.32., 3.2.41.

— —, inorganic compounds, 3.2.19., 3.2.21., 3.2.33., 3.2.36.

— —, minerals, 3.3.10., 3.3.11.

— —, organic compounds, 3.2.19.— 3.2.21., 3.2.32., 3.2.33., 3.2.36., 3.2.41.

— —, rocks, 5.2.18.

— —, steam, water, 3.4.16.

Physical Properties of Rocks under Normal and Standard Temperature and Pressure, 5.2.18.

Physical Property Values of Substances, 5.2.8.

PHYSICAL QUANTITIES, UNITS AND SYMBOLS; BASIC PHYSICAL CONSTANTS; NOMENCLATURE; AND RELATED MATTERS, 6.

Physicochemical Constants of Organo-sulfur Compounds, 5.4.1.

Physicochemical data and standards, IUPAC Commission on, 6.2.3.

Physicochemical properties, crystalline substances, 5.3.27.

— —, elements, 3.6.7.

— —, oxides, 5.4.12.

— —, plutonium, alloys and compounds, 5.4.7.

Physicochemical Properties of Oxides, 5.4.12.

Physicochemical Symbols and Terminology, Manual of, 6.2.3.

Physics Abstracts, 3.1.13., 3.2.14., 4.3.6.

Physics Today, 6.2.3., 6.4.2.

Physikalisches Taschenbuch, 5.2.12.

Piezoelectric, piezooptic constant, inorganic compounds, 3.3.9.

Plasma physics, 3.2.5., 5.3.32.

Plastics, abbreviation of terms relating to (IUPAC), 6.3.1.

Platinum, catalysis of ethylene hydrogenation with, 3.5.3.

Plenum Press Handbooks of High Temperature Materials, 5.4.4.

Plutonium: Physicochemical Properties of its Compounds and Alloys, 5.4.7.

Pockels Effect, *see* Electrooptic constant

Point group, *see* Crystal structure *or* Molecular electronic spectra, structure

Polarizability, molecular, 3.2.13.

Polarization data, Raman spectra, 3.2.27., 3.2.28.

Polyatomic molecules, electronic spectra, structure, 3.2.9.

— —, energy levels, 3.2.9., 3.2.13.

— —, microwave spectra, 3.2.25.

— —, notation for spectra of, 6.2.3.

— —, physical constants, 3.2.13.

— —, spectroscopic data, 2.2.

— —, vibrational spectra, 3.2.9.

Polycrystalline materials, X-ray structure analysis, 5.3.26.

Polymer Handbook, 5.4.17.

Polymers, light scattering data, 4.2.4.

—, molecular weights, 4.3.8.

—, NMR spectra, 3.2.43.

—, radiolytic yields, 3.5.4.

—, thermophysical properties, 3.4.20.

Polymers, steric regularity in, nomenclature (IUPAC), 6.3.1.

Polymorphs, high pressure, crystal structures, 4.3.1.

Polypeptides, abbreviated designations (IUPAC), 6.3.1.

Positive ions, gaseous; appearance, ionization potentials, enthalpy (heat) of formation, 3.2.12.

POTENTIELS d'OXYDO-RÉDUCTION, TABLES DE CONSTANTES SÉLECTIONNÉES, 2.2., **3.4.26.**

POUVOIR ROTATOIRE MAGNÉTIQUE (EFFET FARADAY), TABLES DE CONSTANTES SÉLECTIONNÉES, 2.2., **3.3.16.**

POWDER DIFFRACTION FILE: JOINT COMMITTEE ON POWDER DIFFRACTION STANDARDS, **3.3.3.**

Prandtl number, *see* Transport (thermomechanical) properties

Pressure scale, definition, 4.3.1.

Pressure-volume-temperature relationship, cryogenic fluids, 3.4.21.

— — — —, organic compounds, 5.3.40.

Primary Crystallographic Data, IUCr 6.4.1.

Princeton University, U.S.A., 3.2.1.

Printing Symbols and Numbers, Principles for (ISO), 6.2.2.

Procedures for Inter-Conversion of Values from One System of Units to Another (ISO), 6.2.2.

Progress in Cryogenics, 3.3.17.

Propane, physical, thermodynamic properties, 3.4.17.

Propellant performance calculations, thermodynamic data for, 3.4.4.

PROPERTIES OF ELECTROLYTE SOLUTIONS, **4.3.9.**

Properties of 100 Linear Alkane Thiols, Sulfides, and Symmetrical Disulfides in the Ideal Gas State, 5.4.2.

Properties of Liquid and Solid Hydrogen, 5.4.19.

PROPERTIES OF NEUTRONS, 3.1.7.—3.1.12.

PROPERTIES OF NUCLIDES, 3.1.13.—3.1.18.

Properties of Titanium Compounds and Related Substances, 5.3.44.

PROPERTIES RELATING TO CHEMICAL REACTION RATES, 3.5.

Proteins, crystallographic properties, 3.3.1.

—, optical properties, 3.3.1., 3.6.5.

Proton affinity, atoms, molecules, radicals, 3.2.45.

Publication of Calorimetric and Thermodynamic Data, Resolution on, IUPAC, 6.4.2.

Publication of Numerical Property Values, Recommendations on, 6.4.

Punched card techniques, IUPAC Commission on, 6.3.1.

Purdue University, U.S.A., 3.4.20.

Pure and Applied Chemistry, 3.2.24., 3.4.1., 3.4.25., 6.2.3., 6.3.1.

Pyrometallurgical processes, thermodynamic data for, 3.4.8.

Quantities and Units of Acoustics, ISO R31, 6.2.2.

Quantities and Units of Atomic and Nuclear Physics, 6.2.2.

Quantities and Units for Clinical Chemistry, IUPAC, 6.2.3.

Quantities and Units of Electricity and Magnetism, ISO R31, 6.2.2.

Quantities and Units of Heat, ISO R31, 6.2.2.

Quantities and Units of Mechanics, ISO R31, 6.2.2.

Quantities and Units of Nuclear Reactions and Ionizing Radiations, 6.2.2.

Quantities and Units of Periodic and Related Phenomena, ISO R31, 6.2.2.

Quantities and Units of Physical Chemistry and Molecular Physics, 6.2.2.

Quantities and Units of Radiation and Light, 6.2.2.

Quantities and Units of SI, Basic, ISO R31, 6.2.2.

Quantum fluids (H_2, D_2, He), thermodynamic, transport properties, 3.4.15.

Quantum yield (G value), *see* Radiolytic yield

Quartz, mineralogical, X-ray diffraction data, 3.3.10.

Quinones with isoprenoid side-chains, nomenclature (IUPAC), 6.3.1.

Q-value, *see* Disintegration energy, ground state

Radiation, quantities and units (ISO R31), 6.2.2.

RADIATION CHEMISTRY DATA CENTER, 4.3.3.

Radiation data, alpha, beta, gamma, 3.1.4.

Radiation Dosimetry, 3.2.47.

Radiations from Radioactive Atoms in Frequent Use, 3.1.1.

Radiation shielding, computer program file for, 4.1.1.

— —, engineering compendium on, 3.2.47.

Radical ions, magnetic properties, 2.1., 3.2.50.

Radical-radical reactions, chemical kinetics data, 3.5.2.

Radical yield, *see* Radiolytic yield

Radioactive disintegration, 2.1., 3.1.1., 3.1.2., 3.1.4., 3.1.14.—3.1.17.

Radioactive tracers, diffusion data, 4.3.5.

Radioisotope Data, Table of Isotopes, 3.1.4.

RADIOLYTIC YIELDS, TABLES DE CONSTANTES SÉLECTIONNÉES, 2.2., 3.5.4.

Radiolytic yield (Quantum, radical yield, G value), 3.5.4., 4.3.3.

Radius, atomic, ionic, nuclear, *see* Nuclear radii.

RAMAN SPECTRA, 2.3., 3.2.27., 3.2.28., *see also* Molecular rotational, vibrational spectra

RAMAN SPECTRAL DATA, SELECTED, API RP 44, 2.3., 3.2.27., *see also* 3.2.28.

RAMAN SPECTRAL DATA, SELECTED, TRC, 2.3., 3.2.28., *see also* 3.2.27.

Raman spectral data, hydrocarbons, 2.3., 3.2.27.

— — —, indexes to, 2.3.

— — —, organic compounds, 2.3., 3.2.27., 3.2.28.

— — —, organometallic compounds 2.3., 3.2.27.

Raman spectroscopy, documentation of literature, 3.2.19.

Rare gases (inert fluids), atomic collision data, low energy, 3.2.5.

Rare gases, cryogenic data, 3.4.21.
— —, mass spectra, 3.2.35.
— —, physical properties, 3.4.17.
— —, thermodynamic properties, 3.4.7., 3.4.8., 3.4.15., 3.4.17., 3.4.19., 3.4.21.
— —, transport properties, 3.4.15.
Rare metals, physicochemical properties, 3.4.8.
Rare Metals Handbook, 5.4.6.
Rate constant, bimolecular gas reactions, 3.5.2.
— —, decomposition, inorganic salts, 3.4.13.
— —, homogeneous chemical reactions, inorganic, organic, 3.5.1.
Rate law, catalyzed hydrogenation of ethylene, 3.5.3.
Rayleigh ratio (light-scattering intensity), colloids, detergents, electrolytes, polymers, 4.2.4.
Rayleigh (coherent) scattering cross section, gamma, X-ray, 3.2.47.
Reaction, equilibrium constant, Gibbs (free) energy of, *see* Equilibrium constant, Gibbs (free) energy of reaction
Reaction Kinetics of Catalyzed Hydrogenation of Ethylene, 3.5.3.
Reaction mechanism, catalyzed hydrogenation of ethylene, 3.5.3.
— —, decomposition, inorganic salts, 3.4.13.
Reaction rate, homogeneous chemical reactions, inorganic, organic, 3.5.1.
— —, oxygen, gas phase reactions, 3.5.5.
Reactor applications, evaluated nuclear data file for, 3.1.7.
Reactor calculations, group constants for, 5.3.1.
Reactor characteristics, calculation of, 3.1.6.
Reactor design, computer program file for, 4.1.1.
Reactor materials, cross section data, 3.1.6., 3.1.7., 3.1.9., 3.2.47.
Reactor operation, instrumentation, 3.1.6.
REACTOR PHYSICS CONSTANTS CENTER (RPCC), **3.1.6.**

RECOMMENDATIONS ON PUBLICATION OF NUMERICAL PROPERTY VALUES, 6.4.
Redox equilibria, metal-ion complexes, 3.4.24.
Red System of the CN Molecule, 3.2.22.
Reference Book on Physicochemical Values for Geochemists, 5.2.20.
Reference Book on Solubility, 5.3.52.
Reference Book on Thermophysical Properties of Gases and Liquids, 5.3.62.
Reflectivity (reflectance), thermal, *see* Thermal radiative properties
Refractive index, colloids, detergents, electrolytes, polymers, 4.2.4.
— —, elements, nonmetallic, 3.4.3.
— —, hydrocarbons, 3.2.27., 3.4.2.
— —, inorganic compounds, 3.2.19., 3.4.3.
— —, molten salts, 3.4.22.
— —, organic compounds, 3.2.19., 3.2.20., 3.2.27., 3.4.3.
— —, sesquiterpenoids, 3.2.48.
Refractory compounds, 2.2., *see also* High melting compounds
— —, crystal structures, 5.4.9.
— —, thermodynamic properties, 5.3.42., 5.4.9., 5.4.11.
Relative Atomic Weights, Table of, 3.4.1., 6.2.3.
Relaxation time, dielectric, 3.2.14.
RELAXATION PARAMAGNÉTIQUE, TABLES DE CONSTANTES SÉLECTIONNÉES, 2.2., **3.3.15.**
Rensselaer Polytechnic Institute, U.S.A., 3.4.22.
Reports of Investigations, United States Bureau of Mines, 3.4.5.
Research Institute for Pharmacy and Biochemistry, Czechoslovakia, 3.2.23.
Resistivity, electrical, alloys, 3.4.20.
— —, cryogenic fluids, 3.4.21.
— —, elements, 3.4.20.
— —, —, compounds in steelmaking, 3.4.10.
— —, ferroelectric materials, 5.3.34.
— —, molten salts, 3.4.22.
— —, nonmetallic solids, 3.4.20.
— —, low temperature, alloys, metals, 3.3.12., 3.4.21.

Retention data, gas chromatographic, 3.6.1., 3.6.2.

Retrieval Guide to Thermophysical Properties Research Literature, 3.4.20.

Review of Metal Literature, 3.4.11.

Reviews of Modern Physics, 3.1.4., 3.1.15., 3.1.16., 3.2.3., 3.2.5.

Rhodium, catalysis of ethylene hydrogenation with, 3.5.3.

Richardson constant, elements, compounds, 5.3.31.

ROCK-FORMING MINERALS, **3.3.11.**

Rock-forming Minerals and Rocks, Elastic Properties of, 5.2.19.

Rocks, elastic properties, 5.2.19.

—, physical properties, 5.2.18.

Rotational constant, *see* Moment of inertia, molecular

Rotational spectra, molecular, *see* Molecular rotational spectra

Rotation, specific optical, *see* Optical rotatory power

Rounding Numbers, Rules for (ISO), 6.2.2.

Rowland's Preliminary Table of Solar Spectrum Wavelengths, see Solar Spectrum 2935 Å to 8770 Å

Royal Society, The, U.K., 1.1.2., 1.2.4.

RPCC Newsletter, 3.1.6.

Rubber chemicals, ultraviolet spectra, 5.3.13.

Rubidium, catalysis of ethylene hydrogenation with, 3.5.3.

Rules for the Use of Units of the International System of Units (ISO), 6.2.2.

Sadtler Research Laboratories, Inc., U.S.A., 3.2.21., 3.2.32., 3.2.41., 3.2.43.

Salts, activity properties of water, electrolytes in binary water solutions of, 5.3.53.

—, solubilities of elements, inorganic and organic compounds in, 3.4.23.

—, aqueous solutions, thermodynamic properties, 3.4.1.

—, double, complex, paramagnetic relaxation, 3.3.15.

—, inorganic, *see* Inorganic salts

—, molten, density, electrical resistivity, refractive index, surface tension, viscosity, 3.4.22.

Saturation density, cryogenic fluids, 3.4.21.

Scattering cross section, Compton, gamma, X-ray, 3.2.47.

Schweizerischer Nationalfonds, Switzerland, 3.3.1.

Science Council of Japan, 1.2.3.

Scintillation technique, application of organic luminescent substances in, 3.2.49.

SECONDARY NUCLEAR DATA CENTERS, 4.1.

SEIDELL'S SOLUBILITIES OF INORGANIC, METAL-ORGANIC, AND ORGANIC COMPOUNDS, **3.4.23.**

Selected Infrared, Mass, Nuclear Magnetic Resonance, Raman and Ultraviolet Spectral Data (API RP 44, TRC), *see* Infrared, Mass, Nuclear Magnetic Resonance, Raman, and Ultraviolet Spectral Data

Selenium, semiconducting properties, 3.3.13.

Semiconducting properties, elements, inorganic compounds, 3.3.13.

— —, organic compounds, 5.3.35.

— —, solid solutions, 5.3.33.

Semiconductors, crystallographic, magnetic, mechanical properties, 3.3.13.

—, electrical properties, 3.3.13., 5.3.36.

—, optical properties, 5.3.36.

—, semiconducting properties, 2.1., 3.3.13., 5.3.33., 5.3.35., 5.3.36.

SEMICONDUCTORS, SELECTED CONSTANTES RELATIVE TO, TABLES DE CONSTANTES SÉLECTIONNÉES, 2.2, **3.3.13.**

Sesquiterpenoids, optical, physical properties, ultraviolet spectra, 3.2.48.

Shielding constants, reactor physics, 3.1.6.

Sigma Center, *see* National Neutron Cross Section Center, U.S.A. (NNCSC)

Silica minerals, X-ray diffraction data, 3.3.10.

Silicate minerals, chemical, crystallographic, mechanical, physical, optical properties, 3.3.11.

— —, mineralogical data, 3.3.10., 3.3.11.

Silicates, crystal structures, 3.3.2.
—, phase diagrams, 3.3.11., 5.3.45.
Silicides, thermodynamic properties, 3.4.10.
Silicon (I—IV), atomic energy levels, multiplet tables, 3.2.1.
—, semiconducting properties, 3.3.13.
Silver, thermodynamic properties, low temperature, 3.4.14.
— and compounds, thermodynamic properties, 3.4.8.
Sintered materials (Sinterwerkstoffe), 2.1.
SI (Système International) Units, see International System of Units
Slags, thermodynamic properties, 3.4.10.
Smithsonian Meteorological Tables, 5.2.21.
Smithsonian Physical Tables, 5.2.13.
Soft X-ray spectroscopy, alloys, intermetallic compounds, metals, 4.3.6.
Solar Spectrum 2935 Å to 8770 Å, 3.2.1.
Solid solutions, magnetic moments, 3.3.15.
— —, semiconducting properties, 5.3.33.
Solid state physics (Festkörperphysik), 2.1.
SOLID STATE PROPERTIES, 1.1.1., 3.3., 5.3.26.—5.3.36.
Solubility, alloys, binary, 3.4.11.
—, elements in acids, aqueous, non-aqueous solvents, bases, salts, water, 3.4.23.
—, gases in metals, 3.4.10., 3.4.23.
—, inorganic compounds in acids, aqueous, non-aqueous solvents, bases, salts, water, 3.4.23., 3.4.24., 5.3.52.
—, iron alloys, compounds, solutions, 3.4.10.
—, metal-ion complexes, inorganic, organic, 3.4.24.
—, minerals, rock-forming, 3.3.11.
—, organic, organometallic compounds in acids, aqueous, non-aqueous solvents, bases, salts, water, 3.4.23.
Solubility Products of Inorganic Substances, 3.4.24.
Solution, enthalpy (heat) of, *see* Enthalpy (heat) of solution

Solution equilibria (Lösungsgleichgewichte), 2.1.
SOLUTION PROPERTIES, 3.4.23.—3.4.26.
Solutions, dielectric properties, 5.3.29.
—, light scattering data, 4.2.4.
Solvents, aqueous, non-aqueous; solubility of elements, inorganic and organic compounds in, 3.4.23.
Space group, *see* Crystal structure
Space research (Weltraumforschung), 2.1.
Specific gravity, *see* Density
Specific heat, *see also* Heat capacity
— —, alloys, 3.4.20.
— —, argon, 3.4.19.
— —, cryogenic fluids, 3.4.21.
— —, elements, 3.4.20.
— —, gases, industrial, 3.4.17.
— —, nitrogen, 3.4.19.
— —, nonmetallic solids, liquids, gases, 3.4.20.
— —, oxygen, 3.4.19.
— —, steam, water, 3.4.16.
— —, low temperature, alloys, 3.4.21.
— —, — —, metals, 3.4.14., 3.4.21.
Specific rates, elementary processes, radiation chemistry, 4.3.3.
Specific viscosity, *see* Viscosity
Specific volume, *see* Volume, specific
Spectra, gamma-ray production, neutron induced, 3.1.3.
Spectra of Diatomic, Polyatomic Molecules, Notation for, 6.2.3.
SPECTRAL DATA AND PHYSICAL CONSTANTS OF ALKALOIDS, 3.2.23.
Spectrochemical and other optical analysis procedures, IUPAC Commission on, 5.5.6.
Spectrophotometric absorption data, compounds for colorimetric determination of elements, 5.5.6.
Spectroscopic Data for Diatomic Molecules, Tables de Constantes Sélectionnées, 2.2., **3.2.7.**
Spectroscopic properties, handbooks, 5.3.9.—5.3.25.
Spectroscopic values, fundamental, IAU Commission 14 on, 6.2.3.
Spectroscopy, index of API RP 44-TRC selected data on, 2.3.
—, nomenclature, units, 6.2.3.

Spectrum of the HgH Molecule, 3.2.22.
Spin-parity assignments, 3.1.1., 3.1.16., 3.1.17.
STABILITY CONSTANTS OF METAL-ION COMPLEXES, **3.4.24.**
Standard Alcoholimetric Tables, 5.4.20.
Standard Order of Arrangement of Elements, 3.2.16., 3.4.1.—3.4.3., 3.4.6., 3.4.7.
Standards, American Association, 6.3.5.
—, astronomical, 6.2.3.
—, British Institution, 6.3.5.
—, design, 6.1.2.
—, fundamental, 6.1.1.
—, industrial, 1.1.3., 6.1.2.
—, infrared wavelength, wavenumber, 3.2.24., 5.3.14.
—, measurement, 6.1.2.
—, neutron cross section measurements, 3.1.8.
—, spectroscopic, 3.1.4., 3.2.18., 6.2.3.
—, State Committee, U.S.S.R., 1.1.3.
—, X-ray wavelength, 3.2.3.
Standard states, conventions, 3.4.1.
Stanford University, U.S.A., 3.1.5.
Stark Effect, 3.2.6.
STATE SERVICE FOR STANDARD AND REFERENCE DATA, U.S.S.R. (GSSSD), **1.1.3.**
Status Report: National Standard Reference Data System, April 1968, NBS Technical Note 448, 1.1.1.
Steam, dissociating, saturated, superheated; physical, thermodynamic, transport properties, 3.4.16.
Steam Charts, Tables, ICPS, 3.4.16.
Steelmaking, thermodynamic, physicochemical data for, 3.4.10.
Steel, molten, equilibrium constants of deoxidation reactions in, 4.3.7.
Steroids, infrared spectra, 3.2.20., 3.2.21.
—, NMR spectra, 3.2.42., 3.2.43.
—, nomenclature (IUPAC), 6.3.1.
—, optical rotatory power, 2.2., 3.6.3.
Stretching (bending) frequency, *see* Vibrational frequency, molecular
Structure of Crystals, 3.3.2
STRUCTURE REPORTS, **3.3.4.**, 3.3.7.
Strukturbericht, 3.3.4., 3.4.11.

Sublimation, enthalpy, entropy of, *see* Enthalpy, Entropy of phase change
Sublimation temperature, elements, inorganic and organic compounds, 3.4.1.
— —, semiconductors, inorganic, 3.3.13.
Sulfates, chemical kinetics data, 3.4.13.
—, density, 3.4.13.
—, mineralogical data, 3.3.10.
—, paramagnetic relaxation, 3.3.15.
—, thermodynamic properties, 3.4.5., 3.4.13.
Sulfides, phase diagrams, 3.4.12.
—, properties, ideal gas state, 5.4.2.
—, thermodynamic properties, 3.4.5., 3.4.10.
—, mineralogical data, 3.3.10.
Sulfur, thermodynamic properties, 3.4.5., 3.4.7.
Sulfur compounds, infrared spectra, 3.2.16.
Sulphosalts, mineralogical data, 3.3.10.
SUN Commission, *see* Commission for Symbols, Units and Nomenclature, IUPAP
SUPERCONDUCTIVE MATERIALS DATA CENTER, **3.3.17.**
Superconductive metals, alloys; crystallographic, superconducting, thermodynamic properties, 3.3.17., 4.3.6.
Surface conductance, 4.2.1.
SURFACE TENSION DATA OF PURE LIQUIDS, **4.2.2.**
Surface tension, cryogenic fluids, 3.4.21., 4.2.2.
— —, elements, compounds in steelmaking, 3.4.10.
— —, hydrocarbons, 3.4.2.
— —, molten salts, 3.4.22.
— —, pure liquids, 4.2.2.
Susceptibility, magnetic, *see* Magnetic susceptibility
Swan System of the C_2 Molecule, 3.2.22.
SWEDISH A. B. ATOMENERGI AND THE RESEARCH INSTITUTE OF NATIONAL DEFENSE, **4.1.3.**
SYMBOLS, 6.2.
—, biological chemistry (biochemistry), 6.3.1.
—, chemical, 6.1.2., 6.2.3.

SYMBOLS, electrical, magnetic, 6.1.2.
—, electrical technology, 6.2.2.
—, folic acid, related compounds, 6.3.1.
—, general principles concerning (ISO) 6.2.2.
—, mathematical, 6.2.2.
—, physical, 6.1.2., 6.2.2., 6.2.3.
—, physico-chemical, 6.2.3.
—, printing, 6.2.2.
—, standardization of, 6.1.3.
—, transition probability, atomic, 3.2.2.
—, units, 6.1.2., 6.2.2.
—, terminology and units, IUPAC Commission on, 6.2.3.
Symbols, Units and Nomenclature in Physics, IUPAP, 6.2.3.
Symmetric, asymmetric molecules, physical constants, 3.2.26.
Symmetry class, *see* Crystal structure *or* Vibrational frequency, molecular
Symmetry Groups for X-ray Crystallography, 3.3.6.
Systematic Presentation of Isotopes and Reference Diagrams for Nuclides, 5.3.6.

TABELLEN DER ATOMKERNE, *see* NUCLEAR TABLES
TABLE OF ISOTOPES, **3.1.4.**
Table of Relative Atomic Weights, 3.4.1., 6.2.3.
Tables Annuelles de Constantes et Données Numériques, see Tables de Constantes Sélectionnées
Tables (Charts) of Thermodynamic Functions of Air, 3.4.19.
TABLES DE CONSTANTES SÉLECTIONNÉES, **2.2,** 3.2.7., 3.2.8., 3.2.48., 3.3.13.— 3.3.16., 3.4.26., 3.5.4., 3.6.3.—3.6.6.
Tables des Isotopes, 5.3.3.
Tables for Activity Properties of Water and Electrolytes in Binary Water Solutions of Salts, Acids and Alkalis, 5.3.53.
Tables for Thermophysical Properties of Gaseous and Liquid Methane, 5.3.61.
TABLES OF BIMOLECULAR GAS REACTIONS, 3.5.1., **3.5.2.**
Tables of Chemical Kinetics, Homogeneous Reactions, 3.5.1.

Tables of Experimental Dipole Moments, 5.3.30.
Tables of Frequencies of Nuclear Quadrupole Resonance, 5.3.25.
Tables of Interplanar Distances, 5.3.28.
TABLES OF MOLECULAR VIBRATIONAL FREQUENCIES, **3.2.10.**
Tables of Neutron Resonance Parameters and Neutron Resonance Materials, 5.3.5.
Tables of Physical and Chemical Constants and Some Mathematical Functions, 5.2.2.
Tables of Spectral Lines, 5.3.10.
Tables of Spectral Lines of Neutral and Ionized Atoms, 5.3.9.
Tables of Spectrophotometric Absorption Data of Compounds Used for the Colorimetric Determination of Elements, 5.5.6.
Tables of Thermal Properties of Gases, 5.3.41.
Tables of Thermophysical Properties of Water and Water Vapour, 5.3.55.
TABLES OF WAVENUMBERS FOR THE CALIBRATION OF INFRARED SPECTROMETERS, **3.2.24.**
Tantalum and compounds, thermodynamic properties, 3.4.8.
Taschenbuch für Chemiker und Physiker, 5.2.3.
Technology (Technik), 2.1.
Tellurium, semiconducting properties 3.3.13.
Temperature-entropy diagrams, industrial gases, 3.4.17.
Temperature scales, Geophysical Laboratory, 3.4.12.
— —, International Practical, 3.4.12., 6.2.1.
— —, thermodynamic, 6.2.1.
Termolecular reactions, chemical kinetics data, 3.5.2.
Terms in Nuclear Science, 6.3.5.
Terpenes, NMR spectra, 3.2.42.
Terrestrial abundance, distribution of minerals, *see* Occurrence of minerals
Texas A & M University, U. S. A., 2.3., 3.2.16., 3.2.17., 3.2.27.—3.2.30., 3.2.35., 3.2.36., 3.2.39., 3.2.40., 3.4.2., 3.4.3., 3.4.24.
Thermal conductivity, *see* Conductivity, thermal

Thermal decomposition, sulfates, 3.4.13.

Thermal diffusivity, alloys, elements, nonmetallic solids, 3.4.20.

Thermal expansion, *see* Expansion, thermal

Thermal-neutron capture, 5.3.2.

Thermal Properties of Aqueous Uni-univalent Electrolytes, 3.4.1.

Thermal Properties of Gases, Tables of, 5.3.41.

Thermal radiative properties, alloys, coatings, elements, nonmetallic solids, 3.4.20.

— — —, high temperature materials, 5.4.4.

Thermionic properties, elements, compounds, 5.3.31.

Thermionic (electronic) work function, *see* Work function

Thermochemistry, IUPAC Commission on, 6.2.3., 6.4.2.

THERMOCHEMISTRY FOR STEELMAKING, **3.4.10.**

Thermodynamic calculations, key property values for, 3.4.1.

THERMODYNAMIC CONSTANTS OF SUBSTANCES, 3.4.6., **3.4.7.**

Thermodynamic constants, inorganic, organic compounds, 3.4.7., 5.3.39.

Thermodynamic data, computational techniques for, 3.4.2.—3.4.4.

— —, correlation with molecular structure, 3.4.3.

— —, for propellant performance calculations, 3.4.4.

— —, indexes to, 2.3.

— —, mathematical correlating functions, 3.4.15.

— —, publication of (IUPAC), 6.4.2.

THERMODYNAMIC FUNCTIONS OF AIR, **3.4.19.**

Thermodynamic Functions of Dissociating Steam, 3.4.16.

THERMODYNAMIC FUNCTIONS OF GASES, **3.4.17.**

Thermodynamic functions, calculation from heat capacity data, 3.4.14.

— —, calculation for ideal gas state from molecular data, 3.2.10., 3.4.18.

— —, computer calculation of, 3.4.19.

THERMODYNAMIC PROPERTIES, 1.1.1., 2.1., 2.3., 3.2.45., 3.3.17., 3.4.1.—3.4.21., 3.4.27., 3.6.7., 4.3.6., 4.3.9., 5.2.17., 5.3.37.—5.3.66., 5.4.9., 5.4.11.

Thermodynamic properties, aliphatic alcohols 2.3.

— —, alloys, 3.4.9., 3.4.20., 4.3.6.

— —, ammonia, 3.4.15., 3.4.17., 3.4.18.

— —, electrolyte solutions, 4.3.9.

— —, elements, 2.3., 3.4.1., 3.4.4.—3.4.7., 3.4.10., 3.4.14., 3.4.20., 3.6.7., 5.3.38.

— —, handbooks of, 5.3.37.—5.3.66.

— —, hydrocarbons, related compounds, 2.3., 3.4.2., 3.4.15.

— —, inorganic compounds, 2.3., 3.4.1., 3.4.3., 3.4.5.—3.4.7.

— — , metals, 3.4.9., 4.3.6.

— —, minerals, 5.2.17.

— —, organic compounds, 2.3., 3.4.1., 3.4.3., 3.4.7.

— —, oxides, 3.4.5., 3.4.6., 3.4.10., 3.4.14., 5.4.9.

— —, oxygen, compounds, 2.3., 3.4.2., 3.4.4., 3.4.7., 3.4.15.

— —, refractory compounds, 5.3.42., 5.4.9., 5.4.11.

— —, steam, water, 2.3., 3.4.2., 3.4.16.

— —, superconductive metals, alloys, 3.3.17.

— —, titanium compounds, 5.3.44.

— —, low temperature, 3.4.14., 3.4.21.

THERMODYNAMIC PROPERTIES OF AMMONIA, **3.4.18.**

THERMODYNAMIC PROPERTIES OF CHEMICAL SUBSTANCES, **3.4.6.**, 3.4.7.

Thermodynamic Properties of Combustion Product Components, 3.4.6.

Thermodynamic Properties of the Elements, 3.4.10., 5.3.38.

Thermodynamic Properties of Gases, 5.3.66.

THERMODYNAMIC PROPERTIES OF METALS AND ALLOYS, SELECTED VALUES FOR, **3.4.9.**

Thermodynamic stability, high melting compounds, 5.4.11.

Thermodynamic temperature scale, definition, 6.2.1.

Thermodynamics, Consolidated Index of Selected Property Values, 3.4.27.
—, Index of API RP44—TRC selected data on, 2.3.
—, IUPAC Commission on, 6.2.3., 6.4.2.
Thermodynamics of Certain Refractory Compounds, 5.3.42.
THERMODYNAMICS RESEARCH CENTER (TRC), **2.3.**, 3.2.16., **3.2.17.**, 3.2.27., **3.2.28.**, 3.2.29., **3.2.30.**, 3.2.35., **3.2.36.**, 3.2.39., **3.2.40.**, **3.4.2.**, **3.4.3.**
Thermodynamic Stability of High Melting Compounds, 5.4.11.
THERMODYNAMIC TABLES PROJECT OF THE INTERNATIONAL UNION OF PURE AND APPLIED CHEMISTRY, **3.4.15.**
Thermomechanical properties, *see* Transport properties
Thermophysical Characteristics of Substances, 5.3.65.
Thermophysical properties, air, liquid, and constituents, 5.3.60.
— —, alkali metals, 5.3.59.
— —, alloys, 3.4.20., 5.3.63.
— —, carbon dioxide, 5.3.57.
— —, elements, 3.4.20.
— —, gases, liquids, 5.3.54., 5.3.62.
— —, mercury, 5.3.58.
— —, metals, 5.3.63.
— —, methane, 5.3.61.
— —, nonmetallic solids, liquids, gases, 3.4.20.
— —, oxides, 3.4.20.
— —, water, 5.3.55., 5.3.56.
— —, water vapor, 5.3.55.
Thermophysical Properties of Alkali Metals, 5.3.59.
Thermophysical Properties of Carbon Dioxide, 5.3.57.
Thermophysical Properties of High Temperature Solid Materials, 3.4.20.
Thermophysical Properties of Liquid Air and Its Constituents, 5.3.60.
Thermophysical Properties of Mercury, 5.3.58.
Thermophysical Properties of Metals and Alloys, 5.3.63.
Thermophysical Properties of Monatomic Gases and Liquids, 5.3.54.

Thermophysical Properties of Water in the Critical Range, 5.3.56.
THERMOPHYSICAL PROPERTIES RESEARCH CENTER (TPRC), **3.4.20.**
Thermophysical Properties Research Literature: A Retrieval Guide, 3.4.20.
Thiaalkanes, thermodynamic properties, 3.4.2.
Thiols, properties, ideal gas state, 5.4.2.
—, thermodynamic properties, 3.4.2.
Thorium alloys, phase diagrams, 5.3.46.
Thresholds, nuclear reactions, 3.1.3.
Tin and compounds, thermodynamic properties, 3.4.8.
Titanium and compounds, thermodynamic properties, 3.4.8., 5.3.44.
Tokyo Institute of Technology, Japan, 3.6.1.
Transference number, electrolyte solutions, 4.3.9.
Transients, properties of, 4.3.3.
Transition, enthalpy, entropy of, *see* Enthalpy, Entropy of phase change
Transition metal compounds, magnetic properties, 2.1., 3.3.14.
Transition probabilities, electronic, nuclear states, 3.1.1., 3.1.5., 3.1.14., 3.2.2., 3.2.6., 3.2.25.
Transition temperature (point), elements, 3.4.1., 3.4.3., 3.4.7.
— — —, —, compounds in steelmaking, 3.4.10.
— — —, hydrocarbons, 3.4.2.
— — —, inorganic compounds, 3.4.1., 3.4.3., 3.4.7.
— — —, organic compounds, 3.4.1., 3.4.3., 3.4.7.
— — —, organometallic compounds, 3.4.7.
— — —, sulfate decomposition, 3.4.13.
Transmissivity (transmittance) thermal, *see* Thermal radiative properties
TRANSPORT (INCLUDING THERMOMECHANICAL, THERMOPHYSICAL) PROPERTIES, 1.1.1., 2.1., 3.4.2., 3.4.16., 3.4.20.—3.4.22., 4.3.5., 4.3.9., 5.3.37.—5.3.66.
Transport (thermomechanical) properties, electrolyte solutions, 4.3.9.

Transport (thermomechanical) properties, handbooks of, 5.3.37.—5.3.66.
— — —, hydrocarbons, 3.4.2.
— — —, metals, alloys, 3.4.20., 4.3.5.
— — —, steam, water, 3.4.16.
Triple point, industrial gases, 3.4.17.
Triterpenes, optical rotatory power, 3.6.4.
Tritium, atomic energy levels, 3.2.1.
—, thermodynamic properties, 3.4.7.
Tungsten and compounds, thermodynamic properties, 3.4.8.

UKAEA Health and Safety Branch, Risley, U.K., 3.1.10.
UKAEA NUCLEAR DATA LIBRARY, 3.1.10., 3.1.11.
U.K. National Committee for CODATA, 1.1.2., 1.2.4.
Ultraviolet Multiplet Table, 3.2.1.
ULTRAVIOLET SPECTRA, 2.3., 3.2.6., 3.2.19., 3.2.23., 3.2.29.—3.2.34., 3.2.48., 3.2.52., 5.3.11.—5.3.13., *see also* Molecular electronic spectra
Ultraviolet Spectra of Elastomers and Rubber Chemicals, 5.3.13.
Ultraviolet Spectra of Hetero-organic Compounds, 5.3.11.
ULTRAVIOLET SPECTRAL DATA, SELECTED, API RP44, 2.3., 3.2.29., *see also* 3.2.30.
ULTRAVIOLET SPECTRAL DATA, SELECTED, TRC, 2.3., 3.2.30., *see also* 3.2.29.
Ultraviolet spectral data, alkaloids, 3.2.23.
— — —, aromatic compounds, 3.2.33., 3.2.34.
— — —, elastomers, 5.3.13.
— — —, hydrocarbons, 2.3., 3.2.29.
— — —, indexes to, 2.3., 3.2.52.
— — —, industrial compounds, 3.2.32.
— — —, industrial nonhydrocarbon compounds, 2.3., 3.2.30.
— — —, inorganic compounds, 2.3., 3.2.30., 3.2.33.
— — —, organic compounds, 2.3., 3.2.19., 3.2.30.—3.2.34., 5.3.11.—5.3.13.
— — —, organometallic compounds, 2.3., 3.2.29.

Ultraviolet spectral data, rubber chemicals, 5.3.13.
— — —, sesquiterpenoids, 3.2.48.
ULTRAVIOLET SPECTRA, SADTLER RESEARCH LABORATORIES, INC., 3.2.32.
Unit cell dimensions, *see* Crystal structure
United Kingdom Atomic Energy Authority (UKAEA), 3.1.10., 6.3.5.
United Nations Educational, Scientific and Cultural Organization (UNESCO), 3.3.6.
United States Air Force, 3.4.11.
United States Atomic Energy Commission (USAEC), 3.1.1., 3.1.3., 3.1.4., 3.1.6., 3.1.7., 3.1.13., 3.1.15., 3.1.19., 3.2.11., 3.4.9., 3.4.11., 4.3.3.
United States Atomic Energy Commission, Division of Technical Information Extension, 3.1.19.
United States Bureau of Mines, 3.4.5., 3.4.10., 5.4.2.
United States Calorimetry Conference, 6.4.2.
United States Office of Naval Research, 3.1.15.
UNITS, 6.2.
—, acoustics, 6.2.2.
—, atomic, nuclear physics, 6.2.2.
—, chemical, 6.1.2., 6.2.3.
—, clinical chemistry, 6.2.3.
—, dielectric, 3.2.14.
—, electrical, magnetic, 6.1.2., 6.2.2.
—, general principles concerning (ISO), 6.2.2.
—, heat, 6.2.2.
—, International System (SI), 3.4.16., 3.6.7., 6.1.1., 6.2.1., 6.2.2.
—, ionizing radiations, 6.2.2.
—, mechanics, 6.2.2.
—, molecular physics, 6.2.2.
—, nuclear reactions, 6.2.2.
—, periodic, related phenomena, 6.2.2.
—, physical, 6.1.2., 6.2.2., 6.2.3.
—, physical chemistry, 6.2.2.
—, radiation, light, 6.2.2.
—, radiological, 6.1.2.
—, spectroscopic, 6.2.3.
—, standardization of, 6.1.3.
—, transition probability, atomic, 3.2.2.

Universität Freiburg, Germany-B. R. D. 3.2.26.
Universität Giessen, Germany-B. R. D., 3.2.49.
Universität Heidelberg, Germany-B. R. D., 3.1.17.
University Chemical Laboratory, Cambridge, U. K., 3.3.1., 3.3.7.
University College, U. K., 3.3.6.
University of California, Berkeley, U. S. A., 3.1.3., 3.1.4., 3.1.17., 3.2.22., 3.3.1., 3.4.5., 3.4.9., 3.5.5.
University of Louisville, U. S. A., 3.2.31.
University of Manchester, U. K., 3.3.11.
University of Notre Dame, U. S. A., 4.3.3.
University of Surrey, U. K., 3.1.5.
University of Tokyo, Japan, 3.2.10.
University of Wisconsin, U. S. A., 4.2.3.
Uranium alloys, phase diagrams, 5.3.46.
U. S. National Committee for CODATA, 1.2.5.
U. S. S. R. National Committee for CODATA, 1.1.3., 1.2.6.
U. S. S. R. NUCLEAR DATA INFORMATION CENTRE, 3.1.8., 3.1.11., **3.1.12.,** 3.1.19.
Utrecht Observatory, Netherlands, 3.2.1.
UV ATLAS OF ORGANIC COMPOUNDS, 3.2.19., **3.2.34.**

Vacuum ultraviolet spectra, 3.2.6.
Vanadium and compounds, thermodynamic properties, 3.4.5.
Vaporizable compounds, mass spectra, 3.2.37.
Vaporization, enthalpy, entropy of, *see* Enthalpy, Entropy of phase change
Vaporization temperature, *see* Boiling point (temperature), Sublimation temperature
Vapor pressure, alloys, 3.4.20.
— —, cryogenic fluids, 3.4.21.
— —, elements, 3.4.1., 3.4.3., 3.4.5.—3.4.7., 3.4.20., 5.3.37.
— —, —, compounds in steelmaking, 3.4.10.
— —, hydrocarbons, 2.3., 3.4.2.

Vapor pressure, inorganic compounds, 2.3., 3.4.1., 3.4.3., 3.4.5.—3.4.7.
— —, metals, 3.4.8., 3.4.9.
— —, nonmetallic solids, 3.4.20.
— —, organic compounds, 2.3., 3.4.1., 3.4.3., 3.4.7.
— —, organometallic compounds, 3.4.7.
Vapour Pressure of the Elements, 5.3.37.
Varian Associates, U. S. A., 3.2.42.
Verdet constant, *see* Magnetic rotatory power
Vibrational constant, molecular, *see* Force constant, Vibrational frequency, molecular
Vibrational frequency, molecular, 3.2.10., 3.2.25., 3.4.4.
Vibrational spectra, molecular, *see* Molecular vibrational spectra
Viscosity, alloys, 3.4.20.
—, cryogenic fluids, 3.4.21.
—, elements, 3.4.20.
—, —, compounds in steelmaking, 3.4.10.
—, hydrocarbons, 2.3., 3.4.2.
—, molten salts, 3.4.22.
—, nonmetallic solids, 3.4.20.
—, steam, water, 3.4.16.
VISIBLE REGION SPECTRA, 3.2.31.—3.2.33., 3.2.52., 5.3.12., *see also* Molecular electronic spectra
Visible region spectral data, indexes to, 3.2.52.
— — — —, industrial compounds, 3.2.32.
— — — —, inorganic compounds, 3.2.33.
— — — —, organic compounds, 3.2.31.—3.2.33., 5.3.12.
Vitamins, NMR spectra, 3.2.42.
—, nomenclature (IUPAC), 6.3.1.
Volume, atomic, nonferrous metals, 3.4.8.
—, molar, minerals, 5.2.17.
—, specific, gases, industrial, 3.4.17.
—, —, steam, water, 3.4.16.

Water, activity properties in binary solutions of salts, acids, alkalis, 5.3.53.

Water, physical, transport properties, 3.4.16.
—, radiation chemistry data, 4.3.3.
—, solubilities of elements, inorganic and organic compounds in, 3.4.23.
—, thermodynamic properties, 2.3., 3.4.2., 3.4.16.
—, thermophysical properties, 5.3.55., 5.3.56.
—, vapor, thermophysical properties, 5.3.55.
Wavelengths of Emission and Discontinuities in Absorption of X-Rays, Tables de Constantes Sélectionnées, 2.2.
Wavelength standards, infrared, 5.3.14.
— —, X-ray, 3.2.3.
Wavelength tables, atomic spectra, 3.2.4.
Wavenumber tables, for infrared spectrometer calibration, 3.2.24.
Wayne State University, U.S.A., 4.2.2.
Wiley, John, and Sons, Inc., 3.2.31., 3.3.10.
Work function, elements, compounds, 5.3.31.
— —, semiconductors, inorganic, 3.3.13.
World Meteorological Organization (WMO), 5.2.22., 6.1.2.

Xenon, thermodynamic, transport properties, 3.4.15.
X-ray absorption, wavelengths of emission and discontinuities in, 2.2.
X-Ray Attenuation Coefficient Information Center, 3.2.47.
X-ray crystallography, physical, chemical, mathematical tables for, 3.3.6.

X-ray diffraction data, alloys, 3.3.3.
— — —, crystals, 3.3.3., 3.3.6., 3.3.8.
— — —, inorganic compounds, 3.3.3.
— — —, metals, 3.3.3.
— — —, minerals, 3.3.3., 3.3.10., 5.2.17.
— — —, organic compounds, 3.3.3., 5.3.15.
— — —, organometallic compounds, 3.3.3.
X-Ray Diffraction Powder Patterns, Standard, 3.3.3.
X-Ray Powder Data File, *see* Powder Diffraction File
X-rays, wavelengths of emission and discontinuities in absorption of, 2.2.
X-ray spectra, elements, 3.2.3.
— —, organic compounds, 5.3.15.
X-ray structure analysis, polycrystalline materials, 5.3.26.
X-ray techniques (Röntgentechnik), 2.1.
X-Ray Wavelengths and X-Ray Atomic Energy Levels, 3.2.3.

Yale University, U.S.A., 3.3.10.
Yield, quantum, radiolytic, *see* Radiolytic yield

Zeeman Effect, 3.2.6.
Zeitschrift für Kristallographie, 3.3.4.
Zentralinstitut für Kernforschung, D.D.R., 3.1.2.
Zinc and compounds, thermodynamic properties, 3.4.8.
Zirconium and compounds, thermodynamic properties, 3.4.8.

Country Index

(Chapters 1—4 inclusive)

Argentina	3.6.6.
Australia	3.1.8., 3.4.25., 3.6.3., 3.6.6.
Austria	3.1.2., 3.1.11., 3.2.33.
Belgium	3.1.11., 3.2.7., 3.2.8., 3.3.8., 3.4.20.
Canada	1.2.1., 3.1.6., 3.2.7.—3.2.9., 3.2.16., 3.3.3.—3.3.5., 3.4.16., 3.6.3., 3.6.6.
Czechoslovakia	3.2.23., 3.2.33., 3.4.16.
Denmark	3.1.11., 3.4.24.
France	2.2., 3.1.11., 3.2.7., 3.2.8., 3.2.37., 3.2.48., 3.3.13., 3.3.15., 3.3.16., 3.4.15., 3.4.26., 3.5.4., 3.6.3.—3.6.6.
Germany BRD	1.2.2., 2.1., 3.1.9., 3.1.11., 3.1.17., 3.2.19., 3.2.26., 3.2.33., 3.2.34., 3.2.49., 3.2.50., 3.3.14., 3.4.15., 3.4.16., 3.4.25., 3.6.3., 4.1.4.
DDR	3.1.2.
Hungary	3.2.33.
India	3.4.15.
Israel	3.2.31., 3.3.3.
Italy	3.1.11.
Japan	1.2.3., 3.1.11., 3.2.10., 3.2.16., 3.2.20., 3.2.43., 3.3.1., 3.3.3., 3.3.4., 3.4.15., 3.4.16., 3.4.20., 3.5.3., 3.6.1., 3.6.3., 3.6.6., 4.1.5., 4.3.2., 4.3.7., 4.3.8.
Netherlands	3.1.11., 3.1.16., 3.2.1., 3.2.33., 3.3.3., 3.3.8., 3.4.15., 4.1.4., 4.2.1.
New Zealand	3.1.8.
Norway	3.1.11., 3.3.3.
Poland	3.2.33.
Rumania	3.2.33.

Country Index

Spain	3.1.11., 3.6.6.
Sweden	3.1.11., 3.2.7., 3.2.8., 3.4.24., 4.1.3.
Switzerland	3.1.11., 3.2.7., 3.2.8., 3.3.1., 3.4.24., 3.6.3., 3.6.6.
U. K.	1.1.2., 1.2.4., 3.1.5., 3.1.6., 3.1.10., 3.1.11., 3.2.7., 3.2.8., 3.2.16., 3.2.19., 3.2.33., 3.2.34., 3.2.38., 3.2.44., 3.3.1., 3.3.3., 3.3.4., 3.3.6.—3.3.11., 3.4.15.—3.4.17., 3.5.2., 3.6.3.
U. S. A.	1.1.1., 1.2.5., 2.3., 3.1.1., 3.1.3.—3.1.7., 3.1.13., 3.1.15., 3.1.17.—3.1.19., 3.2.1.—3.2.6., 3.2.11.—3.2.18., 3.2.21., 3.2.22., 3.2.25., 3.2.27.—3.2.33., 3.2.35.—3.2.37., 3.2.39.—3.2.42., 3.2.46., 3.2.47., 3.2.51.—3.2.53., 3.3.1.—3.3.3., 3.3.8.—3.3.10., 3.3.12., 3.3.17., 3.4.1.—3.4.5., 3.4.9.—3.4.16., 3.4.18., 3.4.20.—3.4.24., 3.4.27., 3.5.1., 3.5.5., 3.6.2., 3.6.3., 4.2.2.—4.2.4., 4.3.1., 4.3.3.—4.3.6., 4.3.9.
U. S. S. R.	1.1.3., 1.2.6., 3.1.12., 3.1.14., 3.1.19., 3.2.33., 3.2.45., 3.3.1., 3.3.4., 3.4.6.—3.4.8., 3.4.15., 3.4.16., 3.4.19., 3.6.7.

International Projects — International Unions Index

International Projects

CINDA   3.1.19.
ENEA   3.1.11.
ICPS   3.4.16.
WMO   5.2.22.

International Unions

International Council of Scientific Unions (ICSU)
    1.2., 3.2.1., 3.2.6., 3.2.24., 6.1.2., 6.1.3., 6.2.3., 6.3.1.

International Astronomical Union (IAU)
    3.2.1., 3.2.7., 3.2.8., 3.2.24., 6.2.3., 6.3.2.

International Union of Biochemistry (IUB)
    6.3.1., 6.3.4.

International Union of Crystallography (IUCr)
    3.3.1., 3.3.4., 3.3.6., 3.3.10., 6.3.3., 6.4.1.

International Union of Pure and Applied Chemistry (IUPAC)
    2.2., 3.2.1., 3.2.7., 3.2.8., 3.2.15., 3.2.24., 3.2.25., 3.2.36., 3.4.1., 3.4.9., 3.4.15.,
    3.4.24.—3.4.26., 3.6.3., 5.5.6., 6.1.2., 6.2.3., 6.3.1., 6.4.2., 6.4.3.

International Union of Pure and Applied Physics (IUPAP)
    3.1.1., 3.1.13., 3.1.14., 3.2.1., 3.2.24., 3.4.9., 6.2.1., 6.2.3.

Typesetting and printing: Buchdruckerei Carl Ritter & Co., Wiesbaden